LAUREL

BETTY FRIEDAN
"IT CHANGED MY LIFE"

THE FEMININE MYSTIQUE IS "THE BOOK THAT PULLED THE TRIGGER ON HISTORY."
—Alvin Toffler, author of *Future Shock*

"Her suggestions are not only sensible but mandatory if women are ever to clear away the mists of the feminine mystique and learn to use their full capacities as human beings."
—Marya Mannes

"BETTY FRIEDAN IS A LIBERATOR OF WOMEN *AND* MEN!"
—Amitai Etzioni, Chairperson, Department of Sociology, Columbia University

"Articulated with the insight of a schooled psychologist and with the urgency of a pragmatist who has touched a truth about human experience and will not retreat."
—*America*

"SHE IS A WOMAN OF COMPASSION AND UNDER-STANDING. . . . ["*IT CHANGED MY LIFE*"] SHOULD BE READ AND QUOTED AND READ AGAIN—WHEN-EVER WE NEED TO BE REMINDED OF OUR HUMAN POSSIBILITIES."
—*Christian Century*

ALSO BY BETTY FRIEDAN

The Feminine Mystique

The Second Stage

"It Changed My Life"

Writings on the Women's Movement

Betty Friedan

A LAUREL BOOK
Published by
Dell Publishing
a division of
Bantam Doubleday Dell Publishing Group, Inc.
666 Fifth Avenue
New York, New York 10103

The trademark Laurel® is registered in the U.S. Patent and
Trademark Office

The trademark Dell® is registered in the U.S. Patent and
Trademark Office

ISBN: 0-440-20839-4

Reprinted by arrangement with W. W. Norton & Co., Inc.

Printed in the United States of America

Published simultaneously in Canada

February 1991

10 9 8 7 6 5 4 3 2 1

RAD

We are nearing the land that is life.
You will recognize it by its seriousness.

—Rainer Maria Rilke

Contents

Introduction 1990

It's never finished, I guess, personally or politically. In 1990 the women's movement, which was declared officially dead as the decade ended, its daughters anointed the postfeminist generation, has made choice the critical issue, galvanizing and changing the balance of power in American politics from California and Texas to my own district in eastern Long Island, New York.

When the new majority of the Supreme Court, appointed by Reagan and Bush, ruled the Webster case in July 1989, the enemies of choice were free in every state to pass legislation curtailing the right to choose in the matter of childbirth or abortion, a right essential to the personhood of women. For nearly twenty years American women had taken that right for granted. For the Supreme Court had ruled in Roe vs. Wade that the right of women to decide when, whether, and how many times to bear a child was as basic as any right guaranteed in the Constitution and Bill of Rights as it had been written by and for men, last spring the threat of reversal of that basic right aroused the dormant women's organizations, paralyzed by Reagan-Bush backlash, to organize the largest march in history: 600,000 of us marched in Washington. The daughters, who had taken those rights for granted, marched with their mothers and grandmothers, and so did many sons and husbands and fathers, more men than had ever marched before for women's rights. My daughter, Emily, who had not marched with me since she was thirteen, joined me in Washington with her new baby in a backpack, and went back home to organize her fellow doctors for choice.

Choice was the issue decisive in electing the first black major of New York and the first black governor of Virginia in 1989, as well as the governor of New Jersey and legislators threatened with excommunication by their archbishop in California. It became clear that choice was no longer a radical feminist issue but a gut commitment and necessity for the majority of Americans. In the various states, legislators, fearing for their political future, saw to it that the new repressive bills did not get out of committee for a vote. In Idaho and Louisiana, laws were passed which would have made it virtually impossible for women to get abortions even in cases of rape or incest, but these were vetoed by governors, facing the threat of massive economic boycott. And in 1990, defying the predictions of political pundits, women, firmly supporting choice, won gubernatorial primaries in Texas and California, and women, running on the issue of choice and related concerns of life and environment, were running at five and ten times their previous rates from Pennsylvania and the State of New York to Montana. Buying groceries the other day, I was asked by the young sales clerk, male, if those women had a chance. "Not according to the usual predictions," I said, "but women and people generally are getting pretty fed up." "That's what my mom says," said the grocer. "Those corrupt male bureaucrats aren't helping people's lives."

But there are new problems emerging in women's lives today, and forces are falsely using those problems in an attempt to send women home again—as if the real problem were the new opportunities and aspirations that have changed our lives; where, in fact, the real problem is that the changes haven't gone far enough. The real problem is most women have two jobs today, of home and work, but nothing else has changed. The real problem is that the overwhelming majority of women in the United States today work outside the home— over 60 percent of women with children under two—and most children in the United States today have two parents or a single parent working outside the home, but the United States is the only industrial nation except for South Africa without an official policy on parental leave and child care. And at this writing President Bush has just vetoed a bill that would have provided a minimum of unpaid leave for parents at the birth or adoption of a child or the sickness of a family member.

Some magazines today are promoting a new traditionalism and others a "mommy track" whereby women must choose either to go on a fast career track like men and forgo having children (though that is never a cost demanded of men's careers), or a "mommy track" where they will resign themselves to a permanent sexual ghetto, forgoing advancement to top jobs as the cost of a small amount of flexibility. "Having it all" has become almost a pejorative, as the baby-boom generation comes up against the biological clock and postpones having babies until their forties, using in vitro fertilization for lack of real choices. The implication that they can simply go home again may not be economically possible for most women, but its false promise distracts attention from the urgent need for real options of flextime, parental leave, job sharing, part-time patterns for women or men that would not mean loss of benefits or permanent abdication from professional advance, and the real need for child care, which nations much less rich than ours provide for parents at all income levels. The real problem is that women are being polarized along lines of career versus family, presented with either/or, no-win false choices, instead of uniting behind the further political and social changes necessary for real choice. Even those male politicians who now understand that choice is a potent political issue when it comes to abortion, have not understood that child care and parental leave could be equally potent, as necessary to real choice. And the woman's movement itself has been slow in moving beyond the male model to demand the restructure of work and home, and of political priorities and economic measures of values essential for real choice.

In the think tank that I run every winter now as Distinguished Visiting Professor at the University of Southern California, feminist thinkers from law, medicine, and the humanities, as well as from women's studies, have been joining with policymakers, movie directors, and entrepreneurs, trying to come up with concepts of equality that reach beyond the male model. In rethinking questions of work and power, housing and schooling, competing and creating, and the very measurements of value and productivity, we have been trying to work out a feminist regrounding for marriage and other forms of intimacy and bonding, extending our concern with individual rights to larger concepts of family and community beyond the sexual politics of the first stage of feminism. We have been trying to put names to the new problems of women that are once again being treated as purely personal and not political. Are choices real if they involve impossible superwomen standards for women (or for men) who don't have a wife to take care of the details of life, if they involve violations of values and priorities of family and children, if they involve retreat from the whole idea of equality? But to move to the larger political dimensions of choice involves rethinking the choices of men and the larger issues of our political and economic environment.

The presidential veto of parental leave and child care, and the inadequacy of Democratic or Republican congressional outrage at that veto, is merely a symptom of the philosophy of government during the ten years of the culture of greed of the Reagan-Bush era, from which there was no real dissent: the assumption that government has no real responsibility to the lives, health, and welfare of people—women, children, or men —but merely to the maximization of profit. The unexpected explosion of political ferment catalyzed by the Supreme Court's retreat from choice itself in the matter of abortion may portend the crumbling of our American version of that obsolete wall that was pulled down without a single shot being fired in Berlin because it finally simply did not permit people to live and change their lives.

So male is our own definition of politics that we ourselves do not clearly see that the changes the women's movement has made and is continuing to make in all our lives could be as dramatic and significant as the crumbling of that Berlin Wall and the dissolving of communist autocracy in Eastern Europe, which had seemed so impregnable.

The dynamics of our crumbling wall, however, can clearly be seen in the mass media, which reflect, distort, and shape the reality of our lives in America today as they distorted, shaped, and presaged unforeseen revolutionary change during the time when I wrote *The Feminine Mystique*. I now run a national media monitoring project called Women, Men and Media, which grew out of a course I taught at the University of Southern California, analyzing the changes in the representation and participation of women in newspapers, magazines, broadcast news, film, and television. We discovered that while women are now the majority of journalism students and can be found in entry-level jobs in numbers nearly equal to men, the news itself and media images are still being defined mainly by men. There is a glass ceiling that seems to keep women from top editorial or production decision-making jobs in all the media. Our study of twenty major newspapers showed that over 80 percent of people quoted, cited, reported, or pictured on the front pages were men. There was a virtual "symbolic annihilation" of women, 53 percent of the population accounting for not much more than 10 percent of news.

When editors and publishers began discussing the implication of our study, it was revealed that the crisis of the newspaper industry itself, more than anyone had realized before, was due to a fallout of women readers. Evidently women are too independent and busy in their double lives today to waste time reading what is of no "use" to them. At first glance the pornographers and portrayers of women as sex objects in the predominant action/violence, male-dominated movies that are virtually the only fare offered to Americans today, would seem to be a reversal of our twenty years' breakthrough of feminine mystique and machismo, in film. But the playboy clubs have closed, the bunny is no more, and when male broadcasting executives took Jane Pauley off the *Today Show* as she hit forty, replacing her with a younger blond, the program's ratings plummeted, millions of dollars of advertising were lost, and Jane Pauley, fighting back, emerged to anchor network news with visible new power. At the end of the 80s it seemed as if a new feminine mystique were replacing the strong-spirited television images of women: *Mary Tyler Moore, Maude, Cagney and Lacey*, and *LA Law* are followed by nurses who merely take showers (*Nightingale*), and evil career women who boil children's pet rabbits alive (*Fatal Attraction*) and must be shot dead by housewife heroines. But it becomes increasingly clear that now only children go to the movies and that the television networks are all in crisis today.

On the other hand, there is increasing diversity in women's and men's magazines. The existence of "working women" and "working mothers" is taken for granted by even the traditional women's magazines I used to write for, whose editors now tell me that they lost the new young women when they still tried to speak to them in feminine mystique terms as if only the job itself had changed. And the men's magazines now assume that men are interested in feelings and relationships and not just sports.

As I see my own sons and son-in-law taking so much emotional responsibility and delight in their children, and the men of my generation trying to recreate ties they had no time for before, I refuse to believe that men are also not changing their lives underneath that wall of machismo we still celebrate in our national obsession with baseball and football. The *New York Times* reports on its front page that American men do not do 50 percent of the housework. I consider it of enormous significance, that front-page expectation that men *might* do 50 percent of the housework, and the actual fact that in twenty years, men's share of the housework has gone from less than 10 percent to nearly 30 percent. But if men have not changed their lives even more, it's not just because they are, after all, sons of the feminine mystique whose mothers buttered their sandwiches and picked up their dirty pajamas, but because in the recent culture of greed men have also been working sixty- and eighty-hour weeks. Companies on the cutting edge of American technology, who are facing labor-market shortages because of the recent "baby bust," are beginning to institute child care and flexible working arrangements, not only to attract and keep the able young women now coming out of law school and MBA programs in near equal numbers to men, but on the assumption that these will also appeal to the new young men. Men, after all, in this age of corporate takeovers and savings and loan bankruptcies, know they can no longer count on corporate security to define their lifelong male identity. The new men may not wait for the midlife crisis to demand more choices for themselves.

As for me, politically, I'll keep on marching with the

daughters and help them reach beyond that male model. But I'll also join with any men or women of vision to formulate a new politics of life again, to move with a political passion again to keep on changing all our lives, now that we have gone beyond the polarities of the Cold War, as I think we have gone beyond the sexual politics and confrontations with men that marked the first stage of the women's movement.

Personally, my own life must change now in more subtle ways. I have spent my sixties pursuing a new path to "the fountain of age." I've come to see a mystique of age as devastating as the feminine mystique that denies and distorts the reality of our personhood, for both women and men, in this new third of life that is now open to us. I'm now applying everything I learned from those twenty years of breaking through the feminine mystique and leading the women's movement to the question of age. And I begin to see that the question is not about our national obsession of how to look, live, and love as if we could stay forever young, but how to keep on growing older. I'm trying to break through that definition of age as only a decline from youth, and take it seriously in its own terms as a unique stage of human life and development. In age I see strengths that have no name in women, and wonder why, in fact, we live so much longer than men, and discover that the transformation of age itself may be the greatest by-product of the women's movement, looking back on that time when menopause was considered the end of life as a woman. In age we can finally cross over that sexual polarization of women and men, and all of us become more truly ourselves.

In affirming our own authenticity in the personhood of women, we inadvertently gave ourselves a key to the fountain of age. For we stopped defining ourselves merely in sexual relation to men as objects, mothers, wives, housewives, and we discovered a new joy in ourselves and other women. And without realizing it, we also found ways of knowing-loving men, not just as breadwinners, fathers, sex objects, or enemies in outworn power struggles, but as themselves, fellow survivors in this perilous, passionate human journey. That we can know and love each other personally now, women and men, in so many different ways, and that we will join again in political passion in the largest interest of peace and life before it is too late, is my hope and blessing. As all of us keep on changing our lives, how can I not be hopeful, having seen women who had no power before, give each other the power to change life so immeasurably for ourselves and our daughters and sons. How can I not expect that we will find with changing men the power together to make the larger political turnaround to keep on changing all our lives in the direction of truly human politics.

Betty Friedan
Sag Harbor, New York
July 1990

Introduction 1985

 From the vantage point of 1985, reliving those crucial years of the women's movement's beginnings—those first fearful, nervy struggles in the sixties, the miraculous explosion and triumphant roll of the early seventies, the diversions and stalemates, defeats and regroupings, and the surprising changes in real life—I feel a certain nostalgia, and philosophic rue. Yes, daughters, sisters, curious men, that's the way it happened— that's how I experienced it, then. Now, I smile a little at that nervous movement mother, so distraught when some sisters took their sexual politics to such extremes, so naïve and helplessly dismayed when some sisters fought for their own power through or in that sacred movement and wanted her out of the way, so hurt when that mother-hostility she herself had uncapped was directed at *her.*

But, of course, the women's movement did indeed empower us all in unexpected ways—me, my friends and enemies, the thousands I met in those years and the millions whose lives were touched, including many who still would never call themselves feminists. If you couldn't stand the heat, go back to the kitchen, I would joke, at myself.

And, to be honest, despite the temporary bouts of despair and despondency, and the occasional moments of faintheartedness recorded here—and the little bits of dirty linen I let hang out—I never could distance myself from the women's move-

ment very far or for very long. "It changed my whole life,"
too, as women even today keep stopping me to say, women
who still remember how it used to be, before the movement,
and the moment when it hit them, in high school, or coming
out of college, or in the middle of babies, or in the aloneness of
their thirties, forties, fifties—who remember woman's life
when the problem had no name.

What I see, above all, now is the simple glory of our movement—in all its messy, paradoxical, impossible to pin down,
ever changing complexity—the way it really did empower us
all to change our lives, or even *choose* consciously what before
had been mindless passive destiny, or for some, oppressive
martyrdom. The modern women's movement, in all its political and personal reality—which is already seen as history and
whose totality may never be grasped by history—went so
much deeper and more broadly into life than its own rhetoric.
In those years, when so many of the successive generations of
women who were changing their lives took active part in, and
responsibility for, the movement, in one way or another, it
never could be maneuvered off course, manipulated, diverted,
defeated, for very long. Of course there were, had to be, mistakes, and differences, in tactics, strategy, ideology, styles of
leadership. Not so many mistakes, I do believe, compared to
other movements for social change in our time—or compared
to our nation's highest political leadership, establishment or
opposition, during this period. We have learned to play men's
political games. But that's not the way it was—in those early
years of the women's movement itself. Something new, different, really happened, there; we who empowered ourselves and
other women had to make it up as we went along—we knew
more than we knew.

In any such movement, there have to be tensions, complex
currents—individual ambition serving and/or conflicting with
the general political good; hidden agendas; dangers of corruption and cooption; necessities of compromise; unexpected consequences of victories and defeats. The fact is, in those years
the women's movement had such a life-needed, life-respond-
ing, life-opening momentum, the reality of women's changing
lives kept it growing, sometimes despite its own rhetoric and
mistakes of leadership, sprouting new forms of organization

and new ways of thinking, spontaneously, alongside of or quite apart from the mainstream feminist organizations and spokespersons. Who, then, was immune from the potent virus of live feminism: nun of the conservative church, Junior League socialite, Orthodox housewife, Playboy bunny—perhaps even agents of left and right sent in to infiltrate and destroy our organizations becoming, perforce, feminists.

In actual fact, the women's movement, in those days, fed on everything, even its own defeats, and grew. If excess preoccupation with sexual politics, and the hate rhetoric of the bitterest separatist radical feminists of the early seventies, divided the movement, alienated middle American housewives, and fed the backlash and ERA defeats that stopped the triumphant roll, the consequent necessity to organize NOW and the National Women's Political Caucus, in coalition with established women's organizations, state by state, in that extended seven-to ten-year battle for ERA, brought into the movement sturdy younger women with new zest and confidence, freed from those early mires of raging self-pity, in Maryland and Maine, Montana and Mississippi as well as New York and L.A. And the rhetoric itself, adopted by the mass media, became part of every woman's language.

But, now, twenty-two years since *The Feminine Mystique* was published, nearly twenty years since the founding of NOW, and a decade after these words were written to a movement then still in a crisis of growth, the new young women (you?) simply take for granted their own personhood and choices and the rights and opportunities we fought for. How can we blame them for taking it all for granted when they have never known anything else? The experiences relived here may surprise young women today who do not think of themselves as feminists, do not realize how necessary the women's movement was, how it really did change our lives and give them their choices and opportunities, and how, perhaps, it figured in their own new conflicts, pressures and pleasures.

Now, in 1985, facing war from the right on women's most basic choices, the fundamentalist violence against the right to abortion, the Reagan administration's destruction of the laws against sex discrimination, the impasse of ERA as part of the larger political impasse, the ignominious defeat of the ticket

with the first woman on it, I am told by daughters that feminism is once again becoming a dirty word. The "Yuppies,"
those young urban, upwardly mobile professionals, disdain it.
Are they like the second generation of immigrants, ashamed of
the accent of the loved/hated parents who sent them to college? We, in the experiences relived here, created those Yuppies—the ones enjoying the choices of the two-income professional family and the pressures of the race for success.

Other women today face the realities of divorce, or losing
jobs, or not getting tenure, or supporting kids as a single parent. Others find themselves up against the biological clock, or
facing age alone. In the light of these new realities, we must
remind ourselves again of the diversionary danger of sexual
politics, and its seductiveness. Today, some feminists, disheartened by political and economic defeats, consumed by rage
against those who have blocked ERA and pay equity and
would outlaw abortion, are tempted to put their energies into
a war against pornography—that ugly dehumanization of sex,
women, and men, that vicious sexualization of violence—in
which they would be joined in strange alliance with some of
the worst enemies of women's rights. They face the same
temptation recorded here, in the early days of the movement,
when sexual politics seemed to express so vividly our real anger and frustration—and was so much sexier, to the media,
and to ourselves, than the hard, seemingly insoluble, endless,
mundane realities of fighting for ERA or pay equity, or political clout. After reading these pages, or in retrospect, one
might see that sexual politics also helped build the movement
—it gave expression to real anger, long suppressed. Who is to
say now if it attracted more women than it repelled? Was I too
harsh, or not stern enough, in those early warnings of the
dangers of sexual politics? Still, looking back, one sees that
whatever harm or good it did, sexual politics was not what
empowered us to change our lives.

Reliving this history, one can now ask whether the diversion and division of NOW caused by some members' preoccupation with, for instance, lesbian rights, in the early seventies,
took away energies that might have passed the ERA in those
first seven years. One can still wonder, and probably never
know, whether the obsession with sexual issues that divided

and diverted the movement in this period (not the serious confronting of rape, or lesbian rights or real grievances against men, which I firmly support) was simply an ideological mistake, fed by those long suppressed rages, or a calculated diversion provoked by agents provocateurs within our ranks. Agents of CIA or FBI, the Watergate hearings revealed, had indeed been sent into the women's movement at this time, though even using the Freedom of Information act we never could find out who they were. We do know also that we were infiltrated by agents of far left political sects, attempting to use the life of our movement to advance the extremist ideology that was destroying their own. We may never know the full answer to some of the mysteries I hint at here.

Other movements in this period were destroyed as, for instance, radical extremists, including government agents provocateurs, pushed groups like SDS or Weathermen to such excesses of rhetorical fantasy that they finally alienated their own members, to say nothing of the American public. In our movement—because perhaps, it was more immediately and continually related to, rooted in, checked and validated by life —the extremists did not prevail.

After those sobering defeats and rescindings of the ERA in the early and mid-seventies, the leadership of NOW and other feminist groups decided to go back to "basics"—the issues of economic and educational opportunity, and equality, organizing state by state for ERA, forming coalitions with the large establishment women's organizations (League of Women Voters, YWCA, Junior League, whose members were changing their lives too), pulling off the unprecedented political miracle of extending the seven-year deadline for ERA, and, heartbreakingly, almost but not quite making it—against the rising wave of Reagan conservatism, those last three states could not be won. But the battle brought into movement leadership vigorous, effective, confident young women, who took on the challenge of changing the mainstream.

Good leadership kept emerging in all the organizations; the extremists became a fringe element. Those who chanted the slogan "out of the mainstream into the revolution" in the bitter Philadelphia NOW convention that prompted my "Open Letter to the Women's Movement—1976," which ends this book, gave way, or themselves matured into leaders who took on the hard, grueling responsibility of building a women's movement that could transform the mainstream. It was good that NOW remained outside the political parties, becoming in effect the one political organization whose first priority is women's rights: despite the dismay some sisters sometimes voiced at its "stridency," it was only that independent political pressure from outside that forced the Democratic Party in 1984 to take that history-making step and put a woman on the presidential ticket. It was also good to have the National Women's Political Caucus with the savvy to mount effective floor operations inside the political convention. As violence has mounted against abortion clinics, it is good to have NOW members standing vigil with their own bodies to defend those clinics as the National Abortion Rights Action League (NARAL) and the Caucus press the political battle.

In recent years, I have felt great respect for the leadership of NOW, and NWPC, and NARAL and have been delighted when they asked for my advice or help. I have developed a warm working relationship with the leaders of NOW in New York, where I live. I keep addressing the problems that continue to mount, seemingly insoluble, demanding new solutions, as "Distinguished Director" of the NOW Legal Defense and Education Fund, though I don't go to all the meetings.

Despite the early battles over turf recorded here, I developed great admiration and respect for Bella Abzug, as well as personal friendship, as we worked together in 1980 in Copenhagen to try and prevent the UN International Women's Conference from being diverted from effective world-wide action on women's rights to divisive attacks on Israel and "Zionism as racism." (I wish Bella's own political timing had been better —she would have made a great first woman Mayor of New York, in the La Guardia tradition.) Whether or not Gloria Steinem was ever involved in the CIA, she certainly became a devoted feminist in the women's movement and contributed much of wit and style and shrewdness. Despite my own more recent concern with the "Second Stage" of bringing feminism to new terms with *family*, I think it was important for young women to have an attractive role model like Gloria Steinem who chose not to marry and have children.

Reliving these years, I see how good it was that the women's movement, almost from the beginning, was too big, and encompassed too broad a range of religious, social, generational, and economic differences, to even try to contain itself in a single organization. In the beginning, where I myself was responsible for some of the organizational proliferation, it seemed simply expedient, accidental. If abortion was too controversial for NOW, rather than splitting that organization, I and some others joined with some men in starting NARAL to establish abortion as a woman's right to choose. If NOW was temporarily under leadership determined to get "out of the mainstream into the revolution," the National Women's Political Caucus could get women running for office, organizing to "make policy, not coffee" in the mainstream political parties. When Caucus leaders seemed to get caught in the crossfires of political opportunism in one or another party, NOW's independence and growing political maturity gave the crucial feminist issues mainstream political clout. When *Ms.* was titillating some with sermons about unshaven armpits and pubic hair, others started the Women's Forum to give the isolated women now beginning to move into those boardrooms on the sweep of equal opportunity a new-girls' network of support to counter the old-boys', and a feminist voice for the "dress for success" crowd.

My own experiences recorded here were paralleled in innumerable waves and ripples of innovation and creative energy as women in every town and suburb, office and profession, church and community agency, seemed simultaneously and spontaneously to find their voices and began empowering each other, organizing all those women's caucuses, in medical and law schools, sociological and literary associations . . . began preaching the sermons and reciting the prayers, in every Protestant denomination, Jewish synagogue and Catholic church . . . began teaching women's studies in every community college and university and creating what seemed to be a whole new section of the publishing industry, so that many bookstores set up a separate section of "women" books. And such a spurt of creativity in painting and sculpture as women began to take themselves seriously as artists! And the mothers and grandmothers of the daughters now getting their MBAs restyled themselves as "professional volunteers" if they did not go back to school or into jobs themselves. And all the delicious theorizing, and varieties of personal negotiation, clash and accommodation, as men began to be *expected* to share the housework and the child care.

In those years, we surely took it for granted that women would bring a new and different vision to every art and science, once they rose from invisible, anonymous service to active voice. We surely expected that women who were brought by the movement into positions of political power and economic reward would keep faith and serve the general cause of women as best they could with their new clout. And many did. I used to believe that when, and maybe only when, women reached a point of critical mass in any field, you would begin to hear that other voice, women's own authentic voice, at last.

But will we hear that new voice from the young women who are now entering all these fields in numbers that finally do begin to approach critical mass but do not have the consciousness born of battling for those rights, who do not even know how much of their own confidence and sense of possibility they owe to the women's movement? Will history make them pay their dues, some different way? Less *consciously women*, now, more confident as people, will they hear, express, that other voice more freely, or not at all?

It's ironic to think that the women's movement—which sent its daughters to law school, medical school, into the MBA program and the executive suite—is at least partly responsible for that two-income Yuppie family that is fueling whatever prosperity this nation now enjoys, paying for those proliferating gourmet restaurants and expensive condominiums. Those Yuppies who grew up taking for granted those new choices and opportunities are so busy and preoccupied with that rat race for success on the job, and "having it all," "putting it all together," they do not have the time, or see the need, for a women's movement. The Yuppies take women's rights for granted—but they "aren't feminists." Does it matter? Are they, even now, in danger of embracing a new feminine mystique, if the economy turns down and jobs become scarce again? Before the end of the eighties, will yet another generation of feminists arise to take the women's movement "out of the mainstream into the revolution"? Since I now realize how women, including me, have to keep on changing, this time I might join them.

And then, again, will the women whose lives have changed, as a result of the events recorded here, and those who started from this different place, join with the new men emerging to find that new political direction we all now need for democratic survival, human survival? In the thrashing about for new direction, new leadership, new thinking that is going on now among men and women, it may be reassuring to relive those crucial years when the women's movement improbably became perhaps the greatest revolution of our time—simply by giving voice to the real questions women were facing in their lives: middle-class American women, white and black, including poor women who would rather not be poor and rich women who were not all that secure. As we look back, we can see that as long as that movement tackled real questions with actions that changed and opened lives, as long as the movement, in whatever way, empowered lots of real women to change their own lives, the movement, and women, grew and developed. After years of such movement, women are now in a different place. In 1985, women, and all who yearn for a new human politics in America and peace in the world, are coming to grips with the necessity to define that different place we are in now, so we can move anew from here. Maybe reliving the way we did it then, including the mistakes we made and avoided, could help.

Betty Friedan
New York
January, 1985

Introduction

This is a book that, quite literally, has written itself in history—in actions, and words leading to and from actions, that are now all women's story. I never had time to write it as a book because I was too busy acting it: events were moving so fast, and I was moving with them and sometimes making them happen. Wasn't it Marx who said you can't fight a revolution and write a book at the same time? I did not set out consciously to start a revolution when I wrote *The Feminine Mystique*, but it changed my life, as a woman and as a writer, and other women tell me it changed theirs. I have had to take the responsibility for the revolution my words helped start.

The words I've written in the past dozen years led to or came out of the actions and questions of the modern women's movement—as my own personal experience moved, and confronted, that movement and evolved new questions beyond it. The words as they were spoken in hours of action, or written down in hours between action, are public history; the thoughts I have now, of what it all meant, the memories of surrounding circumstances and events, feelings and problems not then fully understood or shared, are personal: the women's movement as I experienced it. And that new relationship between personal experience and political action is the essence of women's leap into history.

For me it began in the late 1950's with the gradual realization that my own life, and those of other women, didn't fit, couldn't even be understood in the abstract terms of the conventional or sophisticated thought which then defined women and by which we defined ourselves. The unraveling of what I called the feminine mystique from the actual fabric of women's life was my personal consciousness-raising—though I didn't call it that, in the five years it took me to write that book. But those words, rooted in my personal truth, led other women to their own personal truth, truth that had been hidden by the mystique. The public sharing of women's experience led us to a new understanding that its limitations and urgent necessities were more than uniquely personal: they were political. And this new consciousness inexorably led to action: the women's movement. Then women's experience began to be analyzed by new abstractions borrowed from the ideologies of past revolutions . . .

Today, in 1976, the women's movement for equality, human freedom and human dignity—for our own participation in the actions and decisions of human destiny and our own identity in the family of man—clearly emerges as the major movement for basic social change in this decade and possibly the most far-reaching revolution of all time. It affects our daily personal lives immediately, women, men, children; pervades all our institutions, office and home; confronts the economy, politics of right and left, theology, sexuality itself, in unpredictable ways. Today I feel a new need to demystify ideology by relating it to the concrete actions from which it came.

Because words of mine, based on personal truth, led me and others to organize the women's movement, I feel a terrible responsibility, as well as an exultant elation, for the transforming, transcendent actions of the movement, and for its personal reality in every woman's life, including my own. I feel a new urgency to test the words against personal truth again, lest we bind and blind ourselves by a new mystique, in our feminist reaction against the old one.

For with all our elation at the power of the movement, its unprecedented sweep through the world and into the consciousness of women across the bonds of generation, geography, race, class and man-made politics, we need to admit a growing frustration at its problems. There is a certain paralysis of the women's movement now, a turning inward of energies, an eruption and perhaps a manipulation of the rage and bitterness that women for generations took out on themselves. If that rage and bitterness is discharged in blind reactive hatred against men, personally and politically, must it not create a backlash from men, and ultimately, outrage, disillusionment and bitterness from women? Has the rhetoric of sexual politics blinded us to the real political actions and the allies needed to actually open new options in women's lives? Is the promise of our sisterhood—for the first time women able to affirm and work with one another, opening life for us all—now being belied by actions, turning us against ourselves? Is our rage being manipulated by our enemies to paralyze our possibilities of action, to prevent effective responsible leadership from emerging? How do we transcend that rage?

To put it differently, from the very beginning the women's movement for me has involved having to turn new corners: coming to dead ends, looking in vain for blueprints or answers from books and authorities, then trusting my intuition—my gut personal knowledge of something wrong, something missing, something needed—and trying to find the answer in the experience itself. Women's life now for us all means moving on unmapped roads, with signposts nonexistent or not too clear, mapping it as you go along—and maybe not seeing clearly where it's leading until you're almost there, until you look back and see how far you've gone. After a while, you begin to trust the feel of being on the right road, and the warnings that you are off it. But you can come to a dead end and not recognize the new corner to turn. You can get very tired, discouraged. I sometimes wonder what keeps us going.

I started to write *The Feminine Mystique* because the very assumptions of the articles I was then writing for women's magazines no longer rang true to me—though I, as other women in America, was living my personal life according to those assumptions. I began that book with a dimly realized doubt:

> Gradually, without seeing it clearly for quite a while, I came to realize that something is very wrong with the way American women are trying to live their lives today. I sensed it first as a

question mark in my own life, as a wife and mother of three small children, half-guiltily, and therefore half-heartedly, almost in spite of myself, using my abilities and education in work that took me away from home. . . . There was a strange discrepancy between the reality of our lives as women and the image to which we were trying to conform, the image that I came to call the feminine mystique. I wondered if other women faced this schizophrenic split and what it meant.

After five years of figuring out why it had happened and what it was doing to us, I said no to that feminine mystique. But I had a hard time ending that book. They said I had to give some solutions, positive answers, a cure, clear directions as to where we were to go from there. I couldn't see such solutions then, neither in terms of my personal life, nor for women generally. That book had to end with the question:

Who knows what women can be when they are finally free to become themselves? Who knows what women's intelligence will contribute when it can be nourished without denying love? Who knows of the possibilities of love when men and women share not only children, home, and garden, not only the fulfillment of their biological roles, but the responsibilities and passions of the work that creates the human future and the full human knowledge of who they are? It has barely begun, the search of women for themselves. But the time is at hand when the voices of the feminine mystique can no longer drown out the inner voice that is driving women on to become complete.

Over the next few years, I started work on a second book, looking in the United States and other countries for new patterns for women's lives beyond the feminine mystique. I found some exceptional individual women bucking the patterns of society with more or less guilt—and more and more women with new aspirations and new problems—but no new patterns, none at all in America and something disappointing about the ones I began to investigate abroad. And meanwhile there were more and more books and articles and panel discussions and scholarly symposia on the woman problem, and there were reports of commissions on the status of women that no one did anything about, until it looked like the problems of women—finally recognized again in the 1960s in the United States after a sleep of nearly half a century—were going to be drowned again in a sea of words. I began to wonder if these words were meant to take the place of the action that might change society. Virtually all words written about women until recently merely celebrated or rationalized the changeless face of Eve: woman is, man does. I wrote such words once—pre-movement—myself. Part I of this book deals with those experiences that led to and from *The Feminine Mystique*, the reactions it evoked, and those first ideological gropings, from personal to political.

And then in 1966 I saw that nothing was going to happen to most women except talk, words, words, words, unless we organized a movement to change society, as the blacks had done. And I put down that second book and began to organize, with other women, the movement "to take action to bring women into the mainstream of American society now . . . full equality for women in fully equal partnership with men." Part II deals with the organization of the mainstream of the modern women's movement, as I experienced it—which is not quite the same as "women's lib," as the media presented it. Then the rhetoric of "women's lib" and the ideological tracts on sexual politics that began to pour out in the name of radical or Amazonian or separatist feminism forced me to turn another corner. My experience showed me increasingly that the rhetoric was leading to a dangerous dead end. I began to insist to my sisters in the movement that we had to create ideology from our own experience; that we couldn't take a blueprint abstractly from previous revolutions, we had to test our ideology constantly against our real lives of work and home, as women, alone and with men and children.

I look back now at my first attempts to raise such questions, and remember all I felt and didn't say. We really couldn't face uncomfortable questions then; we didn't trust our sisterhood enough, our own strength. I only hinted at such questions in the women's movement at the beginning of the seventies. But my words to the movement then tried to direct energies away from the rhetoric of sexual politics and toward the necessity of political and economic actions that would affect the conditions of all women—the organizing of the Women's Strike for

Equality on August 26th, 1970, the fiftieth anniversary of the vote for women; and the National Women's Political Caucus.

In 1971 I began to write my personal notebook (Part III), in which I tried to relate the words I was using to challenge or lead others politically to the reality of my personal life at the time, and to my encounters with women and men in other countries and other systems. I also began to face more openly my differences with the sexual politics that seemed for a while to take over the women's movement.

Then, in the last three years, I tried to bow out of organizational activity to concentrate on writing, lecturing, teaching and finding the "new yes"—the sex-role revolution, Stage II. For increasingly I have felt the women's movement—and my own—coming to another dead end or a new corner to turn. It cannot continue in a straight line any more just saying no as we have done now to sex discrimination in every institution from baseball fields to banks, saying no to the feminine mystique in all the images bombarding our minds, from school spelling books to TV commercials. Not that the first stage of the women's movement is over: even the gains we have won—outlawing sex discrimination in employment and education, the Supreme Court's interpretation of our constitutional right to choose in the matter of childbirth and abortion, the Equal Rights Amendment and the new concepts of equality in marriage, family and home—are threatened now by reactionary political, economic and religious groups who are attempting to manipulate the hostilities, fears and problems of transition into masculine backlash and feminine retreat.

Inside the women's movement itself, the radical fringe has all but died out from the alienation implicit in its message and tactics. And now the very energies of the mainstream are paralyzed and turned inward, in real or manipulated power battles or ideological disputes. A fringe is trying to take NOW "out of the mainstream." In their personal lives, many women and men who can no longer live the way they used to, are similarly paralyzed in desperate need of a "new yes." In order to move on to that "new yes," I think we must once again put our theories and assumptions to the test of personal truth—of our own lives, and of our movement—and find therein the clue to the new questions, the new thinking we must move into. Our movement must turn a new corner, but we cannot turn this corner with the women's movement turned inward on itself, or separated from men, or even in the isolation from other currents in society that marked our first decade.

For the energies released by the women's movement in the United States now confront an economic crisis and increasing family crises—recession, inflation; layoffs, unemployment; reductions in health and welfare and social service and education budgets; and the enormous increase in divorce rates. Women are coming out of colleges and professional schools in unprecedented new numbers while other women and men are losing their jobs; women young and old have new aspirations and self-respect, and feel an independence they must stress because they don't quite trust it yet; some do not need a man for economic support, and others are suffering from the loss of that support; but still, most of them want to love and be loved by a man, and are able now to decide when and whether to have a child. How, how to put it all together? The new questions are much too complex to answer by simply saying no to the feminine mystique and sex discrimination. If this movement, in political strategy or personal actions, does not lead to a "new yes" for women and for the men and children with whom they share real life, it could even be reversed. Part IV deals with these new questions, and the larger implications of the sex role revolution. In Part V, I begin my own search for the "new yes."

To see where we have come from, where we are going, what it all means, I must look back at our movement—as I myself have helped to create it and truly experienced it—and confront the problems, doubts, emotions and personal realities of the public accomplishments which sometimes seemed almost accidental and still seem almost miraculous to me. Reliving in memory the frantic, mundane, petty, spontaneous and improvised juxtapositions and happenings which led to certain actions and leaps forward that now seem awesome, heroic, I must set out plainly certain problems and reservations that I felt diffident to speak about before. And reliving my personal experience and that of other women, I must try to figure out what really keeps us going—and the new problems we must face and overcome if we are not to be turned back or lose heart. I have come near to losing heart, nearer than anyone ever knew. And yet I know, in the deepest part of me, that the women's movement for equality was and is necessary: it is my personal truth and strength as it has been for other women.

I do not pretend to be writing here either my own autobiography or the history of the women's movement but merely to be sharing my own experience of our leap into history these past twelve years. That experience was shared with many women—and, I suppose, was seminal for more others than I ever knew—but I can only tell it as I experienced it, in political and personal reality.

For the reality of this revolution is that we—the middle-class women who started it—did it for ourselves. Other revolutions, despite the clichés of radical rhetoric, were also started by middle-class intellectuals (the only ones with education to put it into words), but they were always doing it for someone else: the poor, the working class, "them." Liberal whites used to tell blacks what they needed (and middle-class intellectual blacks still prescribe abstract doctrines for "them"). Doing it for *ourselves* is the essence of the women's movement: it keeps us honest, keeps us real, keeps us concrete. And it is that *doing*—not just being, feeling, or sweeping the floor that gets dirty again—which brings women into history. It is *new* for women to be making history—not just a few queens, empresses or exceptional geniuses, but hundreds, thousands, millions of women now entering history, knowing we have made history—by changing our own lives. The most superficial view of the daily paper—front page, sports page, financial page, want ads—shows not only the entrance of women into the actions and professions from which they were barred (the Little League, the police and fire departments, submarines, governor, mayor, Episcopal priest, Conservative rabbi, radical terrorist, orchestra conductor, Wall Street broker), but the transformation of the political, economic, theological and cultural agenda (the very language, the style, the questions addressed) and also the transformation of the women's page: lifestyle, of importance to men.

We otherwise ordinary American women, finding the power to change our own lives, changed the face of history.

We have thus known and experienced the unique human passion as not many men, and almost no women, have known it before. As the men who made the American Revolution knew two hundred years ago—it was the *doing* of it, the process, the participation in the making of our own history that brought us to a new level of human aliveness. For us who made the leap, herstory itself is the reward.

But women from now on will move in history in a new way: it is a qualitative change, that history will be made by women now as well as men. The history of these dozen years already has a different kind of agenda, style, texture from previous history created solely by men. Unlike the linear history of the past, our herstory inevitably deals with the stuff of daily life—in the total, circular, irregular, spontaneously changing flexible gestalt life comes in. As women begin moving into public, professional life—and as men begin to share child care, cooking, cleaning—the whole story is clearly more than a few women reversing roles with men or having a piece of the action, a chance at the jobs only men had before. Something else begins to happen—a bridging, a transcending of the polarization between masculine and feminine, between the abstract and concrete, between eternal values and grubby, sweaty, everyday realities. It will not be a separate story very long. The rights were won after a century of struggle, and then there was a half-century of sleep, and now the women's movement is changing society so women can use those rights. And then it will be human liberation: the next chapter of the human story. After we turn that corner—

—B.F.

New York

PART I

Consciousness

Breaking Through the Feminine Mystique

I keep getting asked "Why did you write *The Feminine Mystique?*" and "What happened in your life that made you start the women's movement?" and I never knew how to answer. Because I did not set out deliberately to found the women's movement; in fact, I had never been particularly interested in women's problems. How I happened to write *The Feminine Mystique* seems almost accidental now. Like Jung, analyzing his childhood dreams eighty years later, I sense "connections which became clear to me only much later in life." It is a mystery, the whole thing—why it happened, how it started. What gave any of us the courage to make that leap? I sometimes feel as if we have been simply acting out a predestined chapter of human evolution, like Jungian archetypes: "They act first and do not know what they are doing. Only long afterward do they reflect on what they have done."

Reflecting, I see now that our movement needs no mystique. It happened at this moment in time from historical necessity; the evolution of society, and the technology made by man, had brought women to this jumping-off point: a massive crisis of identity brewing already in my mother's generation came to a head in my generation of American women. And a certain combination of circumstances in my own life confronted me very sharply with this crisis—and gave me the

3

ability finally to understand it and to put into words what other women were experiencing.

In a certain sense it was almost accidental—coincidental—that I wrote *The Feminine Mystique*, and in another sense my whole life had prepared me to write that book; all the pieces of my own life came together for the first time in the writing of it.

There was my mother, and her discontent, which I never understood. I didn't want to be like my mother. Nothing my father did, nothing he bought her, nothing we did ever seemed to satisfy her. When she married my father, she'd had to give up her job editing the woman's page of the newspaper in Peoria. She could hardly wait until I got to junior high to put the idea into my head to try out for the school newspaper, to start a literary magazine in high school. She could hardly wait for me to go to the college she had no chance to go to, to edit the newspaper there. And at that college I learned the Freudian explanation for my mother's inability to find "feminine fulfillment" as a woman. I also started out to be a psychologist myself, and because the great gestalt psychologists had had to flee from Nazi Germany, learned from Kurt Koffka at Smith, and then Kurt Lewin at Iowa and Erik Erikson at Berkeley how to look at any phenomenon, including my mother's frustration, in its total, concrete, cultural context: the gestalt.

And so I got the authority and tools with which I ultimately was able to pierce through that Freudian mystique of femininity. And also at Smith, that great woman's college, I was taken seriously as a person and inculcated with an ineradicable sense of responsibility for the human destiny, and my own power to affect it. But my passion against injustice—and the chutzpah to think I could help end it—was not, until much later, focused on women or even on myself. (Though it may have stemmed from my own experience of injustice as the daughter of an immigrant Jew in Peoria, Illinois, and from the pragmatic sense of possibility I got nevertheless as I grew up there and was encouraged by my father to leave.) And then in my years after college as a reporter for the labor press, I learned to pierce through the fog of words and even of psychology to the grubby economic underside of American reality. And as a reporter and a writer, I learned to get the story, where the answer is never known at the beginning, as earlier, as a student psychologist and social scientist at Smith and later at Berkeley, I'd learned to test hypotheses and to listen for the hidden clues in the patient's own words and actions. Strangely enough, I remember now a funny feeling, almost of recognition, when on a routine assignment involving a strike at a major electric plant, most of whose workers were women, I discovered that women seemed to be discriminated against not only by the company but in the union. But no one was interested then. I didn't have a word for sex discrimination even when I myself was fired, for being pregnant, from my own newspaper job.

But above all, what drove me to consciousness was the fact that—with all my high-powered education and brilliant promise as a future psychologist or journalist—I too embraced and lived that feminine mystique. Determined that I would find that feminine fulfillment which had eluded my mother, I first gave up psychology fellowships and then even newspaper reporting jobs. I lived the life of the suburban housewife that was everyone's dream at that time. In 1974, *New York* magazine asked me to recall what it was like, being a woman twenty-five years ago—in 1949, which was the year the feminine mystique really hit us. I wasn't conscious of that, then, of course. I just lived it, like most other women in their twenties and thirties at that time. It is only now that I see it as having been the last extreme defense against that necessary evolution which neither I, nor any of us, could evade much longer—the movement to give birth to ourselves as a new kind of woman, to confront our personhood, finally, in human society.

The Way
We Were—1949

 In 1949 I was concentrating on breast-feeding and wheeling Danny, my first baby, to the park, and reading Dr. Spock. I was beginning to wonder if I really wanted to go back to work, after all, when my maternity leave was up. I bought a pressure cooker and *The Joy of Cooking* and a book by George Nelson about *The Modern House*. One Saturday, though we had no money, we went out to Rockland County and looked at old barns that my husband might be able to convert into a house. And I wrote my mother that I wanted the sterling silver—which she had offered us as a wedding present and I had scorned as too bourgeois—after all.

That was the year it really hit, the feminine mystique, though at the time we didn't know what it was. It was just that our lives seemed to have shifted in dimension, in perspective. The last of our group, which had come to New York after Smith and Vassar and shared an apartment in the Village, was getting married. During the war, we'd had jobs like "researcher" or "editorial assistant," and met GIs at the Newspaper Guild Canteen, and written V-mail letters to lonesome boys we'd known at home, and had affairs with married men —hiding our diaphragms under the girdles in the dresser. And we had considered ourselves part of the vanguard of the working-class revolution, going to Marxist discussion groups and rallies at Madison Square Garden and feeling only contempt

for dreary bourgeois capitalists like our fathers—though we
still read *Vogue* under the hair dryer, and spent all our salaries
on clothes at Bergdorf's and Bendel's, replacing our college
Braemer sweaters with black cashmere and Gucci gloves, on
sale.

And then the boys our age had come back from the war. I
was bumped from my job on a small labor news service by a
returning veteran, and it wasn't so easy to find another job I
really liked. I filled out the applications for Time-Life researcher, which I'd always scorned before. All the girls I knew
had jobs like that, but it was official policy that no matter how
good, researchers, who were women, could never become
writers or editors. They could write the whole article, but the
men they were working with would always get the by-line as
writer. I was certainly not a feminist then—none of us were a
bit interested in women's rights. But I could never bring myself to take that kind of job. And what else was there? The
wartime government agencies where some of us had worked
were being dissolved. The group on Waverly Place was breaking up—Maggie, Harriet, Madelon, everyone was getting married (and Abe Rosenthal was waiting greedily to move into
that apartment so that *he* could get married).

It was very hard to find an apartment right after the war. I
had left the group and found a funny apartment in the base-
ment of a townhouse on West 86th. You had to go through the
furnace room to get to it, there were pipes on the ceiling, and
the cold water didn't work in the bathroom so you had to run
the hot an hour ahead to take a bath. It didn't even have a
kitchen, but since I had no interest in cooking, I didn't mind.
It had a brick wall and lots of shelves, and a terrace door, and
when Carl Friedan came back from running the Soldier Show
Company in Europe to start a summer theater in New Jersey,
his best friend, whom I worked with, said he knew a nice girl
with an apartment. He brought me an apple and told me jokes
which made me laugh, and he moved in. We got married in
City Hall, but went through it again with a rabbi in Boston
for his mother's sake. And while I was in the hospital having
Danny, he painted the pipes on the ceiling and made a kitchen
out of the closet and moved our bed into the living room so
Danny could have a nursery.

After the war, I had been very political, very involved, consciously radical. Not about women, for heaven's sake! If you were a radical in 1949, you were concerned about the Negroes, and the working class, and World War III, and the Un-American Activities Committee and McCarthy and loyalty oaths, and Communist splits and schisms, Russia, China and the UN, but you certainly didn't think about being a woman, politically. It was only recently that we had begun to think of ourselves as women at all. But that wasn't political—it was the opposite of politics. Eight months pregnant, I climbed up on a ladder on a street corner to give a speech for Henry Wallace. But in 1949 I was suddenly not that interested in political meetings.

Some of us had begun to go to Freudian analysts. Like the lady editor in Moss Hart's *Lady in the Dark*, we were supposedly discovering that what we really wanted was a man. Whatever the biological, psychosexual reality, a woman was hardly in a mood to argue with that message if (a) she was lonesome and tired of living alone, or (b) she was about to lose her job or (c) had become disillusioned with it. In 1949, nobody really had to tell a woman that she wanted a man, but the message certainly began bombarding us from all sides: domestic bliss had suddenly become chic, sophisticated, and whatever made you want to be a lady editor, police reporter, or political activist, could prevent or destroy that bliss—bourgeois security, no longer despised.

The magazines were full of articles like: "What's Wrong with American Women?"; "Let's Stop Blaming Mom"; "Shortage of Men?"; "Isn't a Woman's Place in the Home?"; "Women Aren't Men"; "What Women Can Learn from Mother Eve"; "Really a Man's World, Politics"; and "Nearly Half the Women in *Who's Who* are Single."

The short stories in those women's magazines we still read under the hair dryer were all about miserable girls with supposedly glamorous jobs in New York, who suddenly saw the light and went home to marry Henry. In "Honey, Don't You Cry" (*McCall's*, January 1949), the heroine is reading a letter from her mother: "You should come home, daughter. You can't be happy living alone like that." In "The Applause of Thousands" (*Ladies' Home Journal*, March 1949), the young woman *pities* her poor mother who dreamed of being an actress; she is going to get married before she can even be tempted by such dreams.

I remember in particular the searing effect on me, who once intended to be a psychologist, of a story in *McCall's* in December 1949, called "A Weekend with Daddy." A little girl who lives a lonely life with her mother, divorced, an intellectual know-it-all psychologist, goes to the country to spend a weekend with her father and his new wife, who is wholesome, happy, a good cook and gardener. And there is love and laughter and growing flowers and hot clams and a gourmet cheese omelet and square dancing, and she doesn't want to go home. But, pitying her poor mother typing away all by herself in the lonesome apartment, she keeps her guilty secret that from now on she will be living for the moments when she can escape to that dream house in the country where they know "what life is all about."

I remember about that time running into a real psychologist, a woman slightly older than I was whom I had known in graduate school. She had been brilliant and ambitious. Unlike me, she had taken the fellowships and gotten her Ph.D. What was she doing now? "I am married," she said with great self-satisfaction, "and I am pregnant." When I asked, she said that she had picked her husband up on the subway. And I understood, because in 1949 I was also becoming infected by the mystique, that it almost didn't matter who the man was who became the instrument of your feminine fulfillment. I was awed by the strength and sincerity of her new psychological awareness, that she would even find him on the subway.

That year saw the last of the spirited, brave, adventurous heroines who had filled the magazines and movies in the thirties and forties—the Claudette Colbert, Myrna Loy, Bette Davis, Rosalind Russell, and Katharine Hepburn types. These heroines, in the end, got their man, but they were usually working toward some goal or vision of their own, independent and determined and passionately involved with the world. They were less aggressive in pursuit of a man, less kittenish than the Doris Day little housewife that followed, and the men were drawn to them as much by their spirit as by their looks. "Career woman" in the fifties became a pejorative, denoting a ball-busting man-eating harpy, a miserable neurotic witch from whom man and child should flee for very life.

In March 1949, the *Ladies' Home Journal* printed the prototype of the innumerable paeans to "Occupation: Housewife" that were to flood the women's magazines into the sixties. It began with a woman complaining that when she has to write "housewife" on the census blank, she gets an inferiority complex. ("When I write it I realize that here I am, a middle-aged woman, with a university education, and I've never made anything out of my life. I'm just a housewife.") Then the author of the reply, who somehow never is a housewife (in this case Dorothy Thompson, newspaperwoman, foreign correspondent, famous columnist), roars with laughter. The trouble with you, she scolds, is that you don't realize that you are expert in a dozen careers, simultaneously. "You might write: business manager, cook, nurse, chauffeur, dressmaker, interior decorator, accountant, caterer, teacher, private secretary—or just put down philanthropist. . . . All your life you have been giving away your energies, your skills, your talents, your services, for love." But still, the housewife complains, I'm nearly fifty and I've never done what I hoped to do in my youth—music. I've wasted my college education.

Ho-ho, laughs Miss Thompson, aren't your children musical because of you, and all those struggling years while your husband was finishing his great work, didn't you keep a charming house on $3,000 a year and paper the living room yourself, and watch the market like a hawk for bargains? And in time off, didn't you type and proofread your husband's manuscripts, play piano duets with the children to make practicing more fun, read their books in high school to follow their study? "But all this vicarious living—through others," the housewife sighs. "As vicarious as Napoleon Bonaparte," Miss Thompson scoffs, "or a queen. I simply refuse to share your self-pity. You are one of the most successful women I know."

That year the *Ladies' Home Journal* serialized Margaret Mead's *Male and Female*, with its deceptively tempting version of a South Sea world where a woman succeeds and is envied by men, just by "being" a woman.

In Bali, little girls between two and three walk much of the time with purposely thrust-out little bellies, and the older women tap them playfully as they pass. "Pregnant!" they tease. So the little girl learns that . . . some day she will have a baby, and having a baby is, on the whole, one of the most exciting and conspicuous achievements that can be presented to the eyes of small children in these simple worlds, in some of which the largest buildings are only fifteen feet tall. . . . Furthermore, the little girl learns that she will have a baby not because she is strong or energetic or initiating, not because she works and struggles and tries, and in the end succeeds, but simply because she is a girl and not a boy, and girls turn into women, and in the end—if they protect their femininity—have babies. . . . In our Occidental view of life, women, fashioned from man's rib, can at the most strive unsuccessfully to imitate man's superior powers and higher vocations.

That it was slightly schizophrenic to try to live through your pregnant belly, as it were, in an increasingly complex world where the largest buildings were a lot taller than fifteen feet—well, we only woke up to that later. In 1949 we were suckers for that apple—we could cop out from the competition, the dull, hard work of "man's higher vocations," by simply "playing our role as women." No more need to rock the boat, risk failure or resentment from men.

That year, the *Ladies' Home Journal* also serialized *Cheaper by the Dozen*, the story of the lady engineer who applied her scientific know-how to raising that newly fashionable large family. Very good reporters were given the assignment of documenting in minute detail every detail of the daily life of the newly glamorous American housewife—cooking in her own kitchen, with all her new appliances. It was also reported in the fall of 1949 that "something new in birth rates has occurred in the U.S. Between 1940 and 1947, the reproductive rate of women college graduates increased 81%, compared with an increase of only 29% among women who had completed only grade school."

It certainly did not occur to any of us then, even the most radical, that companies which made a big profit selling us all those washing machines, dryers, freezers and second cars, were overselling us on the bliss of domesticity in order to sell us more things. Even the most radical of us, in our innocence, wanted those pressure cookers.

We were even more innocent in our sophistication as women. Though I was virtually a virgin myself when I came to New York after college, it was my lot to arrange abortions for our entire Smith group. Why me? Because I was the radical, also a psychologist and unshockable (I knew all the Freudian words). More practically, as a newspaperwoman, I was supposed to know my way around. The men I worked with during the war, necessarily over draft age, were *Front Page* types who taught me to write a jazzy lead after three martinis at lunch. They were avuncular to my innocence, with occasional lecherous lapses. The first time I said, "Trav, you have to help me. A friend of mine is pregnant," the whole office sprang into action. I was told, in serious, sinister secrecy, where to take my "friend." It also cost $1,000, and they were concerned where my "friend" would get the money. Six months later, I had to come to them again. This time, the reaction was not so warm. It was years before I realized that they had assumed each "friend" needing an abortion was *me*.

I myself never had an abortion, though I personally accompanied several of these friends to scary, butchery back rooms, and shared their fear and distrust of the shifty, oily, illegal operators, and sat outside the room and heard the screams and wondered what I'd do if they died, and got them into the taxis afterward. Dear Virginias who read this now—when our efforts have gotten you legal abortion in New York, and an historic Supreme Court decision affirming your right to control your own body, and sexual privacy, and birth control and abortion—you can't imagine how humiliating, traumatic, horrible it was, to need an abortion in 1949. Nor can you whose parents buy you the pill understand the awkward indignity of getting a diaphragm in New York, in 1949, if you weren't married—and sometimes even if you were.

My last task, as the group broke up, was to find an Episcopal priest to marry Maggie and Roger in a fancy church acceptable to her mother. But in 1949 not even a young pacifist minister would perform the ceremony for a man who had been divorced. It was harder to find such a minister than an abortionist. Divorce was unthinkable, in our very buying of the feminine mystique. In fact, no woman I knew personally had been through divorce herself in 1949, and that was still true fifteen years later when the first threat of its personal possibility paralyzed me with terror in the security of my own suburban dream house.

"Security" was a big part of what began to happen in 1949. "Security," as in "risks," was in the headlines, as in atomic secrets, Communist espionage, the House Un-American Activities Committee, loyalty oaths, and the beginning of blacklists for writers. Was it unconscious political retreat that so many who had talked so bravely, and marched, suddenly detoured to the security of the private four walls of that house in suburbia—everything that was "bourgeois." Suddenly we stopped using the word "bourgeois." We were like our parents, it seemed. Suddenly we were very interested in houses and *things:* chairs, tables, silverware. We went to the Museum of Modern Art to study furniture and displays of modern architecture, and bought our first possessions—Eames chairs, a blond free-form sculptured Noguchi dining table, and a Herman Miller couch-day bed with a plain tweed-covered mattress and bolsters, so modern, so different from the overstuffed, tufted davenport at home (whose comfort I have now gone back to).

Toward the end of the year I read a story in the *Times* about a new garden apartment community in Queens called Parkway Village, built for the UN with some vacancies for ex-GIs. It was almost like having your own home: the apartments had French doors opening on to a common lawn where the children could go out and play by themselves, instead of having to be taken to the park. And there was a cooperative nursery school. During my lunch hour I took the subway to the wilds of Queens, and so began the fifteen-year trek of my own particular nuclear family away from the city, to that garden apartment in Queens, to a rented barn in Sneden's Landing, to our own eleven-room Charles Addams Victorian house in Rockland County, where my children (increased to three) grew up, and I chauffeured, and did the P.T.A. and buffet dinners, and hid, like secret drinking in the morning, the book I was writing when my suburban neighbors came for coffee, *The Feminine Mystique.*

I felt that I would never again, ever, be so happy as I was living in Queens. The floors were parquet, and the ceilings were molded white plaster, no pipes, and the plumbing worked. The rent was $118.50 a month, for four and one-half rooms, and we thought that was enormous. And now our friends were the other couples like us, with kids at the nursery school who squealed at each other from the baskets of the grocery carts we wheeled at the supermarket. It was fun at first, shopping in those new supermarkets. And we bought barbecue grills, and made dips out of sour cream and dried onion soup to serve with potato chips, while our husbands made the martinis as dry as in the city and cooked hamburgers on the charcoal, and we sat in canvas chairs on our terrace and thought how beautiful our children looked, playing in the twilight, and how lucky we all were, and that it would last forever.

There were six families in our group, and if your child smashed his finger in the manhole cover and you weren't home, one of the others would take him to the doctor. We had Thanksgiving and Christmas and Passover Seders as a joint family, and in the summer rented houses together, on Lake George and Fire Island, that we couldn't afford separately. And the support we gave each other hid the cracks in our own marriages—or maybe kept them from getting serious. As it is, of the six families, three couples are now divorced, one broken by suicide.

Having babies, the Care and Feeding of Children according to Doctor Spock, began to structure our lives. It took the place of politics. But the mystique was something else—that college graduates should make a *Career* of motherhood, not just one or two babies, but four, five, six. Why even go to college?

I remember the zeal with which we took the classes at the Maternity Center. Our husbands were envious, but then with natural childbirth the husbands could take the classes too, and breathe along, and show off at dinner parties, doing the exercises on the floor. And then there was the moral, political seriousness of our breast-feeding. In the summer of '49, I was frowned on for breast-feeding in public, on the front steps of my husband's summer theater. It wasn't fashionable then. But it's so *natural*, we gloried, feeling only scorn for our superficial

selfish sisters who thought breast-feeding was animal and
would spoil their figures. (Actually, I did not breast-feed in
public—I'd retire to the back row of the darkened theater
where they were rehearsing. But I did sit out on the front
steps afterwards, burping him in the sun.) And how proud I
was, continuing the breast-feeding nearly all that year, even
after the milk began to give out and I had to sterilize bottles
anyway. And how furious I was, when they called from the
office and insisted I come back to work, one month before that
year's maternity leave was over, because it was messing up
vacation schedules.

So twenty-five years later when that grown-up boy is having trouble with his girl, and—knowing Freudian words himself, if not yet Dr. Spock—says his insecurity in love is all my
fault, I still feel the pains of the guilt caused by leaving my
first baby with a nurse when I went back to work. Would all
that guilt have been necessary if Dr. Spock hadn't said, in the
section on "Should Mother Work?": "In most cases, the
mother is the best one to give him this feeling of 'belonging,'
safety and security. . . . If a mother realizes clearly how vital
this kind of care is to a small child, it may make it easier for
her to decide that the extra money she might earn, or the
satisfaction she might receive from an outside job, is not so
important after all."

To be honest, those years were not all products of the
"mystique." I still remember the marvelous dark night in the
spring of 1949 when we were wheeling Danny home in the
baby carriage. I looked down as we passed under a streetlight,
and he was smiling at me, and there was recognition in his
eyes. A person was there, and he knew me.

Besides, the reality of the babies, the bottles, the cooking,
the diapering, the burping, the carriage-wheeling, the pressure cooker, the barbecue, the playground, and doing-it-your-
self was more comfortable, more safe, secure, and satisfying—
that year and for a lot of years thereafter—than that supposedly glamorous "career" where you somehow didn't feel
wanted, and where no matter what you did you knew you
weren't going to get anywhere. There was a guilty feeling,
too: it was somehow your fault, *pushy* of you, to want that good
assignment for yourself, want the credit, the by-line, if the

idea, even the writing, had been yours. *Pushy*, too, if you felt
rejected when the men went out to lunch and talked shop in
one of those bars where women were not allowed—even if one
of those same men asked you out to lunch, alone, in the other
kind of restaurant, and held your hand, or knee, under the
tablecloth. It was uncomfortable, unreal in a way, working in
that kind of office with "career" still driving you, but having
no words to deal with, even *recognize*, that barrier that you
could never somehow break through, that made you invisible
as a person, that made them not take you seriously, that made
you feel so basically unimportant, almost unnecessary, and—
buried very deep—so angry.

At home, you *were* necessary, you were important, you
were the boss, in fact—the mother—and the new mystique
gave it the rationale of career.

The concrete, palpable actuality of the carpentry and cooking you could do yourself, and the surprising effectiveness of
the changes you could make happen in school boards and zoning and community politics, were somehow more real and secure than the schizophrenic and even dangerous politics of the
world revolution whose vanguard we used to fancy ourselves.
The revolution was obviously not going to *happen* that way in
America by 1949: the working class wanted those pressure
cookers, too. It was disillusioning, to say the least, to see what
was happening in the trade unions, and in Czechoslovakia and
the Soviet Union, even if the myth of the Communist menace
was mostly an excuse for red-baiting. In 1949, McCarthyism,
the danger of war against Russia and of fascism in America,
and the reality of U.S. imperial, corporate wealth and power
all made men and women who used to have large visions of
making the whole world over uncomfortable with the Old
Left rhetoric of revolution.

Suburbia, exurbia, with the children as an excuse—there
was a comfortable small world you could really do something
about, politically: the children's homework, even the new
math, compared to the atomic bomb.

The feminine mystique made it easier for a woman to retreat smugly, without the pangs of conscience and self-contempt a man might feel while using all his wits to sell cigarettes that would cause cancer, or deodorants. We could be

virtuous and pure of compromise, and even feel a smug contempt for the poor man who could not so easily escape the
ulcerous necessity of really conforming and competing. For a
long while, it looked as if women had gotten the better of that
bargain. It was only later that some of us discovered that
maybe we had walked as willing victims into a comfortable
concentration camp.

Shortly after 1949, I was fired from my job because I was
pregnant again. They weren't about to put up with the inconvenience of another year's maternity leave, even though I was
entitled to it under my union contract. It was unfair, *wrong*
somehow to fire me just because I was pregnant, and to hire a
man instead. I even tried calling a meeting of the people in the
union where I worked. It was the first personal stirring of my
own feminism, I guess. But the other women were just embarrassed, and the men uncomprehending. It was my own fault,
getting pregnant again, a *personal* matter, not something you
should take to the union. There was no word in 1949 for "sex
discrimination."

Besides, it was almost a relief; I had begun to feel so guilty
working, and I really wasn't getting anywhere in that job. I
was more than ready to embrace the feminine mystique. I took
a cooking course and started studying the suburban real-estate
ads. And the next time the census taker came around, I was
living in that old Charles Addams house we were fixing up, on
the Hudson River in Rockland County. And the children
numbered three. When the census taker asked my occupation,
I said self-consciously, virtuously, with only the faintest stir-
rings of protest from that part of me I'd turned my back on—
"housewife."

If I hadn't wasted a whole year, 1956–57, doing an alumnae questionnaire of inappropriate and unnecessary depth on the experiences and feelings of my Smith college classmates fifteen years after graduation . . . if their answers had not raised such strange questions about that role we were all then embracing . . . if the article I finally wrote raising certain of those questions had not been turned down by one woman's magazine (McCall's) because its male editor didn't believe it, and rewritten by another (Ladies' Home Journal) to deny its evidence so I wouldn't let them print it, and received by a third (Redbook), in a shocked rejection note, as something with which "only the most neurotic housewife could possibly identify" . . . I might never have written that book, The Feminine Mystique.

During the five years I was writing it, asking other women questions they hadn't asked themselves before, tracing clues from the case histories and puzzled side comments of marriage counselors, psychoanalysts, sociologists and the like, and finally tuning in to the Geiger counter of my own personal truth, I led a double life. I took the bus into the city from Rockland County three days a week, and wrote at my carrel in the Frederick Lewis Allen Room of the New York Public Library, and endured jokes at lunch from the professional writers working in that room because I was writing a book about women, of all things! It was supposed to take one year, and it

18

took five, and neither my husband nor my publisher nor anyone else who knew about it thought I would ever finish it. And when the writing of it took me over completely, I didn't want to waste time taking the bus into the city. I wrote every day, on the dining-room table, while the children were in school, and after they went to bed at night. (It didn't do any good to have a desk of my own; they used it for their homework, anyhow.) The summer I was finishing *The Feminine Mystique*, for some strange reason—maybe a last gasp at denying my seriousness—I dyed my hair blond!

Checking the footnotes in the fall of 1962, I sensed the inescapable implications of the trail of evidence I had followed—that if I was right, the very assumptions on which I and other women were basing our lives and on which the experts were advising us were wrong. I thought, I must be crazy! My then agent refused to handle the book when it was finished, and the publisher only printed several thousand copies. But all along I also felt this calm, strange sureness, as if in tune with something much larger, more important than myself that had to be taken seriously. At first I seemed alone in that awareness.

And then in the spring of 1963, in the weeks and months after the publication of *The Feminine Mystique*, I and other women knew we were not alone. It was a great relief to realize how many others had come up with the same painful questions in trying to live the mystique.

It was a relief, more important to more women than I had even dreamed, to have those questions put into words. The words enabled some women to begin to make changes in their lives almost immediately. And they wrote me personal, impassioned letters, expressing their relief. They also wrote me of the insuperable problems they now had to face trying to move in society not just as "my husband's wife, my children's mother, but as myself."

The emotions that book stirred up in women were not simple. In addition to the dozens, then hundreds, by now thousands of letters of relief, I received many angry letters from women. In fact, I would hear of cocktail parties being broken up by women arguing over my book who hadn't even read it, who in fact seemed afraid to read it. I would hear later that such a woman, attacking me as a destroyer-of-the-family, an enemy-of-motherhood, a betrayer-of-femininity, would finally be driven by her own problems that she hadn't dared face before to go back to school, or to look for a job—and she would be passing my book around to her neighbors. I decided that women were sitting on such painful feelings that they didn't dare open the lid unless they knew that they were going to be able to do something about them.

A woman called in to a television program in Detroit where I was publicizing the book. "Tell her to go back and take care of her own children and stop putting ideas into my daughter's head," the woman sputtered angrily. "Being a mother is all women were meant to be; I would never leave any child of mine with a baby-sitter." Thinking to suggest she might feel different a little later, I said, "How old is your youngest child?" "Twenty-three," said the lifelong mother.

Another time, on a program called *Girl Talk*, Virginia Graham, the hostess, turned to the camera and said to the studio audience and the women out there: "Girls, how many of us really need by-lines? What better thing can we do with our lives than to do the dishes for those we love?" Well, I knew that her agent fought for every foot of the size of her by-line on the television screen, and I wondered when the last time was she'd done the dishes for someone she loved. I turned to the camera and said, "Women, don't listen to her. She needs you out there doing the dishes, or she wouldn't have the captive audience for this television program, whose by-line she evidently doesn't want you to compete for." I realized then that this kind of "career woman" didn't really identify with other women at all. For her, there were three kinds of people in the world—men, other women, and herself.

The book was thus strangely threatening to some of those few career women who had defied the feminine mystique in those years to make it, as freaks or exceptions, in man's world. I think they also were sitting on painful feelings—the sacrifices and conflicts and bitter choices some had had to make to get there.

I got very few angry letters from men. From the very beginning, there was much less hostility from men than one might have expected. Many women told me their husbands had bought *The Feminine Mystique* for them to read. It was much more of a threat to women—the challenge, the possibility, the risk and test of moving in society as a person on one's own—than to their husbands. From the beginning, many men seemed to sense that women's liberation would liberate them. It was women who felt the fear—and the relief.

The letters I got came not only from those who had bought the book itself, but also from those who had read excerpts of it printed simultaneously—in unprecedented inexplicable defiance of custom—by the major competing women's magazines whose very feminine mystique I was attacking, the *Ladies' Home Journal* and *McCall's*, and earlier, *Mademoiselle* and *Good Housekeeping*. In this fashion, I suppose the book reached five times the 3,000,000 or so who actually bought it. The unprecedented passion of their response was such that later that year *McCall's* asked me to do an article about the letters.

Angry Letters,
Relieved Letters

"Who am I? What shall I do with my own life?" These seem to be troubling questions for more and more American women, questions that have brought strongly worded responses in the hundreds of letters women have written to me from all over America since the publication of *The Feminine Mystique*.

Many were violently outraged at the charge that American women have been seduced back into the doll's house, living through their husbands and children instead of finding individual identity in the modern world. As the proponent of this heresy, I was cursed, pitied, told to "get psychiatric help," to "go jump in the lake," and accused of being "more of a threat to the United States than the Russians."

Many correspondents suggested that American women would not be discontented in their "sacred role of housewife" if words like mine did not *make* them discontented.

But there were also hundreds of letters of another kind. A Florida mother of four: "I have been trying for years to tell my husband of my need to do something to find myself—to have a purpose. All I've ever achieved was to end up feeling guilty about wanting to be more than a housewife and mother." A woman from South Attleboro, Massachusetts: "I have for the past ten years now been asking myself, 'Is this all there is to life?' I am a housewife and mother of five children. I have a very poor education. I am thirty-eight years old, and if this is all there is for me to look forward to, I don't want to go on."

A twenty-six-year-old from Lansing, Michigan, whose three children are ready to begin their own lives: "Here I am! I feel like an appliance. I want to live! I want more education and a chance to compete in this world. My brain seems dead, and I am nothing but a parasite."

How often letters have come in, postmarked from small towns across the country, that have echoed and reechoed each other, as if a whole generation of women were humming together the same song of their lives.

From a small town in Georgia: "I had truly come to distrust anything I had read concerning women. None of it seemed to fit the picture of 'women' I had experienced by being a woman. My feelings are those of complete exhilaration. . . . You set up a challenge to me. I do not know that I have the strength or the perseverance to go through with it. I never thought of having a career, for I was not particularly bright.

"I felt I probably could not have really made the grade in a profession had I tried, so I considered marriage a career and tried to teach my children as much as they would allow me about the advanced thinking of the day. As they have reached teen-age they no longer listen but in fact rebuff whatever I may say. When my youngest starts to college I intend to go back too. So long as I can think of obtaining further education even if I never use it to earn money, the future seems exhilarating to me. . . . Otherwise, death pangs grip at my very being and a depression sets in that nearly drowns me."

Somehow, that either/or choice built into the feminine mystique seemed to doom women to contempt and self-contempt, loneliness, hostility, resentment whatever path they took.

A distinguished woman scientist wrote describing her growing depression and discontent. "You see, I am the other side of the coin. I am a career woman without husband or babies—somehow emerged from a bigoted Southern background for a few years, only to be smacked back again by the advent of the feminine mystique. My career has been so successful that it sometimes surprises even me, but I am cut to shreds by the glances and comments and pity from my sisters and brothers in this, my chosen field—physics—because I am obviously a frustrated sexual freak. I would not deny it for a moment, but the reason I am is now clear. My life has spanned from the mid-Victorian era (the South!) to the orbiting of the earth—from the hate and bitter ridicule of the feminist movement to the namby-pamby return of the mystique and woman to her nest. I haven't said, 'Women are people,' since I was twenty-six. The nothingness didn't just hit the women who bought, but also those who couldn't buy because for them the price was simply too great. This silly business is indeed a fester that mankind can not delay opening any longer. I work almost exclusively with men, and their hostility to women (not to me—I'm a freak—I'm unfeminine because I have ideas and act upon them) is phenomenal and it grows daily. It's worse than it ever was down on the Southern farm—and that was little short of contempt."

A housewife who also comes from the South wrote bitterly about her experience of that hostility and contempt in marriage. "For years I have despised the drudgery part of housekeeping. The endless picking up after a thoughtless family, the continual battle to keep up with mountains of laundry, the stacks of dirty dishes, mending rips and tears and sewing on buttons, removing spots and stains from clothing, upholstery and rugs, because the lordly male can't be bothered changing into work clothes before he paints the fence nor can he remove his greasy trousers before he sits in the best chair. I was ashamed of my resentment because I had been brainwashed into believing that drudgery was my lot in life and all of this was what I was born to do. Finally, our financial situation gave me an excuse to go back to work. He put every possible obstacle in the way to make it difficult for me. What to others must seem a lovely home, to me is both a prison and an endless treadmill. I can't look at my husband without being overwhelmed with bitter resentment. I can't face spending the rest of my life as a mindless zombie, existing only to do his bidding or living in a state of constant hostility and open warfare between us. I now have the consolation of knowing I am not a freak of nature. I was just born thirty years too soon and I compounded the error by marrying a man who can no more accept a woman as an equal than a poor, white trash, tenant farmer down in Mississippi can accept a Negro as an equal, even if the Negro has the IQ of an Einstein and several doctor's degrees to 'prove' it."

But even women who were encouraged by their husbands in their efforts to find new paths faced implacable barriers, blocks, prejudices when they tried to go back to school or work. An Ivy League graduate described her interview with an alumnae vocational agency when she decided to look for a real job. "I asked what vocational opportunities were possible for a reasonably intelligent, energetic woman, holder of an A.B. degree. I was ready and willing to pursue future study or training, and I wanted some information about possibilities. I shall never forget the advice I received from the woman in charge of the agency, and I quote: 'Go back to your kitchen and stay there and make jam.' I was a sissy—I paid attention to her! I wonder how many other frustrated housewives have been similarly discouraged."

Many, it would seem—like this woman who tried to go back to her profession after the years of diapers and P.T.A. meetings: "I was very happy doing it. My children have been honor students. Now they are almost grown and I am forty-five years old and find myself with time on my hands. Naturally I expected to go back into teaching. What a foolish dream! I was told that I was 'too old.' 'But,' I protested, 'there are women who are much older than I am teaching in schools all over town.' And back came the answer, 'Oh, but they have been teaching all these years. They don't have a twenty-year break in their teaching experience. A woman who has spent twenty years just being a housewife has nothing to contribute to the teaching profession.' Again I pleaded my cause: 'I am sure I have just as much to offer as the young girls just out of college.' 'No, that is not our point of view. The way we see it, the young girl is naïve and inexperienced. We can build her and shape her thinking the way we want it.' "

From a woman in Wisconsin: "I am grateful because you have dispelled some of the loneliness I have felt in a lifetime struggle for knowledge and achievement. And given me an incentive to continue, for one begins to think it is time to lie quietly in the grave when clods of dirt keep plopping you in the face. I married at nineteen, a junior in college—completed my B.A. at twenty-three, a mother of one, obtained another year of college and a teaching certificate at twenty-six, the mother of two. I could not believe that the pleasure I gained teaching a classroom of young people was neurotic, nor did it seem apart from my own 'femininity,' whatever that is. But I met with hostility everywhere. 'Go Home, Young Woman.' Parents, husband, other women, an occasional professor, sometimes a colleague. So I fought in addition to hostility a sense of guilt which caused me to do all my own housework in spite of the demands of my job—and for some time, for the simple pleasure of teaching I renounced all social life and rec-reation in order to spend time with my children. My regret is the fatigue, the sorrow, the emotional drain spent in an effort to be what I am. . . . You see, one can struggle against that lethargy for only so long. I had been ready (from fatigue, per-haps) to pitch it all, convinced that after all THEY must be right—devotion and another go at the kitchen floor are the answer and have been just ready to turn my two independent, vital and charming daughters into the kitchen where all of society seems to want them to be."

Are there two distinctly different kinds of American women, or merely different *stages* in our growth as women? And if the latter is the case, isn't it possible for women at these different stages to help one another?

Even among these letters, I found that one woman's ques-tion became another woman's answer; one woman's answer, the question another woman had failed to ask . . .

Can a woman find herself by simply *being* "feminine," pas-sive, and dependent on her husband? A California woman, who married at nineteen and quit college to stay home and have babies, wrote: "I happen to love the rewards of being completely passive, with just a hint of the aggressor at the right time. I don't want to compete with my husband. I want to respect and admire and love him. He's not working as hard as he is for himself. He's doing it all for me, for the same reason I'm keeping his house nice for him, cooking his meals, and being dependent on him. My whole life isn't *completely* centered around my home and family, but you can bet your bottom dollar ninety-five per cent of it is, and I love it. I'm sick of having my station in life referred to as trapped. Interview the young widow, and see if she wouldn't gladly call back the days she was 'submissive, dependent, and childlike, in her husband's shadow'!"

But from Forest Hills, New York, a young widow replies: "Where is a woman's SECURITY when her husband goes to war and never comes back? For ten years before, she has allowed every day to pass without learning anything she could use and forgetting everything she once learned. In 1941, when my husband was away in the war, I took a part-time job as a doctor's receptionist to keep myself from dying alone in the house day and night with only my eight-month-old baby for company. Mama told me, your job is your little son, stay home, it's safer, close the door. Five months later, my husband was missing in action, and two years later he was presumed dead. There is no security; the only security is within yourself."

Are American men so weak that *they* cannot compete unless their wives dedicate themselves to help them—or is this a measure of a man's strength? A New York university graduate cum laude who worked her husband's way through graduate school found then that she could not "compete" herself in the field that interested her. Now she "chooses" to stay home and help her husband with *his* work.

"It is more important for me to have one worthwhile career involving both our efforts, than two mediocre ones," she writes. "I'm being coldly realistic about our capabilities. There's nothing wrong in a wife's pride in her husband's achievement if she has honestly been a part of it. It is difficult for men to retain pride and masculinity if the wife is more successful in her career."

But a woman who was divorced after twenty-three years as a "selfless housewife" writes: "While I was disturbed, it was also with an enormous sense of relief that I went back to college, got my M.A., and also found another husband. A man fosters the 'feminine mystique' because he can't tolerate a wife who is strong and independent. But if she habitually stays her hand and 'gives in' gracefully to his 'superior wisdom,' he is likely to know how phony he is—and they both wind up feeling that she is much brighter and more competent than she actually would be if forced to measure herself in reality against him, or alongside him. Men need to grow up enough to be able to act independently without the constant validation of somebody weaker. So do women. If they can't, they'll either encourage a 'child-husband' or have child after child."

What is real womanhood? "Real women are loved, needed, wanted, and desired because we are happy, having learned the finest lesson of all: selflessness," says one woman. And an unhappy echo comes from another: "It takes a real woman to sit home every night raising his kids while he's living it up high, wide and handsome in a nice clean shirt she washed and ironed and starched for him, so some other woman could smear lipstick all over it. I am fighting for a man I have always loved and always will."

The mother who considers femininity her "blessing" from God may have a daughter who curses its name. "Being a good housewife and mother is a most fulfilling role which God planned for all womankind and for which He especially equipped her with such assets as the ability to be all-loving, self-sacrificing, gentle, feminine," says a New Jersey housewife. "It is reward enough for me to see my husband busy but happy, my children leaders in their schools, because I am at home each day making beds, cooking good meals, and ready to listen with a full heart and ear to problems, sorrows, and joys."

But the daughter of a "buried woman" writes: "After my father's death, my mother, who had entirely given up her identity as an individual, then gave herself 'unselfishly' to us. She was afraid to walk on the street by herself. The children did the marketing 'because you are so smart,' she used to say, while she stayed at home, mended our clothes, and wheedled finances from the rest of her family. She never could and never will feel like a whole person without us. At fifty-seven, my mother expects the children she raised to reap beautiful rewards for her. But believe me, I will have to be paralyzed, deaf, dumb, and blind before I become a preying, bigoted 'femininity-ist.' "

"Did God ordain woman's weakness?" writes one from Connecticut. "For the benefit of my fellow Catholics, the great saints who have been women were rarely those who just stayed home and did the wash. In fact, I can't name one. But I can name Joan of Arc, Saint Bridget of Sweden, Saint Teresa of Avila, the parables of Mary and Martha, and the one where the Master goes off, having issued His assorted servants money —it's funny that the coin should once have been called a 'talent'—and rewards the ones who have doubled what was entrusted to them, and punished the one who hid his two in the hill. All this concerns me because I've got two daughters who are at least as intelligent and creative as their brothers. I don't want them waking up to stimulating days of dishes and diapers."

"Don't our husbands work every dreary day, as cogs in that big, workday world, just to support us at home?" asks a writer from Natchez, Mississippi. "My husband, in a sense, offered his life and purpose to me when we married. He's the one who has to go to the same job at the same time every day forever, just to feed and clothe me and his three children. He's the one who should feel trapped, but he doesn't."

But a woman in Grandbury, Texas, found that her husband did, and this discovery "knocked the wind out of my sails, it was so unexpected. I never felt he begrudged my staying home while he earned the living, especially after the children were all in school. Only now I am a player who has been thrust out onto the stage with no lines to speak. The fact that my grades, twenty years ago, ranked third in a high-school class of 895 isn't much of a wedge to pry a thirty-nine-year-old woman into the world of arts, sciences, and professions."

"The real answer would seem to be for today's women not to produce children," says a letter from Anaheim, California, bitterly. "That way they could write, paint, compete with men in the world of business, work side by side with the scientists, participate in politics, and express themselves all over the place."

How many women—and children, marriages and talents— have been maimed by the perpetuation of that either/or choice? One woman, in Eau Gallie, Florida, developed a recurrent toxic condition which required surgery rendering her sterile. Her relationship with her husband deteriorated; her gifted oldest child developed personality problems; and she finally became so "tired, listless, and bored with the humdrum routine that books were too much effort to get through, and even my house was beginning to look neglected." Finally she broke away, went back to school, "and came alive again."

Eleven years ago, one person from New York walked away from a teaching job she truly loved to devote herself "for good" to motherhood. "Even loving the three boys as deeply as I did, I must confess that the climate of motherhood never elevated me as I had anticipated. When they went to school, I became a mop. Each morning, my little speck of humanity left cheerfully through the door, leaving me behind with myself and an inanimate house, which I cleaned and cleaned without any elation or enthusiasm. I ran the gamut of deep depression, fainting spells, migraines of the eye, and finally heart palpitations. I felt myself sinking in a terror too frightening to describe." When she went back to teaching, the terror went away, and "slowly began to emerge the inner image of myself, and I began smiling again at my family."

How ingenious an American woman can be when she really wants to! An Illinois mother of six does her shopping early, picks up her baby-sitter, and retypes the paper she wrote at midnight before her first class at the University of Illinois at 12:30. Her youngest child is just a year old, her oldest child nine, and she is graduating this summer with honors and a degree in elementary education.

"Most of my neighbors think I'm crazy. Nevertheless, I doubt that many women are as happy as I. The children accept the fact that I have a life of my own. There are scholarships and loans; I have both in sufficient amounts to take care of baby-sitting expenses. All that is really needed is a husband who sees his wife as a real person in her own right."

From a young mother recently returned to college: "After two years of hard work, I will be a sophomore at the university. The discovery that I am a person with abilities and a desire to contribute to the world something more than a biologic function is heady stuff. Learning is the hardest work I have ever done. The competition keeps me off my husband's back, so that I can be a person to him rather than merely a physical thing. There is limitless satisfaction in being able to reply to the question, 'What did you do today?' with 'I learned how genes are carried,' rather than 'I scrubbed the bathroom floor.' I still scrub the bathroom floor, but it is no longer the be-all and end-all of my life. I don't *hate* kids any more; I have begun to see them as something more than voracious birds with mouths open. I *like* my children now."

"Some of us are trapped, with no hope of freedom," one woman wrote me. "After twenty years of home, husband, and children, I finally got a chance to fulfill a dream. I went to college four evenings a week for two and a half semesters and then had to drop out. My husband gave me a choice—school or him. Many men resent their wives becoming persons in their own right. I love my husband and so gave up school. However, I will try to raise my sons to realize that women are people with the same dreams, hopes, and feelings as men. Maybe they will help their wives to be women in every sense of the word. I will also try to help my daughter realize you can be feminine, a woman, and a full person at the same time. It is too late for me, but not for them."

It is not too late for a Philadelphia college girl, who wrote: "Believe me, it has been quite an encounter I have fought with myself. The emotional escape route which I had built was a picture of my deliverance, via marriage and a home and ten babies, from the mental discipline of organic chemistry and advanced metaphysics. I had convinced myself that any discontent I experienced was because I am a female and hence not fashioned for abstract creativity. I saw in marriage the opportunity to 'become a woman' by completely immersing myself in husband and home. I still want to marry, but now I know I can only give to my marriage what I am as a person. And I know I cannot be a full person if I live exclusively in a ghetto of diapers and dishpans. It comes as no small upheaval to realize that my future happiness requires the use of some of this stuff I am presently wrestling with! It is no mean jolt to see that my future home is merely the center of my life—not all of it. I begin to know myself."

From a woman in Iowa whose education stopped at high school: "Thank God someone had the insight and courage to write it. It struck at the center of my being. I am finally confident of myself and my desire to launch the career I've wanted for so long. The last of the cobwebs of guilt have been swept away, and what a marvelous free feeling! The release of women from this subtle bondage can only be good and right.

How can it help but add a new dimension to the lives of the
male as well as the female, even if it might be unwelcome by
the male at first. How great the responsibility to be the superior sex. How it must weigh on those who prove inadequate to
live up to the myth. I have been able now to rid myself of the
resentment I have felt towards my husband in particular and
men in general. I am on the threshold of a new life. I feel alive
and excited for the first time in years."

And from Maine:

"I want to say this at least—I'm with you. I would like to
join with others to improve our image and help other women
to make their lot less difficult in the world and in the home.
What can we do?"

As the message of *The Feminine Mystique* spread, the women's magazines began to be in trouble. The younger, more educated readers with money to spend were somehow not responding to those full-page pictures of luscious red tomatoes with which male editors filled the vacuum of their assumption that "they" were not interested in ideas, issues or anything in the world outside of the care and feeding of their husbands and kids. One day in 1964 I got a call from a man named Clay Felker, who had been hired as a consultant to revive the *Ladies' Home Journal*.

He wanted me to turn the *Ladies' Home Journal* around, to give me a completely free hand, and would I meet him for lunch Wednesday at the Oak Room of the Plaza to discuss it? I got to the Plaza at twelve-thirty, didn't see Clay, and told the headwaiter at the Oak Room to tell Mr. Felker I'd be in the bar. I'd often been to the Oak Room bar in the evening with my husband. The waiter said, "No, madam, you cannot wait at the bar. Women are not allowed." Well, then, show me to Mr. Felker's table, I said. "I'm sorry, madam," he said, "we do not serve women in the Oak Room at noon." In my existence as a suburban housewife-writer I'd not been to many business lunches in the city. Wasn't I dressed right, what was wrong with me? It didn't really sink in, that they didn't serve women. There must be something I didn't understand. The headwaiter said he could transfer Mr. Felker's reservation to the Edwardian Room, and they would seat me there. By the time Felker found me in the Edwardian Room, I was feeling so humiliated and insecure that I didn't even take seriously his proposal that I edit a special issue of the *Ladies' Home Journal*— articles, fiction, fashion, service—according to my idea of women as people. In that shaky, self-doubting state, I knew he couldn't possibly mean it, and even if he did, I wouldn't be able to do it.

The next day my new agent, Martha Winston, virtually dragged me to meet the editors of the *Ladies' Home Journal*. The meeting lasted a long time; we stopped off at the ladies' room on our way out. My agent still remembers me shaking my head in a kind of wondering disbelief. It was so different, the way they were treating me now—asking for my ideas with something that almost felt like respect—compared to the patronizing, almost contemptuous way they and the other men who edited those women's magazines used to treat me and other women who wrote for them.

And now they were going *to let me* (note the apologetic tone, the way a woman like me felt then, "I was lucky to be allowed") edit a whole issue of the magazine dealing in that dimension women's image of women had denied: her own personhood, her definition of herself not as a husband's wife, a children's mother or a housewife, but in terms of her own actions in society. As I put it to them, that fourth dimension did not necessarily deny the other three, but it made the whole gestalt different.

In addition to my own lead piece, I was going to have a man express his own honest feelings—of relief and pleasure as well as threat—about a wife who was now going to be a person in her own right. And an article, the first in any women's magazine, about child-care centers. I planned an article about women and money: the specific facts of what she earned, if she worked, and how much she should contribute to the family budget, and if she worked inside the home, how she handled or could handle her share of the husband's income.

I wanted real women, in action, with character, modeling the clothes in the fashion pages—not those flat, boring, innocuously pretty model housewives. For fiction, I wanted *heroines* who did or thought or *felt* as subjects of their own stories—not just girl-gets-boy, or can-this-marriage-be-saved. I asked people like Doris Lessing, Joan Didion and Marya Mannes—women who didn't usually write for such magazines, in whose fiction I sensed this new image of women—to contribute, and I asked Gwendolyn Brooks, a fine black poet, to do me a poem about black women.

That singular issue, "Woman: The Fourth Dimension" or "Beyond the Feminine Mystique," did not turn out quite as I had planned. My own article was all right, and Alvin Toffler's on the man's welcome of the new woman, and the article on child-care centers that indicated for the first time that it might be good for children to be exposed for some hours in the day to someone else than their martyred mothers. I suppose just that was revolutionary enough for a mass Middle American women's magazine.

But the deeper economic and emotional implications of that new dimension must have gotten too powerfully close to some vital nerve center. The article on "Women and Money" was vetoed by the same male editors who had offered me that free hand. So was *all* the fiction, with its deeper personal truth. No real, ordinary women could be shown modeling clothes. Finally, and the bitterest battle between me and the editors, they simply wouldn't print Gwendolyn Brooks' passionate angry poem about the black woman. They got so annoyed at my "stridency" on that one, they suggested that I could pay them $5,000 and run it as an ad. And at the last minute they put my new image, a double-headed woman, a strong woman's face emerging from the vapid one, which was to have been the cover and the logo, on an inside page, and substituted the usual pretty women's magazine model on the cover.

Rereading "Woman: The Fourth Dimension" now, I sense the built-in limitation, the tentativeness, the timidity that still permeated my own thinking. Those women I found who combined work and family life had almost of necessity to be "exceptional." For surely here I found no new patterns, no new structures in society—merely individual women who juggled the chores of maintaining *Good Housekeeping* homes, raising Spockian children, and keeping husbands happy and ego-fulfilled, while finding some precarious foothold in society.

My own sights were still so modest that I barely sketched as vague possibility, dared as some hope for a remote future, that girls might make serious commitments to real professions and not take ten to fifteen years out to have children; that such women might have fewer children, later, spaced differently; that the location of the home might possibly be decided in terms of her future as much as his; that women might expect to get educational or professional credit, or even be paid, for that innovative volunteer work; and, fantastic notion, that a woman might seriously run for President or Vice President. It surely did not occur to me that all this would *happen* within ten years' time.

But the very hint of these things, in my new image of women, was revolutionary enough in 1964 to cause some unusual reactions among the five million readers of the *Ladies' Home Journal.* The circulation manager later told me it was the one issue in those years that elicited a significant readership from the more affluent, under-thirty, educated readers. It also elicited outraged, threatened, vituperative letters from what the editors called "the little old lady in Nebraska." The editors of the *Ladies' Home Journal* panicked. Clay Felker was liberated to become editor of *New York* shortly thereafter. And the *Ladies' Home Journal* retracted, *apologized* for even suggesting that women could be people in their own right, by quickly putting together another special issue in which Phyllis McGinley, the Pulitzer Prize poet, acclaimed that the greatest thing she or any woman could achieve was to bake a perfect custard pie. And the very by-lines on the cover were listed as "Mrs. Stuart Udall," "Mrs. Arthur Goldberg." (As if a woman could *write* as her husband's wife—writing has to be a personal act.)

Disillusioned at the possibility of really turning the existing women's magazines around, I tried to interest five or six publishers in starting a new mass women's magazine aimed at that market. It was about six years too soon. It wasn't until after 1970 that they saw the commercial possibility of *Ms.*

Woman:
The Fourth Dimension

 All at once even the arguments about the feminine mystique seem obsolete, swept aside by a massive breakthrough in the lives and minds of American women.

"Now I can see a future before me—not just marriage as my inevitable destiny," a high-school graduate on Long Island told me. After seven years of going steady, she has canceled plans for marrying right away and working to put her boyfriend through law school. Instead, she will work her own way through college. "The difference is—I am an individual human being. I still want a home and children, but I know now about a world big enough for me to become a part of it myself."

A forty-four-year-old mother in Greenbelt, Maryland, is learning to become an orbital programmer—one day she will be tracking satellites in space: "You go through life as Joey's mother, Helen's mother, and you come to a dead end. Two years ago I felt my life was all over. My mother died at forty-seven, and in her day that was beyond middle age. But the numbers don't feel the same now. It's the new things that keep opening up in my life."

Even words like "fulfillment" seemed inadequate as I listened to Marty Camp, Seattle housewife, tracing her progress from den mother, Sunday-school teacher, frustrated campaigner for better schools, to her own weekly television program, *What's New in the Schoolhouse.* " 'Fulfillment' sounds so selfish," she said. "Actually, it's suddenly feeling that you are part of the world before and the world after, of something bigger than you are. And the excitement of making your own ideas become realities. You can sit around and talk till hell freezes over, but it's just daydreaming unless you have the courage to take the next step and get personally committed to real action that tunes you in to other people, and to the community."

I have filled twenty notebooks with the words of such women this past year. They are creating, in their own lives, the new image of women I was groping toward in my book *The Feminine Mystique.* So far I have received more than a thousand letters from women who have made decisions and taken action "that changed my whole life" as a result of breaking through the feminine mystique. I have been traveling too, talking with women across the country, from small towns in the Pacific Northwest to the suburbs of New York, Boston, Dallas, Detroit, Minneapolis, Baton Rouge, Los Angeles, women who seem to have found a new dimension of existence untroubled by the old dilemmas—"marriage-motherhood-career" and "self-fulfillment-femininity." Somehow, in actions of individual commitment to society, they have found that sense of their own identity which eludes so many women, young and old, who are caught in the narrow confines of the feminine mystique.

Far more American women than I had realized have now moved *beyond* the feminine mystique, which defines woman solely in terms of her three-dimensional sexual relationship to man: wife, mother, homemaker—passively dependent, her own role restricted to timeless, changeless love and service of husband and children. Millions of women in mid-twentieth-century America have broken through, or are on the verge of breakthrough, to a fourth dimension in their existence: woman as a person *herself,* using her abilities in a changing world. And the new identity she finds there does not deny her age-old three-dimensional femininity, but meshes with it in patterns that can only be seen in that other fourth dimension: time.

The emergence of this fourth dimension involves a subtle

but profound change in the whole gestalt of women's lives. It changes the way they see themselves and the way others see them; poses new problems for women, men, and society; creates new patterns in marriage, motherhood, homemaking, education and all the professions; even impinges on American politics and the national economy.

Women who *use time* to create the fourth dimension of their world, who serenely accept *change* as the normal state of life, simply bypass the conflicts caused by regarding marriage-motherhood-career as changeless, separate states of being. A woman cramped within the narrow, three-dimensional terms of the feminine mystique sees the relatively young years of childbearing as the peak of life. She dreads the years beyond, the so-called empty years, which for a young mother today, if she has her last child at thirty and expects to live till nearly eighty, can span half a century. She lives in fear of the rapid changes in our complex society, which seem to be leaving her behind. The experts on woman still debate "careers" for women as if time did not exist, as if she could remain forever a young mother, as if the world would stop moving while she devoted twenty years to having babies.

But it is the new years which medical science has added to woman's life, her future *beyond* childbearing, which demand and make possible the fourth dimension: her own identity in society.

After a woman becomes keenly aware that she has nearly eighty years of life to plan for, a qualitative difference is evident in her use of time; in her choices and her goals; in the timing by which she marries and has babies; even a difference in the maturity she achieves, and in the way she ages. The women I have met who have broken through to their own identity as persons move with a new serenity and freedom in the three other dimensions of marriage, motherhood and home.

Bette Kurtzman of Detroit told me how she went back to school as a young mother of three, and emerged with a brand-new job in communications: "The day I came home from work and realized that one of my ideas had contributed something—they had listened to me not as a pretty woman but as a person with something to contribute—that's the day I began to enjoy being a pretty woman, and clothes and cooking and taking care of my house and children. Suddenly I had a new kind of energy and freedom and tranquillity, and everything became different. I put my whole mind to it, and fitted the pieces of my life together."

Such a woman is a "heroine" in the Greek sense, which defined a hero as any free man who took his own part in the Trojan War, and about whom a story could be told. For the Greeks understood that "courage" is involved in leaving one's private hiding place and showing who one is.

As the political scientist Hannah Arendt put it, courage "is in fact already present in a willingness to act or speak at all, to insert oneself into the world and begin a story of one's own. . . ." In this sense there are no heroines today on television, in movies or conventional fiction. Instead, there are sex objects, mindless household drudges devoted to cleaning the sink, keeping their bodies feminine, being Jimmy's mother or John's wife, kissing husband and children good-bye as they depart for adventures in the world.

That obsolete image, the feminine mystique, makes the woman on the verge of breaking through feel guilty for being more than the doctor's wife, Jimmy's mother, the cleaner of kitchen sinks. She feels uncomfortably "different" from her suburban neighbors, or from the other girls at college, not realizing how much company she has, among women her own age, in women older, younger, in other suburbs, other cities, across this nation—more company every day. Perhaps she has company right on her own block, for that obsolete feminine mystique impels many women to keep secret their entry into a fourth dimension. The woman who writes and sells short stories uses a pseudonym "for fear of being lynched by the other housewives," she tells her editor. The woman who has an absorbing job pretends that she's working only "to help pay the mortgage."

The human abilities of women, now being released, are as various as the evolving needs of society. They may be as familiar as the mothering of children or as strange as mapping outer space. And the four-dimensional pattern in any woman's life evolves and changes, as it meshes now one way, now another, with marriage, motherhood and homemaking. That's why it's so confusing for any woman to measure herself in terms of what she is doing at any one moment. The curse of so many housewives—and men and women who hold jobs—is that fragmented *dailyness*.

As the great architect Eero Saarinen said to his wife, Aline, "You've got to stop living in rabbit time. Architects live in elephant time."

The fourth dimension in any woman's life does not emerge in one day, full-blown; indeed, it is often found by trial and error.

"It's not one big choice," said Rosalind Loring, an engineer's wife and mother of two children, who after fourteen years of volunteer activity and part-time teaching jobs in Los Angeles became adult-education coordinator for the University of California. "You make minor decisions at first. The first decision is yes, I will travel sixty miles twice a week to take the course, for credit. Or I will find some other mothers to start the cooperative nursery school, and take turns baby-sitting, so I can take the part-time job or work in the voters' campaign. Or that you will apply for the grant to get the new degree in adult education. And put the kids in camp two weeks, and travel three thousand miles for the leadership training program.

"That year was the turning point for me. I was thirty-seven, and suddenly all the possibilities in the big wide world became apparent. But by then you know what kind of a person you are, you don't keep asking yourself the same piddling question, 'Am I right to do this?' You're making other decisions that produce results."

I have observed six patterns by which women in the United States today seem to be achieving a fourth dimension in life:

FIRST: The Job. The 23,000,000 women who work in the United States today have at least emerged from the isolation of household "labor" to face the world. But to be fourth-dimensional a job must involve *choice*, entail a future, and permit a meshing with marriage, motherhood, and home. A girl who takes a "nothing" job to fill the time before marriage or to put her husband through graduate school is evading choice. Per-

sonnel experts call it a "terminal job"; it has no "future." An
untrained widow or divorcee or wife who must take a routine
job to earn money is not free to choose. In the United States,
most jobs are difficult for women to keep when they begin
having children. This job pattern is responsible for employers'
prejudices against hiring or training women for jobs with a
real future, and for the general impression that children are
neglected when their mothers work.

But there is a great influx in the working force today of
women who are married and living with their husbands, with
children over six, who work from "choice." Four out of ten
such women work in the United States today, a 400 percent
increase in twenty years. According to recent research by sociologists F. Ivan Nye of Washington State University and Lois
Hoffman of the University of Michigan, these women differ
basically from the working mother of 1940 who was "forced
into an unskilled, physically tiring, low-paying job by direct
economic necessity." Women who work because of commitment are more aware of themselves as individuals, take a
greater joy in their own children, and know greater physical
well-being than housewife-mothers or mothers "forced" to
work. The forced workers often have to quit a "job" to find a
fourth dimension. One of them wrote me: "An outside job as a
stenographer meant working eight hours a day for someone
else, leaving my baby with someone else, eating quickly prepared meals, cramming a day's housework into an evening,
and, at the same time, taking a bath, curling my hair, bathing
the baby and putting her to bed, without spending much time
with her. I got no more thrill out of typing a letter than cleaning the toilet bowl. After I quit my job, my flexible schedule at
home gave me time for my husband and baby and for myself. I
now take a nursing course two nights a week. . . ."

For a different woman, a typist's job became fourth-dimensional. When her youngest child was enrolled in kindergarten,
Harriet Bassett, wife of a chemical engineer in Rockland
County, New York, took shorthand lessons to become a clerk-
typist at the Lamont Geological Observatory. Though she has
never finished college, she is now assistant to the director of
the observatory. Last year she was given a sabbatical to study

in the physical and biological sciences, on a fellowship from Columbia.

SECOND: Commitment to a Profession. Women who have made a firm and early commitment to a life work or profession, integrating it with marriage and motherhood as they come along, keep moving in the fourth dimension with the evolution of their own field. In the past twenty years, these women have been in a distinct minority, not only because the feminine mystique has dissuaded girls from such commitments, but because society itself has made it difficult for a woman to keep progressing in any profession during the years when she has duties toward children and home. The world of work is still so much a "man's world" that professions such as medicine are only now beginning to arrange training schedules for the human beings who give birth to babies.

Margaret Menzel of Tallahassee, Florida, research geneticist and mother of three, spent three and a half years "arguing the strategy for combining two careers into one marriage" before she married a fellow biologist. They decided against working as a husband-and-wife team; they did not want to compete, nor did they want her to be a restive subordinate member of the team. "We agreed—one—to give his career first precedence in selecting locations, but to seek positions where there were some possibilities for me. Two, when children came, I should try to work at least part time to keep abreast of my field. Three, I should be responsible for seeing that the household was run and look upon domestic help as a necessary professional expense. He doesn't enjoy housework, but he volunteers cheerfully when I'm in a pinch.

"We have three children, now ten, six and five. I worked right through all my pregnancies until the day of delivery, and bore them easily and with great exhilaration. They are bright, affectionate, self-reliant children with no serious problems.

"Of course there *are* other problems—the overt and subtle professional discrimination; the necessity of saying no to a lot of minor pleasures and community duties; the hostility mixed with envy of other women; the difficulty of fitting children's school schedules into a working day; the crises when a child, or worse, the maid, is ill; the guilt you sometimes feel when a child gets into difficulty.

"Let's not pretend combining a career and children is easy work. You've got to put more into your job than a man would to get ahead (or just stay even) and, despite all the modern gadgets, a household takes some executive attention. But once you've overcome the initial inertia, employers prove surprisingly cooperative, children adaptable, husbands admiring. Parkinson's law even runs in reverse and time begins to expand to meet the work required."

THIRD: The Committed Volunteer. A great many women who wrote "housewife" on the census blank while their children were young followed a fourth-dimensional commitment—to politics, education, art, mental health—through voluntary or paid action in community projects. Some who never thought of themselves as career women are being tapped, at thirty-five or forty, for posts on the new frontiers of our time. For their movement, tuned to the evolving needs of their own communities, keeps them abreast of change, unhampered by the blind spots of professional conformity. Others move on to still higher levels of responsible leadership, often breaking through to run for political office instead of serving in the safe backwater of the women's auxiliary or forever seconding the nomination. Instead of the painful, often tortuous period other women often experience before the breakthrough—that "first decision" at eighteen or thirty-eight—this woman suffers a period of self-questioning each time one commitment is fulfilled, and her growth forces her to move on to the next.

Priscilla Jackson of Birmingham, Michigan, felt that she should be home with each child until he entered school—she organized cooperative nursery schools for each one of them. Then—

"I was so thrilled to explode out into the world that I joined everything, volunteered for everything—and had to retreat and say, 'No, I can only be room mother for one child at a time.' I then found my niche in the League of Women Voters, and became active on foreign policy. Running a public meeting on foreign aid, I discovered that to make it top-flight we needed more resources, so I contacted the Dean of Continuing

Education of Michigan State. The conference was one of the best he'd ever seen, so he offered me a job.

"I said, 'But I have children and a house and a demanding husband . . .' who said: 'You've been getting pretty restless around here, why don't you try it?' (He was also starting a new business and we could use the money.) I agreed to try, but only if I could have a ten-month appointment like a faculty member, and a six-hour day. I also refused to do routine work.

"Any woman who has gotten *volunteers* to raise money and accomplish real goals has better administrative and management training, I have discovered, than men who have simply bought the talent they needed, and when it didn't fit, fired it."

Women of commitment are emerging as the new political pros in many parts of the country. In the state of Virginia, Kathryn Stone, housewife and mother of three, moved from leadership in the League of Women Voters to the state legislature. There she stood alone—not only as a woman but as the only legislator to oppose the so-called legal "massive resistance" to desegregation of schools. The barrage of insults from male legislators finally reduced her to tears (not of weakness, she insists, but massive outrage). The tears made newspaper headlines. Refusing to retreat, she has since been reelected for the third time to the Virginia legislature, and is now chairman of the Governor's Committee for Youth.

In their concentration on the issues, such women often are not aware of the degree of professional stature they have won. They are held back by the vestiges of timidity and diffidence (not on the issues, only on the question of asserting their own candidacies). Some months ago I met the retiring national president of a large women's organization, one that is effective in combating discrimination. She was depressed and uncertain about her future. She had to retire as national president, she told me; it was time to let a younger woman take over, but she couldn't bear the thought of staying home and "succumbing to the menopause." She'd thought of going back to school, but maybe she was too old to attempt that.

Six months later I met her at a luncheon. Gay, energetic and slightly frantic, she drew me aside. "I'm not going to get my M.A. after all," she said. "I don't have time. You know, they've been asking me for years to run for City Council. I was afraid to run and risk defeat. In a volunteer women's organization, you don't have to run; if you're nominated, you're elected. Well, I began to go to City Council meetings, and suddenly I decided I'd run—there is such a mess to be cleaned up. . . ." (She was elected.)

FOURTH: Creation of a Fourth-Dimensional Career. The creation by a woman of a new fourth-dimensional job for herself, which meshes her work with her marriage-motherhood-home commitments, can constitute a breakthrough for all women in the chosen field.

When Marian Gartler's husband was transferred to Seattle, there seemed no way she could continue in her highly specialized profession of textbook editor. This kind of editing simply wasn't done outside the publisher's office, three thousand miles away in New York.

But as soon as she finished decorating her house in the Spooky Hollow section of Seattle, she set up what might be called a subcontracting textbook "cottage industry"—using her whole house as the publishing office. Among the other wives and mothers around her age, the middle thirties, she found four with good backgrounds in education or journalism who "were at the turning point all women are reaching in our society, as their youngest children go off to school."

Another modern version of the old "cottage industries" pattern sprang up five years ago in a new field, computer programming, when Mrs. Elsie Shutt of Harvard, Massachusetts, left her job to have her first baby. Soon afterward she launched Computations, Inc., recruiting other mothers trained in high-level mathematics who wanted to be home while their babies were young. (Their joint production of twenty-seven babies, so far, has earned them the title "the pregnant programmers.") They work in their own homes, charging only for time actually spent at the desk, which they regulate themselves, as their babies nap or exercise in the playpen. The caliber of their professional work has won contracts from such giants as Minneapolis-Honeywell, Raytheon, the Air Force, and Harvard itself, on computer-programming projects too sprawling for their own staffs to handle.

Some women have even created the fourth-dimensional

pattern they need in rigidly traditional professions—which need women. A breakthrough has finally been made in medicine. Dr. Helen Kaplan, mother of three children, and Dr. Kathleen Shanahan, mother of two, are midway through their residency training in psychiatry, under a new program initiated by New York Medical College for women who want to be both homemakers and doctors. Instead of the twenty-four hours a day, twelve-month regimen of the male resident, the women's residency is divided into four nine-month periods, with Christmas and Easter vacations, and night and weekend duties modified. The women spend morning and evening with the children, and work the usual forty-hour week at the hospital, their resident's salary being prorated according to the time spent on the job.

The whole program has been organized to meet strict professional standards, and as a pilot project, forecasts a general reshaping of medical training for women. What they have proved, these women say, "is not that we are the same as men, but that we are different, and that there is room in psychiatry for this difference."

A similar program, one that recognizes that women who are needed as pediatricians may also have children of their own, is under way at Children's Hospital in Boston. There, two mothers carry a pediatric residency in tandem, completing in two years the residency a man would carry on a round-the-clock basis in one year. An equally important breakthrough has been made by a number of hospitals in their desperate need for nurses. To entice back some of the millions of mothers who have nurses' training, they have set up nursery schools for their children right in the hospital.

FIFTH: Second-Chance Education for the Late Bloomer. A great many women today are making a late and unnecessarily painful breakthrough into their fourth dimension. The "late bloomer" can be encouraged by the promise of a second chance, such as the Minnesota Plan for Women's Continuing Education. This plan offers women educational retreading, after fifteen years of housewife hibernation, at hours—and for fees—that are acceptable for a woman whose oldest child may be on the expensive brink of college, or who still has young children to care for at home.

Knowing how many other women are in the same boat makes it somehow easier to swallow one's pride and go back to school, or risk rebuff at a first job interview.

The miracle is how many women in America in 1964 have the strength—and the desperation—to break through at thirty-five or forty or more, with little help from society, even active opposition, and move into the world with skills unused for ten or fifteen years.

Virginia Gibson Allen of Pittsburgh told me: "I left school and married in 1951. Since then I have moved thirteen times, lived in eight states and produced two children. But I have also studied alone and at home, privately, and at school; I have worked till two in the morning ironing because I don't need light for that, and I do for painting. I have conducted, alone, my first one-man show, coping with the measles, and finally, when I fill out the income tax now, I put down—occupation: painter, not housewife.

"I may still be a business loss, but I am a net gain. Never, in the six years since I broke out of the trap, has one concession been given, nor one iota of recognition of my effort been forthcoming from any source except my husband and my children. A woman who undertakes to become herself, to find her work, also finds that the people who are the proudest are her own family—the ones she most feared to deprive of her tender loving care."

The hostility some women show to women who've made the "breakthrough" is understandable. There is an open nerve end here; growing numbers of women are facing the need to make their own breakthrough, but if they are afraid to do something about it—or don't see anything they *can* do—better to believe that they were meant to be "just housewives."

For many women in their late forties and fifties the opening up of a fourth dimension in their lives comes like a miracle. Edith Mucke was graduated from high school in 1931, got a job in an office, was married at twenty-five "to a great, wonderful guy."

"Nobody was ever as fulfilled a mother as I was. I loved raising my children at every age. But the last few years I've been feeling I'd like another crack at living my life, either to teach young people, or to be a ballet dancer. I've done all the things active, intelligent women do, been president of the Women's Club, bowling, bridge. But last year, with my Jane a senior in high school—my boy is already in college—I would wake up in the middle of the night, tears streaming back on my pillow, just thinking how sad it was going to be. I'm not really awfully smart, just curious about things, but what was I going to do?

"I began to have trouble with my feet. The doctor said I was getting arthritis. I've always had a feeling people with arthritis have a terrible sadness within, even though they're cheerful outside, like custard pudding.

"And then there was the Minnesota Plan and I took the seminar. And I did the paper. On what the philosophers and psychologists have found out about creative thought. For some reason I ended on the question of what possible creativity I, as a human being who has lived forty-eight years, had to offer. And my adviser on the paper told me it was *important* for me to come back and get my degree. It seemed to me a very selfish thing, to spend money on myself. He told me of the seven thousand young people who would be coming here every year, and of how so many more mature people would be needed to teach them how to think and live. And I could do that. I know it's not going to be easy. But I have no pain now in my joints. It's been like a fountain of youth within me, that this is what I'm going to do with my life."

SIXTH: The Second or Third Dimension Becomes a Fourth. Some women may find their fourth dimension as astronauts in outer space, but for many the third, or even the second dimension, simply becomes a fourth. There are, for instance, women whose abilities are particularly suited to the mothering of babies. Instead of having baby after baby when our society has no room for so many babies, such a woman could find a lifelong fourth dimension by providing a new kind of professional baby care for mothers whose abilities lie elsewhere. In recent years many women, like Eleanor Siegl in Seattle, have found their own future in starting cooperative nursery schools or summer day camps for their children's benefit. The new federal funds for training workers to run and staff new kinds of day-care programs could provide the breakthrough for hundreds of thousands of mothers: women meeting women's new needs.

Similarly, a woman whose true creativity is cooking cannot use this ability fully by cooking for a family of four or five. How many gourmet dinner parties can she give in one week, even if her husband's career benefits from such hostessing? Cooking has already become the fourth dimension for many women, who have made it into a creative business or a new service to society. It doesn't have to be a "big business," either —the woman who expanded her own bread-making into the million-dollar Pepperidge Farm. In Detroit, some fourth-dimensional women were complaining that they couldn't manage the ordering and cooking for the dinners they once gave. "Face the fact that you can't do it all yourself," one woman said. "I've made a deal with a friend of mine whom I consider the best cook in Detroit. She comes into my house two days a month and cooks a vast supply of gourmet dishes. They're in my freezer, for use when I entertain or when I don't have time to cook dinner for my family."

As more and more women begin to lead four-dimensional lives, America must face the true challenge of women as full members of society. This challenge is more revolutionary than the "equal rights" which women won many years ago and did not use. What are the real feelings of men who suddenly must see women, their own wives, as people with lives of their own? What are the new patterns that have to be worked out, when women's dependence on marriage as her only dimension is no longer the cement that keeps the marriage together? What are the implications of her new paycheck?

For instance, I keep hearing (from women, not from men) that "the real problem is the male ego." Some women in Texas —a lawyer, a psychologist, an artist, a newspaper editor, a volunteer leader, a young scientist, several teachers—were discussing how they "handled" their husbands. "You must never talk about your work, or let him see you working," one said. "It would be threatening to him." "You must keep thinking of yourself as the subordinate partner, and be prepared at all times to sacrifice your career for his," another said.

But one of the Texas women suddenly broke in: "I thank God every night of my life for the man I'm married to. I can't imagine not talking to him about such an important part of my life as my work. Besides, he's interested." Dr. Conchita Winn, who teaches Spanish at Southern Methodist University, clinched it: "Are American husbands so weak we need to pamper their egos? Mine isn't."

Actually, some husbands of four-dimensional women seem to enjoy being asked for an opinion on a wife's business problem. It's the wife, after all, who is generally the acknowledged expert on the domestic front. Indeed, there's a growing suspicion that women have become too much the "boss" at home.

The fact is, as women move into the world of work and large decisions, they become less dominating, more "feminine," at home. The massive research of Hoffman and Nye has shown that the husbands of working mothers actually have much more decision-making power in their own homes than other husbands.

A man who has started his own electronics business told me with some puzzlement about his "problem" with his wife, a department-store buyer: "I didn't want a woman who would be completely dependent on me, and live through me. The burden would be too great. But the funny thing is, Marge tries to wait on me, fetch my slippers, act as if she doesn't have any opinion of her own. Sometimes it makes me feel as if we're living an act, and I can't be myself."

Occasionally a woman's breakthrough into the fourth dimension helps to free a man from the masculine mystique. In a Midwestern city I interviewed a young minister, with four children, who had given up a successful automobile agency to study theology—the same year his wife applied for her teaching certificate. She had set him "completely free," he said. He couldn't have made his decision if she hadn't been willing to give up their expensive house and car and suburban trappings. It was a two-way street:

"A decision has to be made that you're going to turn the other person completely loose, free to grow and develop by themselves. It's a little frightening. But because Jane set me free from the burden of being a model breadwinner, I don't feel as if I have to put pressure on her to be a model housekeeper and a model mother the way I did before. I didn't have any complaints about our sex life before, but now it's taken on a new dimension—a complete freedom. Before, I had the impression that she felt used. If I dominate her, it isn't really *her*, and I'm not free to be myself."

Of the thousand women who have written me about their "breakthrough," a great majority report "delight," "100 percent support," "cheers and hallelujah" from their husbands. Far more report problems *solved* in their marriages than problems created by their new moves. In Seattle, Detroit, in Oakland, wherever I have seen four-dimensional women with their husbands, there is a sense of mutual knowledge, openness, respect, delight in each other—and a complete absence of that war between the sexes, the manipulations, boredom and antagonisms, that have seemed epidemic in America recently.

"I suppose I would rather have only myself to think about," a young husband told me. "It would be more comfortable for me. But then I wouldn't be married to her. And I *like* her." The research of Hoffman and Nye showed more "arguments" between man and wife when the wife worked, but interpreted this as a temporary adjustment to change (and to the wife's being less dependent on her husband). It does seem to take a secure, mature man to welcome his wife's breakthrough. The truly insecure male ego may not be able to take it, even if his own problems have nothing to do with his wife.

As for children, the specter of "problems" raised by child psychologists turns out to be largely illusory. Only recently have sociologists and psychologists examined what actually happens to the children of working mothers. Findings reported by Hoffman and Nye showed no significant difference between children of working mothers and children of housewife-mothers.

For mothers who worked from "choice," the commitment to work did not mean a lessened commitment to motherhood. But their children sometimes had problems caused not by neglect, but by the mother's feeling of guilt. Their children were given fewer household chores to do than other children. Because the mother did not want her outside work to inconvenience the child, he was not given enough responsibility to develop his own effectiveness.

By adolescence, the report showed, this problem had disappeared. For sons, self-development was modeled by their fathers. And the daughters of four-dimensional working mothers showed in their teens an initiative, responsibility, autonomy—"an independence of thought and values generally rare in girls." They were much more active—in taking household responsibility and jobs outside the home, in clubs, sports, hobbies, school achievement, and in dating—but were less likely to go steady before sixteen. They had strong goals for the future: to achieve something themselves—and in partnership with their future husbands. They "tended to perceive women as freer to move more widely, to behave more vigorously and to achieve more freely" than other girls. They loved and respected their mothers, and wanted to be like them. "More often than other girls, they chose their own mothers as adult ideals."

These girls may set a new pattern to replace the early-marriage-and-early-motherhood routine that has been America's shame since World War II. Early marriage prevented too many women in this generation from finding their own talents of mind and spirit, their own identity. One reason for their escape into too-early sexuality was their lack of an independent self-image. Perhaps our daughters will use their education not as a way to get a man, but as the door to their own fourth dimension, now that mothers are breaking through the feminine mystique to give them images of women as full people.

Such girls will have dreams beyond that dream house in the suburbs. (In fact, that house may be a 3-D dream that will not even appeal to four-dimensional women.) Such women may prefer to stay with their husbands in the mainstream of civilization—creating a new kind of city living with close neighbors to organize cooperative nursery schools and swap babysitting with; buses children can take themselves rather than having to be chauffeured by their mothers; universities, technical schools, libraries, laboratories and offices where the new frontiers of our society can be joined. Maybe that suburban house will turn into a weekend retreat for the whole family instead of that onerous daily commute for the husband and a separate, isolated world for the wife and children. And as women commit themselves to these new frontiers, they will feel less guilty about using labor-saving devices to speed their housekeeping chores.

Certain new patterns implicit in woman's mass break-through are yet to come. As women prove themselves in professions which badly need their brainpower, there will be more part-time work schedules for mothers; leaves for motherhood; nursery schools or day-care centers in laboratories and offices, as they are provided now for nurses in the hospitals. Women may even surmount their self-denigration and contempt of other women, and vote for a woman for President—or at least lots of women for the Senate.

But the most remarkable new pattern of all is emerging right now, under our eyes: there is evidence that the aging process is different for four-dimensional women. The lifetime work of Dr. Charlotte Buhler at the University of Southern California—work begun nearly forty years ago in Vienna—and the implications of a massive study still in progress at the University of Chicago indicate that women who use their abilities don't suffer the menopause as a "little death" but as a new stage of growth. From Dr. Buhler's work, it would seem that women who pursue a conscious goal for their life, expressed in creative work, reach the height of their human powers in the last half of their life, long after the so-called bloom of physical maturity. For men and women who live by larger purposes—scientists, artists, statesmen, teachers, philosophers—the peak is not yet in sight at fifty. The new millions of women with such purposes—the fourth-dimensional women—seem to follow such a "human curve of life." Physically, they appear to age differently than other women.

I could see this as I went around the country, seeking them out. They all looked ten or twenty years younger than they were—not in the embalmed sense of a woman who dyes, diets and tries to hide her age with make-up, but in the bloom of their eyes and skin, and in the vitality that burned inside. They were intensely alive women; many, in fact, described their breakthrough as a "fountain of youth that keeps bubbling inside."

Such women have done for themselves what doctors and drug researchers have not been able to do with their hormones. Hormones may relieve physical symptoms, but not the suffering of "the little death"—which menopause is to a woman who lives only as sexual object and bearer of children, never as a person herself. This is the real breakthrough, for each woman to take her own life seriously, to *choose*, to use finally all of her human power.

For no one will hand women anything except cheap dreams of perpetual youth, the limbo of passive, effortless, unlived days. The new dreams, the real dreams, women must make come true themselves. There are real problems yet to be solved before this world becomes a truly human world, and woman no longer walks as a freak in the "man's world" of art and science, war and politics, exerting a power she does not really enjoy in the "woman's world" of home. Man is not the enemy here, but the fellow victim. The real enemy is women's denigration of themselves, fostered by the feminine mystique. Now that women have broken through the mystique, they can attack the problems that remain, from the discrimination in paychecks and income tax to child-care centers. All they need to do is simply to become themselves, and help each other; to ask for, affirm and create the new patterns all women need—in voices loud enough to be heard. For no woman can truly make this breakthrough by tolling the bell alone.

In the wake of the reaction to the *Feminine Mystique*, *TV Guide*, improbably, asked me to analyze the television image of woman. I'd never watched television much, except for national political conventions, the McCarthy hearings, and the irritating subliminal fallout of *Howdy Doody* or *Captain Kangaroo* keeping my children busy while I was making dinner, or doing breakfast dishes.

So I stayed home watching television morning, afternoon and night for two straight weeks—commercials, soap operas, family situation comedies, the serials as well as the news. The image of women that television presented—once one really examined it, instead of just taking it for granted—was outrageously insulting. And yet it was used to sell things to women; millions of dollars were spent developing those dumb commercials, series and soap operas whose message was that women were too repulsive to endure unless they bought those powders, deodorants, and detergents. Those soap operas in their very tone of voice—sepulchrous, falsely pious—reeked of guilt: unspeakably evil sexual shame. (Did they have to make us feel so dirty, guilty, bad to make us buy so many things we didn't need?) At four o'clock, when my children came home from school, I used to come up for air with the most terrible headache. When "Television and the Feminine Mystique" came out as a two-part series in *TV Guide*, it got more letters than any other piece they'd ever run. These weren't letters from Radcliffe graduates; lots of them were on lined school tablet paper. It seemed an awful lot of women out there in Middle America were also insulted by television's image of them.

The first necessity—and I hope ineradicable accomplishment—of the modern women's movement was to overcome that image of women as it was perpetuated by all the mass media. In the dozen years since my first analysis of the sexual sell, numbers of scholarly studies have been done in every field, demonstrating the damage to women's self-confidence that resulted from growing up with that image bombarding them day and night.

More important, as a result of the women's movement, the television image of women had begun to change dramatically by 1976. A number of popular new television series—even family situation comedies and soap operas—offer heroines who are bright and gutsy, have good jobs and are also sexually attractive—heroines, single, married and divorced, who are no longer passive sex objects or silently wave goodbye, but who act adventurously in their own lives: Cloris Leachman in *Phyllis*, Maude, Rhoda, Mary Tyler Moore, Angie Dickinson in *Police Woman*, moving even to the farthest reaches of science and space in *Bionic Woman*. The sassy heroine of *One Day at a Time* is not only a sympathetic, likable divorced mother, as attractive as her teenage daughters, but she has a younger boyfriend who adores her!

The amazing success of the camp soap opera *Mary Hartman, Mary Hartman* also says something new about the intelligence of American housewives; at least, all those women who still presumably turn the dial out there seem to be coming out of their state of misery and hate, and laughing, and liking themselves more.

And as a result of class action suits and other pressures from the women who work in television, both local and network TV are using more and more women as news commentators, producers, directors, and even behind the camera, where women never worked before. In 1976, Marlene Sanders, a feminist and a founding member of NOW, became the first network vice-president for news and public affairs at ABC.

Television and
The Feminine Mystique

 If the image of women on television today reflects—or affects—reality, then American women must be writhing in agonies of self-contempt and unappeasable sexual hunger. For television's image of the American woman, 1964, is a stupid, unattractive, insecure little household drudge who spends her martyred, mindless, boring days dreaming of love—and plotting nasty revenge against her husband. If that image affects men—or at least reflects the men who created it—then American men, in their contempt, loathing and fear of that miserable obsessed woman, must be turning in revulsion against love itself.

This is the rather horrifying feeling I had after sitting for several weeks in front of my television set, trying to reconcile the image of women projected by television commercials, family situation comedies, soap operas and game shows, with the strangely missing, indeed virtually nonexistent image of woman in all the rest of television: the major dramatic shows; the witty commentary, serious documentary and ordinary reportage of the issues and news of our world.

In fact, the most puzzling thing about the image of woman on television today is an eerie *Twilight Zone* sense that it is fading before one's eyes. In the bulk of television programs today, and even, increasingly, in commercials, one literally sees no image of woman at all. She isn't there. Even when the face and body of a woman are there, one feels a strange vagueness and emptiness, an absence of human identity, a missing sexual aliveness—is it a woman if it doesn't think or act or talk or move or love like a person?

Behind that fading image, the nonwoman on the television screen, I found, talking to producers, network decision-makers, agency executives, an even more unpleasant image: their image of those millions of American women "out there" watching that television, controlling that dial, determining those ratings—the American housewife who, they say, "has taken over television" as she is supposed to have taken over control of her husband, children, home, the U.S. economy and the nation in general. Put the two images together—the woman on the screen and the one watching it—and you see how television has trapped itself in the feminine mystique.

This whole process of the feminine mystique is projected on television to such an extreme that the question is not only what the mystique and its stunted, dehumanized, sick image of woman is doing to real women, and their respect for themselves, or men's love and respect for women—but what it is doing to television.

Consider first that drab, repulsive little housewife one sees on the television screen. She is so stupid that she is barely capable of doing the most menial household tasks. Her biggest problem is to get the kitchen sink or floor really clean, and she can't even do that without a kind, wise man to tell her how. ("To think that just a few months ago I was in college and now I'm a wife and mother," she weeps on the television commercial. "I want to be everything Jim wants in a wife and mother. But he says I'm inefficient. I can't cook and clean. I've tried and tried and I just can't get that sink clean.") Her biggest *thrill* is when, with that old man's magic help (which comes in a can), she gets that sink *clean.*

Her other biggest problem is how to keep doing all that cleaning and still keep her hands *"feminine."* She is so unattractive and feels so insecure that she needs all the help and mechanical contrivances modern science and industry can supply to keep her man from leaving her. ("How long has it been since your husband took you dancing . . . brought you flowers . . . really listened to what you said? Could it be that gray in your hair?" Bad breath? Irregular bowels?)

She isn't even adequate as a mother to her children. ("Even the most careful mother can't completely protect her family from household germs," the kind, wise man reassures her. "Is there really more than one vitamin?" she asks him, having never finished fifth grade herself.) In fact, she is barely capable of feeding the dog. (That wise old man has to tell her how to get the mutt out of his "mealtime rut.")

Less than a fifth-grader, more like that simple animal in her capacity to understand or take part in modern human society, this television-commercial woman has no interest, purpose or goal beyond cleaning the sink, feeding her kids, and going to bed.

The whole world beyond her home—its politics, art, science, issues, ideas and problems—is evidently beyond her comprehension. For not only is there no television image of a woman acting in the world, but the programming of daytime television and, increasingly, even prime time, assumes she has no interest in it or ability to understand it. She lives only for love.

But beneath the sacred exaltation of marriage, motherhood and home in the soap operas and the religious tones of the commercials, there is a crude assumption on the part of television decision-makers that all those women out there are panting through their boring days of mindless drudgery in a state of permanent unappeased sexual hunger. From a little after eight in the morning until the late, late hours after midnight, they evidently want from that television screen only the image of a virile male. At least this is the superficial reason given for that disappearing image of woman on the television screen, and the preponderance of male cheesecake ("beefcake," is it called?). "It's women who control the dial, and what a woman wants to look at is a man—a man with sex appeal, a man who's available to her," I was told over and over again up through the ranks of television decision-makers.

Several years ago, when the networks were under attack from the Federal Communications Commission, CBS put on a daytime news program. The producer, new to daytime, suggested a woman commentator. The network brass said he was

out of his mind. In simple four-letter words, they explained to
him that of all things the dames didn't want to see at 10 A.M., it
was a woman. They wanted a man they could jump right back
into bed with. But CBS did put a news-oriented show, *Calendar*, into that 10 A.M. time period, and hired actress Mary Fickett to act as Jill-of-all-trades. She did the household commercials and acted as pretty little straight man to commentator
Harry Reasoner. The condescension with which he talked to
the women out there may have marred his sexual charm. *Calendar* died.

On the MGM lot, producer Irving Elman explained to me
why his show *The Eleventh Hour*, and *Dr. Kildare* and *Mr. Novak*
at the same studio, and several other major series are built
around two men—a young bachelor and a middle-aged widower. The bachelors such as Dr. Kildare and Ben Casey are
available for a fantasy affair with the younger housewives; the
widowers like Dr. Starke in *The Eleventh Hour* are available for
the older housewives. In *The Defenders* the older lawyer, Lawrence Preston, is the object of affection for the over-forty
crowd; his son, Kenneth Preston, can be embraced by the
young mothers. "There is more sex appeal if he is a widower,"
Elman explained. "It makes him more available. If he were
married, his wife would be in the way. And if he were divorced, the women wouldn't like it. It would be too threatening. Marriage is sacred."

The double standard involved here almost seems unfair to
men. Madelyn Martin, long-time writer of the *Lucy* shows,
explained: "You can't package a dramatic show around a
woman because women want only to look at a man, and they
don't want their husbands to look at other women." The
housewives "out there" are evidently so insecure that they
can't face fantasy competition from a woman on the screen
not only for their own husbands, but for their fantasy extramarital amours either. "We have to be very careful to keep
Kildare from getting seriously involved with a woman,"
MGM executive producer Norman Felton said. "Women love
stories where there's the suggestion of romantic involvement,
but they resent it if he even kisses the girl on the screen. That
kiss jars the viewer's fantasy that she is the one with whom
he's having the love affair." This, of course, is one of the great

advantages of the hospital to television; the romance never has to be consummated because the woman patient neatly dies. "One of the high spots was Kildare's romance with that girl who died of leukemia," Felton reminisced.

If housewives control the dial, why, with no women at all, are Westerns so popular? "Beefcake," of course. *Bonanza*, for instance, really gives the panting women a choice of sizes and ages—four unmarried men: Daddy and his three sons. According to reports, the producer has been toying with the idea of letting one of the four get married, but, evidently out of consideration for all those women "out there," hasn't had the nerve to let it happen yet.

If the image-makers are right in theorizing that a woman "never wants to look at a woman, only men," is sex really the reason? "Love" is hardly the emotion the television woman seems to feel for that man she clutches so possessively. In the soap operas it is more like a martyred suffering, a noble endurance. ("Get married, stay home, suffer," a high school boy summed up woman's fate after he had spent a week at home, sick in bed, watching daytime television.) On *I Love Lucy*, *The Danny Thomas Show*, and other family comedies, that television housewife, far from "loving" or even "liking" her husband, seems positively obsessed with the need to wipe him under the doormat, get revenge against him, control him, manipulate him, show him up for the despicable, miserable worm he really is, and establish once and for all who's really the boss of the house. As if over and over she must show herself to be somebody by forcing him to his knees—getting him to admit her unquestioned superiority as the boss of the family.

Since the women in these comedies aren't ever allowed to overreach that definitive level of dullness and unattractiveness (otherwise would they offer too much competition for the supposedly dull, unattractive housewives out there?), the husbands must also be shown as stupid, unattractive boobs for even a semblance of believable suspense or conflict. It is perhaps a tribute to real male vanity, or real male contempt of the female, that television critics often complain of this silly-boob image of the husband, never noticing that the wife in these situation comedies is an even sillier boob. Evidently, in order to retain her "femininity," that wife always has to lose the battle in the end—or rather, demonstrate her true superiority by magnanimously letting the poor fool think he won it. (As on *The Danny Thomas Show* when, after he had subverted her complicated plot to make him give her a mink coat for Christmas, she shames him—by bringing him his rubbers and raincoat in the rain and catching near-pneumonia—into tape-recording abjectly that he loves her, in front of the whole Tuesday afternoon bridge club.)

In the daytime soap operas, the martyred superiority of the wives doesn't even have to be demonstrated; it's just mysteriously, axiomatically *there*. Since the housewives in *As the World Turns* and all the rest must conduct their warfare with men day after day during the day, the major dramatic problem seems to be to get the men home to be manipulated. It is amazing how often those busy lawyers and doctors and businessmen on television soap operas come home for lunch! But the neatest trick—which simultaneously accomplishes revenge and keeps the man home permanently to be controlled, or perhaps just to provide the soap-opera housewife with someone to talk at—is to paralyze the husband and put him in a wheelchair.

However it is accomplished, the real emotion played to by this image of woman who supposedly lives for love is hate. As a former network vice-president in charge of program development put it: "They [those housewives out there] don't want to look at husbands who are nice or strong. They only want to look at attractive younger men or old codgers out of the battle between the sexes. In the average dame's life the husband is the enemy, the guy you have to manipulate, push around, be happy in spite of. When the daytime serial features a strong husband, and the wife is not the controlling one, the rating is invariably low. The husband becomes acceptable only if he is manipulated by the good, kind, loving, all-wise wife."

But why is there no image of women on television engaged in anything else but that so-called war between the sexes? After all, it is only in the family comedies that men appear as such stupid boobs. The bulk of television features men engaged with more or less valor in action with the world—curing the sick, coping with social problems in *East Side/West Side*, Mr. Novak teaching in the classroom, cowboys in Westerns, supermen zooming into outer space, detectives, and variously engaged individuals in dramas and specials that are concerned with something beyond intramarital warfare, to say nothing of news and documentaries about real issues of the world beyond one woman's house.

Could the very absence of any image of women active or triumphant in the world explain the dream of revenge and domination over the male, the sexual insecurity and self-contempt and even that supposedly unappeasable sexual hunger which television plays to, in its nasty image of the American housewife?

•   •   •

Actresses complain, and producers and directors confirm, that there are fewer parts for women on television today. Network brass may say that this is because those sex-obsessed housewives who control the dial only want to look at men. But I submit that television, in its literal embrace of the feminine mystique, has narrowed the image of women to an emptiness that simply cannot be dramatized in terms of human action.

According to television's image, the only action or dramatic adventure possible for an American woman today is to get sick, preferably with an incurable disease. Virtually the only exceptions are *The Nurses* and the commercial in which a woman plumber fixes the kitchen sink. "Actresses beat down the doors to become our psychiatric patients," says Irving Elman, producer of *The Eleventh Hour*. "They say they're the only parts that give them anything to do. On the other shows, the women just stand in the door, kissing the men good-bye."

It's not strange that the unwritten law which permits only the drab "average housewife" image of women on television is causing this fade-out of any image of women at all. For the daily tedium of a life whose biggest challenge is to clean the sink is simply too devoid of human action, involvement with other human beings, or human triumph to provide the basis for drama—or even the basis for a sense of human identity. That's why real housewives who live within that empty image have so little sense of themselves that they need a man to make them feel alive—even a man who talks down to them on television—and why they also are choking with resentment against men, whose lives at least provide enough action to dramatize.

Beneath the clichés of the feminine mystique, television plays consciously to this tedium, and to the resentment it engenders —narcotizing woman's very capacity to act and think into a passive, sullen, vengeful impotence.

After all, if it weren't for the real tedium of the so-called average housewife's day, would she ever willingly endure the tedium of daytime television, or the sneering contempt for women explicit in the game shows? *The Price Is Right, Truth or Consequences, Concentration,* and *Queen for a Day* seem to assume an average IQ of 50 (submoron) in the American woman; surely, if my psychology doesn't fail me, *most* women are not feeble-minded, though years of bombardment by television in that isolated house could make them so. Why else would middle-aged women dress up in children's dresses and hair bows to lumber through an obscene reincarnation of themselves as high-school cheerleaders? The suave man at the mike can hardly veil his own contempt at those fat grown-up women making such a public spectacle of themselves ("a siss and a siss and a siss boom bah!").

What does such a denigrating image of real women do to young mothers watching, who are no longer sure who they are, or to girls who don't even know who they can be? What does it do to women or girls—or the boys and men whose love they want—to see no image at all of a self-respecting woman who thinks or does or aims or dreams large dreams or is capable of taking even small actions to shape her own life or her future or her society?

One hesitates to accuse television of a conspiracy to keep women confined within the limits of that demeaning housewife image, their minds anesthetized by the tedium and lack of challenge of those empty hours, their very confidence in their own abilities to act or think for themselves destroyed so that they meekly buy whatever the kind, wise, authoritative man tells them to. Undoubtedly there are such mindless, passive housewife robots among American women, but why is television doing its best to create more in their image?

Why is there no image at all on television of the millions and millions of self-respecting American women who are not only capable of cleaning the sink without help, but of *acting* to solve more complex problems of their own lives and their society? That moronic-housewife image denies the 24,000,000 women who work today outside the home in every industry and skilled profession, most of them wives who take care of homes and children too. That image also insults the millions of real American housewives, with more and more education, who shape U.S. culture, politics, art and education by their actions in the P.T.A., the League of Women Voters and local political parties, and who help to build libraries, art galleries and theaters from Detroit to Seattle, and even strike for peace.

Why, for instance, isn't one of the leads in a program like *Mr. Novak* a woman teacher? I asked MGM executive producer Norman Felton. He explained: "If you have a woman lead in a television series, she has to be either married or unmarried. If she's unmarried, what's wrong with her? After all, it's housewives we're appealing to, and marriage is their whole life. If she's married, what's her husband doing in the background? He must not be very effective. He should be making the decisions. For drama, there has to be action, conflict. If the action is led by a woman, she has to be in conflict—with men or women or something. She has to make decisions; she has to triumph over opposition. For a woman to make decisions, to triumph over anything, would be unpleasant, dominant, masculine. After all, most women are housewives, at home with children; most women are dominated by men, and they would react against a woman who succeeded at anything."

But that housewife in the family situation comedies is only too unpleasant, dominant and masculine. She is always triumphing, not over forces in the outside world, but in that endless warfare against her own husband or children. "In comedy it's all right," Felton said. "You're not supposed to take her seriously; you laugh at her." Could there be a serious drama about a woman in the home, a housewife? "We couldn't make it dramatic—and honest," he said. "Most of a housewife's life is too humdrum. If you showed it honestly, it would be too dull to watch. Maybe you can get away with it in a hospital. After all, how many dramatic cases does a doctor or lawyer have in a year? But if you tried to do it with a housewife, no one would believe it. Everyone knows how dull the life of a housewife really is."

Thus if television's only image of women is such a "dull"

housewife, there is in the end no action or dramatic conflict she can engage in except that warfare with her own husband or children. Unless she gets sick and goes to the hospital, where she can die nobly of a brain tumor. "It makes sense that women are only figures of comedy," said Madelyn Martin, writer of *Lucy*. "When you think of traditional figures of comedy—the short guy, the ugly one, the man with the big nose, the Negro or Jew or member of any minority group—comedy is a way of turning their misfortune into a joke. It's a way of being accepted—'Look at me, I'm funny,' and, 'Don't anybody laugh at me, I'll laugh first.' "

If women are the one majority in America that resembles an oppressed minority, it's not because of actual deprivation of right or opportunity or human dignity, but simply because of that self-ridiculing image—the mystique of the mindless female, the passive housewife, which keeps girls and women from using their rights and opportunities and taking their own lives seriously, in time. In an examination scene in a *Mr. Novak* episode, a high school girl takes the blame for her boyfriend's crib sheet to protect his future as a would-be physicist. "It's all right," she says, "let them blame it on me. I'm not going to college or anything. It won't matter to me." Why doesn't it matter to her—her own life and future? Why, in high school, does she already play the martyred, passive wife? No need to work or study in school herself, or plan her own future, the image says. All she has to do is get that boy to marry her—the sooner, the better—and he'll take care of her life.

Do anything you can to hook that man, all those images of women on television say, because you aren't or can't be a person yourself. But without studying or working or doing anything yourself, you can be a "housewife" at eighteen. And get all those expensive things for wedding presents, just like on *Queen for a Day*—a lounge chair, a dishwasher, a whole set of china, baby furniture, even a free trip to the beauty parlor every week.

Is it a coincidence that millions of real girls who have grown up watching television—and seeing only that emptily "glamorous" housewife image of women—do not, in high school, have any goal in their own future except being such a passive housewife? Is it partly from lack of any self-respecting image of a woman as a person herself that so many stop their own growth in junior high to start that frantic race to "trap" a man, get pregnant in high school, or quit college to take a "housework" job in industry to put their husbands through medical or engineering school? By seducing real girls into evading the choices, efforts and goals which would enable them to grow to maturity and full human identity in our society, television's image of women is *creating* millions of unnecessarily mindless, martyred housewives, for whom there may never be a thrill or challenge greater than that dirty kitchen sink.

Thus television's little housewife monster becomes a self-fulfilling prophecy. You can see it happening in the increasingly drab looks, whining voices and general stupidity of the new young housewives in the commercials. Not very many years ago, the average American woman could supposedly identify with a pretty, bright, self-confident dame, eager to grow and educate herself and seize any challenge that came along. For instance, Betty Furness. That was *her* image—and it certainly sold refrigerators and stoves to millions of American women, who evidently shared her eager, life-loving self-confidence.

All of a sudden it was decided that Betty Furness's image was making "the average little housewife" uncomfortable. She looked too intelligent or independent or individual, or maybe just too eager and alive. Couldn't she dim herself down somehow, put on a housedress, give off a smell of dirty diapers and unwashed dishes and burned chops in the background to make that "average housewife" feel less inferior? Betty Furness looked "smart" as well as "feminine," and she was proud of it. She had the assured professional air of authority, which is necessary to sell anyone anything: "I try not to open my mouth unless I know what I'm talking about," she said. "I know who I am and I like it. I can't look dumb. I can't dim myself down to that so-called average housewife." [*TV Guide* here added, "An agency spokesman said there was no attempt to temper the Furness 'image.'"]

So she moved on, from commercials to daytime television. And then it was decided her image was too "intelligent" for daytime television; she went to radio, like Arlene Francis and the few other intelligent women on TV with whom evidently the new "average" housewives could not identify.

But these new teen-age housewives—the growth-stunted young mothers who quit school to marry and become mothers before they grew out of bobby socks themselves—are the female Frankenstein monsters television helped create. And they may writhe forever in that tedious limbo between the kitchen sink and the television game show, living out their century-long life ahead, in a complex world which requires human purposes, commitment and efforts they never even glimpsed. How long can even television channel their pent-up energies into vicarious love affairs with Dr. Kildare, vicarious death by leukemia, even vicarious revenge against that husband who is surely not their real enemy?

How long will boys and men love women if this nasty, vengeful martyr is their only public image of woman, and becomes an increasingly vengeful private image? The female Frankenstein monsters, after all, are created by the minds of men. Does the new plethora of widowers, bachelor fathers and unmarried mature men on television, who pay a maid or houseboy or soon perhaps a robot to get the household drudgery done, signify unconscious rebellion against that "housewife" altogether? Do they really want her for a wife? One suddenly realizes that there are no real love stories on the television screen—in the sense of the love stories that one can still see in the old movies, with Ingrid Bergman, Joan Crawford, Norma Shearer, Claudette Colbert and all the rest. No love stories, no heroines—only those housewife drudges, the comic ogres who man the war between the sexes.

Television badly needs some heroines. It needs more images of real women to help girls and women take themselves seriously and grow and love and be loved by men again. And television decision-makers need to take real women more seriously—not for women's sake but for their own. Must women only be used as weather girls or "straight men" diaper-and-pot-holders for the male news commentators? Must they be shown only as paid or underpaid dishwashers for fear of making real housewives uncomfortable?

I've had letters from thousands of these real women, and

whatever the reasons why they tried to settle too soon for this narrow, humiliating image, a lot of them want a second chance to grow. Television could help them get it, not keep cutting them down. Is it a coincidence that daytime network television, which has banished real women with minds like Arlene Francis and Betty Furness to radio, is having less success with that "average housewife" than radio, which feeds their minds with intelligent talk, much of it from women—not only Betty and Arlene but also the Martha Deanes, Ruth Jacobs, and all the bright women on local radio and television?

The men who decide the image of women on television could take a tip from a blonde who interviewed me on a local TV show in Los Angeles last summer. She called me at my hotel the day before to ask me some questions, explaining she'd stayed up all night finishing my book. It was refreshing for someone to take the trouble to read my book before interviewing me, and it was a good interview. Over breakfast later she said she liked reading such "tough" books; she hadn't been to college herself. She also said she was taking a pay cut from $750 a week as a night-club singer to accept this job as television commentator at $250 a week.

"It's the mental challenge of it," she said. "It makes me feel alive. I'm sick of just being a body. I want a chance to be someone myself—and give something of myself—in this world."

By now, the writing which I had more or less kept secret from my suburban neighbors—they didn't read most of the magazines I wrote for—was out in public. I was on television programs, I was asked to lecture at universities, women's clubs, professional groups—and had to hire a cab to take my turn at the car pool for the children's art or dancing classes.

And suddenly I was a leper in my own suburban neighborhood. The children were kicked out of the dancing-class car pool. We were no longer invited to the dinner parties. Maybe I was Joan of Arc to some women far away, but in my own suburb they wanted to burn me at the stake. It wasn't any fun, being *that exceptional*. I didn't like being a freak, alone, the target of all that hostility from the other suburban women whose children played with mine—my only pool for friends at that time. It was only later that I understood the reason for their hostility: *I threatened them because I was acting out the secret desire that they did not yet dare to face in themselves.* (Some years later, long after we had moved to the city, Jonathan went back at Christmas to a party at his friend Peter's house, three doors down from our old suburban homestead. "Where are the cookies?" he asked Peter's mother, one of those ideal housewives who baked and always kept a cookie jar full for her kids and their friends. "I'm working," she said drily. "Tell your mother we're all working now, more power to her.")

There were powerful forces that kept us filling those cookie jars, even when our children didn't need them any longer. I was assistant den mother in the Cub Scouts, for instance, out of duty to Danny, my oldest son. One year the outfit that gives the Emmy Awards—the American Academy of Television Artists—decided to train a few writers from other fields to write for the quality-aspiring television market. I was one of those writers. The TV seminar turned out to be the same day as the Cub Scout meetings. To take the bus into the city on time, I'd have to skip my den mother duty every other week. I did it twice, and had such a guilty asthma attack—and writer's block on the TV script—that I simply resigned the seminar, honor and professional opportunities notwithstanding. And I tried in vain to persuade the chief den mother to drop the packaged plans for adventures on the trail. Some months later, my ten-year-old Danny said apologetically that he hoped I wouldn't mind if he stopped going to Cub Scouts, it was too boring.

Apologetically, I began campaigning to exchange that suburban life—where the children had to depend on me too much for chauffeuring, and my own commuting now kept me from spending as much time as I wanted with them—for a city apartment, where they could take the bus by themselves, and a house on Fire Island, where we could be together on weekends and no one had to drive. (And in the city, I would no longer be a leper, "exceptional," because other women also undoubtedly worked.)

It's not *comfortable* to be an "exception"—a woman in man's world, or a freak among women in the suburbs. But the women I was meeting as I began to be asked to lecture at universities, cities, and schools across the country, and the women writing in answer to my book and to those subsequent magazine articles, were not all that exceptional. The obstacles I found—trying to go back to school for a belated, now never-to-be Ph.D. in psychology; the hostility from other women and the toll on my children as I deviated from the housewife norm and began to take my own work as seriously as their schoolwork; the hostility from my own husband, the guilt and pain and fear that made me hold dependently on to a marriage more and more imbued with hate than love for fear of being alone—those problems were not exceptional.

The problems and conflicts seemed insoluble because I was so afraid of being alone, as long as we all felt alone. But in the midst of my personal conflicts and near despair, I guess I was moving to that crucial step that would give us all the support we needed to really change our lives. I was beginning to realize how very many women in all age groups were trying to change their lives—and thus facing those obstacles in society.

Around this time, I talked to some Oklahoma housewives who'd gone back and gotten those graduate degrees, and were now grading freshman English with no hope of advance— captive slave labor because of their husbands' jobs in that university town. "Forget what we told you," they telephoned me after I got home. "Nothing can be done about it. We should be grateful to be taken back at all, women of our age." These women who stood poised to move were the potential armies of the women's movement.

By the spring of 1964, the woman question, or the problem of the trapped housewife, was being talked to death, going around in circles that got nowhere.

President Kennedy had appointed a Commission on the Status of Women, which had gone into all the problems (I'd been drawn in to its work on the image of women, as a consultant), had issued a report—and had been discharged, with no provision at all for implementing its recommendations. This process was being repeated with state commissions, educational meetings, symposia. The professionals whose trade was women—counselors, psychoanalysts, home economists, appliance manufacturers, advertisers, and television producers— were having conferences whose thrust, it seemed to me, was a great wish to embrace "Woman" in the abstract so that the real women erupting all over the place with their messy irritating unpigeonhole-able problems would just shut up and go away.

In the spring of '64, some member of that anonymous female underground who were refusing to shut up and go away somehow sneaked me in as a speaker in an otherwise bland bill of fare at two conferences on "Professional Opportunities for Women: Choice or Chance" held by various government agencies and state commissions on the status of women, in San Francisco and Seattle. There was something about the hushed, expectant way those western women listened to me, gave me a standing ovation, and came up afterward, that wasn't just my celebrity; it was as if they counted on me, needed me, expected something of me. I felt the burden of that expectancy, and the guilt over that second book I should have been writing. Why was I wasting so much time running around the country talking to women? I was supposed to be writing a book on patterns that would enable women to move beyond the feminine mystique. But to be honest, I really hadn't found such new patterns. In every city where I lectured, I insisted the institution hosting me gather together all the women it could find combining marriage, motherhood and professional work in new ways. All I found was the same old apologetic, makeshift, hassles. But I did find an awful lot of women who couldn't solve their problems alone unless society changed. And in my naïve search for those solutions that did not yet exist, I had inadvertently stumbled on the force, the source of energy, that could and would coalesce to change the whole gestalt: the women with those problems, those yearning, helpless, defensive, apologetic guilt-ridden women, who were unconsciously getting ready to move—just as I was.

I had a dream about that time. I dreamed I was meandering, fooling around, doing this, doing that, evading some task, some appointment I was supposed to keep. A lecture, maybe; a whole audience I was keeping waiting behind a curtain. And finally I sort of sidled up to the curtain and peeked through. And there were thousands, thousands of women sitting out there on their chairs as if waiting for something, for some signal. And I turned away from that glimpse in the hole in the curtain. And I thought—because I do take dreams seriously— God, I must be guilty about not working on my next book. But I now know that wasn't what that dream was about.

At a meeting of women in radio and television, most kept their eyes averted when I attacked television's put-down of our sex, but their leader, Muriel Fox, sent me a note: "If you ever start an N.A.A.C.P. for women, count me in." I had no such intention. I was a writer, period. But my own words were moving me as they were moving other women to our time to act.

The Crisis
in Women's Identity

(University of California,
San Francisco, 1964)

I am delighted to be here. Women all over this country are on
the verge of completing the massive delayed revolution that
needs to be won for women. It is a delayed revolution because
all the rights that would make women free and equal citizens
of this country, persons able to develop to their full potential
in society, were won on paper long ago. The last of these
rights, the right to vote, was won the year before I was born.
But we are not really free and equal if the feminine mystique
keeps us from freely using our rights; if the only world we
really are free to move in is the so-called woman's world of
home; if we are asked to make an unreal choice no man is ever
asked to make; if we think, as girls, that we have to choose
somehow between love, marriage and motherhood and the
chance to devote ourselves seriously to some challenge, some
interest that would enable us to grow to our full human potential.

Are we really free and equal if we are forced to make such a
choice, or half-choice, because of lack of support from our society—because we have not received simple institutional help in
combining marriage and motherhood with work in the profes-

sions, politics, or any of the other frontiers beyond the home? If girls today still have no image of themselves as individual human beings, if they think their only road to status, to identity, in society is to grab that man—according to all the images of marriage from the ads, the television commercials, the movies, the situation comedies, and all the experts who counsel them—and if therefore they think they must catch him at nineteen and begin to have babies and that split-level dream house so soon that they never have time to make other choices, to take other active moves in society, to risk themselves in trial-and-error efforts, are they, are we, really free and equal? Are we confined by that simple age-old destiny that depends only on our sexual biology and chance, or do we actually have the freedom of choice that is open to us as women today in America?

I say that the only thing that stands in women's way today is this false image, this feminine mystique, and the self-denigration of women that it perpetuates. This mystique makes us try to beat ourselves down in order to be feminine, makes us deny or feel freakish about our own abilities as people. It keeps us from moving freely on the road that is open to us. It keeps us from recognizing and solving the small, but real problems that remain.

Whether you know it or not, you have—in your own lives, in your own persons—moved beyond this false image. You yourselves deny the feminine mystique; you deny the very images of women that come at you from all sides. There are no heroines today in America, not as far as the public image is concerned. There are sex objects and there are drudges. We see this on television every day.

You here, however, are the new image of women: as person, as heroine. You live actively in society. You are not solely dependent on your husbands and your children for your identity. You do not live your life vicariously through them. You do not wait passively for that wise man to make the decisions that will shape your society, but move in and help shape society yourself, and begin to make it a more human world. You bridge that old, obsolete division that splits life into man's world of thought and action and woman's world of love. With little help from society, you have begun to make a new pattern in which marriage, motherhood, homemaking—the traditional roles of women—are merged with the possibility of women as individuals, as decision-makers, as creators of the future.

But because of the feminine mystique, you have not felt fully free and confident even as you have moved on this road. You have felt guilty; you have endured jeers, sneers, snickers, perhaps not from your own husband—who, I suspect, supports you more than the image would admit—but from the image-makers, and perhaps from your less adventurous neighbors, who are less willing to assume the role of heroine.

Your presence here today, however, is a testament to the fact that you are beginning to become conscious of the task that is before you. You are beginning to become conscious of the moment in history in which you stand, and this consciousness is what we need now.

Someone said to me in St. Louis that I wasn't actually telling women to do anything new, that I was only helping to make them conscious of the road on which they were already moving. I would accept this. I think we must become conscious of it in order to finish the job. Otherwise we keep repeating over and over again the same arguments with ourselves, the same conflicts, the same decisions, instead of moving ahead and facing the new problems that need to be solved, and asking, in voices loud enough to be heard, for what we need from society. We do not know how strong we could be if we affirmed ourselves as women and joined together, instead of each woman feeling freakish and isolated, as if no one else but herself had the brains and the courage to look beyond that young peak of marriage and childbirth that the feminine mystique enshrines.

You know that you have brains as well as breasts, and you use them. You know what you are capable of, but you could use it for yourselves and for other women with so much more freedom if you could only break through those self-denigrating blocks. It is not laws, nor great obstacles, nor the heels of men that are grinding women down in America today. Men as well as women are victims of the feminine mystique. We must simply break through this curtain in the minds of *women* in order to get on with the massive delayed revolution. And there *are* massive numbers of us, if we stop to realize how many of us have already moved beyond the feminine mystique and how many more are ready to move.

I am speaking not only of the women who work outside the home in industry, but of every woman who works in society, for they all have made a certain advance from the isolation of household drudgery. Unfortunately, far too many women are taking jobs too soon in order to put their husbands through law, engineering, graduate or theological school, because these women do not take themselves and their own abilities seriously enough to put themselves through schools. Consequently, too many women of the one-out-of-three who work outside the home are concentrating on the housework jobs of industry—which are going to be replaced by the machine, anyway, just as much of the drudgery of our housework at home has been replaced by the machine. Even more of this household drudgery could be done by machines if the massive resources of American technology were devoted to it, instead of to selling women things they do not need and convincing them that running the washing machine is as creative, scientific and challenging as solving the genetic code.

All of these women in industry housework, however, are now in a position, with the proper training, to move ahead to the kinds of work that cannot be replaced by the machine. With them in the massive revolution are the great numbers of women who engage in volunteer community leadership, work that requires a great deal of human strength, thought and initiative. To a certain extent, their work is often more in tune with the rapid change in our society than that of the existing professions. Committed, innovative volunteer work is done almost completely by women in America, and thus is not recognized for what it is by our society. Therefore, by sneaking around the corner, it manages to innovate in ways that the conformity, the resistance to change, structured into the existing professions does not permit.

I think, however, if we break through that denigrating image of women enshrined in the feminine mystique and take ourselves seriously, society may begin to take us seriously. The disparagement of volunteer work in America will stop, and the false line between the professional and the volunteer will be redrawn. As it is, professionals have such a low opinion of the woman volunteer that they dream up work to keep her busy, use her far below her own ability merely to raise money or hold teas or lick envelopes—or they break the jobs up into little segments that someone with even a small IQ could do. And yet we hear that they cannot find the professionals that they need to solve the social problems in the community, and that there aren't enough trained group workers to do what needs to be done in the hospitals, the schools, and the health and welfare agencies.

If all the volunteers resigned tomorrow, much of this work, not all, would still have to be done, but it might be done with a more serious use of women's real abilities.

I would add also to the massiveness of this revolution the great numbers of women who are doing the housework of politics, who, trapped in the feminine mystique, acquiesce merely to lick envelopes, take nominal posts in ladies' aid auxiliaries, collect furniture for auctions, and second nominating speeches. Freed from their self-denigration, however, they could hold policy-making positions, run for the county committee, serve on the town committee, run for the state Senate or Congress, go to law school and become a judge, or even run for Vice President. I won't say President, for I think that may be premature, but it might help the revolution if a woman had enough courage to try. Above all, women in America need higher aspirations in politics. We know more than we think we know politically, and we are not using this knowledge.

Of all the passions open to man and woman, politics is the one that a woman can most easily embrace and move ahead in, creating a new pattern of politics, marriage and motherhood. Only self-denigration stops women in politics.

In addition, there are the great number of women who could be artists, who *are* artists but do not take themselves seriously as such. In *The New York Times* recently, there were some interesting figures that showed an enormous increase in the number of Americans who answered "Artist" on the census blank, who defined themselves professionally as painters, sculptors, art teachers, writers, poets, playwrights, television writers, all the rest. This great increase was almost completely made up of men. All that keeps a woman of talent from being an artist is her false image of herself, the fear of making the commitment to discipline herself—and of being tested. She doesn't even run across the problems that an American woman has, say, in wanting to become a physicist. Even if as a young girl she does not absorb the notion that physics is un-feminine, she may find it hard to want to have children and go to the physics laboratory at the same time. However, you can paint at home. It is only for lack of taking herself seriously that a woman who paints does not become an artist—or that a woman who wants to become a physicist doesn't work out some sort of accommodation for both children and a career.

I also add to the massive, delayed revolution many of the young women who fell hook, line and sinker for the feminine mystique, used it as a rationalization for evading their own choices, and married early. They thought that all they had to do was to get that man at nineteen and that would take care of the rest of their life, and then they woke up at twenty-five or thirty-five or forty-five with the four children, the house and the husband, and realized they had to face a future ahead in which they would not be able to live through others. Such a woman, whose children are already moving out the door, fi-nally asks herself what she is going to do with her life, and begins, even if late, to face and make some choices of her own. These great numbers of women are now trying to go back to college to get the education they gave up too easily and too soon, and they are getting more or less—too often less—a help-ing hand from the educators. Some of the universities are breaking through formal barriers and helping these women to grow to their full potential by admitting them to part-time college or graduate work—since part-time study is usually the only answer today for a woman who is still responsible for small children. Some universities may even provide part-time nursery schools so that women may continue to study even during those years; in this way they will not emerge as dis-placed people when their last child goes off to school, and they will not have to contribute to the population explosion by having baby after baby for lack of anything else creative to do. Perhaps the colleges and universities will even begin to be a little less rigid and understand that a woman who has had the strength to innovate in the community—who has led in solv-ing new problems in education, politics, mental health, and in all the other problems that women have worked on in their suburbs and cities in recent years—may have learned something that is the equivalent of an academic thesis.

Finally, there are the great numbers of young girls for whom, thank heaven, the choices are still ahead. If they only see through the false image, they can so easily make the little choices—not the false big ones such as marriage versus career, but the little ones—that, if made all along, will easily create a new image of woman. And even if their choices involve effort, work, a few conflicts and problems that have to be solved, these are easier problems than that desperate emptiness a woman faces at thirty-five or forty after she realizes that all her life cannot be lived in lifelong full-time motherhood. These young girls can decide in high school "I would like to be a physicist, I would like to be a teacher, I would like to be a nurse, I would like to be an astronaut." Not "What do you want to be, little girl?" "I would like to be a mommy." "What do you want to be, little boy?" "I would like to be a cowboy." Of course he is going to be a husband and father; of course she is going to be a wife and mother. But the choices she must make in school are to learn what else she can be and do herself, because if she does not make these choices when she is young, she will not even try to do the work, to make the effort that will take her to our new frontiers.

Of course, if the revolution is going to be so massive, there is going to be resistance to it. In the last year or so, the problem of women in America has been put on the table. The President's Commission on the Status of Women has made its report. My book and others like it have stimulated discussions among women who have too long suppressed their own aspirations as people, and we are beginning to see some resistance.

There was a story in the *New Yorker* a few months ago called "An Educated American Woman," by John Cheever. It was about an educated woman who fought a zoning battle in her neighborhood, who was taking a French course at Columbia and who was writing a book. She was punished. The baby-sitter left her child alone and he died. Her husband left her for a motherly woman. No more education, no more zoning battles, and, heaven forbid, no more books.

In one of the Doris Day movies, she too was fighting a

zoning battle, and the implication was, as a result, no sex: her man left her bed. Obviously, no more zoning battles for her. In the latest one, *The Thrill of It All*, Doris Day is an obstetrician's wife who gets a chance to do television commercials. She enjoys it, but her husband doesn't like it very much. He, by his great scientific ingenuity, is helping one of his patients, a poor, embittered, sophisticated career woman, to finally have a baby at the age of forty. In the end, the baby is born in a taxicab on the East River Drive, with Doris helping to deliver it and the obstetrician galloping up on a horse. Doris Day says, "Now I know what life is all about, helping you to deliver this baby." But of course, how foolish can the audience be, she can't help him deliver a baby in the operating room tomorrow, so what will she do? Aha, she'll have another baby herself, that's the answer. But the real life Doris Days can't go on having babies forever.

Recently you may have seen an advertising campaign by one of the women's service magazines. There are three obviously neurotic women. One says, "I read this wonderful poem; it was such an escape." Dreamy, neurotic escape. A second one, a very hard, bitter, career woman with a hat pulled down, says, "I read this article about India in such and such a magazine. It kept me occupied coming home on the five thirty-five." Another woman who looks as if something is wrong with her says, "I read a wonderful novel by so-and-so." Then we see the fourth one, healthy and wholesome, Mrs. Average Housewife: "I read about a new paint for the children's room. I won't use it, Jim will." The magazine only a homemaker could love. No articles about India, no poems, no great literature here, only service to home and children.

Redbook magazine had a story about a woman who felt guilty because she just sat home and baked cookies and fooled around while her neighbor made petitions to improve the schools. This neighbor said, "Goodness, how are women ever going to assume their equality if you are just going to sit on your behind and make cookies?" Then a mousy little wren came to town who wouldn't even *sign* the petitions; she literally did nothing but bake cookies. And the guilty woman discovered that this mousy little wren, who didn't even bother to look attractive, had been a physicist. But she saw no greater thing in the world to do now than to bake cookies in her own home. This was evidently supposed to mean that it was all phony, the idea that women could make petitions and campaign for the school board or be physicists or dream of doing something else besides bake cookies in their own kitchens.

Margaret Mead, who has contributed much to our knowledge of the plasticity of the human male and female but who has also helped to create the feminine mystique, had an article in *Redbook* attacking the report of the President's Commission on the Status of Women because, she said, it assumed that political life and work would be important to women and did not emphasize enough that women must be full-time wives and mothers. This woman, who is a world-famous, far-traveled anthropologist, declares approvingly that more and more educated women are choosing to be full-time wives and mothers. Margaret Mead even asked that if women really finish the job that the President's Commission says needs to be done, "who will be there to bandage the child's knee and listen to the husband's troubles and give the human element in the world?" Somehow she never explains how the woman is going to listen to the husband's troubles during the eight hours of the day when the husband is at the office, and how she is going to bandage the child's knee when the child isn't there but is at school.

Thus the resistance to the revolution even shows up in the ranks of what I call "capital C" Career women, women who would not be caught dead themselves behind a dishpan, and who from their vantage point back from the expedition in New Guinea or behind the television microphone, say, "But what greater thing can a woman do but drudgery for those she loves, and how many really rewarding, satisfying things in the world are there to do anyway—look at taxi drivers?" Somehow this is always at Radcliffe or Harvard, where the choices open to women, or men, are far more than being taxi drivers. Or, they sneer, how many women have abilities to do anything beyond housework? Of course, these women know *they* have such abilities, but they are exceptional.

I don't think they are so exceptional. I think that 50 percent of the women are above average, just as 50 percent aren't. And I think that while all women have to get dressed, eat dinner, make meals and keep houses clean, these tasks can hardly use all the abilities of an above-average woman—or the whole life-span abilities of a below-average woman, either. For we are going to live, my generation, to be seventy-five, and our daughters may live to be one hundred. No matter how much they will love their children, how much they will want to be wives and mothers and truly enjoy motherhood, it will be such a small part of their lives. It would deprive them of their real choices to say that they should think of themselves only, or even primarily, in terms of their sexual difference from man (long live it) and never in terms of their unique human abilities, whatever they may be.

There is also resistance on the part of some men, but not of as many as you think. I am increasingly surprised at the numbers of men who really do have a full regard for their wives as human beings, who want them to have full lives of their own, who are weary of the burden and the guilt of having to make up to a woman for all the life she misses beyond the home, for the world she has no part in. Men are weary of coming home from that tough, complex rat race in society only to be met by a pent-up wife who feels short-changed in the narrow world of home—and finds him somehow inadequate because he can't give her all that magic fulfillment she has been told to expect from marriage. But perhaps he is not inadequate at all; perhaps she is merely asking for too much from marriage. Perhaps for a woman, as for a man, marriage and love, while two of the basic, great values of life, cannot be all of life. For it is a fact that most men do not spend most of the hours of their day, most of the years of their lives, preoccupied with love or sex, as much as those passions are overglorified in the public image today. These images are directed at women, and they are directed at women to sell them something.

Do we really have to keep on acquiescing to the sexual sell, and is it really essential to the American economy? I have a hunch that if women were released to develop their full potential, they might want things that would keep the American economy alive just as much as those eighty-eight ways to get that man or keep him, or those magical powders that will keep the sink pure white. Perhaps more of the American economy might go to research and education, perhaps there might be other changes, but I hardly think keeping the American housewife in a state of perpetual frustration and emptiness and nagging discontent is essential to the American economy.

I think there are some men who may resist this massive, delayed revolution because they have had too much smothering from mothers who need them for an identity, and thus feel insecure in their own ability to move as human beings in the world. They may think they need a woman as a doormat. They may need someone whom they can think of as inferior so that they can feel superior. But I doubt that it is really going to solve any man's problem for his wife to beat herself down, to project a phony inferiority. Isn't it pretty contemptuous of man to say that his ego is so weak that he needs her to pretend to be something that she isn't, in order to make him feel like a big boy? I happen to think men are stronger than that. It might be better for both men and women if they could accept each other for what they are. It might even free men from the binds of the masculine mystique. Someone else will have to write a book about that.

I think all of these resistances are not that great. Our own self-denigration of ourselves as women and perhaps our own fears are the main problems. For it is an unknown road we now must take, and if we move on it, we take risks. It takes courage. We face a more complex life when we begin to create this new image of woman and to put all of these pieces of ourselves together. We risk being tested, being measured. We risk exposing ourselves if we insert ourselves into the human story instead of living through our husbands and children. The longer we hide in our homes evading the challenges of the society that is moving and changing so fast outside our doors, the more we may be afraid to move, the more we may wish, insist, somehow, that we can and only need to be wives and mothers, this is all, this is the greatest thing in life. And it is indeed the bedrock of life, the beginning.

But it isn't all, it can't be all for women today. And if it has to be all for some women too old or too frightened to risk a more complex road, it is not too late for most women. Most women have more strength than they imagine. We do not know what strength we have.

I will tell you something that might make you feel good; it

makes me feel good. There is a study not yet published that is being done at Washington University Medical School about the growth of the self in women, the ego, identity, whatever you want to call it. Do you know who has the most mature and the strongest self of all, the most autonomous ego? The committed woman volunteer. Her sense of identity is much stronger than that little housewife. Much stronger, interestingly enough, than the professional social worker in the same field. Why? Because she pioneered on an unknown road; because she had to structure a growth pattern for herself, not a pattern already there and structured by society; because in many cases she innovated; and because she imposed a discipline on herself that was not imposed by the demands of the paycheck. She is living this new image of woman, she is showing the way. And so are you, whether you realize it or not.

We must all say yes to ourselves as women, and no to that outworn, obsolete image, the feminine mystique. We must stop denigrating ourselves, stop acquiescing in the remaining prejudices the mystique enshrines. We must recognize and affirm each other in the massiveness of our own numbers and our own strength and ask for all women what we all need to move freely ahead. One does not move freely and joyously ahead if one is always torn by conflicts and guilts, nor if one feels like a freak in a man's world, if one is always walking a tightrope between being a good wife and mother and fulfilling one's commitments to society—with no help from society. If we ask, I think we can get simple institutional solutions from society to these real problems. Well-run five- or eight-hour-a-day nursery schools or day-care centers are needed, and maternity leaves that are real and not just on paper—so that the staff doesn't become mysteriously reduced when you get pregnant. Real credit needs to be given for the work you have done as volunteers. More part-time patterns are needed in all professions for mothers. Above all, women must assume real political equality and take their place as decision-makers in political life.

We must ask for these things ourselves, for no one will hand women anything, any more than society has handed Negroes anything. It was only when they said for themselves, in 1963, the young ones and the old ones, we will no longer eat, live, work, go to school, or even go to the toilet as anything less than free and full and equal human beings, that the rights they won on paper a hundred years ago began to be a reality, and our society began to take them seriously.

American women—the only majority, perhaps, that is still treated like a rather unequal minority—do not have the uncomfortable suffering of the Negro. But they will not be free and equal members of society until they take themselves seriously and finish the work of the delayed revolution. Each and every woman must in her own life stop denigrating herself and must help to win these things for other women.

I have three children. I love them. I would not have missed having them for the world. They are a great fulfillment of my life. But my children no more fulfill, no more define me as a woman; my love for and my life with my husband no more defines or fulfills me as a woman, than the work I do, the nonsexual passions, the questions and the search that made me write my book—and the wish to help write the human story that makes me urge you to affirm your own identity as full human beings and to help create this new image of women as *people*, both for your daughters and for our society.

PART II

The Actions

Organizing the Women's Movement for Equality

The most extraordinary thing about the women's movement is that it happened. Because the facts of our lives as women kept getting in the way of herstory. Questions which men who move and shake the world take for granted would have seemed impossible for us to solve—if we had stopped to ask them. Even asking them now, as people do of me, I have to laugh. *How did you find each other? Where did you get the money? Did you know what you were doing? Did you have any idea where it would lead? What gave you the power—the nerve—to do what you did, in the name of American women, of the women of the world?*

We didn't know each other personally, at all. Nobody ever gave us any money to start the movement. It was hard enough to pay for our own plane tickets, to get together nationally—most of us didn't have jobs with expense accounts; it was impossible to take time off during the week, unthinkable to leave husbands and children to fend for themselves the whole weekend.

None of us had any experience organizing a national movement. The ones who had grown up in the McCarthy conformist years had never taken part in any movement of dissent. None of us had ever acted on our own behalf as women. There was a *dread* I remember—I expect we all felt that dread—as from our various vantage points, in 1965 and 1966, we began realizing the necessity of organizing the women's movement.

The dread you feel before any crucial, decisive action . . . the dread that keeps Americans from taking public actions that rock the boat . . . the dread that women feel of taking any action that might seem unfeminine, immodest, aggressive, selfish.

Yes, we knew what we were doing. We couldn't possibly know where it would lead, but we knew what had to be done. But why me, why us? Who wants to take the responsibility, to commit oneself to carry it through and risk being laughed at, getting people mad at you, maybe getting fired? Now that the women's movement has become big national business, and women have come far enough to compete openly, even fight, for power, it is worth noting that we who started it all were reluctant heroines.

These problems weren't solved but were somehow bypassed by the improbable power we found in ourselves and each other. The power came from the personal truth of burning need; we were all acting not as "exceptional" women or for others but for ourselves. We identified, as women, with Everywoman. Like most Americans, the women who started the movement would be considered, or considered themselves, middle class, though not all had been to college, not all were white, and their fathers might have worked in a factory or as janitors or started out as peddlers, like mine. All of us, by whatever combination of need, talent, or opportunity, had already moved further than most women, to overcome the dread. But none of us could have found the power to organize a movement in ourselves alone. We came together as crucial molecules, finally reaching a critical mass—catalyzing each other into the actions that became a chain reaction, until the movement of women exploded through all the strata of American society.

It is more than a historical fluke that the organization of the women's movement was ignited by that law, never meant to be enforced, against sex discrimination in employment. Women were ready to work *now*. They were ready to move into the mainstream, and watching the blacks refuse to work or ride the bus in less than human dignity, they could finally say, "Me, too." Confronting the issue of equal opportunity in employment, women were able to bring themselves out of the psychological murk to the brink of action; to bring themselves out of housewife isolation and the apologetic timidity it fostered. Coming together with other women, they made up that critical mass that was ready to explode.

In that unconscious underground, where each one had been operating alone, not even knowing the others existed, how glad, how relieved we were to find and recognize each other. But the fears and frustrations of women isolated in their jobs made them almost as impotent and powerless in their rage as those scared Oklahoma housewives grateful for any chance of work, no matter how humiliating or unfairly paid. The women who for many years had worked for a living under conditions of outrageous sex discrimination, full time, were no longer bemused by false gratitude. But they were beaten down; some had even become mouselike in appearance or voice. And the bitterest of all were the closet feminists who had their noses rubbed every day in the dirty treatment women were getting in the government agencies and labor unions and continuing education programs, even in some of the volunteer women's organizations—the bureaucracies which in the name of service to women were helping to keep them in their place. The token women who sometimes got to fairly high posts in such agencies—the "Aunt Toms"—were especially threatened by women who wanted to really fight for women.

For this reason, I had to keep secret the identity of the valiant, incorruptible woman who eventually maneuvered and cajoled me into the act of starting NOW. For all these years, Catherine East of the Women's Bureau of the Labor Department has been the pivot of the feminist underground in Washington spreading from government agencies to Capitol Hill. Midwife to the birth of the women's movement, she has served its development with research, intelligence, and alerts to sabotage or strategic possibilities that the movement itself would never have been able to afford. She never violated any Government Secrets Act, but if it had been known by her superiors in the Women's Bureau how actively she was supporting and servicing the organization of an independent, activist women's movement, she would have been fired. From the beginning, the government, first, through the Women's Bureau, later, through the FBI and the CIA, has tried to prevent and then control the organization of the women's movement. And women like Catherine East have tipped us off to the sabotage and helped us fight it.

•   •   •   •

I was a third of the way through that second book about patterns beyond the feminine mystique, and I couldn't go on with it because I knew there weren't any real patterns, only women with problems. And I was beginning to be worried about all those women whom I had helped make conscious of wanting to do more with their lives. If all that happened was just talk, those women were going to be faced with even more practical problems than those first would-be career women whose disillusionment fueled the feminine mystique. I could already see the pendulum swinging again—a feminine backlash. Trying to write that book which I never did finish, I realized: "Unless something happens to really change the role of women in society, the best and brightest of the new generation of women may turn their backs completely on motherhood, marriage, and even sex and love with men. . . ."

And then that uncanny moment I have often recalled: on a plane to Washington to look into the new law against sex discrimination in employment, I swear I saw a student carrying a book whose title hit me in the face—*Consciousness Is the First Stage of Revolution*.

Around that time, I got in touch with Pauli Murray, an eminent black woman scholar then studying law at Yale. I had heard that she had shocked a staid convention of women's clubs by stating that Title VII would never be enforced "unless women march on Washington like the blacks." She and Catherine East tuned me into the underground network of women. I didn't have to work underground, however. As the author of a best-selling book on women, I was often invited to the White House in the Johnson years, when token women were needed to give a Good Housekeeping seal of approval to some new program like Head Start. There was a subliminal awareness of the potential of the women's vote out there, though the women's auxiliaries of the political parties were never taken seriously. In 1965-66, Lyndon Johnson, already preparing for the reelection battle in 1968, was with much fanfare appointing supposedly more women than ever before in history to the government. Not to the Cabinet or the Supreme Court, of course, but appointments important enough to call the press to the Rose Garden of the White House to meet the lady. He had even ordered members of his Cabinet to find out where the women were in each department and if, as turned out to be the case, 90 percent of the women were in the lowest, clerical grades of Civil Service, to do something about it, to *find* some women to promote, and to "report back" to him.

I did my research in Washington now. And I learned from Martha Griffiths, the intrepid congresswoman from Michigan, how the House almost had to be adjourned in hysterical laughter the day Howard Smith of Virginia proposed adding "sex discrimination" to Title VII of the Civil Rights Act of 1964, outlawing race discrimination in employment. And she and the few other women then in Congress cried from sheer outrage and vowed to make those men stop laughing. With help from that feminist underground, she had managed to persuade the Johnson administration to *keep that joke* in the Civil Rights Act, or she would force the men to be counted on the floor in "a vote against women." Senator Margaret Chase Smith made the same threat to Dirksen. And though women in 1965–66 were still thought to vote with their husbands, and no one took the women's vote seriously, still all the *talk* of women was beginning to have enough effect to make that threat effective. Sex discrimination was kept in the Civil Rights Act, but nobody expected the ban against it to be enforced.

As I went from agency to agency in Washington, I found those appointments of women, and the new programs to advance women—the precursors of "affirmative action"—weren't serious either. I found patterns, all right—patterns of tokenism and sex discrimination that aren't even touched by laws like "Equal Pay for Equal Work" which has long been on the books in the U.S.A.

The highest jobs to which women were being promoted had titles like "Assistant to the Assistant Secretary of State" in charge of flower-arranging. A new job would be created—to arrange fashion shows or pick out paintings for embassies—outside the regular line of promotion to decision-making jobs.

One woman given such a token title to fill the new woman quota at the State Department closed the door of her office and told me, in tones of the bitterest frustration, that she'd been sitting here for six months, and no one had given her anything to do but study the department phone book. The word was she didn't have the experience, the competence to do the real work. I wondered why there weren't more women available to be promoted from within—among, for instance, the young women who took and passed the foreign service examinations. And I learned that they had to resign when they married. This was a rule that would never be changed, a State Department official told me; otherwise imagine the embarrassment, a foreign service woman privy to diplomatic secrets she might betray on the pillow to her husband. And if he were also in the service, quite impossible, having to place both together. The men, of course, did not have to resign when they took wives to their pillows, but even I did not seriously make that comparison out loud. I remember meeting a very few senior women, in diplomatic posts then, and they were all spinsters, having had to make that choice their male colleagues never faced. And I heard the pitying jokes and shrugs and sighs of these comfortable men about those spinster ladies.

I discovered that the poverty program, then headed by Sargent Shriver, had no women at all in decision-making posts, and no programs for high school dropouts or job training for women, though statistics showed 80 percent of the welfare load in the cities to be women and children supported by women. Sargent Shriver said to me: "Why should I try to train a woman, who would rather be my wife and the mother of my children, to use a computer?"

At the very agency empowered to administer Title VII against sex discrimination as well as race, there were no women at all in top decision-making posts except the one Presidential appointee on the commission itself, a black woman named Aileen Hernandez. And no attempts were being made to find or hire such women.

One day in the White House Rose Garden, the young wife of one of the top economists on that commission was listening to the President of the United States extol his sincerity about utilizing that great source of unused talent, the women of this country, and she believed he meant it. She had been hired as an economist herself, childbound from serious job-hunting, to do a quick personnel study of the job needs of the E.E.O.C. And she knew exactly where women could and should and so far were not being hired to really enforce that law against sex discrimination. Her husband was now being promoted to a job beyond that agency, and she had rehearsed, down to one succinct sentence, how when she shook the President's hand in the Rose Garden receiving line, she would tell him about those job openings she was sure *he* would want to fill with women, even if others hadn't taken his instructions seriously.

The day after, her husband got a telephone call from the White House to "tell your wife to shut up"—or he would lose his job.

Even that first year of Title VII, with very little publicity about the sex discrimination provision except the jokes about it, thousands of complaints were being filed by women, in factories and offices. And the field investigators told me it was a cinch investigating those complaints, because the employer didn't even try to deny sex discrimination, like he did on race. "I wouldn't hire a woman for that job." "We just don't hire women." And now I learned that the E.E.O.C. was going to issue a "guideline" saying that it was all right to go on advertising "Help Wanted, Male" for all the good jobs, and "Help Wanted, Female" for clerks and gal Fridays—even though the law specifically said no discriminatory advertising. "Help Wanted, White" or "Help Wanted, Colored" was illegal. But as for sex, such advertising could be done "for the convenience" of the reader. They would simply need to run a disclaimer in the upper left hand: "No advertiser here discriminates on the basis of race or sex."

Richard Graham, a real fighter for women who had emerged on that commission, told me that he personally had gone to see the heads of the League of Women Voters, the American Association of University Women and other women's organizations with national headquarters in Washington, to get them to use pressure to have Title VII enforced on behalf of women. And they had been appalled at the very suggestion. They were not "feminists," they had told him.

And then a young "Assistant to the General Counsel" of

the Equal Employment Opportunities Commission started to talk. She had been avoiding me for months. Some of those supposed to enforce that law against sex discrimination had begun to get uneasy about my research. Sonia Pressman shut her office door and said, "I'm not a feminist. I've never been interested in women. I like men. I don't want to keep realizing how this law could be used to get rid of discrimination against women, and have to keep shutting myself up, every day. I get so mad at the way they're not doing it. I go home every night with a headache. Who appointed me to worry about women? But I'm not free to do anything about it. I'd lose my job. I need the job. At least a woman like me has to stay here and watch. But you can do what has to be done. Nobody can fire you. Your fame is based on speaking out for women. You have to start a national organization to fight for women, like the civil rights movement for the blacks." And there were tears in her eyes.

It was as if the whole female underground was maneuvering me to the point where I would do what they knew had to be done and weren't free to do themselves. After my research days in Washington, Catherine East and Mary Eastwood of the Justice Department would come up to my hotel room after dinner and somehow start me making hypothetical lists of women I had met in my research around the country, women who were the keys to certain crucial segments of women needed to form a national organization of sufficient clout to get that law against sex discrimination enforced.

Why didn't the unions do it? They showed me the cases of sex discrimination where the union was actually siding with the bosses against the women. And they got me to go out to Detroit, and Dorothy Haener and Caroline Davis of the U.A.W. brought young women and old from the plants, and I learned about the hassle, the run-around, the intimidation when women tried to speak up for themselves or other women, even in the progressive U.A.W.-C.I.O.

I've never been an organization woman. I'd never even joined the League of Women Voters: I couldn't stand the programmed "lesson plan" approach, the nit-picking, parliamentary procedure, the ladies' tea parties. I was a writer, a loner. Still, as a result of my book and this "research," I did know various people in different fields who were at this same point of impatience.

"What about those commissions on the status of women?" I equivocated to those irritating underground gadflies. "They are organized in every state to do something about these problems, aren't they?"

My Washington friends were less sanguine about those commissions. They had done the staff work for the national Commission on the Status of Women. Marguerite Rawalt, a salty lawyer from I.R.S., had headed the legal task force. They had fought all the way, and in vain, for demands and teeth to implement them—and had watched in dismay as the President disbanded the national commission, with thanks, and filed its report to be forgotten. Didn't I realize the same thing was happening now in every state? And the women who were appointed by their governors to those state commissions could be counted on not to rock any boat. They were beholden to the governor; the only power they had came from his appointment. Even if some of the members of those commissions got outraged about women's situation, as a result of their work, they couldn't do anything about it, since the commissions were set up specifically with no power to act. My underground informants didn't specifically suggest that those commissions were set up to keep women from acting, but . . . Anyhow, it so happened all those state commissions on the status of women were meeting in June, in Washington. I could cover that meeting, get official credentials, as a writer. There would be women there, from every state . . .

That's where it actually began.

How did we know each other? We recognized the honest fire. I still remember running into Dorothy Haener and Pauli Murray on the escalator the first morning at the Washington Hilton, and agreeing, somewhat less than enthusiastically, that we would invite to my hotel room that night anyone we met who seemed likely to be interested in organizing women for action. So after I heard Kay Clarenbach, head of the Wisconsin Commission, give a biting talk on how far from equality the very terms were in which the status of women was being discussed, I invited her to my hotel room. The others were horrified. Kay was the darling of the Women's Bureau, they told me. We'd be stopped before we could even get started. I was very naïve. Then, I trusted anyone who dared to speak out.

Just before that conference in Washington, I'd gotten another one of those middle-of-the-night calls from one of my new friends in Washington telling me that Richard Graham was not going to be reappointed to the E.E.O.C. He had evidently become too serious in his honest conscientious attempt to do his duty about sex discrimination.

There were maybe fifteen women in my hotel room that night. They all felt we had to do something about Dick Graham, and to stop those guidelines which would tell employers to disregard the law about sex discrimination. But surely women did not have to organize anything as radical as a civil rights movement, like the blacks. I didn't recognize it then, but their reluctance, queasiness, and fear was exactly the same I'd been feeling against my gadflies from the underground. How many times has that process repeated itself—in me and all the others, each time we face a new necessity to act? And the very fury of our resistance may mask our underlying sense of the urgency of that action, and our reluctant awareness of our need and responsibility to take it. It is existential dread. And then, acting, we evoke that dread in others until they too bring themselves to act.

How could we trust each other, then, women who didn't know each other personally, who hadn't yet acquired the trust we would later earn in action together? The McCarthy period was barely over; radicalism, nonconformity had been so dangerous, destroyed so many lives and careers, that people, including women, had learned the lesson—not to act, not to speak out from conscience on political issues.

The argument went on till after midnight. The ladylike rows . . . the timidity . . . the suspicion. That afternoon we'd all been bussed over to the Rose Garden at the White House and Lady Bird had given us tea and L.B.J. had appeared, a bit late, and had figuratively patted our heads and said how happy we must all be now that the job had been done —those reports on the status of women—and now we must all go back home and volunteer again our service to help the children, the poor and all the others who depended on our good-ness and our dedication to service, etc., etc. —not one word about discrimination against women. If anything, the officials speaking to these women would send them home feeling guilty about ever concerning themselves about the status of women.

They didn't want to recognize that, those women in my hotel room. So no organization was necessary, but Kay Clarenbach and some of the others would insist tomorrow that a resolution be voted by the women present from all fifty states, demanding the reappointment of Dick Graham and the enforcement of Title VII. And they left, in what I felt was sanctimonious disapproval of *me* for suggesting anything so radical as independent organization. And Pauli Murray, the black scholar who'd triggered me first, and my indefatigable friends from the Washington underground and Dorothy Haener from UAW and I just looked at one another and shrugged. *Women*—what can you expect? Not for the last time in these ten years, I thought the battle was over before it had even begun, not realizing that the same fears and finally the daring necessary to act despite those fears were now under way in the others, just as in me. I went to bed, relieved at least that those pious self-appointed consciences of the Washington under-ground couldn't pester me any longer.

But the next noon those very reluctant women were wait-ing for me, fighting mad because they couldn't even get a reso-lution on the floor at this convention. Looking harassed, deter-mined, somehow more in focus than the night before, Kay Clarenbach, the darling of the Women's Bureau, was abso-lutely outraged, that—with all her politeness, her responsible request, her put-down of my rabble-rousing—she had been told officially that this particular conference of the official status of women commissions of all the sovereign states had no power whatsoever to take any action, even pass a resolution, not even on sex discrimination.

So we took two tables at lunch to discuss forming the orga-nization I had said was needed—we had to do it at lunch be-cause most of us had plane reservations that afternoon, when the conference ended, to get back in time to make dinner for our families.

I wonder if Esther Peterson and the other Women's Bureau officials and Cabinet members who talked down to us at lunch knew that those two front tables, so rudely, agitatedly whispering to one another and passing around notes written on paper napkins, were under their very noses organizing NOW, the National Organization for Women, the first and major structure of the modern women's movement, "to take the actions needed to bring women into the mainstream of American society, now, full equality for women, in fully equal partnership with men."

Those words, which in June 1966 I wrote out on a paper napkin in the Washington Hilton Hotel and which became the keystone of the Statement of Purpose of NOW, were the crux of the qualitative change that the women's movement brought about in all our lives. Everything was different—the problems *looked* different, the definitions of the problems, the solutions sought, once we dared to judge our conditions as women by that simple standard, the hallmark of American democracy—equality, no more, no less.

After that lunch in Washington, we met for an hour before people had to make their planes and agreed we would have a formal organizing conference for NOW in the fall. Kay Clarenbach, who at least had an office and a secretary, would draw up a membership blank, and I would send out invitations to that list I had been compiling. Others would also recruit.

Drafting the Statement of Purpose for NOW, I was forced to spell out in my own mind the implications of "equality" for women. "The time has come to confront, with concrete actions, the conditions that now prevent women from enjoying the equality of opportunity and freedom of choice which is their right, as individual Americans, and as human beings." The ideology of the mainstream of the women's movement—and the agenda of its actions against sex discrimination over the subsequent ten years—are clearly set out in the NOW Statement of Purpose, which was adopted basically as I wrote it, with one exception. (As I wrote it, it also spelled out the right of the woman to choose, and to control her own childbearing, which meant access to birth control and abortion—

the others said that was too controversial. It wasn't until its second year that NOW confronted abortion.)

The crux of the ideology and the actions was simply the concept of "equality" and the value of the individual: dignity, self-fulfillment, self-determination—which seem like no ideology because they are simply the values of the American Revolution (of all human revolutions, basically) applied to women. "Equality" is the basic word: it cut through the confusion of the symposia and the talk, the psychological claptrap, the mystique, and exposed the apologetic token half-solutions which were all that women had been offered, or had even dared to demand, up until now.

The logic was inexorable. Once we broke through that feminine mystique and called ourselves human—no more, no less—surely we were entitled to enjoyment of the values which were our American, democratic human right. All we had to do was really look at the concrete conditions of our daily life in the light of those lofty values of equality which are supposed to be every man's birthright—and we could immediately see how unfair, how oppressive our situation was. And it was our actions confronting those concrete conditions—not the later apocalyptic rhetoric of overthrow of male dominion—which began to change the system.

Just before that organizing conference, four months later, I realized we would need to make its decisions public, and asked Betty Furness, Muriel Fox and Marlene Sanders over to my apartment to discuss "public relations" for the about-to-be-born women's movement. It really amazes me now, that all these high-powered high-salaried women knew, even before it was born, that the women's movement was going to be big. Muriel Fox, who was one of the few women at the top in the public relations professions, said she would "consult," for free of course, but someone else would have to do the work. But there was never "anyone else" to do the work of the women's movement. The one thing, by definition, we all hated to do was secretarial work. The night after we adopted the Statement of Purpose in Washington, Muriel Fox, and a half-dozen women economists and lawyers stayed up till five A.M. running off NOW's first press releases on Senator Hart's mimeograph machine, and taking them by hand to the newspaper offices.

On the day NOW officially began, October 29, 1966, there were some three hundred members, and around thirty of them were present at the meeting in Washington, adopting the Statement of Purpose and skeletal bylaws which were then finalized during the first year. In the archives is a document signed by those who were present: Muriel Fox, Inka O'Hanrahan, Alice Rossi, Carl Degler, Marguerite Rawalt, Ollie Butler-Moore, Phineas Indritz, Gene Boyer, Catherine Conroy, Mary Eastwood, and many others. A few were never heard of again. A few were perhaps the government "agents" whose purpose was to prevent the organization of NOW altogether. Kay Clarenbach was not present, but she was elected chairman of the board, and I, president of NOW. Dick Graham, who had not been reappointed to the Equal Employment Opportunity Commission, would be vice president—a male visible in NOW from the beginning, not as a token but as a fighter for equality. Caroline Davis of the U.A.W. would be secretary-treasurer, not only as a fighter for women but so she could get us a free ride for our printing, mailing, and membership records on the U.A.W.'s facilities. A lot of employers less sympathetic to women's cause than the leadership of the U.A.W. would be surprised to know that their Xerox machines, mimeograph machines, and WATS lines were doing NOW's work, as a result of that women's underground, in every office. It was the only way the work could get done: our treasury in those days seldom had more than several hundred dollars. It was three years before we even had an office. During my presidency, the membership records and mailings were handled out of Caroline's office in the U.A.W. building in Detroit, the board notices and minutes out of Kay's office at the University of Wisconsin, the P.R. out of Muriel's office in New York, and the policy and organizing of the women's movement out of my apartment on 72nd Street.

I started out suspicious of Kay as an agent of the Woman's Bureau, and she surely saw me as a wild New York radical. But I would always call Kay—that tall, bony, plain-speaking Midwesterner—before embarking on my wildest schemes, and discovered that where principle was involved, she was not afraid of rocking any boat. I began to trust and rely on her judgment, which fueled my sparks of vision.

A young Catholic nun had been particularly eloquent and commonsensible, breaking through the quibbling over detail that could have kept the organization from getting born. Her name was Sister Mary Joel Reed, later president of Averno College in Milwaukee. I asked if I could nominate her for the NOW board. She was modest and suggested instead that she would nominate Sister Mary Austin Doherty of Chicago. Walking across the street to the hotel where we were going to have a drink before the election, I said I still wanted to nominate her. Would she join us? "No, Betty," she said regretfully, "it wouldn't be right wearing this habit, but someday maybe." In the years to come, Sister Joel, like so many of the militant nuns who have been at the heart of our movement while they were liberating themselves from the cloister, abandoned that habit, revolutionized the order and the college she now heads, and is now pioneering in "relevant" education for women. After she came out of her habit, we drank together, agonizing over abortion and other crises. In the actions of the women's movement, we knew ourselves and each other as women never did before, and the trust growing from these actions was real. The mushy words about "sisterhood" that gloss over differences, purporting to be universal, automatic, and thus unearned, deny the complex toughness of the real sisterhood which was forged in the movement.

Shortly before we adjourned Sunday afternoon, we shared a moving moment of realization that we had now indeed entered history. Pauli Murray passed on to us a medallion that had been handed down to her by one of the survivors of the battle for the vote for women in America a half-century ago— a woman who had been imprisoned, and tried to starve herself in protest, in a jail near where we were meeting. And Alice Rossi recalled that exactly one hundred years ago two British women took the first petition for the vote for women to the British Parliament—and did not know how to get it inside except by hiding it in the bottom of a cart of apples being taken in for the members to eat. We suddenly realized the confidence and courage we must share—to confront the complex unfinished business of the revolution they started so long ago, to launch this new movement for full equality for all women in America, in truly equal partnership with men.

So NOW began . . .

The National Organization for Women (NOW)

 Statement of Purpose

We, men and women who hereby constitute ourselves as the National Organization for Women, believe that the time has come for a new movement toward true equality for all women in America, and toward a fully equal partnership of the sexes, as part of the world-wide revolution of human rights now taking place within and beyond our national borders.

The purpose of NOW is to take action to bring women into full participation in the mainstream of American society now, exercising all the privileges and responsibilities thereof in truly equal partnership with men.

We believe the time has come to move beyond the abstract argument, discussion and symposia over the status and special nature of women which has raged in America in recent years; the time has come to confront, with concrete action, the conditions that now prevent women from enjoying the equality of opportunity and freedom of choice which is their right as individual Americans, and as human beings.

NOW is dedicated to the proposition that women first and foremost are human beings, who, like all other people in our society, must have the chance to develop their fullest human potential. We believe that women can achieve such equality only by accepting to the full the challenges and responsibilities they share with all other people in our society, as part of the decision-making mainstream of American political, economic and social life.

We organize to initiate or support action, nationally or in any part of this nation, by individuals or organizations, to break through the silken curtain of prejudice and discrimination against women in government, industry, the professions, the churches, the political parties, the judiciary, the labor unions, in education, science, medicine, law, religion and every other field of importance in American society.

Enormous changes taking place in our society make it both possible and urgently necessary to advance the unfinished revolution of women toward true equality, now. With a life span lengthened to nearly seventy-five years, it is no longer either necessary or possible for women to devote the greater part of their lives to child rearing; yet childbearing and rearing—which continues to be a most important part of most women's lives—is still used to justify barring women from equal professional and economic participation and advance.

Today's technology has reduced most of the productive chores which women once performed in the home and in mass production industries based upon routine unskilled labor. This same technology has virtually eliminated the quality of muscular strength as a criterion for filling most jobs, while intensifying American industry's need for creative intelligence. In view of this new industrial revolution created by automation in the mid-twentieth century, women can and must participate in old and new fields of society in full equality—or become permanent outsiders.

Despite all the talk about the status of American women in recent years, the actual position of women in the United States has declined, and is declining, to an alarming degree throughout the 1950's and 1960's. Although 46.4 percent of all American women between the ages of eighteen and sixty-five now work outside the home, the overwhelming majority—75 percent—are in routine clerical, sales, or factory jobs, or they are household workers, cleaning women, hospital attendants. About two-thirds of Negro women workers are in the lowest paid service occupations. Working women are becoming increasingly—not less—concentrated on the bottom of the job ladder. As a consequence, full-time women workers today earn on the average only 60 percent of what men earn, and that wage gap has been increasing over the past twenty-five years in every major industry group. In 1964, of all women with a yearly income, 89 percent earned under $5,000 a year; half of all full-time year-round women workers earned less than $3,690; only 1.4 percent of full-time year-round women workers had an annual income of $10,000 or more.

Further, with higher education increasingly essential in today's society, too few women are entering and finishing college or going on to graduate or professional school. Today women earn only one in three of the B.A.'s and M.A.'s granted, and one in ten of the Ph.D.'s.

In all the professions considered of importance to society, and in the executive ranks of industry and government, women are losing ground. Where they are present it is only a token handful. Women comprise less than 1 percent of federal judges; less than 4 percent of all lawyers; 7 percent of doctors. Yet women represent 53 percent of the U.S. population. And increasingly men are replacing women in the top positions in secondary and elementary schools, in social work, and in libraries—once thought to be women's fields.

Official pronouncements of the advance in the status of women hide not only the reality of this dangerous decline, but the fact that nothing is being done to stop it. The excellent reports of the President's Commission on the Status of Women and of the state commissions have not been fully implemented. Such commissions have power only to advise. They have no power to enforce their recommendations, nor have they the freedom to organize American women and men to press for action on them. The reports of these commissions have, however, created a basis upon which it is now possible to build.

Discrimination in employment on the basis of sex is now prohibited by federal law, in Title VII of the Civil Rights Act of 1964. But although nearly one-third of the cases brought before the Equal Employment Opportunity Commission during the first year dealt with sex discrimination and the proportion is increasing dramatically, the commission has not made clear its intention to enforce the law with the same seriousness

on behalf of women as of other victims of discrimination.
Many of these cases were Negro women, who are the victims
of the double discrimination of race and sex. Until now, too
few women's organizations and official spokesmen have been
willing to speak out against these dangers facing women. Too
many women have been restrained by the fear of being called
"feminist."

There is no civil rights movement to speak for women, as
there has been for Negroes and other victims of discrimination. The National Organization for Women must therefore
begin to speak.

WE BELIEVE that the power of American law, and the
protection guaranteed by the U.S. Constitution to the civil
rights of all individuals, must be effectively applied and enforced to isolate and remove patterns of sex discrimination, to
ensure equality of opportunity in employment and education,
and equality of civil and political rights and responsibilities on
behalf of women, as well as for Negroes and other deprived
groups.

We realize that women's problems are linked to many
broader questions of social justice; their solution will require
concerted action by many groups. Therefore, convinced that
human rights for all are indivisible, we expect to give active
support to the common cause of equal rights for all those who
suffer discrimination and deprivation, and we call upon other
organizations committed to such goals to support our efforts
toward equality for women.

WE DO NOT ACCEPT the token appointment of a few
women to high-level positions in government and industry as
a substitute for a serious continuing effort to recruit and advance women according to their individual abilities. To this
end, we urge American government and industry to mobilize
the same resources of ingenuity and command with which
they have solved problems of far greater difficulty than those
now impeding the progress of women.

WE BELIEVE that this nation has a capacity at least as
great as other nations, to innovate new social institutions
which will enable women to enjoy true equality of opportunity and responsibility in society, without conflict with their
responsibilities as mothers and homemakers. In such innova-

tions, America does not lead the Western world, but lags by decades behind many European countries. We do not accept the traditional assumption that a woman has to choose between marriage and motherhood, on the one hand, and serious participation in industry or the professions on the other. We question the present expectation that all normal women will retire from job or profession for ten or fifteen years, to devote their full time to raising children, only to reenter the job market at a relatively minor level. This in itself is a deterrent to the aspirations of women, to their acceptance into management or professional training courses, and to the very possibility of equality of opportunity or real choice, for all but a few women. Above all, we reject the assumption that these problems are the unique responsibility of each individual woman, rather than a basic social dilemma which society must solve. True equality of opportunity and freedom of choice for women requires such practical and possible innovations as a nationwide network of child-care centers, which will make it unnecessary for women to retire completely from society until their children are grown, and national programs to provide retraining for women who have chosen to care for their own children full time.

WE BELIEVE that it is as essential for every girl to be educated to her full potential of human ability as it is for every boy—with the knowledge that such education is the key to effective participation in today's economy and that, for a girl as for boy, education can only be serious where there is expectation that it will be used in society. We believe that American educators are capable of devising means of imparting such expectations to girl students. Moreover, we consider the decline in the proportion of women receiving higher and professional education to be evidence of discrimination. This discrimination may take the form of quotas against the admission of women to colleges and professional schools; lack of encouragement by parents, counselors and educators; denial of loans or fellowships; or the traditional or arbitrary procedures in graduate and professional training geared in terms of men, which inadvertently discriminate against women. We believe that the same serious attention must be given to high school dropouts who are girls as to boys.

WE REJECT the current assumptions that a man must carry the sole burden of supporting himself, his wife, and family, and that a woman is automatically entitled to lifelong support by a man upon her marriage, or that marriage, home and family are primarily woman's world and responsibility—hers, to dominate, his to support. We believe that a true partnership between the sexes demands a different concept of marriage, an equitable sharing of the responsibilities of home and children and of the economic burdens of their support. We believe that proper recognition should be given to the economic and social value of homemaking and child care. To these ends, we will seek to open a reexamination of laws and mores governing marriage and divorce, for we believe that the current state of "half-equality" between the sexes discriminates against both men and women, and is the cause of much unnecessary hostility between the sexes.

WE BELIEVE that women must now exercise their political rights and responsibilities as American citizens. They must refuse to be segregated on the basis of sex into separate-and-not-equal ladies' auxiliaries in the political parties, and they must demand representation according to their numbers in the regularly constituted party committees—at local, state, and national levels—and in the informal power structure, participating fully in the selection of candidates and political decision-making, and running for office themselves.

IN THE INTERESTS OF THE HUMAN DIGNITY OF WOMEN, we will protest and endeavor to change the false image of women now prevalent in the mass media, and in the texts, ceremonies, laws, and practices of our major social institutions. Such images perpetuate contempt for women by society and by women for themselves. We are similarly opposed to all policies and practices—in church, state, college, factory, or office—which, in the guise of protectiveness, not only deny opportunities but also foster in women self-denigration, dependence, and evasion of responsibility, undermine their confidence in their own abilities and foster contempt for women.

NOW WILL HOLD ITSELF INDEPENDENT OF ANY POLITICAL PARTY in order to mobilize the political power of all women and men intent on our goals. We will strive to ensure that no party, candidate, President, senator, governor, congressman, or any public official who betrays or ignores the principle of full equality between the sexes is elected or appointed to office. If it is necessary to mobilize the votes of men and women who believe in our cause, in order to win for women the final right to be fully free and equal human beings, we so commit ourselves.

WE BELIEVE THAT women will do most to create a new image of women by *acting* now, and by speaking out in behalf of their own equality, freedom, and human dignity—not in pleas for special privilege, nor in enmity toward men, who are also victims of the current half-equality between the sexes— but in an active, self-respecting partnership with men. By so doing, women will develop confidence in their own ability to determine actively, in partnership with men, the conditions of their life, their choices, their future and their society.

Our first official act was to petition the Equal Employment Opportunity Commission to rescind those guidelines permitting discriminatory "help wanted" advertising, and to issue the finding, long delayed, of sex discrimination in the case of airline stewardesses forced to resign at age thirty or thirty-five or at marriage. We also requested a meeting with President Johnson to demand that sex discrimination be added to the executive order banning discrimination by federal contractors and subcontractors. It is that Executive Order, which we demanded and won in the first year of NOW, which has enabled women to get affirmative action programs insuring their hiring and promotions in thousands of universities, law schools and companies.

With the organization of NOW, and the declaration that token appointments and mere words about women were not enough, I was suddenly persona non grata at the White House. But the implicit threat of that women's vote insured that the White House would have to deal with us. That was clear when President Johnson had John Macy, head of the Civil Service Commission and Johnson's domestic trouble-shooter, meet with us. Sitting around that mahogany conference table, John Macy quickly lost that avuncular head-patting patronizing courtliness that used to be handed down to me and the status-of-women ladies at those earlier White House tea parties.

The executive order on government contracts! As if, how did we even know about that one! The stewardesses, now that was just plain embarrassing, how could we expect the government to act on a matter so—well, silly or smutty, he seemed to be saying. And I remember insisting that the stewardesses' case was serious—that making stewardesses quit at thirty, or marriage, when pilots could age in the skies and even have children, was the essence of sex discrimination.

We hurried out of that meeting to confront the head of the Equal Employment Opportunity Commission, in person. We said how could women hope to get protection against sex discrimination from the E.E.O.C. when they didn't even have any women in their own top ranks. "Why, I am interviewing girls right now for an opening as Assistant General Counsel," said one of the commissioners. "I hope, Commissioner, that you're not interviewing girls for such an important job," I said. The others in our delegation laughed. The men looked uncomfortable. "Did I say something wrong?" he asked. I explained that since the lawyers applying for such a job were surely over twenty-five, to call them "girls" was a little like calling a forty-five-year-old black man "boy" to shine your shoes. That was the first time, in public, a government official got a lesson in sexist language. He tried "ladies"—and we wrinkled our noses—and he began to sweat. "What do you want to be called?" "Women," we said.

But to treat stewardesses like people—women, not girls— was something else! On Christmas Eve, 1966, I was subpoenaed and hauled down to the federal district courthouse—I had never had either of these things happen to me before—to be questioned about NOW's involvement in the stewardesses' case. They wanted a list of our members. I knew my rights and refused to give it to them. We had all agreed to keep the membership list of NOW secret, for in those early days no one was sure she wouldn't be fired or otherwise excommunicated for belonging to an organization to overthrow sex discrimination. The lawyer for the airlines—now dead—was so famous that even I, untutored in law, had heard of him. He got more and more exasperated as the hour for Christmas Eve stockings got nearer and I somehow wasn't answering his questions. And the lawyer for the government, who happened to be a young woman, objected whenever I didn't. The E.E.O.C. had finally voted that the firing of stewardesses after they had lost nubility *was* sex discrimination, and the airlines were trying to enjoin the ruling as "conflict of interest" by proving that Aileen Hernandez was a member of NOW.

But why, I wondered, would they go to such lengths—hiring those expensive lawyers, subpoenaing Aileen on the West Coast and me on the East Coast, on Christmas Eve—just to prevent that finding of sex discrimination? Surely, they didn't really think that men rode the airlines because of those nubile stewardesses, they flew to get from New York to Chicago on business. And then it occurred to me how much money the airlines saved, having all those women resign at thirty or thirty-five or marriage—how much money in raises, pensions, vacations, Social Security. Sex discrimination *was* big business, I began to see.

I didn't go to jail that Christmas, but months went by and the decision on the stewardesses was still held up, and there was no word at all on the "help wanted" guidelines. So NOW planned to hold a nationwide action.

On a given day in February—our first use of Susan B. Anthony's birthdate, I believe—a small delegation of us simultaneously descended on the offices of the government's Equal Employment Opportunity Commissions in New York and Washington and Pittsburgh, etcetera, bearing bundles of newspapers all tied up in red ribbon tape, and dumped those bundles at the government agents' feet, in view of the TV cameras (we had tipped off the networks).

I told the regional commissioner in New York it had been months since our petition for a hearing on the advertising guidelines had been filed, and asked him what was happening. And when his run-around answer made it clear that nobody even was considering any longer doing anything about either the discriminatory advertising or the stewardesses, I felt an enormous sense of pure, indignant outrage. I asked the regional director if I could have a blank to fill out a complaint of sex discrimination myself. And I filed a complaint that the U.S. government was discriminating against the women of America by not enforcing Title VII equally on behalf of women. I handed the complaint to the government agent and said, "I am filing this complaint formally against the government of the United States." And I asked his secretary if I could use her phone. The TV cameras were waiting outside the door, so while the others were exchanging final courtesies with the regional director—a rather nice Puerto Rican man who seemed to be getting a big kick out of whatever we were doing—I went into his secretary's cubicle, called Mary Eastwood at the Justice Department, and said, "Quick, don't ask me any questions, just tell me is it possible to sue the government, and if so, what do you call it. Like, to sue them for not enforcing Title VII for women, and not even answering our petition for a hearing on the guidelines." And she thought a minute and then told me what to say.

And I announced in front of the television cameras that NOW was going into court for a writ of mandamus against the U.S. government for not enforcing Title VII on behalf of our sex and spoke of this "national demonstration" as an expression of women's acute outrage—our patience had been exhausted. "And while we here are acting in New York, our sisters in Washington and Pittsburgh and Chicago and Atlanta and Los Angeles are simultaneously showing their displeasure and will join us in the suit on behalf of all American women." And it was all true enough. No matter that so far we had only two members in Atlanta, six in Pittsburgh, a dozen in Chicago and California and not much more in between—all of them that day were visibly doing that action, in the name of the others who had not yet been able to join us. The government did not want a cause célèbre suit from women in 1967. And so the hearings were held. And we got men from the unions—and even some male publishers and advertisers—to join us in testifying at the hearings. Martha Griffiths cut through the airline executives' line by saying, "If you are trying to run a whorehouse in the sky, then get a license." And it was ordered that the stewardesses could grow up and still fly, and the newspapers could and must advertise jobs by alphabetical order, without sex discrimination—or danger of sexual disorder.

The orders finally released merely put a coda to the new consciousness created by the actions. For the stewardesses' unions began perforce to demand and get these matters written into the union contracts with the airlines, including the right of these newly liberated female Peter Pans to have babies as well as grow up, and keep flying. And today I pick up the hoary gray *New York Times*, whose business manager told us patronizingly on that first day of national action that it would be out of the question, suicidal for newspapers to change their sex-segregated advertising; the customers would rebel. It gives me joy to see (*New York Times*, September 2, 1975) "Help Wanted—Male-Female: Wall Street Bank Reconciliation Supervisor, Warehouse Supervisor, Buyer/Sales Person, Lunch Counterperson"—not exactly singing poetry, but the earthy fruits of herstory.

* * *

So we got NOW organized, knowing we needed some structure to get things done and to insure responsibility and continuity. We expected the major actions of NOW to be carried out by women in their own communities. We wanted them to move in their own style, according to their own priorities, toward the general goals set forth in the Statement of Purpose. We didn't want the women's movement to be stultified by the kind of bureaucratic organization whose officers—or, heaven forbid, paid staff—spend most of their time maintaining their own power.

We knew also that national actions were necessary to accomplish our goals—to focus, spotlight and strengthen the women in their communities. Those would be decided by the members meeting once a year in national convention, who would then elect a board to execute policy between conventions. From the beginning, there was great reluctance among NOW members to hand over their individual autonomy and decision-making power to any body of leaders. Women had had enough of being manipulated, passively, into performing other people's agendas. Leaders could be locked later in power struggles, or even co-opted at the top, but the local autonomy and individual participation built into the structure of NOW insured the continued development and emergence of leadership among women at the grass roots, as they took responsibility for actions.

The vehicle for actions was the "task force" set up nationally to carry out each major goal—Task Forces on the Image of Women, Textbooks, Marriage and Divorce, Employment,

Sports. The first few years, those task forces only met at the national conventions. Composed of members concerned and expert in those areas, they assessed the needs of the situation and formulated policies and targets for action to be approved by the convention. Later, when membership had reached a point where the treasury could finance officers' travel, the task forces themselves met during the year. Each chapter mirrored that structure. Thus any woman, or man, in NOW with a project s/he genuinely wanted to do, easily got the responsibility and authority to initiate it—and developed into a leader, in the doing.

With no money, no office, no staff, it was impossible to answer all the letters and calls from women who wanted to join NOW. When someone would get so impatient that she'd call long distance—Eliza Paschall in Atlanta, Karen De Crow in Syracuse, Roxey Bolton from Florida, Wilma Scott Heide from Pittsburgh, Mordeca Jane Pollack in Boston—I'd make her the local NOW organizer—if she didn't sound too crazy. It was a chancy method, and the style of the women's movement in different cities varied enormously according to that initial self-appointed NOW organizer—nurse, secretary, colonel's lady, academic or embittered divorced housewife.

I would leave a NOW chapter behind, in the wake of my own lectures, accept a Southern finishing school or college of home economics in an attempt to recruit where we were weak. From the very beginning, I was especially interested in getting black women involved in the South, made special visits to Coretta King, and Julian Bond's sister Jane, and the young women with their afros at the S.N.C.C. headquarters in Atlanta. "We don't want anything to do with that feminist bag," one of them said. The important thing for black women, they said, was for black men to get ahead. And when the black men got the rights they had been denied so long, they would give black women all the equality they desired. Well, I didn't blame any black women for giving priority to the cause of black civil rights. But I couldn't buy that line that equality was for white women only.

When Muriel Fox and I went to see the men at the N.A.A.C.P. Legal Defense Fund to ask their help in setting up such a defense fund for women and in getting NOW into the

Leadership Conference on Civil Rights, we were told: "Women are not a civil rights issue." I saw the battle for women's rights as part of the total struggle for human rights, and had committed NOW unequivocally against racism from the very beginning. I knew how some of our feminist foremothers schooled in the battle to free the slaves later turned bitterly against the blacks, in their own frustration that "women" was not added to the amendment that gave black males the vote. This time many of us were determined not to let the women's movement and black civil rights be pitted against each other. But black male leaders seemed to resent the women's movement and made black women feel guilty about joining it.

Nevertheless, at our first national convention in Washington in 1967, we felt conscious of our responsibility to all women . . .

"The First Year": President's Report to NOW, Washington, D.C., 1967

 It is slightly over a year since we met here in Washington to organize a "new movement toward full equality for all women in America." In this incredibly fast-paced year, we have been so busy organizing and acting on behalf of that equality—and so harassed by the day-to-day problems involved, with no resources but our own energy, persistence, and dedication—that we are hardly aware of how far we have come. I do not measure this distance by the fact that our membership has quadrupled from three hundred to more than twelve hundred men and women committed to action in NOW, or by the fact that chapters are being organized almost weekly in California, Illinois, Wisconsin, Ohio, New England, Pennsylvania, New York, the nation's capital, and the South. It is, rather, the lengths that these first twelve hundred members have gone to, to become active in NOW—too impatient to wait for an answer to a letter sometimes, they have been ready to go to great trouble to track down an officer who would tell them what they could do right away. It is the intensity of their dedication to our purpose that impresses me, the seriousness, perseverance, ingenuity, and indeed, elegance by which NOW members in this past year have already begun to create the new image of women which America sorely needs.

Consider the distance we have traveled. In the spring of 1966, when some of us first began discussing the need for an

"N.A.A.C.P. for women," the outlawing of sex discrimination in employment in Title VII of the Civil Rights Act was a joke. No one was supposed to take it seriously. Spokesmen for the E.E.O.C. joked at press conferences about the right of a man to become a Playboy Bunny. Without a blush of shame or a murmur of protest from any organized group, the commission whose mandate was to end sex discrimination reversed guidelines which forbade segregated advertising to *permit* employers to advertise "help wanted—male," "help wanted—female," though they could not advertise "help wanted—colored," and "help wanted—white." That summer, there was a good deal of talk at various high levels in Wasington about taking sex *out* of Title VII. It was a "nuisance" when the cases of women suffering job discrimination began to pour in in a volume no one had expected. Neither the labor unions nor women's organizations nor the civil rights movement seemed interested in these cases. "It was just a fluke that sex got into the Civil Rights Act," according to the Establishment party line; "women don't really want job equality." There was indeed "no civil rights movement to speak for women, as there has been for Negroes and other victims of discrimination." So NOW began to speak.

Our first order of business was to make clear to Washington, to employers, to unions, and to the nation that someone *was* watching, someone *cared* about ending sex discrimination. When we went to the Hill to meet with Mr. Macy, with the Attorney General, with the Equal Employment Opportunity commissioners to ask that the mandate against sex discrimination be enforced as seriously as that against race discrimination, to ask that the President use his powers to do more than make token speeches and token appointments of women and that he issue an executive order to end sex discrimination in the government and by government contractors, to ask that new civil rights legislation forbid sex discrimination in jury service, they listened. We were speaking for the New Woman in a tone of voice that had not been heard from women before. We were not afraid or ashamed to be called feminists, but we seemed to be a new breed of feminists. We were not battle-axes nor man-haters. Indeed, there are men in our own ranks. The officials we interviewed, the men who interviewed us, treated us as attractive women, but without that glint of contempt that so often belies men's flattery of women. Because we were and are *serious* about real equality, and because we really meant it (*real* equality, *not* half equality), they treated us with real respect. Unlike most women's organizations and official spokeswomen, we are not timid about taking our case to the nation through the mass media. For we know the importance of bringing the question of sex discrimination out from under the table, where it can be ignored or sniggered away, to confront the human rights consciousness and conscience of this country.

When nothing happened about the help-wanted guidelines, we used our best legal skills to force the E.E.O.C. to hold public hearings. NOW members in New York and other cities began to put pressure on the newspaper publishers and even to picket the newspapers. When we learned through the grapevine that there was a possibility of merely a token addition of sex to the executive order on government contracts—sex discrimination would not have been handled by the same agency and procedures as would other forms of discrimination—we made it clear to the White House that we would consider this a betrayal of equal opportunity. Women all over the country began coming to NOW for help in fighting sex discrimination in their jobs: women who had no unions to fight for them, sometimes women whose unions didn't seem to want to know how to fight for them. We helped them. The members of our volunteer legal committee had to work nights and weekends on top of their own demanding jobs and law practices. Where we had no NOW member lawyer, our legal committee taught women to act as their own lawyers. We helped by shedding the light of publicity on particularly infamous cases of sex discrimination such as the Pauline Ziob case, a woman who was sent to us by the UN when she was pulled off her job as yeoman typist aboard a ship at sea because this was said to be a "man's job." Again and again, as in the Mengelkoch case in California and the Colgate-Palmolive case in Indiana, we found that sex discrimination, now forbidden in employment by the federal laws, was hiding behind the so-called state protective laws whereby women, but not men, might be prevented from lifting thirty-five pounds or working overtime—

and thus denied promotion to good jobs or recall after layoffs. The courts so far have been singularly deaf to our plea that women are being denied equal protection of the law as guaranteed by the Fourteenth Amendment to the Constitution. But we have just begun to fight. It is amazing, considering the powerful adversaries we have had to take on, that we are not intimidated. The airlines probably spent a small fortune on nationally famous lawyers to keep us from supporting the airline stewardesses in their battle against forced retirement at age thirty-five or marriage. Despite the fact that we suffered indignities in the subpoenaing of our officers when we first offered support to the stewardesses, we offered it again when a new hearing was called this spring, and not only testified on the implications of their case for the twenty-eight million working women in America, but saw to it that the mass media understood the serious implications of the case.

So now we have that long-overdue Presidential order outlawing sex discrimination in the government and by government contractors. The word, according to industry newsletters, is that new guidelines are about to be released on help-wanted ads and that the decision on the stewardesses' case is due. Perhaps even more important, sex discrimination is out in the clear light of day and is now being talked and written about all over the country. In the last two weeks, five major magazines have approached us for material for major articles on sex discrimination and NOW. There is no more talk about taking sex out of Title VII. But in 1968 we must ask why so many of the cases of sex discrimination brought to the E.E.O.C. have been lost by women and why the Attorney General has not yet used his powers to interfere in cases of sex discrimination. And why there are still no women in major policy-making positions on the E.E.O.C. itself. Moreover, we must organize ways to police the executive order on government contracts, so that every company and educational institution which works on a government contract clearly posts notices to all executives and employees that sex discrimination on the job is now forbidden. And where it continues, we must take steps to see to it that that company or that institution pays the penalty and loses its government contract!

We have also in this past year begun to raise our voices on

issues even more complex than this, issues where women's voices had not been heard. We protested the absence of women on the Urban Coalition on the emergency in our cities, noting that the problems of those cities will not be solved as long as the women who with their children make up 80 percent of the welfare load are considered unemployable for lack of job training and day-care facilities. We protested the use of women as mere window-dressing in the war on poverty. We protested the kind of day-care legislation that would have *forced* women to work and put their children in day-care centers while adequate standards for those centers were lacking. At a conference in August of the National Students Association, we were asked to help students confront sex discrimination on the campus and discovered that the students felt that discriminatory and segregated living arrangements were as injurious in keeping women second-class citizens as the existing quotas against women in fellowships and graduate school admissions. A representative of NOW helped expose the fact that a much-publicized international conference on abortion was rigged not to open but to prevent free discussion of that issue. Individuals in the leadership and membership of NOW laid the groundwork for the decision by the governing assembly of the United Presbyterian Church in 1967 to inaugurate a study of women in society and the church. The church will restructure its own attitudes and prioritites on the employment and education of women, their sexual relationship with men, and the effect of separate women's organizations within the church, "a subtle as well as overt discrimination against women in ecclesiastical matters," and women's lack of responsibility in decision making within the church. With similar movements under way in other Protestant denominations, in the Roman Catholic Church, and in Judaism, our own task force on religion may address itself to an ecumenical congress on equality for women in 1968.

In California, NOW spoke out forthrightly against legislation supposedly designed to help workingwomen that would have undermined labor standards for men and women alike. In New York, NOW has won support from men in our battle against sex discrimination in employment on the basis of our principled approach to divorce, alimony and abortion reform.

Nationally, NOW has won membership in the leadership conference for civil rights despite the attempt of some Negro leaders to say that civil rights do not include women. We are now engaged in a dialogue with leaders of other civil rights groups, including the black power movement, out of a belief that the question of full equality for women is inextricably linked with equality for all victims of discrimination. We have and must continue to resist efforts to use women to put down the Negroes' new militancy just as we resist the efforts of some misguided Negro leaders to put down women.

And now we enter a Presidential election year. In 1968, when women represent 53% of the electorate, the New Women could prove a significant factor in the Presidential election *if* we organize our potential power properly. I propose that our first order of business for 1968 be the organization of women and men committed to our goals into a true voting power bloc. I will not call it "woman power," for it includes men. We must find a synonym for "sexual equality power."

As a touchstone for the evaluation of all political parties and candidates in 1968, I propose that we here proceed to draw up a *Bill of Rights for Women for 1968*, and that we present this Bill of Rights to the platform committees of both parties and to all major candidates for President, to all senators and congressmen running for reelection and to all aspiring for nomination. And I propose that we, ourselves and others who share our goals, cross party lines to work for and support those candidates who will commit themselves to our Bill of Rights and to defeat those who are its enemies. We must also, every single member of NOW, become active in the mainstream of our parties and not in the ladies' auxiliary. We must insist that for our support we must sit on a major decision-making committee of the party. And everywhere possible we must use the same courage and confidence in running for political office that we have found in fighting for our own equality in employment. We must make it understood that there are many issues facing our nation today of as great or even greater importance to many of us as equality for women, but that it is by the very nature of our commitment to that equality that we wish to speak out and act on those issues in the decision-making mainstream rather than as members of women's ghettos, whether these be Democratic or Republican Women's Divisions, the League of Women Voters, or Women's Strike for Peace.

My own revulsion toward the war in Vietnam does not stem from the milk that once flowed from my breast, nor even from the fact of my draft-age sons, but from my moral conscience as a human being and as an American. And it is to that conscience which most Americans share—our common commitment to human freedom, equality, individual dignity—that we must address our Bill of Rights for women in 1968.

I would suggest that the first article be the long overdue amendment to the Constitution to provide that "Equality of rights under the law shall not be denied by the United States or any state on account of sex."

Second, since bearing and rearing children is important to society, the right of women who want to or have to work not to suffer because of maternity must be protected by a law insuring their right to return to the job within a reasonable time after childbirth, and to be given paid maternity leave as a form of Social Security and/or employee benefit.

Third, the right of women to equal opportunities in employment must be implemented by immediate revision of tax laws to permit the deduction of full home and child-care expenses for working parents.

Four, to insure the right of women to participate on an equitable basis with men in the world of work, education and political service, child-care facilities must be established by federal law on the same basis as parks, libraries and public schools, adequate to the needs of children from preschool years through early adolescence, as a community resource to be used by all citizens from all income levels.

Fifth, the right of every woman to be educated to her full potential on an equal level with men must be *secured* by federal and state legislation eliminating all discrimination by sex, whether written or unwritten, in colleges, graduate and professional schools, and loans and fellowships to women.

Sixth, the right of women in poverty to secure job training, housing and family allowances on equal terms with men must be secured by revision of welfare legislation and poverty programs which today deny women dignity, sexual privacy and self-respect.

Seven, the right of women to full sexual equality with men and to the dignity and privacy of their own person must be secured by federal statute recognizing the right of every woman to control her own reproductive life, and giving her the means to do so by giving her access to contraceptive devices and information and by removing contraceptive information and abortion from the penal code.

Whether or not you wish to include what I have outlined in our Bill of Rights for Women in 1968, we must begin a major national dialogue on the sexual implications of full equality between women and men if we are ever to enjoy it for ourselves or for our children. The sex-role debate, as I learned to call it in Sweden last month, cannot be avoided if equal opportunity in employment, education and civil rights are ever to mean more than paper rights. In Europe this fall I went to some of the Communist countries, where such equality is enjoyed on paper by women, but these women were working eighty and ninety hours a week, carrying the full burden of housework as well as the most menial work on their jobs, suffering the same kind of sexual discrimination which we are finding here. And they were beginning to organize a version of NOW to fight against a campaign that said it might be cheaper to pay women to stay home rather than pay for maternity leaves and child-care centers. In Sweden, where for about twenty years the sex-role debate *has* been engaged, a version of NOW has almost as many men actively committed to it as women. In their own lives, too, these people are acting out their commitment to real equality in ways that would seem almost fantastic to us. Because this is so, not only is their whole attitude toward sex more enlightened than ours, but matters such as child-care centers are near the top of the agenda for politicians of all parties.

In France I also saw the equivalent of NOW. Organized in the last few years, they have begun already to do what we should now begin to do—to run for political office themselves, as well as working on the economic and educational activities that we have been doing so far.

One final plea as we begin our serious work here. I ask not

so much for unity, for I assume that we are united in our goals or we would not be here, but for a serious respect for our honest differences, and for an ability to overcome our prejudices and to see beyond the moment to the future.

The 1967 NOW convention faced two major crises of decision: the Equal Rights Amendment and abortion. Many feared those controversial issues would split the women's movement apart before it was off the ground. In fact, in facing and airing our "honest differences" over abortion and the Equal Rights Amendment as I had urged the conference to do, we forged the crucial generational links between the century-long battle for women's rights that was our past and the young women who were the future.

Some of the women who had chained themselves to the White House fence to win the vote in 1920 had been trying ever since to amend the Constitution, to guarantee its rights and protection equally to women. For fifty years, they had been pestering senators about the Equal Rights Amendment. They had become a Washington eccentricity. Senators even signed their petitions to get rid of them, knowing ERA would never get out of committee to be voted on. The labor unions, the left, and the liberals when I was growing up opposed the ERA because it would destroy state "protective" laws which supposedly protected workingwomen from lifting heavy weights or working long hours.

But now those "protective" laws were being used in state after state to deny women equal employment opportunity. A weight-lifting component would be arbitrarily added to a job so that women couldn't be promoted to it. Or a state law "protecting" women against working more than eight hours would be invoked to deny her a promotion or lucrative overtime pay. The first court cases which led us to set up the NOW Legal Defense Fund involved blue-collar Southern factory women—working for Colgate-Palmolive and Southern Bell Telephone—who were denied jobs that they needed to support their families under the guise of those state "protective" laws, and then were harassed by employers and union leaders when they fought for their rights under Title VII.

The Equal Rights Amendment was designed to put a guarantee in the Constitution that would cover not only the limited areas of employment that come under Title VII, but every area of American life—a guarantee that would take precedence over those state laws now "protecting" women from good jobs and pay, that could not be rescinded at a mere whim of Congress or state legislature. With it, the courts low and high, state or federal, could no longer rule that women were not "persons" under the U.S. Constitution, as they have done so frequently over the years.

At five A.M. on the morning of the vote, I was warned by the NOW sisters from the U.A.W. that we would lose the U.A.W. facilities for our mailing if we took a stand on ERA. Turning the NOW convention into a committee of the whole, I let debate continue as long as anyone wanted to speak. Alice Rossi had impressive demographic warnings of the urgency of getting the Equal Rights Amendment into the Constitution before the changes which she saw coming in the economy and the population threatened the very jobs and gains women were now making in universities and industry.

As I listened and watched the women all over that hall who spoke, I saw that very few were opposed to taking a stand on the ERA. When those very old suffragettes sitting in the front row got up to speak on the Equal Rights Amendment, I saw that they *spoke to* those very young women who had never heard of it before and were kindled by it as they had not been by narrow job issues.

On abortion, I noticed the Catholic sisters seemed to be abstaining. And the women speaking up passionately for it were not only the young women from everywhere, but the square middle-aged housewife types from Indiana and points south.

I handed the gavel over to Kay. As a member of NOW, I spoke of our responsibility to history, to take the torch of equality from those tired, valiant women who'd grown old, lonely, keeping it alive. I spoke of our responsibility to the future, to the young women coming up to take that torch from us.

The vote was not unanimous in either case, but those "honest differences" I had exhorted the members not to gloss over had been aired to everyone's satisfaction. Caroline Davis of U.A.W. resigned as secretary-treasurer and we were forced to find printers and mailers in New York, but we now had enough members' dues in the treasury to pay our own way. Barely one year later Dorothy and Caroline convinced the national board of their union, the U.A.W.-C.I.O., to come out in support of ERA officially.

Today, not only the U.A.W., but the A.F.L.-C.I.O. as a whole support the ERA and understand the urgency of workingwomen's need for equality. Today the reactionary political and economic forces who have been flushed out as the real enemies of ERA are trying to use housewives to block the ERA, with the similarly false claim of "protecting" them.

In actuality, the Equal Rights Amendment and abortion were and are the two gut issues of the women's movement essential to real security—and equality and human dignity—for all women, whether they work outside or inside the home. Only a few older women who insisted NOW had to "choose" between them and the young on abortion walked out and started W.E.A.L. (Women's Equity Action League)—which later joined forces with NOW over the ERA and employment. As long as we kept acting and moving, confronting the issues of women's equality as they emerged, even our own differences helped build the movement.

•   •   •

As NOW began to grow into the truly nationwide organization it was meant to be, problems of internal housekeeping vexed us more and more. All we wanted was enough organization to keep women in touch with one another and to provide some leadership, ammunition and coordination for their own activity. In those days, we regarded any time spent at board meetings or national conferences on structure or details of internal housekeeping as time wasted—time stolen from the real business of the women's movement. If we could have foreseen the day—1974, 1975—when whole board meetings, whole days of NOW national conferences would be spent in power squabbles over details about structure, staff and internal housekeeping—that money would even be spent preventing the membership from making their own decisions until no time was left even to consider the issues or plan action on them—we would have been horrified. We would have wondered where and why and how the decay and corruption started. Even in 1966 and 1967, I began to get headaches and to start impatiently tapping my foot under the table when our finicky lawyers went on and on about how there was yet more red tape before we could get tax-deductible status for the Legal Defense Fund, or about why the bylaws had to be changed yet again to be sure lawyers would always have the majority of the fund board.

The questions kept multiplying. Should we allow more than one NOW chapter in a city? If ten members ascribing to the goals of NOW and paying dues could constitute a chapter —should we insist that all NOW members in a city like Chicago or New York be herded into a single chapter, which might grow to be a thousand people or more? Wouldn't that prevent leadership from developing? On the other hand, wouldn't it weaken the impact of NOW in any city if too many different women were speaking, maybe even disagreeing with each other, in the name of NOW? Should the dues be $25 or scaled even higher according to ability to pay so we'd have money in the treasury to hire services to do the things that were taking up so much time—or should we reduce them to $5 so the women in direst poverty could join NOW? And could we continue as an organization where every single member of NOW could come to the convention, one member, one vote, and make its basic policy decisions—or, now that we were beginning to organize in state after state, didn't we need a clear, orderly structure where chapters elected delegates responsible to their own members, to vote the actual numerical strength of the chapter membership, like the House of Representatives?

One Saturday noon, the second year of NOW, the national board meeting in the Hotel Biltmore in New York adjourned for lunch after such a tedious lawyerish discussion that some of us had no appetite for food. We went to the Biltmore Bar to calm our nerves. "Can't serve you ladies," the bartender said cheerily, though in fact he wasn't busy—the bar was virtually empty. But of course it was an ancient fixture at the Biltmore: "The Men's Bar and Grill." No women allowed. We tried to kid him out of that old-fashioned "for men only" nonsense; we wanted a drink. He stopped being so cheery.

We went back up to the NOW board meeting, thinking—and, laughing at the irony of it all, reported the incident to our sisters. "Maybe we should do something about it," someone said. "I mean, it's the height of ridiculousness to be sitting here pretending to be an organization to end sex discrimination and shut our eyes to it in the very hotel we're meeting." And of course all of us had been subjected to such indignity. It wasn't just a matter of hurt feelings or humiliation—in her company, Muriel Fox told us, the men would go for lunch in a bar like that after crucial account meetings, and she'd actually miss out on information, even important decisions. We decided to go down en masse to the Men's Bar and Grill and stage a sit-in.

Suddenly someone's husband raised a violent objection: it would make us look ridiculous; women really had no business in men's bars; it had nothing to do with equality; *his* wife, at least, would have nothing to do with it. Well, I thought, what would happen at a male board meeting if someone brought his wife along and she interfered like that? We ignored him and sent people off to various pay phones to alert the media.

At four o'clock we adjourned and moved, twenty strong, down to that Men's Bar and Grill. The TV cameras and the reporters were waiting—but the Men's Bar and Grill was closed, shut for business; in fact, it was padlocked. And a big CLOSED sign on the door—that *fink* of a husband must have tipped off the management. Now we couldn't have our sit-in. But we'd made our point by forcing them to close down on

Saturday. And the TV newspeople interviewed us picketing the Biltmore Men's Bar and Grill—with the CLOSED sign on it.

And we went back upstairs and planned our second national day of action against sex discrimination in public accommodations—for Susan B's birthday, the day after Valentine's Day, 1968. I personally and with enormous satisfaction led the invasion of the Oak Room at the Plaza, where I had been so humiliated four years earlier.

In Pittsburgh, they sat in at the fancy Stouffer's grill. Karen DeCrow and other New Yorkers even invaded the superjock McSorleys Old Ale House. The reverberations of this action were far from frivolous. Shortly thereafter, measures were introduced in Pennsylvania, New York and elsewhere to ban sex discrimination in public accommodations.

That year, on Mother's Day, we demonstrated for "Rights, Not Roses" in front of the White House, demanding that the Equal Rights Amendment be brought before Congress for a vote. And symbolically, on the spot where the suffragettes fifty years earlier had chained themselves to the White House fence to demand the vote, we made a ceremony of dumping aprons in a huge trash pile. Later, in the protest against the Miss America beauty contest in Atlantic City, women dumped girdles and bras. Somewhere in all that was the genesis of the "bra-burning" image. But to my knowledge, no one in the American women's movement ever really burned a bra. The braless fashion, launched at about that time by male designers Rudi Gernreich et al., may have had deep unconscious psychosocial links to the emergence of the women's movement, but we can't take the actual credit for it.

That image, however, was fueled by the rage that was beginning to explode now in women—the ones who in the fifties and early sixties had evaded their own education to marry young or to put their husbands through school, or who had been running the mimeograph machines in SDS and S.N.C.C.

In the student strike at Columbia in 1968, the girls were supposed to make spaghetti while the men made and carried out the strategies in the occupied buildings—and the girls said no. They presented a resolution about the liberation of women to the SDS convention, were laughed off the floor and decided to start their own, separate "women's liberation" group. And because they had cut their political eyeteeth on the doctrines of class warfare applied to the problems of race, they tried to adapt, too literally, the ideology of class and race warfare to the situation of women. Stokely Carmichael had originated the concept of "black power"; separatism, black nationalism, black studies programs—all these things could be adapted to women's situation, and that rage, suppressed so long, could even make them seem plausible.

But there was something about this new, abstract ideology of man hatred, sex warfare, that made me uneasy from the beginning. It sounded more ideological, more startling—the phrases literally borrowed or adapted from Communist or black power jargon and applied to sex. It seemed, in fact, more sexy than the NOW actions addressed to the concrete social and economic situation of women, but it also seemed to be leading us away from the reality of our movement—and its real possibilities for changing the situation of women. But because it was fueled by the real, legitimate rage erupting in women as a result of the very oppressive conditions our movement was organized to change, it was harder to fight than male oppression. The pathology caused by oppressive institutions was being mistaken for, and was in danger of perverting, the revolution women needed to change those institutions.

Then in 1968 a woman named Valerie Solanas shot Andy Warhol in the guts, though she aimed lower, and was hailed as a "heroine" of the feminist movement by Ti-Grace Atkinson, then president of New York NOW, who also smuggled her "SCUM (Society for Cutting Up Men) Manifesto" out of the mental hospital where Solanas was confined.

No action of the board of New York NOW, of national NOW, no policy ever voted by the members advocated the shooting of men in the balls, the elimination of men as proposed by that SCUM Manifesto! Ti-Grace Atkinson was repudiated by her NOW board. (Ironically, it was I who first pushed Ti-Grace into leadership. Her Main Line accent and ladylike blond good looks would be perfect, I thought, for raising money from those mythical rich old widows we never did unearth.) Then she began to spout theories of an Amazonian army of women, advocating absolute separatism from men. Ti-Grace's "radical chic" had a certain allure for the young women hippies then emigrating to the East Village and San Francisco. But she certainly did put off the women from the cities and suburbs of Middle America who were beginning to identify with the women's movement. When she began to lecture, I would often have to undo the hostility she had aroused. When the National Conference of Christians and Jews agreed to hold an all-day conference on the women's movement with NOW in New York, Ti-Grace started out by announcing that the only honest woman was a prostitute. Since married women were merely dishonest prostitutes, they should get into the women's movement by working for better conditions for the honest prostitutes. Women began to leave immediately.

It was very clear that Ti-Grace Atkinson would not be re-elected president of New York NOW. So, using that rationale against "elitism" that permeated all movements in the late sixties, Ti-Grace came up with a proposal to abolish the office of president and the democratic election of officers altogether in NOW—a "drawing lots" anonymous nonleadership scheme that would enable the "crazies" to take over and manipulate decisions, with no accountability to the membership. Ti-Grace and her "nonelitist" scheme were soundly defeated by the members of New York NOW, and she walked out to start her own movement. It was short-lived, but the media continued to treat Ti-Grace as a leader of the women's movement, despite its repudiation of her. And her kind of thinking has from time to time crept up again to disrupt the women's movement in the years that followed.

•　　•　　•

I encountered another kind of problem when I helped Sheila Tobias plan an Intersession on Women at Cornell, in January 1969. We had to steer between the fearful conservatism of timid academic women and threatened academic men and the reactionary opposition of suspicious New Left radicals. Or at least the vocal opposition of the radical young men, and a suspicious—auspicious—quiet from the radical young women. A bearded young radical leader (there were virtually no female leaders in SDS then) accosted me at the end of my Cornell lecture. He had been particularly incensed at my questioning the current practice of girls giving up their own education to Put their Husbands Through graduate school (Ph.T., they called it at Cornell) or to support them as revolutionary leaders of SDS, or in their draft resistance. If the women listened to me, what would it do to the real revolution, to *them*? I had no right to use the word "revolution" in talking about women like this, he said. Revolution had to do with socialism, the masses. If I wanted to talk about revolution to women, I should go to the beauty schools and talk to girls from the working class who got jobs in beauty parlors, not to girls who went to colleges like Cornell. ("Don't put ideas in my chick's head.")

"You'd better read Marx again," I told that righteous bearded young radical. "The only ones who can tell women how and where to run their revolution are women themselves. Any woman, every woman. Who are you to tell me which women I can't talk to, in the name of revolution? This is my revolution." There at Cornell, a young woman student passed me a mimeographed essay called "The Chick as Nigger." The women who would bring the women's movement, our revolution, to critical mass were not in the beauty schools, they were his own "chicks."

The Cornell intersession became the model for "women studies" which by 1976 are being offered in virtually every college and university in the United States and were permeating the course offerings of academic departments from Greek and Latin and French literature to business administration, economics and art. And the young women who are now putting themselves through graduate school gave those first fearful academic feminists the courage to begin organizing the women's caucuses in the American Sociological Association, the Modern Language Association, the American Psychological Association, the American Bar Association, all the associations of managers and professionals: women invading "the power elite" and subtly beginning to transform it.

"Our Revolution
is Unique"

 (Excerpt from the President's
Report to NOW, 1968)

It is not an accident that the first sentence of NOW's statement of purpose is a commitment to action.

We have begun to learn certain differences between our
revolution and the black one. We can cut no corners; we are in
effect where the black revolution was perhaps fifty years ago.
Yet there can be no illusion on our part that a separatist ideology copied from black power would work for us. Whatever
sexual-equality power or woman power is, we cannot conceive
of a single-sex society. We cannot conceive of fighting a revolution to achieve full equality between the sexes, cannot fight
our revolution in single-sex terms.

We have become aware of the reality of our revolution as
opposed to the fantasy. The reality of change we have already
brought about can be sensed in the new seriousness with
which women are taking themselves, and are finally beginning
to be taken, in America: sex discrimination is not a joke any
longer. We are treated very seriously, even with trepidation,
when we move against *The New York Times* to end sex-segregated want ads and against the Conrad Hilton in Pittsburgh or
the Plaza in New York to oppose for-men-only public accom-

modations, restaurants and bars. Whether launching a seminar at Wayne State in Detroit on women's revolution, or planning an intersession at Cornell at the invitation of the faculty and administration, or challenging help-wanted advertising, or suing the federal government for not enforcing the law equally on behalf of women, or demanding a voice for women *within* the political parties, or proposing new doctrine on the question of abortion, we are being taken seriously. That's reality, not fantasy.

It is because we are real, because this is a really serious new historical phase in the evolution of women and men toward full equality and therefore a fuller humanity, that we are beginning in action to recognize our historic and real responsibility. We are not operating in a fantasy world; we are not doing something for our own private kicks or personal self-aggrandizement, though we most certainly are doing something for ourselves; we are not telling ourselves fairy stories about the natural superiority of women to make ourselves feel better—we are really changing society. We have *begun to change society in reality.* Therefore, we have the responsibilities that reality imposes. We then begin to distinguish the women from the girls, if you will, and the men from the boys.

We begin to distinguish the women of all ages who accept responsibility for the real society-changing possibilities in our revolution, from the girls who operate as if they're playing childish games. The girls do not understand that we are really doing something here that is changing history. Our movement has brought change that is visible in this country and that is already having its reverberation around the world; it is showing its potential to effect this change with amazing speed, as all revolutions in this new postindustrial era are advancing with amazing speed.

Man is not the enemy, as we said in our statement of purpose, but the fellow victim of the bind of half-equality we are in now. And in our every action this past year, as we speak, act, demonstrate, testify and appear on television concerning matters such as sex discrimination in employment, public accommodations, and education, or divorce-marriage reform, or abortion rights—I see so clearly and hear from the mouths of men how they also are sensing that they are going to be freed to greater self-fulfillment as human beings as we women are released from the binds that now constrain us from full development of our own human potential.

We can say with absolute assurance that we do not speak for every woman in America, but we speak for the *right* of every woman in America to become all she is capable of becoming—in her own right and/or in partnership with man. And we already know now that we speak not for a few, not for hundreds, not for thousands, but for millions. Especially for millions in the younger generation that have enjoyed more equality than the older ones.

In Canada, they want to have an affiliate National Organization for Women, and propose that ultimately there will be a World Organization for Women. WOW! From Great Britain, France, Italy, from many countries over the past year, from the Scandinavian countries, from Germany, Japan, New Zealand, women—young, vital new feminists—have asked me for guidance. High school students are asking for speakers and for guidance from NOW in New York. From Bennington College I received a letter saying that their decision to go coeducational was based in part on their awareness of the thinking of NOW.

We cannot approach matters of employment in such a way that still prescribes a choice: that somehow a woman must *choose* between marriage and child rearing—a commitment in full consciousness and conscience to her own children as a mother—and a serious aspiration to the decision-making ranks of professions or politics in society. If more than a very few women are to enjoy equality, we have an absolute responsibility to get serious political priority for child-care centers, to make it possible for women not to have to bow out of society for ten or fifteen years when they have children. Or else we are only going to be talking of equal opportunities for a few. This year we got sex discrimination out from under the cobwebs where it had been buried, out from under the jokes and hilarity to where it was taken seriously. Now we must confront some of the much more difficult questions of social innovation, the new institutions that are going to be needed to make equal opportunities possible for all women, not just a few.

144

The denigration of women implicit and explicit in languages and practices is not only symbolic but perpetuates the second-class status of women in employment, education, politics. It is not frivolous; it is not even a question of how many people it affects that United Airlines bars women from executive flights; or how many people it affects that in the Rifle and Plow Restaurant in Gateway Center in Pittsburgh, or in the Oak Room at the Plaza in New York, where so much business gets settled, women can't have lunch—they are welcome only at night, escorted by men. (But isn't this the basis of women's denigration and self-denigration: that woman is defined only as a sex object, that unescorted by men she is a prostitute, never welcome as a person on ordinary business at lunch?) We are also confronting the fact that equality for women and men means something new and different in the relationship between women and men—not fantasies of destroying men or illusions about the superiority of women, but actual confrontations of the need to evolve to a new stage in the relationship between the sexes and in the mores and the laws that govern marriage. We have to ask the questions that will open up alternative lifestyles for the future, alternatives to the kind of marriage and nuclear family structure that not only women but men want out of today.

By 1972 we must be determined that we will have our own Julian Bonds, that we will find some way to confront and break through the travesty of women visible in American political conventions only as miniskirted greeters or at ladies' luncheons. We must begin to use the power of our actions to make women *visible* as people, finally, in America, as conscious political power; to change our society *now* so all women can move freely, as people, in it.

"Tokenism and
the Pseudo-Radical
Cop-out"

 Ideological Traps for
New Feminists to Avoid
(Cornell University, 1969)

All of us have been thinking about revolutions in this postindustrial era—how they are in danger of being aborted by Establishments, the traps we can fall into. This is no less true of the sexual revolution. I use the sexual revolution in its larger sense—not to mean simply when and with whom we go to bed and how we enjoy intercourse, but also the actual relationships between the two sexes, men and women.

Here we are talking about equality. We are exploring how to achieve it. The danger of the "liberal arts fallacy," especially in discussions about the sexual revolution (or the woman question, as it's so often called), is that it is terribly easy to use words and psychological concepts and very glib formulations to somehow rationalize the status quo. This is enormously easy for men to do by a clever transposing of some study of the sexual differences of children or animals, or an application of Freudian thought. To say, like Erik Erikson, that little girls are concerned with inner space and little boys with outer space and *therefore* there are some differences between men and women, and we must make an analogy with the black problem and affirm the right of women to be different—this is a rationalization of the status quo. It's a way of saying that this is a world of happy problems, that we need to do nothing.

One should simply say by definition that both men and women have inner space, and both men and women—as human beings in American society, or in any society in 1969—must move into outer space. Whether we are talking about the race to space or the problems of American society, these problems are being decided *out there*, in society. So for men and women outer space is a must.

As James Baldwin said in the letter to his nephew, Whitey has always spelled your name. You don't know how to spell your own name, and until you know, you won't know the truth about anything. There are differences between men and women—I am not denying that. But we will not know what these differences are until women have begun to spell their own names and define themselves in the human dimension more than they've been able to do in the past. One of the reasons that women have not done this is that they have accepted the denigrating image society has of them; they have kept it in the form of self-denigration. Above all, they haven't had the actual active experiences that tell a human being who he or she is.

We won't know for quite a while how much of the difference between men and women is culturally determined and how much of it is real. But let's at least start with the assumption that men and women are human. Women are female, but they are not cows—they are people. There is only one place you can be people and that is in outer society, in human society.

We rationalize all the time and whine in endless self-pity. "The poor trapped housewife, but what can we do? Someone's got to do the dishes and who's going to do it? He is out there, and he has to bring home the groceries and he's got to get up from associate professor to full professor, so you can't ask him to baby-sit. Besides, who has the money for her to go and get a Ph.D.? All right, she made a mistake and married too young, but what are you going to do about it now?"

And then we get into abstractions. "What's wrong is marriage altogether. What's wrong is having babies altogether;

let's have them in test tubes. Man is the oppressor, and women are enslaved. We don't want jobs because who wants to be equal to unfree men, and all jobs today are just rat-race anyway." And so again we rationalize, only now we're rationalizing in radical terms, not in terms of the Freudian analyst but perhaps in terms of the SDS activist. We are rationalizing again to accept the status quo, because in the end we're going to weep and go home and yell at our husbands and make life miserable for a while but then we'll conclude that it's hopeless, that nothing can be done.

Endless self-pity or abstract discussions of a miserable situation that do not lead to a transcendence in action are no good if we are going to try to arrive at a revolutionary theory. But if we are going to address ourselves to the need for changing the social institutions that will permit women to be free and equal individuals participating actively in their own society and changing that society—with men—then we must talk in terms of what is possible, and not accept what is as what must be. In other words, don't talk to me about test tubes because I am interested in leading a revolution for the foreseeable future of my society. And I have a certain sense of optimism that things can be changed.

It is my educated guess as an observer of the scene—both from what I know of psychology and what I've observed of actual women and men, old and young, conservative and radical, in this country and other countries—that for the foreseeable future people are going to want to enjoy sexual relationships and control the procreative act and make it a more responsible, human decision whether and when to have babies. If we use test-tube babies as some glib solution for the whole problem, we are going to move away from the concrete engagement with the need to change certain institutions that *can* be changed.

Similarly, we need not accept marriage as it's currently structured with the implicit idea of man, the breadwinner, and woman, the housewife. There are many different ways one could posit marriage. But it seems to be a reasonable guess that men and women are going to want relationships of long-term intimacy tied in with sexual relationships, although we can certainly posit a larger variety of sex relationships than

seem conventional in the square towns and cities of America
or in other parts of the world. But at least we can engage
ourselves with the realities of what seem to be basic needs of
people in life. Women have to eat; as long as bread and houses,
clothes and books cost money—if women can't get good jobs
they are going to be dependent on men or welfare or alimony.
And it's not possible, much less conducive to health, happiness
or self-fulfillment, for women or men to completely suppress
their sexual needs—a basic Freudian finding which even those
who object to its distortion, misuse and exaggeration do not
deny.

We can change institutions but it is a fantasy deviation
from a really revolutionary approach to say that we want a
world in which there will be no sex, no marriage, that in order
for women to be free they must have a manless revolution and
down with men. It is just silly to say that a woman who shoots
a man is a heroine to the new feminist because man is the
enemy. It's worse than silly—it's a bit sick. We have to deal
with the world of reality if we are going to have a real revolution. Here at Cornell a few weeks ago I asked the girls in SDS
why they had to have a separate organization, why they
couldn't speak up in SDS, and they said that they might not
get married because the men would think they were too aggressive. As long as this is still going to be the hang-up of even
the most radical young girls, don't tell me that anybody can
posit a possible revolution—for which there would be any following or any possibility of fulfillment for most women, much
less most men—if it says, "We're going to kill off the men and
refuse to breed male babies."

A revolutionary theory must be applicable to all. There is
no special breed of woman. I am no "exception" because I
have a high IQ and am able to write a book. Any revolutionary
theory or theory of women that doesn't include me is by definition wrong because it must spell my name too. But at the
same time I do not accept a revolution that will make me a
special class of person and say that 85 percent of other women
are going to be in a drone class. Any theory that we accept
must be applicable to the 15 percent as well as the 85 percent.
It must be applicable to all women—even the nuns who are

leaving the nunneries—and it must take the realities of sex into account.

A reality we must also face in this revolution is the fact that even the most enlightened of men have got to give up certain things. Just as there were benefits that the Southern plantation owners got out of the slaves, there are benefits that men have gotten out of the prime role. And I don't think it's very realistic to expect any large group of people to voluntarily move over and give up the central place in the sun and by largesse hand it to anyone else. So women are going to have to organize, just as the blacks and any oppressed peoples have had to, not to destroy or fight or kill men or even to take the power away from men, but to create institutions that will make possible a real life of equality between the sexes.

It is possible for some men to understand this. I don't happen to think that women and men are so completely different that it is impossible for us to see each other as human beings. I think that it is as possible for men to put themselves finally in woman's place by an act of empathy or by guilt or conscience or simply by a human rights consciousness as it has been possible for whites to do it for blacks. But it's perhaps not much more possible than that. There are more bonds between men and women, and really men's stake in this revolution is greater because a woman can make life hell for you if it isn't solved. But I think that we would make as much of a mistake if we expected men to hand everything to women as we would if we expected that all men were the enemy, all men were the oppressor. This revolution can have the support of men, but we've got to take the lead in fighting it as any other oppressed group has had to.

To enable *all* women, not just the exceptional few, to participate in society we must confront the fact of life—as a temporary fact of most women's lives today—that women do give birth to children. But we must challenge the idea that it is *woman's primary* role to rear children. Now, and equally, man and society have to be educated to accept their responsibility for that role. And this is first of all a challenge of education—to the college, the university and the graduate school.

I was in Sweden a year ago, and I was impressed that these expectations are considered absolutely normal not only in

Stockholm but even "in the sticks" in Sweden. The need for child-care centers is accepted as so absolutely important by all the fathers as well as all the mothers of the younger generation that every major young politician has it high on his agenda. In Sweden, the equivalent of the Sunday editor of *The New York Times* or of a rising state senator would tell me how he and his wife both have part-time schedules so that they can both go on with their professions, and how this is fine but they realize it's only makeshift because what's really needed is more child-care centers. And the editor would pick up the baby and say proudly that she relates to him more than to the wife. These are not queer, freakish hippies but the successful men of society. And in the Volvo factory, even the P.R. man with a crew cut says the same thing. I couldn't believe it! I asked, how do you explain this? How does everybody have these attitudes? And they said, education. Eight years ago, they decided that they were going to have absolute equality, and the only way you can have this is to challenge the sex-role idea. The sex-role debate is not considered a woman question, not even an individual woman question or a societal woman question, but a sex-role question for men and women alike. In the elementary schools boys and girls take cooking and child care, and boys and girls take shop. Boys and girls take higher mathematics. In the universities the dormitories are sexually integrated and they all have kitchens; thus boys and girls learn to cook, to sleep together and study as equals at the same time. The kitchens are very important—a boy will boast how good a cook he is, and the idea that this is woman's work is gone.

This can be done in the course of one generation, and if Sweden can do it, the United States can do it. There is no excuse for an educated person or an educator who gives lip service to the need for this revolution not to recognize that it can and must be confronted not in the slums but in the universities and the places that are training the teachers. It can be done in time to affect our own lives. Even if we had an economic revolution tomorrow, we'd still need to do this. If you don't have the sex-role debate you could have socialism and women would still be playing a menial role. But if you address yourself to the urgencies of this revolution in education as it really can be done, then you can do an awful lot in a short amount of time.

Let's talk about what the academic community could really do that isn't just tinkering or tokenism. Every single university should have a child-care center, and a Child Development department in any university that doesn't address itself to this need is not confronting its own professional challenge. Another thing you could do, which NOW is trying to do, is to tackle sex discrimination in the universities in the broadest sense. If we got sex into Title IX of the Civil Rights Act, so that sex discrimination in education was outlawed as well as race discrimination in education, we could then demand the removal of government contracts from any university that discriminated against women in assigning fellowships. We could then establish, by going to the Supreme Court, that it was discrimination against women not to give them maternity leave and instead to make them drop out of medical school if they get pregnant or else have to diet so much that the belly isn't visible. It is as much discrimination against women not to give them a maternity leave as it would be unconscionable to make a boy lose his chance to get back into graduate school if he has to go into military service. And it is discrimination against a woman for the graduate school not to have a child-care center.

There are many things we can do about sex discrimination in an activist way as educators, as students, and simply as political animals that are not tokenism. Faith that tokenism or continuing education will solve this matter is setting our sights down to a "culture of poverty" for women, in which any woman with four children who gets into graduate school at *all* is ecstatic. But every woman with four children should be able to get in and not have to pay the penalties that some have had to pay. Problems must be confronted. If an exceptional few are able to do it happily, don't tell me that all the problems are solved. Everybody—widows, men, children—has problems today, but the problems that are holding women back, and that you can confront very concretely in the university, are as sharp and special in their own nature and need as much concrete attention as the problems facing the blacks.

When women began to speak for themselves on the question of abortion, we in fact and in deed changed the very terms of the debate. In the first year of NOW, a young woman from Chicago persuaded me to come to the National Student Association Congress in College Park, Maryland, to hold a workshop discussion with young women. I knew we needed the young, even the most revolutionary of the young, for the women's movement to catch fire. High on their list of priorities—as it was on mine—was the right to abortion. I called up Janey Hart and asked her if it would scare all the Catholic women away if the NOW board began a serious consideration of the question of abortion. "Don't be silly," said Janey. "Catholics are doing some serious consideration of such questions themselves right now." (Some months later Janey Hart, a senator's wife and a Catholic mother of seven was arrested along with some young Catholic priests and lay people for picketing a bishops' meeting in protest against the new papal edict forbidding Catholics to use the pill or any birth control.)

So all during the winter, spring and fall of 1967, the NOW Board "considered" the questions of abortion and ERA. And our Catholic members—Sisters Mary Joel Reed and Mary Austin Doherty, nuns moving out of the cloister, theologian Elizabeth Farians—seemed annoyed as I kept trying to "protect" them, assuming that their religious stand against abortion would put them in a untenable spot if NOW acted on it. On a snowy wintry weekend we holed up in the University of Chicago Theological Conference Center and didn't leave for three days. Until finally one of the sisters snapped at me: "Will you please stop palming this off on the Catholics? You're just using us to evade the issue. Figure out what needs to be done according to your conscience, and we will act according to ours." They told me that Catholics would have less trouble with assertion of the right of the woman to choose according to her conscience—which meant repeal of all criminal abortion laws —than the previous approach to abortion reform, which had implied state sanction of abortion under limited circumstances. The position we first tried out in New York NOW was virtually identical with one being advocated by the Catholic priest and jurist Father Drinan of Boston. After NOW painfully confronted this challenge, the whole issue moved from the obscurity of an unspeakable dirty sexual secret to being the proud political symbol, and final essential right, of full personhood for women. I remember the shock of even the most benevolent abortion reformers—the ministers, civil libertarians, liberal doctors, the radical wing of Planned Parenthood—at the simple boldness of women, when we finally spoke for ourselves.

The hearings which were held on abortion by Governor Rockefeller in New York were reported on the front pages of the newspapers. The very word "abortion" had been taboo in the papers, before. In preparing to testify at the New York hearings, I suggested to the younger women that they actually talk about their own abortions—the way abortion really happened, their feelings, the pain, the humiliation—that they be personal about it. "At a public legislative hearing?" asked the young Episcopal churchwomen, and new NOW members. To talk about your own abortion, then, was more than embarrassing—women never told anybody if they had an abortion, much less bared the bloody details at a public legislative hearing. Not that at that point any of us had had any experience testifying at such hearings. "Why not?" I said. "At least maybe it will make them listen to us."

I expect that none of us will ever forget the way those fusty dusty old male politicians and those smooth oily younger male politicians, white and black, snapped to attention, woke up and started listening when Barbara Seaman and the others began to describe in gory detail their own abortions.

At the 1969 meeting in Chicago where we organized N.A.R.A.L.—the first National Conference for Repeal of Abortion Laws (after the Supreme Court decision we changed the name to National Abortion Rights Action League)—our best male protectors were still a little disturbed when the women they were "protecting" talked, themselves.

I was sent out to drum up publicity on television while Larry Lader and the others, in their own version of the smoke-filled rooms, made the decisions about the charter and structure of the abortion rights coalition. When the preamble of that charter was read out in the plenary session on Sunday, I was horrified to hear not one single mention of the right of woman to decide and choose in her own childbearing. It was all about the right of the doctor to perform an abortion without going to jail. Well, some of us in the women's movement were beginning to wonder if doctors were even necessary to perform operations as simple as abortion. A self-help women's abortion underground had started in California. We, the women, were not sticking our necks out on this abortion issue from any great interest in the doctor's right to perform abortions and earn a lot of money from them without going to jail. (Though we were grateful, then, to find doctors who would perform that service for women. They *did* risk jail.)

I certainly was not interested in abortion for the doctor's sake, or even in abortion as such, but because spelling out that right to choose would—and did—force church and state to confront the personhood of women in the most basic sense. That Sunday morning I took the floor mike and proposed to preamble the N.A.R.A.L. charter with the clear statement: "Asserting the right of a woman to control her own body and reproductive process as her inalienable, human, civil right, not to be denied or abridged by the state, or any man." Some of the leading abortion reformers and Planned Parenthood types were aghast at that. Protesting, they took the mike: "Abortion is not a feminist issue." "We have nothing to do with feminism." "What have women's rights got to do with abortion?" But behind me now, at that floor mike, a line formed: a middle-aged Baptist woman minister from Philadelphia, white-haired Nan Wood from Chicago NOW, and any number of young women whom I'd never seen before, like the ones who dared to describe their own abortions at the hearings in New York. So despite the well-laid plans of the male abortion politicos and medicos, the right of woman was spelled out as the basis of the abortion movement. And later, when the first law embodying women's right to choose and to have medical help in abortion was passed in the New York State legislature in 1970, it was women—who had marched, lobbied, and now stood filling the legislative chamber, breathing down the assemblymen's necks—who were given clear credit for its passage. And in 1973, for the first time in my life I sat in the Supreme Court chamber to give moral support to the young women lawyers from Texas and Georgia, and to share the moment in our history when the Supreme Court finally interpreted the Constitution to acknowledge the personhood of women—stating that our right to sexual privacy and the control of our own bodies in the matter of childbearing and abortion was more basic than many of the rights spelled out in the Bill of Rights, as it was written of, by and for men.

After the Supreme Court decision, maternity mortality dropped to an all-time low in the United States, for abortion-related deaths dropped by nearly 600 percent. In 1974, 900,000 American women had safe, legal abortions.

Abortion:
A Woman's Civil Right

(First National Conference for Repeal
of Abortion Laws, Chicago, 1969)

This is the first decent conference that's ever been held on
abortion, because this is the first conference in which *women's*
voices are being heard and heard strongly.

We are in a new stage in the sexual revolution in America.
We are moving forward again, after many decades of standing
still—which has been in effect to move backward. Belatedly,
we have come to recognize that there is no freedom, no equality, no full human dignity and personhood possible for women
until we demand control over our own bodies.

Only one voice needs to be heard on the question of
whether a woman will or will not bear a child, and that is the
voice of the woman herself: her own conscience, her own conscious choice. Then, and only then, will women move out of
their definition as sex objects to personhood and self-determination. This new stage of consciousness is like that of the
black revolution. Blacks are no longer accepting anyone else's
definition of what their liberty, equality and identity should
be, no matter how paternalistic or beneficent it is, whether
from sheriffs with bullwhips or kindly white liberals. The
blacks finally have the dignity and the self-respect and the guts

156

to say: we're writing our own names; we are the ones to say what we want and where we're going.

Women are finally saying that, too. We are the ones to say what will happen with our bodies, with our lives. We are finally demanding the voice that has not been accorded us, despite all the paper rights that women are supposed to have in America: all the tokenism, the lip service, the pats on the head, the sexual glamorization. The use of sex to sell everything from detergents to mouthwash, the glorification of breasts and behinds are finally being understood by women for what they are: the ultimately denigrating enshrinement of women as sex objects.

Yesterday, an obscene thing happened in the City of New York. A Committee of the State Legislature held hearings on the question of abortion. Women like me asked to testify. We were told that testimony was by invitation only. Only *one* woman was invited to testify on the question of abortion in the state of New York—a Catholic nun. The only other voices were those of men. It is obscene that men, whether they be legislators or priests or even benevolent abortion reformers, should be the only ones heard on the question of women's bodies and the reproductive process, on what happens to the people that actually bear the children in this society.

The right of woman to control her reproductive process must be established as a basic, inalienable, civil right, not to be denied or abridged by the state—just as the right of individual and religious conscience is considered an inalienable private right in both American tradition and in the American Constitution.

This is how we must address all questions governing abortion, access to birth control, and contraceptive devices. Don't talk to me about abortion reform. Abortion reform is something dreamed up by men, maybe good-hearted men, but they can only think from their male point of view. For them, women are the passive objects that somehow must be regulated; let them only have abortions for thalidomide, rape, incest. What right have they to say? What right has any man to say to any woman—you must bear this child? What right has any state to say? This is a woman's right, not a technical question needing the sanction of the state, or to be debated in terms of technicalities—they are all irrelevant.

This question can only be confronted in terms of the basic personhood and dignity of woman, which is violated forever if she does not have the right to control her own reproductive process.

It is quite remarkable what has happened in the little more than a year during which some of us have begun to talk about abortion in these terms. The people who first began talking about it loudly were women. We've had a lot of support from men, but I remember how they laughed when my group, NOW, decided that there had been enough talk about women, we wanted action; when we decided to define a new Bill of Rights for women, and one of the rights had to be the right of women to control their own reproductive process. At that time, New York State was having a constitutional convention and Larry Lader invited me to the meeting of all the different groups—church groups, medical groups, Planned Parenthood, and the rest—who were working on abortion reform. I said, we're going into the New York State constitutional convention demanding a Bill of Rights for women, and we are going to demand that it be written into the Constitution that the right of a woman to control her reproductive process must be established as a civil right, a right not to be denied or abridged by the state. Most of the people at that table, people working on abortion reform, were men. They looked at me in absolute horror, as if I was out of my mind. They said, you don't know what you are talking about, you're not an expert on this, you women have never done anything like this. You're just going to rock the boat—this isn't the way to go about it—you listen to us: A.D.A., A.C.L.U., the clergymen, the medical people.

If I were easily intimidated, I would have slunk out. But I said well, you may be right but as far as we are concerned, this is the only way that abortion is worth talking about; we're going to demand it and let's see what happens. As I left, a couple of the women who were sitting quietly at the table came up and said, "We'd like to help." Then, lo and behold, I began to hear ministers and A.D.A. and A.C.L.U. and others begin to voice the same position, in terms of woman's basic right. We began to get to the nitty-gritty of it. In the rest of this conference, you can talk about all the technical reasons that different abortion reform laws are inadequate or have worked or haven't worked. It's hardly interesting. What interests me is the basic position, and the resonance it gives to the whole revolution toward sexual equality today.

Women, even though they're almost too visible as sex objects in this country, are invisible people. As the Negro was the invisible man, so women are the invisible people in America today: we must now become visible women who have a share in the decisions of the mainstream of government, of politics, of the church—who don't just cook the church supper, but preach the sermon; who don't just look up the ZIP codes and address the envelopes, but make the political decisions; who don't just do the housework of industry, but make some of the executive decisions. Women, above all, who say what their own lives and personalities are going to be, and no longer listen to or even permit male experts to define what "feminine" is or isn't.

The essence of the denigration of women is our definition as sex object. To confront our inequality, therefore, we must confront both society's denigration of us in these terms and our own self-denigration as people.

Am I saying that women must be liberated from sex? No. I am saying that sex will only be liberated to be a human dialogue, sex will only cease to be a sniggering, dirty joke and an obsession in this society, when women become active self-determining people, liberated to a creativity beyond motherhood, to a full human creativity.

Am I saying that women must be liberated from motherhood? No. I am saying that motherhood will only be a joyous and responsible human act when women are free to make, with full conscious choice and full human responsibility, the decisions to become mothers. Then, and only then, will they be able to embrace motherhood without conflict, when they will be able to define themselves not just as somebody's mother, not just as servants of children, not just as breeding receptacles, but as people for whom motherhood is a freely chosen part of life, freely celebrated while it lasts, but for whom creativity has many more dimensions, as it has for men.

Then, and only then, will motherhood cease to be a curse

and a chain for men and for children. For despite all the lip service paid to motherhood today, all the roses sent on Mother's Day, all the commercials and the hypocritical ladies' magazines' celebration of women in their roles as housewives and mothers, the fact is that all television or night-club comics have to do is go before a microphone and say the words "my wife," and the whole audience erupts into gales of guilty, vicious and obscene laughter.

The hostility between the sexes has never been worse. The image of women in avant-garde plays, novels and movies, and behind the family situation comedies on television is that mothers are man-devouring, cannibalistic monsters, or else Lolitas, sex objects—and objects not even of heterosexual impulse, but of sadomasochism. That impulse—the punishment of women—is much more of a factor in the abortion question than anybody ever admits.

Motherhood is a bane almost by definition, or at least partly so, as long as women are forced to be mothers—and only mothers—against their will. Like a cancer cell living its life through another cell, women today are forced to live too much through their children and husbands (they are too dependent on them, and therefore are forced to take too much varied resentment, vindictiveness, inexpressible resentment and rage out on their husbands and children).

Perhaps it is the least understood fact of American political life: the enormous buried violence of women in this country today. Like all oppressed people, women have been taking their violence out on their own bodies, in all the maladies with which they plague the M.D.'s and the psychoanalysts. Inadvertently, and in subtle and insidious ways, they have been taking their violence out, too, on their children and on their husbands, and sometimes they're not so subtle.

The battered-child syndrome that we are hearing more and more about from our hospitals is almost always to be found in the instance of unwanted children, and women are doing the battering, as much or more than men. In the case histories of psychologically and physically maimed children, the woman is always the villain, and the reason is our definition of her: not only as passive sex object, but as mother, servant, someone else's mother, someone else's wife.

Am I saying that women have to be liberated from men? That men are the enemy? No. I am saying the *men* will only be truly liberated to love women and to be fully themselves when women are liberated to have a full say in the decisions of their lives and their society.

Until that happens, men are going to bear the guilty burden of the passive destiny they have forced upon women, the suppressed resentment, the sterility of love when it is not between two fully active, joyous people, but has in it the element of exploitation. And men will not be free to be all they can be as long as they must live up to an image of masculinity that disallows all the tenderness and sensitivity in a man, all that might be considered feminine. Men have enormous capacities in them that they have to repress and fear in order to live up to the obsolete, brutal, bear-killing, Ernest Hemingway, crew-cut Prussian, napalm-all-the-children in-Vietnam, bang-bang-you're-dead image of masculinity. Men are not allowed to admit that they sometimes are afraid. They are not allowed to express their own sensitivity, their own need to be passive sometimes and not always active. Men are not allowed to cry. So they are only half-human, as women are only half-human, until we can go this next step forward. All the burdens and responsibilities that men are supposed to shoulder alone makes them, I think, resent women's pedestal, much as that pedestal may be a burden for women.

This is the real sexual revolution. Not the cheap headlines in the papers about at what age boys and girls go to bed with each other and whether they do it with or without the benefit of marriage. That's the least of it. The real sexual revolution is the emergence of women from passivity, from the point where they are the easiest victims for all the seductions, the waste, the worshiping of false gods in our affluent society, to full self-determination and full dignity. And it is the emergence of men from the stage where they are inadvertent brutes and masters to sensitive, complete humanity.

This revolution cannot happen without radical changes in the family as we know it today; in our concepts of marriage and love, in our architecture, our cities, our theology, our politics, our art. Not that women are special. Not that women are superior. But these expressions of human creativity are bound to be infinitely more various and enriching when women and men are allowed to relate to each other beyond the strict confines of the *Ladies' Home Journal*'s definition of the Mamma and Papa marriage.

If we are finally allowed to become full people, not only will children be born and brought up with more love and responsibility than today, but we will break out of the confines of that sterile little suburban family to relate to each other in terms of all of the possible dimensions of our personalities—male and female, as comrades, as colleagues, as friends, as lovers. And without so much hate and jealousy and buried resentment and hypocrisies, there will be a whole new sense of love that will make what we call love on Valentine's Day look very pallid.

It's crucial, therefore, that we see this question of abortion as more than a quantitative move, more than a politically expedient move. Abortion repeal is not a question of political expediency. It is part of something greater. It is historic that we are addressing ourselves this weekend to perhaps its first national confrontation by women and men. Women's voices are finally being heard aloud, saying it the way it is about the question of abortion both in its most basic sense of morality and in its new political sense as part of the unfinished revolution of sexual equality.

In this confrontation, we are making an important milestone in this marvelous revolution that began long before any of us here were born and which still has a long way to go. As the pioneers from Mary Wollstonecraft to Margaret Sanger gave us the consciousness that brought us from our several directions here, so we here, in changing the very terms of the debate on abortion to assert woman's right to choose, and to define the terms of our lives ourselves, move women further to full human dignity. Today, we moved history forward . . .

In January 1970, I got a call from Catherine East in Washington tipping me off that Judge Harold Carswell, whom Nixon had just nominated for appointment to the Supreme Court, had a clear-cut record of sex discrimination. He also, she indicated, had a record of race discrimination and had been a prime mover in a racist country club; the black groups were opposing him. But the civil rights groups and the liberals in Congress had fought so hard to prevent the ratification of Haynesworth, Nixon's previous nomination to this vacancy on the Court, that they did not have any real heart for, or expectation of success in, starting all over again now to block Carswell. Why didn't I ask permission to testify for NOW on the Carswell appointment? Even in Carswell's own state, Florida, the women's movement was getting strong enough to put real pressure on senators if they were alerted to Carswell's record against women.

Senator Eastwood of Mississippi, presiding over the Senate Judiciary Committee hearings, kept staring down at me incredulously from his high podium as I testified. He told a reporter later: "It's the first time ah eveh heard of anybody objectin' to a Supreme Court justice for discrimination—against wimen!" I met Joe Rauh of A.D.A. and Birch Bayh, and the men from the Leadership Conference on Civil Rights, but they weren't very confident of stopping Carswell. Some of the votes they could count on in hard-core racial issues were not going to be available this time around. They were interested in my idea that women might provide the extra strength needed—but skeptical.

On the way back to New York, I decided to have a press conference to call on women everywhere to put pressure on their senators to block Carswell's nomination. With crucial cases such as that of abortion due to reach the Supreme Court in the next few years, an all-male Court was bad enough, even without the addition of an outright sexist. But NOW's demand that a woman be appointed to fill that vacancy on the Court had been treated as a joke. I wanted to have a press conference that would indicate that women were strongly united on such issues, and would demand more serious treatment than the media was giving to "women's lib."

So, in addition to NOW leaders, I got some of the women from the YWCA and the National Conference of Christians and Jews with whom I'd been working on the abortion issue. And some of the Democratic party women leaders I'd been talking to about starting a women's political caucus, and Beulah Sanders, black leader of the welfare mothers, and someone from Redstockings whose consciousness-raising sessions I'd looked in on. A woman had just come in from Michigan to offer to help organize NOW—a Republican, the wife of a Detroit executive, a former Miss Michigan beauty contest winner who wore a hat and gloves! I made sure Patricia Burnett *said* she was a Republican and had been "Miss Michigan," in front of the press. (The "bra-burning" innuendoes had begun to build; it was important to show that women who wore bras and even women who had won beauty contests also objected to sex discrimination on the Supreme Court.)

The young woman from Redstockings, carrying her baby in one of those kangaroo pouches on her back, sat on the couch in my apartment next to Pat Burnett, who looked like she'd dropped in from the Grosse Point Country Club. The Redstockings sister pulled out a very big bare breast and started to nurse the baby in the middle of the press conference. Then Beulah Sanders, who is black and weighs several hundred pounds, huffed up my stairs, apologizing and explaining that she was late because she had to see someone off to jail. The church ladies and my new friend Pat went right on explaining how they, all women, were outraged at the idea of appointing a sexist to the Supreme Court. The bare-breasted young mother and Beulah made their own protest in quite different language, flamboyant and revolutionary. "Do you mean to say you dames have anything in common—that you agree with her?" the reporters pressed Pat Burnett in her ladylike hat, and in turn, the bare-breasted young "hippy" and Beulah. This was not the usual political mix trotted out at press conferences in New York for liberal causes.

And amazingly, despite the pessimism of the civil rights politicos, the liberals and insiders, the nomination of Carswell was indeed blocked. Joe Rauh and others in Washington told me that the fuss made by women had made a crucial difference —votes they hadn't expected, from states where the blacks and civil rights forces hadn't been that strong, came through as the result of unexpected pressure from women. It wasn't just rhetoric, then, that the women's movement and black civil rights movement might present a formidable united front against what often were the same enemies—if they could get together. The Carswell incident showed me it was possible for women to unite on specific issues of equality across a much broader spectrum of age, politics, style and race than the media image of "women's lib," the existing state of NOW, or the more radical new women's liberation groups had revealed.

Judge Carswell and the "Sex Plus" Doctrine

 Testimony Before the Senate
Judiciary Committee, 1970

I am here to testify before this committee to oppose Judge
Carswell's appointment to Supreme Court Justice on the basis
of his proven insensitivity to the problems of the 53 percent of
United States citizens who are women, and specifically on the
basis of his explicit discrimination in a circuit court decision
in 1969 against working mothers.

I speak in my capacity as national president of the National
Organization for Women, which has led the exploding new
movement in this country for "full equality for women in
truly equal partnership with men," and which was organized
in 1966 to take action to break through discrimination against
women in employment, education, government and in all
fields of American life.

On October 13, 1969, in the Fifth Circuit Court of Appeals,
Judge Carswell was party to a most unusual judiciary action
which would permit employers, in defiance of the law of the
land as embodied in Title VII of the 1964 Civil Rights Act, to
refuse to hire women who have children.

The case involved Mrs. Ida Phillips, who was refused employment by Martin Marietta Corporation as an aircraft as-

sembler because she had pre-school-age children, although the company said it would hire a man with pre-school-age children. This case was considered a clear-cut violation of the law which forbids job discrimination on the grounds of sex as well as race. The E.E.O.C., empowered to administer Title VII, filed an amicus brief on behalf of Mrs. Phillips; an earlier opinion of the Fifth Circuit filed in May upholding the company was considered such a clear violation of the Civil Rights Act by Chief Judge John Brown that he vacated the opinion and asked to convene the full court to consider the case.

Judge Carswell voted to deny a rehearing of the case, an action which in effect would have permitted employers to fire the 4.1 million working mothers in the U.S. today who have children under six. They comprise 38.9 percent of the nearly 10.6 million mothers in the labor force today.

In his dissent to this ruling in which Judge Carswell claimed no sex discrimination was involved, Chief Judge Brown said: "The case is simple. A woman with pre-school children may not be employed, a man with pre-school children may. The distinguishing factor seems to be motherhood versus fatherhood. The question then arises: Is this sex-related? To the simple query the answer is just as simple: Nobody—and this includes judges, Solomonic or life-tenured—has yet seen a male mother. A mother, to oversimplify the simplest biology, must then be a woman.

"It is the fact of the person being a mother—i.e., a woman —not the age of the children, which denies employment opportunity to a woman which is open to men."

It is important for this committee to understand the dangerous insensitivity of Judge Carswell to sex discrimination, when the desire and indeed the necessity of women to take a fully equal place in American society has already emerged as one of the most explosive issues in the 1970's, entailing many new problems which will ultimately have to be decided by the Supreme Court.

According to government figures, over 25 percent of mothers who have children under six are in the labor force today. Over 85 percent of them work for economic reasons. Over half a million are widowed, divorced or separated. Their incomes are vitally important to their children. Perhaps even more important, as a portent of the future, is the fact that there has been an astronomical increase in the last three decades in the numbers of working mothers. Between 1950 and the most recent compilation of government statistics, the number of working mothers in the United States nearly doubled. For every mother of children who worked in 1940, ten mothers are working today, an increase from slightly over 1.5 million to nearly 11 million.

In his pernicious action, Judge Carswell not only flaunted the Civil Rights Act, designed to end the job discrimination which denied women, along with other minority groups, equal opportunity in employment, but specifically defied the policy of this administration to encourage women in poverty, who have children, to work by expanding day-care centers, rather than having them depend on the current medieval welfare system which perpetuates the cycle of poverty from generation to generation. Mothers and children today comprise 80 percent of the welfare load in major cities.

Judge Carswell justified discrimination against such women by a peculiar doctrine of "sex plus," which claimed that discrimination which did not apply to all women but only to women who did not meet special standards—standards not applied to men—was not sex discrimination.

In his dissent, Chief Judge Brown said, "The sex plus rule in this case sows the seed for future discrimination against black workers through making them meet extra standards not imposed on whites." The "sex plus" doctrine would also penalize the very women who most need jobs.

Chief Judge Brown said, "Even if the 'sex plus' rule is not expanded, in its application to mothers of pre-school children, it will deal a serious blow to the objectives of Title VII. If the law against sex discrimination means anything, it must protect employment opportunities for those groups of women who most need jobs because of economic necessity. Working mothers of pre-schoolers are such a group. Studies show that, as compared to women with older children or no children, these mothers of pre-school children were much more likely to have gone to work because of pressing need . . . because of financial necessity and because their husbands are unable to work. Frequently, these women are a key or only source of income for their families. Sixty-eight percent of working women do not have husbands present in the household, and two-thirds of these women are raising children in poverty. Moreover, a barrier to jobs for mothers of pre-schoolers tends to harm non-white mothers more than white mothers."

I am not a lawyer, but the wording of Title VII of the Civil Rights Act so clearly conveys its intention to provide equal job opportunity to all oppressed groups, including women—who today in America earn on the average less than half the earnings of men—that only outright sex discrimination or sexism, as we new feminists call it, can explain Judge Carswell's ruling.

Human rights are indivisible, and I, and those for whom I speak, would oppose equally the appointment to the Supreme Court of a racist judge who had been totally blind to the humanity of black men and women since 1948, as the appointment of a sexist judge totally blind to the humanity of women in 1969.

To countenance outright sexism, not only in words, but by judicial flaunting of the law in an appointee to the Supreme Court in 1970, when American women—not in hundreds or thousands but in the millions—are finally beginning to assert their human rights, is unconscionable.

I trust that you gentlemen of the committee do not share Judge Carswell's inability to see women as human beings, too. I will, however, put these questions to you.

How would you feel if in the event you were not reelected, you applied for a job at some company or law firm or university, and were told you weren't eligible because you had a child?

How would you feel if your sons were told explicitly or implicitly that they could not get or keep certain jobs if they had children?

Then how do you feel about appointing to the Supreme Court a man who has said your daughters may not hold a job if they have children?

The economic misery and psychological conflicts entailed for untold numbers of American women, and their children and husbands, by Judge Carswell's denial of the protection of a law that was enacted for their benefit suggest only a faint hint of the harm that would be done in appointing such a sexually backward judge to the Supreme Court. For during the next decade I can assure you that the emerging revolution of the no-longer-quite-so-silent majority will pose many pressing new problems to our society, problems which will inevitably come before the courts and which indeed will probably preoccupy the Supreme Court of the 1970's as did questions arising from the civil rights movement in the 1960's.

It is already apparent from decisions made by judges in other circuit courts that Judge Carswell is unusually blind in the matter of sex prejudice and that his blindness will make it impossible for him to judge fairly the cases of sex prejudice that will surely come up.

Recently, courts have begun to outlaw forms of discrimination against women long accepted in society. The Fifth Circuit Court of Appeals (convened as a three-judge court without Judge Carswell), on March 4, 1969, in *Weeks* v. *Southern Bell Telephone* ruled that weight-lifting limitations barring women, but not men, from jobs, were illegal under Title VII. The Seventh Circuit Court of Appeals, on September 26, 1969, in *Bowe* v. *Colgate Palmolive Co.* ruled that, if retained, a weight-lifting test must apply to ALL employees, male and female, and that each individual must be permitted to "bid on and fill any job which his or her seniority entitled him or her." Separate seniority lists for men and women were forbidden.

Here are a few existing instances of discrimination against women, that are or will be before the courts:

1. In New York City, male, but not female, teachers are paid for their time spent on jury duty.
2. In Syracuse, New York, male, but not female, teachers are paid for athletic coaching.
3. In Syracuse, an employer wants to challenge the rule that forbids her to hire female employees at night in violation of New York State restrictive laws.
4. In Pennsylvania, a woman has requested help in obtaining a tax deduction for household help necessary for her to work.
5. In Arizona, a female law professor is fighting a rule that forbids her to be hired by the same university that employs her husband in another department.

6. In California, a wife is challenging a community property law which makes it obligatory for a husband to control their joint property.

7. And all over the country the E.E.O.C. regulation, which made it illegal to have separate want ads for males and females, have not been followed by most newspapers.

The Honorable Shirley Chisholm, a national board member of NOW, has summed it all up in her statement that she has been more discriminated against as a woman than as a black.

It would show enormous contempt for every woman of this country and contempt for every black American, as well as contempt for the Supreme Court itself, if you confirm Judge Carswell's appointment.

I spent a lot of time in 1969 and 1970 trying to find ways of bringing together the enormous wave of women I sensed building up "out there" as my own lecture requests began to come from unlikely cities in the Deep South, Catholic colleges, and states like Kansas, Oklahoma, Texas, Maine, and Alabama. (As an ironic footnote, I took advantage of a lecture engagement at the Episcopal Cathedral of Jackson, Mississippi, to get my divorce, which I could no longer avoid, across the border in Mexico. I did not tell the Episcopal church ladies who met my plane in Jackson why it was coming from that direction. I kept my divorce as quiet as possible, to "protect" the movement.)

The young women I had been trying to interest from the beginning were now organizing their own "women's lib" and consciousness-raising groups. I also sensed a new readiness to move on the part of older, Establishment women who used to be afraid of being called "feminist." And then there were the black women, organizing now as welfare mothers, Beulah Sanders and others whom I'd joined in their marches and who had readily responded to me on the Carswell appointment.

In San Francisco, in the summer of 1969, I had persuaded the board of NOW to forgo our own next board meeting, and organize instead a "Congress to Unite Women" in each city where we were organized. I said we should make a special effort to bring in the young, new, radical "women's lib" groups, as well as organizations of black women and church women, the League of Women Voters, the P.T.A. housewives and professional career women who had been afraid of being called "feminist" in the beginning.

I had no idea of getting them all together in one organization. It seemed to me problems of difference in style would be insurmountable, much less those of structure. In San Francisco, I met with some of the younger, radical women from Berkeley and the Bay Area in the Candy Factory, at Ghirardelli Square, and asked their help in organizing these congresses. I told my NOW sisters—and the young radicals, too—that we should stay away from issues of "socialism" and "capitalism." We should try not to be shocked or put off by differences of language or style. I did not think we should attempt to create organizational structures or bylaws or get them all into NOW. We should just try to see if all these women who were beginning to move might not be able to get together on the specific issues of the greatest importance for women.

But those Congresses to Unite Women didn't really jell. The radicals seemed to take over. Their tactics invited sabotage.

At the Congress to Unite Women in New York, the abusive language and style of some of the women, their sexual shock tactics and man-hating, down-with-motherhood stance quickly alienated the women from the Establishment and church groups, and even disgusted the NOW members who had come in from Syracuse, Buffalo, and the suburbs of Westchester, Long Island, and New Jersey. I was sitting next to one of the younger, responsible women from Redstockings when Bill Baird and a male television camera crew tried to break in on a discussion of abortion where the women had voted men wouldn't be allowed. The doors of the public school we were meeting in were locked; he insisted on breaking in; and a crew of young women who had begun to study karate went, physically, to eject the men. This young woman said to me, "If you were a CIA agent trying to bust up the movement, wouldn't this be just the way to do it?"

Later that night all discussion was stopped by a hysterical episode in which women came up on the stage to cut off all their hair; the message some were trying to push was that to be a liberated women you had to *make yourself ugly*, to stop shaving under your arms, to stop wearing makeup or pretty dresses—any skirts at all. Marlene Sanders, charter member of NOW and the only woman commentator then on ABC, had persuaded the network to do a commentary on the women's movement and was filming the Congress to Unite Women. She called me at home in the middle of the night, after the hair-cutting binge. Someone had stolen her cans of film; they had objected to the male cameramen. The next day when I made an appeal that the film be returned, I was countered with a taunting attack on the idea that women should be bound by any values of honor or morality when it came to dealing with a male network or with the women who worked for it. I was later told that the film was on the bottom of the Hudson. It had to be destroyed because it showed the full hair-cutting episode. I suppose it was just as well that hair-cutting episode never got on TV, though Marlene had assured them she would not consider using it. (The women in the media had already become quite an effective underground, protecting the movement from its own excesses in their coverage.) But I would dearly love to have the evidence today—who was egging on the women to cut their hair off?

There was a sense, then, of the women's movement beginning to surface as one of the major movements for social change of the late 1960's—and of all kinds of unseen forces moving in on it to rip it off, to turn it to their own agenda. I thought the women's movement was much larger in its potential than those other radical movements which were beginning to alienate Americans by their shock tactics and their violence. (We didn't know, then, how much of that violence in the student movement and the New Left was being engineered by *agents provocateurs,* CIA and FBI agents, the infiltrators of Operation CHAOS.) To me, the women's movement was by definition a radical movement—it was going to, had to, bring about radical change in society. It needed its own radical voices. It needed the emotional verve and style of the young radicals. I admired that verve and style in the Miss America protest. When the Communist Party of the U.S.A. wrote to the NOW office, asking for our suggestions as to a really revolutionary program for American women, I sent them the NOW Bill of Rights. I wasn't even alarmed when I heard the Socialist Workers Party had told women to join NOW. They would simply become feminists, I thought. But the movement would die out, like the other radical movements were doing, if the "bra-burning" image and hate rhetoric alienated the broad groups of women who I sensed were ready to come in.

I remember at one of those conferences that a young woman from New Jersey named Florence Dickler was beside herself because no one would let her talk about child-care centers. I encouraged her to set up a NOW Task Force on Child Care; I knew, from my study of the situation in Sweden, that "without child-care centers, it's all just talk." But the women who started NOW had had their fill of child care, or they were young professional women who had no children. And some of these younger radical women were pushing a line that liberated women either should refuse to bear children or, as a revolutionary act, leave their own, refuse to bring them up. Yet to women like my bare-breasted sister at the Carswell press conference, a child-care center was a real issue. She and her husband were taking turns working and staying home to take care of the kids; most couples couldn't make such arrangements.

More and more women were facing the problems of divorce. We had fallen into a trap, in the first years of NOW; when divorce laws began to be reformed in New York and other states, leading to the no-fault divorce law, we were so anxious to espouse full equality that we repudiated the very concept of alimony. Now women who had been housewives, who hadn't worked in years or who made very little money, found themselves divorced, with no provision whatsoever for their maintenance or for training for a job to earn real money, and often with the whole responsibility for the children to boot. Betty Berry, who had found herself in such a plight, was organizing a NOW Task Force on Marriage and Divorce, and we'd discussed the possibility of marriage insurance.

More and more women were beginning to recognize how they were put down in their jobs—and universities and professional schools—even if they hadn't filed sex discrimination suits under Title VII. And abortion was a real issue, already uniting women in New York in unprecedented ways as they began confronting abortion concretely, from their own experience. None of these issues fired all women alike, but when we took action on such issues in NOW, women did get together—and they turned their anger against the situation—the real enemy—not against one another.

But NOW members were beginning to turn their energies against one another over what seemed to be differences of sexual ideology. The attempt to equate feminism and the women's movement with lesbianism had always been a favorite device of those who wanted to discredit the women's movement—or to frighten women away from it. Now that note was beginning to be pushed within the women's movement. And the most responsible lesbians didn't like it. I was warned by one, shortly before the Chicago convention of NOW, that certain lesbians in NOW were going to take over the organization, using me as a "straight front" only as long as they needed me. She told me they had even assigned someone to "seduce" me, to insure my cooperation.

It seemed such a wild story, I didn't know whether to believe it or not. I was not "seduced," but—betraying, I suppose, my own Middle American roots—I was beginning to feel very uneasy about this talk of lesbianism. I stopped off at the airport in Madison, Wisconsin, on my next lecture trip west, to tell Kay Clarenbach about this, because I thought it was so politically damaging to NOW I'd better not discuss it on the phone.

I was going to step down as president of NOW. I'd been spending virtually full time as an activist for nearly four years. Divorced myself now, I had to get back to my writing and otherwise pay the rent. And Aileen Hernandez wanted to run for president. A black woman—and a good administrator—could be right for NOW at this time. I've often been asked if I voluntarily bowed out of NOW leadership. That's a hard question to answer. I had such great support from the NOW membership that I had no fear of being defeated if I ran again as president. (In those days, women only ran for office if they were uncontested; a nominating committee decided the slate ahead of time, and it was very rare to run from the floor or oppose the official slate.) But in addition to the conservative sector of NOW—who feared me as too radical but whose grudging respect I was beginning to have—there were those murky new currents I didn't know how to handle. I didn't want to be a "straight woman" fronting for a lesbian cabal, I didn't want that issue even to surface and divide the organization, as it surely would have in 1970, and almost did, later. (Not that I knew, or asked, or, until then, even cared who was a lesbian, or what anyone's sex life was, in the women's movement or NOW. Admittedly square in that respect, I'd only just begun to realize that some of the best, most hard-working women in NOW were in fact lesbian. But they didn't make an issue of it or try to proselytize others, and they were very leery indeed of others who—for whatever reason—began to push that issue. Recently, *Majority Report*, a radical feminist weekly, ran the article "I Was A Lesbian for the F.B.I." In 1970, that wouldn't have occurred to me.) Anyone who understood how her own strength as a woman derived from the growing strength of the women's movement felt threatened, then, by issues that would divide us, turn us against one another, or alienate the women "out there" who we sensed identified with us.

The media was still treating the women's movement as a joke. And fear of ridicule still kept a lot of women from identifying themselves as feminist, from identifying with the women's movement—especially if they were isolated in all those cities and suburbs and offices and universities where there weren't any NOW chapters or consciousness-raising groups. (In 1970, there were about 3,000 members of NOW in thirty cities. The more radical groups, such as "Redstockings," "Bread and Roses," and "BITCH," came and went in locales like Boston, New York and San Francisco, with no permanent structure or national organization and no focus for action or continuity.) And despite the new consciousness and the media attention, our real demands weren't as yet being taken seriously by politicians, employers, church or state.

We needed an action to show them—and ourselves—how powerful we were. And if I was right, and all those women across the country were ready to identify with the women's movement, we needed an action women could take in their own communities without much central organization. A woman from Florida, Betty Armistead, had written me about a general strike of women that had been proposed in the final stages of the battle for the vote, reminding me that the fiftieth anniversary of the vote was August 26, 1970.

On the plane to Chicago, I decided to propose such a strike for August 26, 1970, on the unfinished business of women's equality. I told Mary Jean Collins-Robson and the others from Chicago NOW who met my plane, and they were immediately fired by the idea. I hid in my motel room, writing my speech in advance for once. The ones that were fighting to get control of the NOW board were disconcerted that I wasn't politicking. We were a very small organization, then, to mount such a huge action—but I sensed that the women "out there" were ready to move in far greater numbers than even we realized. To call on women anywhere to get together in their own place, and strike, symbolically, would give scope to all the ingenuity surfacing in the women's movement, channel the energies into action, transcend the differences—and kindle a chain reaction among women that would be too powerful to stop or divert or manipulate—or laugh at or ignore.

We were meeting at a motel near O'Hare Airport, outside the Chicago city limits in protest against Mayor Daley's gassing and clubbing down of the war-protesting youth the year before. I had to go into Chicago to do a broadcast the local NOW leaders had agreed to. The M.C. said I and the other women in the studio would watch and then discuss the new midiskirt and braless styles which models would now show. I said no, if black leaders were assembling in Chicago to plan, say, the march on Washington, would you ask them to sing darky songs or swap soul-food recipes?

I went back to the motel, and some Chicago NOW volunteers must have stayed up all night mimeographing my speech. I was told later that I talked for nearly two hours—"like Castro, or some Communist commissar," Kay Clarenbach teased me. But the women of NOW listened. It was late in the afternoon, and intense. I was so tired when I finished that I held on to the lectern. I ended, knowing it was so—"I have led you into history. I leave you now—to make new history." They gave me a standing ovation, the members of NOW, and I was moved.

The NOW members had gasped and cheered at the idea of

the strike. But the next morning, at the board meeting of NOW at the convention's close, Aileen Hernandez and some others opposed wasting NOW's resources on such a wild scheme, which would be embarrassing if it flopped. Since I had dreamed it up, I would have to take the responsibility of organizing it (and the blame if it failed). And I said it wouldn't, shouldn't be solely a NOW venture; it would only work if launched by a larger coalition. But the NOW convention had voted to support it. And I knew that NOW leaders would organize actions with all their newfound ingenuity in Chicago and other cities, as I would, to keynote it nationally, in New York.

Call to
Women's Strike
for Equality

 Our movement toward true equality for all women in America in fully equal partnership with men has reached a point of critical mass. All of us this past year have learned in our gut that sisterhood is powerful. The awesome power of women united is visible now and is being taken seriously, as all of us who define ourselves as people now take action in every city and state, and together make our voices heard.

It is our responsibility to history, to ourselves, to all who will come after us, to use this power *now*, in our own lives, in the mainstream of our society, not in some abstract future, when the apocalypse comes. There is an urgency in this moment. We face recession in this country, and repression, with the babies overproduced in the postwar era of the feminine mystique moving into the job market; with inflation eating up all our dollars; with men taking over even those professions that used to be female, as automation replaces blue-collar work. And in this era of recession, if we are going to compete for jobs with men, as we must to support ourselves and our families, there is bound to be more resistance than we have yet encountered. We are going to have to show that we mean it, and use our economic power to break through the barriers of sex discrimination once and for all, if women are not again to be the first fired, the last hired, as they have been in all other economic depressions.

As we visibly become the fastest-growing movement for drastic social change in this country, it would be naïve not to recognize that there are, and will be, many trying to destroy our strength, to divide us and divert us. I have said from the beginning that the enemy is not man or men, though individual men among bosses, politicians, priests, union leaders, husbands, and educators must be concretely confronted as enemies. Men are fellow victims; ours is a two-sex revolution.

The rage women have so long taken out on themselves, on their own bodies, and covertly on their husbands and children, is exploding now. I understand the conditions that cause the rage, the impotence that makes women so understandably angry, but if we define that rage as sexual, if we say that love and sex and men and even children are the enemy, not only do we doom ourselves to lives less rich and human, but we doom our movement to political sterility. For we will not be able to mobilize the power of that great majority of women who may have been oversold on love as the end of life, but nevertheless have a right to love; who may be overdefined as sex objects, but nevertheless cannot be asked to suppress their sexuality. Nor will we be able to use the political power of the men who are able to love women, and perhaps even more importantly, to identify with them as people. We will not be able to use their power to help us break through sex discrimination and to create the new social institutions that are needed to free women, not from childbearing or love or sex or even marriage, but from the intolerable agony and burden those become when women are chained to them.

I would warn you that those societies where women are most removed from the full action of the mainstream are those where sex is considered dirty and where violence breeds. If we confront the real conditions that oppress men now as well as women and translate our rage into action, then and only then will sex really be liberated to be an active joy and a receiving joy for women and for men, when we are both really free to be all we can be. This is not a war to be fought in the bedroom, but in the city, in the political arena.

I do not accept the argument that to use this power to liberate ourselves is to divert energies needed to stop repression and the war in Vietnam and the crisis in the cities. Our movement is so radical a force for change that as we make our voices heard, as we find our human strength in our own interests, we will inevitably create a new political force with allies and a common humanistic frontier, with new effectiveness against the enemies of war and repression that affect us all as human beings in America. Either that energy so long buried as impotent rage in women will become a powerful force for keeping our whole society human and free, or it will be manipulated in the interests of fascism and death.

I therefore propose that we accept the responsibility of mobilizing the chain reaction we have helped release, for instant revolution against sexual oppression in this year, 1970. I propose that on Wednesday, August 26, we call a twenty-four-hour general strike, a resistance both passive and active, of all women in America against the concrete conditions of their oppression. On that day, fifty years after the amendment that gave women the vote became part of the Constitution, I propose we use our power to declare an ultimatum on all who would keep us from using our rights as Americans. I propose that the women who are doing menial chores in the offices cover their typewriters and close their notebooks, the telephone operators unplug their switchboards, the waitresses stop waiting, cleaning women stop cleaning, and everyone who is doing a job for which a man would be paid more—stop —every woman pegged forever as assistant, doing jobs for which men get the credit—stop. In every office, every laboratory, every school, all the women to whom we get word will spend the day discussing and analyzing the conditions which keep us from being all we might be. And if the condition that keeps us down is the lack of a child-care center, we will bring our babies to the office that day and sit them on our bosses' laps. We do not know how many will join our day of abstention from so-called women's work, but I expect it will be millions. We will then present concrete demands to those who so far have made all the decisions.

And when it begins to get dark, instead of cooking dinner or making love, we will assemble, and we will carry candles symbolic of the flame of that passionate journey down through history—relit anew in every city—to converge the visible power of women at City Hall—at the political arena where the larger options of our life are decided. If men want to join us, fine. If politicians, if political bosses, if mayors and governors wish to discuss our demands, fine, but we will define the terms of the dialogue. And by the time those twenty-four hours are ended, our revolution will be a fact.

Somehow, improbably, August 26th worked: a political miracle experienced personally by the women who made it happen. We got the word out. The call to the strike resonated that gut identification women in their different places were beginning to feel for the movement, and gave them a way to join it, to act themselves. August 26th, 1970, elicited a creativity in women that cut across the political inhibitions of the organized women, both conservative and radical, and the timidity of the unorganized. It transcended—or for a while at least suspended —their suspicions and self-distrust, the incipient power struggles and hidden agendas, or even turned them to the service of the day: the joyous coming of age of the modern women's movement, the peak experience of the women's strike for equality, on August 26th, 1970.

I stopped off, my next trip out, at the Syracuse Airport, to check plans with Karen De Crow, who would coordinate August 26th for NOW. I would concentrate on organizing a broad coalition and center for strike materials and information in New York, and on putting together a march to give it all focus, as women had marched down Fifth Avenue fifty years earlier to win the vote.

We began to meet in New York, from Republican women working for Governor Rockefeller and Mayor Lindsay—closet feminists coming out to organize in City Hall and Statehouse, using their know-how gained in servicing power to service the movement—to newly rebellious professional women, not yet organized or just beginning to organize, to the young radical women flocking into the movement in their blue jeans and afros and thrift-shop costumes.

We would sit around on the back terrace of my apartment on West 93rd, or in the auditorium of the National Conference of Christians and Jews on West 57th, and agree that the "strike" would not really be a strike. How could we actually ask women to walk out on their jobs when they weren't organized in unions and the movement itself wasn't strong enough to protect them? And we would agree that information, leaflets, posters had to get out to all the possible interested women —secretaries and stewardesses in singles bars, mothers in playgrounds, suburban women in the commuter stations and shopping centers, the women that worked on Madison Avenue and Wall Street and in the garment district, and the cleaning women when they got on the subways to go home.

The young radical women were the ones who volunteered to write the leaflets and distribute them. And when they switched the meetings away from midtown, down to lofts in the East Village, the Establishment women wouldn't come along. A loose steering committee had been set up, with actual decisions being made by whoever showed up at the strike meetings, now being held weekly. I was "convenor" or "coordinator"—some title that conveyed the least amount of power compatible with the fact that the people I was raising money from, and otherwise getting help from in the matter of permits and the like, held me responsible. When the young radicals looked like they were scaring all the most respectable middle-class, middle-aged elements away—including NOW members—I held a private little session with Ruth Ann Miller, the efficient young organizer for the Socialist Workers Party. If this became solely a radical affair, in the old political style, it wouldn't serve the purposes even of the radical women, I insisted. We could either have the radicals work by themselves in the loft and do their own thing, and the rest of us would meet uptown and do our thing. Or we could all organize separate events for August 26th, in our own style, but combine forces for the march, and agree to respect one another's differences. I said I would try to raise enough money to pay at least baby-sitting expenses so she could work days at strike headquarters.

The women from one of the Democratic clubs got us a midtown strike headquarters for free, and as the pace intensified, the young radicals abandoned their loft locus and joined the rest of us in the frantic mimeographing, leafletting, telephoning, and organizing that began to go on, day and night there.

On the weekends, I would go out to East Hampton to my "commune," a big house I rented with four other friends who were also in the process of divorce or were otherwise unmarried. They were friends male and female from my writing and personal life, which I'd always kept separate from my movement life. But those rich widows we always expected to give us the money for movement projects still hadn't materialized. Our "commune" went to one of those "radical chic" fundraising affairs for the American Indians at a huge estate in the Hamptons, and some women recognized me and wanted to talk about their problems. I said, "I wish someone right here would have a party to raise money for a strike of American women like you're doing for the Indians."

The women loved the idea and said they'd ask their husbands. But I thought our strike benefit should be run by women. Ethel Scull, then wife of a taxi baron pop-art collector, was one ambitious hostess who had shown an interest in "women's lib" since I had first interviewed her for a magazine series. She agreed to have a pool party for the strike; I asked the socially most interesting women who might be willing to co-hostess it—and Gloria Vanderbilt Cooper, Edith de Rham and Gloria Steinem agreed. And the dear members of my "commune"—Betty Rollin, Arthur Herzog, Si Goode, Martha Stuart—with their friends and women we met at the beach and parties in East Hampton, spent weekends organizing the socialites to raise the money for the leaflets and posters and August 26th sound trucks we were trying to put together for the march in New York.

In the city I was battling to keep the broad political coalition together; some of the radicals were insisting on slogans like "free abortion on demand," which other feminists said was ridiculous when other kinds of medical care weren't free. I finally got the radicals to go along with "the right to abortion" and "the right to child care," "equal employment opportunity," etc. I went to see Bella Abzug, who was just starting to run for Congress, to get Women Strike for Peace into the act.

Meanwhile, NOW chapters in Chicago, Kansas City, Minneapolis, Boston and elsewhere were organizing their own events, and New York NOW, at first leery of the march, was organizing a whole series of actions for August 26th. In order not to precipitate too daring a walkout from the job for women at work, and in order to get the crowds on their way home, we had decided to hold the march in the late afternoon. And we figured women could come in from the suburbs, and spend the evening in town with their husbands.

I once heard that the war protest moratorium cost $1,000,000; that for each one of those nationwide demonstrations against the war in Vietnam, hundreds of thousands of dollars were raised and spent. That party in Ethel Scull's swimming pool netted maybe $5,000—with all the money we raised by selling buttons or posters, or mainly just by chipping in from our own pockets, we carried out the August 26th strike for a total of less than $10,000.

There were no professional fund-raisers involved in our fund-raising event; the women who were my new socialite friends in East Hampton were doing this for women, *for themselves*, and used their own brains as well as their social expertise. They began to take a lot of flak from their husbands. Ethel Scull wondered if her name on the invitation shouldn't read "Mrs. Robert Scull"; that was the way ladies' names appeared in the society news and on engraved invitations for such benefits, after all. I said, "Ethel, you are not giving this party as your husband's wife."

The party didn't raise much money, but busloads of press came out from New York, probably because of the lure of a free party at a fancy swimming pool in the Hamptons rather than out of an interest in women. Still, the happenings at that party—as distressing as they seemed at the time—made news and began to attract not only national but international attention to the women's strike. Jill Johnston, a *Village Voice* columnist who later wrote *Lesbian Nation*, took off her clothes and jumped into the swimming pool in the middle of a speech (I forget if it was my speech or Gloria Steinem's; the whole thing was so traumatic that I didn't even realize that the drawstring on the neck of my own demure red-and-white-checked cotton summer evening dress had broken—there were pictures of me speaking in the papers next day with my own bosom veritably hanging out). I will not apologize for that hilarious, glamorous event—if you are serious about anything in America, to make it fashionable helps.

We also raised enough money to get those leaflets printed. And, first sign that something big was happening, none of those leaflets handed out were left on the street—the women were evidently taking them home.

Even the problems helped build the day. Mayor Lindsay refused to let the women have Fifth Avenue—it would tie up traffic, interfere with business. "What are you going to do?" the press would ask, visions of mounted policemen with billy clubs and tear gas bombs riding down the women. "I don't believe the mayor will persist in this insult to women," I would say coolly. After all, Irish, Italians, ethnic minorities of every shade were allowed to parade up Fifth Avenue, every month, every year. For women, not once in fifty years? For the women of 1970 not to be allowed to do what women had done fifty years before! I kept insisting the mayor would change his mind . . . but up to the eve of August 26th we didn't have a permit for Fifth Avenue. How could we have a gigantic parade down the sidewalk?

On the Sunday of strike week, the women of Massachusetts got the Protestant churches turned over to the women to preach, as the suffragettes had done a half-century before. And I went to Boston and preached from the pulpit of the famous Arlington Street church in Boston, joined, at my request, by Mary Daly, who was being threatened with discharge as a professor of theology by the Catholic hierarchy for her book on *The Church and the Second Sex*. And a historic caravan went, by land and sea, to the birthplaces, homes and graves of the feminist foremothers, ending at Seneca Falls, where the Governor of New York proclaimed August 26th a holiday, and paid historic respects to Susan B. Anthony, Elizabeth Stanton, and me!

As August 26th approached, creativity flowered from women everywhere, and the excitement and pace of activity became so intense in New York that the differences got lost. The women at City Hall turned the grounds of City Hall into a day-care center, bringing their own children and inviting other women's, to demonstrate their demands for day care and other needs of working women in the city.

And NOW task forces had forays organized—Betty Berry demanding of the state insurance commissioner a way to put economic value on the work women did at home, to insure them for old age in their own right, in case of divorce . . . a foray to advertising agencies with "This ad insults women" medals . . . a putting up of mock statues of ignored women of history at various places in the city . . . a huge banner "Women of the World Unite" smuggled over by boat and draped on the Statue of Liberty. Elsewhere, bulletins were coming in: the women in a Louisiana newspaper put the *men's* pictures in the engagement and marriage society news that day . . . Women at a beach resort had their husbands bake cakes for a strike-money cake sale. As a result of all the foreign coverage, Dutch women marched on the U.S. embassy in Amsterdam to demonstrate their support of their American sisters.

Lois Beck, a woman working at my bank, asked me for some strike buttons, and we got talking—about the need for a woman's bank. I had asked a friend who was administrator of the Whitney Museum to have an exhibition of women artists that had perhaps been buried because they were women. He was horrified: no sex discrimination in the art world, said he. On August 26th, the women at his museum—ticket takers, candy sellers, elevator and switchboard operators, assistant curators . . . and his own secretary—left in midafternoon to assemble for the march, leaving instructions for the men to take their place.

The mood was lighthearted: "Don't iron while the strike is hot!" I joined my NOW sisters on Wall Street, where they'd protested the absence of women from the Stock Exchange by eating lunch at White's, a venerable "men only" landmark. At all the tables around us, I could hear the men talking about what was going on that day, with their wives, the women at the office. "My wife said she would mow the lawn and I would make dinner." "I started to tell my secretary to go out for coffee, and she sort of stared at me."

Wearing a sign she'd drawn herself, "Women Strike for Equality" a woman named Madeline Collins—a quiet suburban housewife and mother of four, now going back to school herself—marched the whole route up Fifth Avenue two hours before the march began. She'd addressed invitations and made hors d'oeuvres for the strike benefit, but she had to appear with her husband at an important business-social event of his that night and couldn't march with us. She felt such a strong need to show herself to be part of it that she marched all that way alone.

I took a bus up Madison Avenue from the strike headquarters at four o'clock, up to 59th at the entrance to Central Park, where we were to assemble. I couldn't understand why traffic was so jammed up. Why was the bus so crowded? It was a weekday, the middle of the afternoon—where were all the people going? I hadn't had time, so fast were things breaking all week, to let myself think what it would be like if only several hundred women turned up on Fifth Avenue—if the police didn't let us even march on the street.

And I got off the bus and walked the block over to Fifth Avenue, and saw women hurrying, and they smiled at me and waved. And I turned the corner on to the park, and there were more women than anyone had ever seen. The crowd was estimated at 50,000, 35,000—we kept jumping up to look back, and couldn't believe it.

Not just women. A lot of men, too, some carrying kids on their shoulders or babies on their backs and walking with their wives. All those suburban housewives who'd gotten the leaflets at the stations had come in . . . and the women from Harlem. A huge banner "Women Strike for Peace—and Equality." Another artistic banner, a whole contingent from M.O.M.A (the Museum of Modern Art). And successful women who'd been afraid of being labeled feminist—that afternoon, Shana Alexander stopped to pick up Helen Gurley

Brown, to march with her. And Betty Furness—and women with their daughters and their grandmothers.

We came out of the park onto Fifth Avenue, and sure enough there were the police on horses, trying to shunt us off to the sidewalk. But there were so many women. I was walking between Judge Dorothy Kenyon, who in her eighties refused to ride in the car we'd provided for the suffragette veterans, and one of the young radicals in blue jeans. I took their hands and said to the women on each side, *take hands and stretch out across the whole street*. And so we marched, in great swinging long lines, from sidewalk to sidewalk, and the police on their horses got out of our way. And people leaned out of office windows and waved and we said, "Join us." And after the first few blocks, we didn't hear any whistles or catcalls from men. Many reporters, male, wrote afterward that they'd never seen so many beautiful women as the proud and joyous crowd who marched down Fifth Avenue that day. But as the women, afterwards, wrote to me of August 26th: "It made all women feel beautiful." "It made me feel ten feet tall."

Strike Day,
August 26th, 1970

After tonight, the politics of this nation will never be the same. By our numbers here tonight, by women who marched curb-to-curb down Fifth Avenue—women who had never marched before in their own cause with veterans of the first battle of the vote with young high school students, black women with white women, housewives with women who work in factories and offices, women whose husbands are rich and who discovered that all women are poor—we learned. We learned what none of us had dared to hope—the power of our solidarity, the power of our sisterhood. We learned that we have the power to change the conditions that oppress us. We learned that we have the power to restructure the social institutions that today are so completely man's world. We learned who the enemy was, and I say *was*, because by the very act of learning this, by our actions tonight, that enemy went away. We faced the enemy and the enemy was us, was our own lack of self-confidence, was woman's self-denigration. We know now, if we didn't know before, that the enemy is not man. Many men joined us in this march, men who are part of our true sex role revolution, who dare by wearing their hair long to say no to that tight-lipped, muscled, obsolete image of masculinity, to say, "No, we don't have to be dominant and superior to everybody in the world to prove our manhood. We can be compassionate. We can be tender. We can be gentle. We can be sensitive. We can admit sometimes we are afraid and we can even cry, and we are men."

These men will welcome their liberation, with ours, from this tyranny of roles as they have been defined by others. And they will welcome women who finally and at last are beginning to spell their own names. We spell our own names here tonight. We spell our names as people first. And the liberation involved here is true sexual liberation. The sexual liberation from the Playboy bunny image that is just the other side of the repression, of the puritanical obsession that says sex is dirty. We will not only free ourselves, we will free men from the torment that makes it impossible to make love not war, for when we liberate ourselves from the discrimination and the barriers that keep us from being full people, then men also will be free.

Anthropologists know that in any society that denies women full humanity and full participation in the mainstream, in that society, sex is an obsession or a repression, and in that society, violence breeds. The violence that is napalming the children in Cambodia is linked to the loneliness, anguish, guilt and hostilities of the war between the sexes that we transcend tonight. In liberating ourselves, we must find our human voice and the strength to unite with our brothers, with the youth, with the blacks, in a common coalition against repression in this country, against fascism, against death and war.

There is nothing inevitable about this or any other revolution. We make it happen ourselves. The meaning of this strike is that we have no more time to waste in navel-gazing rap sessions, we have no more time to waste in sterile dead ends of man hatred, mistaking the rage caused by the conditions that oppress us for a sexual rage that is simply a temporary aberration. This is not a bedroom war. This is a political movement and it will change the politics. We are not a small minority— we who are now 53 percent of the people. We have the power to act against the conditions that oppress us and to change them. We will use it. Our strike has just begun. It will not end until we have real equality of opportunity in education and employment, a whole network in this and every city of universal twenty-four-hour child-care centers, and the right, the inalienable human right, to control our own bodies, to medical help in abortion. It will not end until our political movement stops voting for the best of two men and we have fifty women in the Senate.

We serve notice, in our strike here tonight, that any senator who dares to trifle in any way with the Equal Rights Amendment trifles with his political future, for women will not forgive and will not forget. There is no way any man, woman or child can escape the nature of our revolution, of this great movement as it manifests itself here tonight and in other cities where women are marching. What we do here will transform society, though it may not be exactly what Karl Marx or anyone else meant by revolutionary. We are all the Karl Marxes of this revolution. We, the women, must create—existentially—our own ideology, though we have much to learn from others. It will mean a new kind of structuring of professions, of work, of the economy. What will happen to the economy when women are no longer so mired in self-denigration from prenubility to late senility that they can be sold anything and everything in order to catch and keep a man? What will happen to architecture, to city planning, when women are no longer the unpaid free servants of the home?

Part of the unfinished business of our revolution is to put a real economic value on the work women do in the home. All of us are housewives, but from now on it shouldn't be housewives—"housespouses" is a better word. Both of us will share the world inside the home and walk equally in the world outside the home.

And finally, there will be a new kind of creativity, not only a new definition of love, but, as we define ourselves, a new image of woman and of man, and a new theology. The great debate of the 1960's in theology was "Is God Dead?" The debate of the 1970's will be "Is God He?" I do not say that God should be She, but unless we can see the highest possible creation and creativity in female roles as well as in male, we have not reached the next step of human evolution.

In the joy on every woman's face here tonight, in the sense that all of us have that we are sisters, that all women are beautiful, in our ability to transcend the lines of nation, class, manmade politics and race that divide us, in our affirmation of ourselves as women, we have felt a transcendent joy tonight. Woman's life has been confined by dailyness—cooking the dinner that gets eaten, and must be cooked again, sweeping the floor that must be swept every day—and transcended only by the biological birth of our children. It has never been completely human because so few of us have had this great experience that all of us have had tonight, of creating in history, of taking the torch from those great women who won us the vote fifty years ago and carrying that torch high so that it shines on the lives, not only of our daughters, but on our own selves in self-affirmation.

In the religion of my ancestors, there was a prayer that Jewish men said every morning. They prayed, "Thank thee, Lord, that I was not born a woman." Today I feel, feel for the first time, feel absolutely sure that all women are going to be able to say, as I say tonight: "Thank thee, Lord, that I was born a woman, for this day."

It's been said that the women's movement had three golden years, in which we discovered, ourselves, that "sisterhood is powerful." But after August 26th, 1970, the day that made that power visible to the world, the women's movement became the target —the vulnerable, even willing victim—of others' political and economic ripoffs, and of women's own hunger (greed, or desperate need) for a personal taste of that power and its economic payoff. At first we were afraid of really using that power for ourselves, because our personal need was maybe too desperate even to admit to ourselves. So it was very easy to turn us against each other—against any one of us who began to show that power all of us so needed. We also had too little experience in the use of power to understand the limits and the difference between the building of personal or economic power in the service of the larger cause, and the using of the movement to build one's own political or economic power. Why do I castigate myself or other women for our mild sins in this regard, in these years of the serious misuse and near-destruction of the far greater power of American democracy by the self-serving dirty tools of the Watergate gang—why, indeed? Because women still feel guilty at the mere hint, the faintest scent, of power; our need for it is so great. Often now I say in my lectures, trying to bring this out into the open, "Absolute power corrupts absolutely, but absolute powerlessness is worse." It seems to me even now that our absolute powerlessness explains, if not justifies, any sins women may have committed or will commit in their struggle for equality. As it also explains, if not justifies, the sins of Communist dictators or black power-mongers.

We were complete suckers to ripoff by others, too naïve even to be aware of the degree we were being manipulated. We couldn't bear to face the possibility of such calculating manipulation, least of all by one of our own. In fact, we didn't want to face any differences in political or sexual ideology which would divide us, and diminish that power. And that made us even more vulnerable, because the real differences which were not faced could thus be played upon in masked battles for personal power within the movement, or manipulated by those who wanted to destroy it before it rocked their own boat.

In the beginning we hardly dared disagree, publicly at least, with one another for fear of destroying that illusion: "Sisterhood is powerful." Women had been told too often that "women can't get together on anything." So how then to express uneasiness—to take one's responsibility to object—when ideology seemed to be taking a dangerous turn, tactics were becoming self-defeating, power was being mishandled—if it meant somehow attacking another woman, revealing to the public differences among ourselves?

Who am I to take a holier-than-thou attitude about all this, now? I already had a certain amount of fame, and thus power, which other women envied and wanted for themselves. Okay. But there was also the women's movement, a real commitment —or it should have been—underlying and essential to, and also serving, all our individual struggles. The different power agendas made it very difficult indeed for us to deal with the real differences as they emerged: the real differences which had to be confronted if the movement was going to be strong enough to make the social changes needed and to protect us all —and in fact the differences, when confronted, did not in the end destroy us.

In any event, women who had come together for the first time on August 26th organized new NOW chapters, or a women's caucus or group at work, or a continuing consciousness-raising group in the suburb. Aglow with the success of August 26th, I went to the next NOW board meeting in Syracuse to propose that NOW take leadership in organizing a permanent, ongoing political coalition of women on the basis of the diverse elements we had brought together. But the new NOW leadership did not seem interested in building such a broad political coalition. To be blunt, I had the disconcerting experience I now know has been the lot of many in the women's movement of reaping hostility from my sisters for the very success of August 26th. If it had been a flop, they would have commiserated with my tears and apologies. That has been one of the problems of the women's movement. We are so unused to success, recognition, even a taste of power, that we hardly know how to handle it when it is offered to us, and begrudge it, enviously, for one another. Much easier to identify women, now and forever, with the "outs," the lowliest of the low, and to base your feminism on—rationalizing as positive feminist values—the worst attributes of powerlessness, the diffidence, inhibitions, obsequiousness, and meek self-abnegation that is caused by the dependence, enforced passivity, and impotent rage which was our lot as women—and that is so hard to lift ourselves out of. Easy to wallow in that victim state.

That's what seemed to me the fatal flaw in Kate Millet's *Sexual Politics*, which was being hailed as the ideological Bible for the new feminism. But I hesitated to express my real disagreement with her ideology. It was unwritten law that we not publicly disagree with each other. I refused several requests to review her book, for that reason. But because that general ideological thrust which I variously call "sexual politics" or "sex-class warfare" was being advocated now by a number of women—without the brilliant insights which Kate Millett interspersed with her rage—and because I thought that thrust genuinely dangerous to the movement, I agreed to do a general critique of sexual politics for *Social Policy* magazine. (*Playboy* had asked me to do an article about the disagreements in ideology within the women's movement, but I refused. I offered instead to do a critique of Hugh Hefner and the Playboy Bunny as sexual philosophy, but they didn't want that.)

I didn't have time to write the article for *Social Policy* because I was too harassed trying to keep the strike coalition together, so Frank Riesman, the editor of *Social Policy*, finally came and did it as an interview, on tape. (He and Amitai Etzioni and other sociologists and economists on *Social Policy* were the kind of allies I felt the women's movement should be making, in moving for public service employment and other such larger measures necessary for women's equality.)

That same month, the Women's Strike Coalition—which I was feebly trying to hold together—was going to hold another action in New York focused on abortion and child-care centers. Those issues were under particular threat then even in New York State, where medical help in abortion was now legal, and admittedly inadequate but real child-care centers were about to have funds cut off.

My own fund-needing hectic out-of-town lecture schedule kept me from attending most of the meetings of the Women's Strike Coalition. I would get indignant telephone calls, first from my Establishment allies, telling me that they were pulling out, then from Jacqui and my other NOW friends advising me that they were leaving and warning me that my name was being used as a front for ends I might not wish to endorse. The general fear seemed to be that the Socialist Workers Party was taking over the August 26th coalition, now that I and others were too busy to come to meetings every week.

There was real need for an action on abortion and child-care centers. There was a real imperative for keeping together that enormously broad and politically powerful political coalition that had put together August 26th. (For the Equal Rights Amendment, buried in Congress for fifty years, had been passed by the House of Representatives just before we marched on August 26th, 1970—and was defeated then by the Senate after we disbanded and went home.)

And so on December 12, 1970, in a miserable freezing sleet storm, I went out again to Fifth Avenue to march with the others on the Mayor of New York, this time for child care and abortion. Well, there weren't the twenty or forty or fifty thousand of August 26th, but several thousand at least, despite the freezing sleet, and I recognized allies from the suburbs, the churchwomen from the abortion battle, and the various professional women and housewives from NOW, as well as the young radicals. And men, too; Larry Lader marched with me, trying to fill me in on the latest abortion developments.

And we crossed the avenue, to Gracie Mansion. Kate Millett was to speak, Gloria Steinem, Flo Kennedy, others and myself. Suddenly, as the speeches began, women wearing purple armbands began distributing purple armbands for others to put on, with leaflets signed "Women's Strike Coalition," explaining "why we're ALL wearing lavender lesbian armbands today." A woman marching next to me, who might have been a suburban housewife or a social worker or secretary, anyone of the proper Establishment types flocking into the movement, looked at me with horror. "Did you know about this?" "Did you have anything to do with this?"

And in fact I didn't. Kate Millett had told a reporter for *Time* magazine that she was "bisexual" and a new furor was mounting that the women's movement was just a bunch of lesbians. (I didn't know then that enormous pressure amounting finally to blackmail had been put on Kate Millett to make such a public pronouncement of what was—and surely she had a right to keep to herself—her private sexual life. Kate's editor told me that the reception of her book suffered enormously as a result, and Kate later suffered a nervous breakdown herself, as did, in a certain sense, the movement. I wonder now who put that pressure on her, even threatening blackmail, and why it was done.)

It seems the "Women's Strike Coalition" had decided—without informing me, though my name was still listed as convenor—to "issue lavender lesbian armbands" to all members of the march. The leaflet said: "It is not one woman's sexual experience that is under attack—it is the freedom *of all women* to openly state values that fundamentally challenge the basic structure of patriarchy. If they succeed in scaring us with words like 'dyke' or 'lesbian' or 'bisexual,' they'll have won. AGAIN. They'll have divided us. AGAIN. Sexism will have triumphed. AGAIN. . . . That's why we're ALL wearing lavender lesbian armbands today—to show that we stand together *as women*, regardless of sexual preference. They can call us all lesbians until such time as there is no stigma attached to women loving women. SISTERHOOD *IS* POWERFUL!!!"

Today, five years later and light-years advanced, maybe, in my own consciousness, I might feel the validity of such a statement. But on that sleeting December Saturday in 1970, it only aroused the creeping horrors in me—and I am not that far from everywoman (that is part of whatever political wisdom I may have—that I do come from Peoria, Illinois). For me, for everywoman—or most women, surely—the women's movement, women's liberation, the equality we now demand, had nothing whatsoever to do with lesbianism. Or giving up, renouncing, denouncing the love of men. Et cetera, et cetera.

Besides, there was something fishy about the whole thing. The leaflet said: "On Tuesday, December 8, *Time* magazine decided to try this time-honored method of intimidation on the Women's Liberation movement by publicly attacking Kate Millett for her courageous statement that she is bisexual." (But who pressured her to make that announcement? And who was now trying to equate the whole movement with lesbianism—and divert that force?)

I didn't have time to figure it out, but I did not myself put on a purple armband. And when it was my turn to speak, I climbed up on that precarious ladderlike rostrum in the sleety rain, and spoke of this march and the issues for which it had been called—the right to abortion, the right to community child care. And the strength in ourselves we had discovered August 26th. And the necessity now to use that strength for the real needs of women, to not let it be diverted by sexual irrelevances, to not let it be divided.

Afterwards, I went into a bar, the nearest one to Gracie Mansion, with Kate, and Ivy Bottini, then president of New York NOW, and, I believe, Gloria Steinem, and others. I was shocked by the purple armband caper—as I suppose they knew I would be, which is why they didn't tell me about it. And I now learned they were going to follow it with a press conference, in which Gloria Steinem and others would echo that note: "We are all lesbians"; "Feminism is lesbianism."

I begged them not to do it. I said the women's movement was too important to too many people who were not necessarily lesbians at all and had no intention of becoming such, to be sacrificed to such a cause. I said this would do a terrible disservice to a lot of good women in the women's movement who happened to be lesbians in their sexual preference. And I and others hadn't known or couldn't have cared less about that until now. But if they insisted on making such an issue of lesbianism—introducing it as such an insistent sexual red herring in the women's movement—I was sure it would boomerang into an era of sexual McCarthyism that might really paralyze the women's movement, and hurt *them* and everyone. I didn't succeed in convincing them. And in fact that sexual red herring of lesbianism did preoccupy and divide—or was used and manipulated to divide—NOW and the women's movement for months, for years thereafter.

The August 26th Women's Strike Coalition was never heard of again. I pulled out of it altogether; called them up the next day and told them if my name was ever used again in conjunction with their activities, I'd sue. They had not consulted me on an issue of importance on which they'd used my name as a front. They evidently did not expect or want me to pull out like that. So since I objected to the language of their leaflet—"Free Abortion on Demand" again, "Free Twenty-four-Hour Child-Care Centers"—they now suggested maybe I was right, politically; they'd change it to "The Right to Abortion" if I'd stay. But now I didn't trust them. Now, I was learning, you couldn't necessarily trust anyone and everyone who jumped on that bandwagon "Sisterhood is Powerful"— that so many people, powers, groups and interests were finally taking us seriously enough to try to co-opt.

But the only way to handle it, any of it, was finally to confront it straight on.

Critique of
Sexual Politics

(*Social Policy* Magazine,
November 1970)

*What do you think of the new trend in the women's
movement which seems to be primarily concerned with
orgasm, sexual relationships, etc.?*

I'm quite disturbed by it. I think the whole trend is highly
diversionary. It builds up a straw-man enemy by packaging
together all the negative characteristics in man and making
him the main enemy, the oppressor.

Why do you describe this as diversionary?

Because I think it diverts us from serious political action.
Women fighting for the basic changes necessary in society will
at once affirm themselves and produce much more positive
relationships with men both inside and outside the bedroom.
But if the main enemy is seen as the man, women will wallow

around in self-pity and man-hatred and never really be moved to action.

The sexual relationship is not the issue. The concern of some women to be on top in the sexual act strikes me as quite ridiculous. The problem is that the sexual relationship is soured and dehumanized by the workaday relationships of men and women in society. Its converse is the equally obsolete image of masculinity—*machismo*—which enjoins men to dominance.

Do you feel that machismo is characteristic of men today?

Machismo is the extreme. It is certainly not characteristic of the younger generation. Men wearing their hair long is, in fact, a revolt against *machismo*, with all its sadism and brutality.

Why do you think that there is so much emphasis on the new bedroom politics? Why is the trend occurring?

There are two reasons: first, because it's sexy; it suits the communications media, the TV. It's more glamorous than talking about jobs and discrimination, and women in politics.

But secondly, and even more important, the extremity of the condition that needs changing is what's causing the fulmination. I predicted four years ago, when I could see nothing happening except talk, that if this country did not really begin to confront the situation and do something to change it, the most spirited of the upcoming generation would turn their backs completely on love and sex and marriage and having children, and that's what's happening.

This trend is dangerous in that it diverts women from the necessary positive action; but it is even more dangerous in that it fits in with the rise of hatred developing all over society, which a fascist movement, a fascist demagogue could easily appeal to and capture. A random hatred of men, a hatred that can lead nowhere, with no allies, will produce no significant changes; but it can serve as the soil for a fascist appeal.

What do you think about all this talk about clitoral orgasms, vaginal orgasms, and so on?

I think, to each her own, and all the fuss is very misleading. I think as women become freer and improve their own status, their sexual response will be fuller, more positive, and will not be eroticized rage or frigidity. Kinsey, Masters and many others have shown that as women have improved their status in life, their sexuality has also grown. The point is not to focus on the kinds of sexual orgasm, but on the basic human relations that need to be changed. Unfortunately, the new sexual theorists do not seem to see the possibility of sex and love combined, of joyful sex as part of a larger, meaningful relationship. And some are badly exaggerating the presumed positives of lesbian sex. We don't want a society in which there are two separate sexes, men and women, with each getting their pleasure by themselves—men with men and women with women. Such a vision is hardly the radical future. It is only pseudo-radical because it does not lead to any real institutional change of any kind. In essence, we cannot permit the image of women to be developed by the homosexual. The male homosexual omits the strength of women just as the bull dyke omits the essential tenderness of men. What is the point of reacting against one's sexual role as man or woman merely to adopt the stereotype of the opposite sex? The *machismo* image hurts men as much as it hurts women. They can't live up to it, and a good deal of the sexual war created by the new bedroom politics is simply exacerbating the difficulties between men and women, not overcoming them. The difficulties are not being transcended, they're just being expressed. As women were the scapegoats before, so now man is becoming the new scapegoat, the monster.

What action flows from orgasm politics?

No action flows from it. All that flows from it is talk and hate, and the potential manipulations of left or right demagogues. You ought to note that De Gaulle and Reagan and Nixon were all elected with the strong help of the women's vote. It is extremely important to win the women who are 53 percent of the population to their own best interests and not to permit them to go in a rightist direction. This requires allies, and men are important allies.

What do you think of the bra burning?

Sometimes it's nice not to wear a bra, but this is not the major issue of the world. And I think it's kind of silly for women to lean over backwards and want *not* to look pretty because that, presumably, is being seductive and was determined by the patriarchal society. I guess you might say that my whole approach is less titillating and less glamorous. But the other approach is a dead end. I don't want a lot of navel-gazing and consciousness-raising that doesn't go anywhere. I want people to recognize that there are tremendous positive aspects in both men and women, that both men and women have been seriously hurt by the sex roles they've been required to play in our society; and that they frequently take their anger out on each other and on their children. The new understanding that women are developing must be channeled into political action, not into a highly verbalized sexual emphasis with a lot of whining and wallowing.

Do you want to sum up?

The essence of the matter is that sexual politics is highly dangerous and diversionary, and may even provide good soil for fascist, demagogic appeals based on hatred. No serious meaningful action emerges from a sexual emphasis. There is simply talk, anger, and wallowing. It is also based on a highly distorted, oversimplified view of our society, men and women, family relations, relations to children. The reason that I called the strike on August 26th is that I felt the movement had reached its stage of critical growth. It now must channel its energy into action that can really change political life. I feel the strike is going to help our whole movement to overcome the wallowing, navel-gazing rap sessions, the orgasm talk that leaves things unchanged, the rage that will produce a backlash —down with sex, down with love, down with childbearing. I think love and sex are real and that women and men both have real needs for love and intimacy that seems most easily structured around heterosexual relationships.

The great majority of women are not going to renounce their own need for love and shouldn't be asked to do so. My own experience tells me that family life and children can be positive experiences. And I don't want to retreat from building on those positive dimensions because of the distortions— rather, I want to fight against those factors in society that are producing the distortions. And although I think that childbearing shouldn't be the end-all of a woman's life, there is a real generative impulse in women. So if we define our movement in antilove, antichild terms, we are not going to have the power of the women and the help of increasing numbers of men who can identify their liberation with women's liberation. This is not just my theoretical view of the situation; this was evident beyond anyone's question on August 26th, when perhaps as many as one-third of the people who marched were men. Women in a coalition with students and blacks and intellectuals can build real change in society.

You have a vision, a hope?

Yes, it is happening, it is happening. And I know that we have the power to make it happen. The next step is human liberation!

The National Women's Political Caucus was an abortive attempt to introduce a new kind of political power onto the American scene. My concept may or may not have been valid, but it certainly threatened a lot of people because they ultimately did not let it prevail. At best, the Women's Political Caucus galvanized a lot of women into running for office in 1972 and afterwards who had not thought of running before, and introduced some new issues, relevant to women, on the political agenda. At worst, it prematurely siphoned off the political power implicit in the women's movement, to be too easily controlled and manipulated by a few ambitious women who served—inadvertently perhaps—the interests of those who didn't want women to control their own new power themselves.

In the beginning, the women's movement was insistently "nonpolitical" and was not considered of political relevance. So although I protested as a writer against the war in Vietnam and marched with my children for peace, I kept my "politics" out of NOW.

But in 1968, with the nation corroding in the war in Vietnam and with my own sons of draft age, I couldn't separate my own concerns as a woman from the larger political agonies of the nation. When Eugene McCarthy, who was the chief Senate sponsor of the Equal Rights Amendment, ran for President in order to end the war in Vietnam, I joined that campaign. It was, for me, the first connection between the women's movement and mainstream politics. I was severely criticized by my NOW sisters for this radical political stance, as Martin Luther King was criticized by blacks in his organization for his protest against the Vietnam war. The members of NOW were of varied political allegiances, but many were so single-minded in their feminism that they felt women should have nothing to do with any male politics.

On the other hand, while McCarthy welcomed my support as a name writer, neither he nor his advisers wanted me to talk about his support for the Equal Rights Amendment in the campaign literature I helped to write, or in my speeches for him in primary states. Even the women who were doing most of the work in the McCarthy campaign—and whose support for it was as crucial, and less clearly understood, than young people's—did not then see the political relevance of the issues of women's equality. On McCarthy's campaign plane in California, I was scolded by Tom Hayden and by the editors of *Ramparts* for even wanting to bring up such "irrelevant" issues as women's equal rights, which McCarthy had in fact championed, while all the other Presidential candidates had ignored it. (As a footnote to history, Arthur Herzog, who ran McCarthy's campaign in Oregon, was the only one to stress the women's issues and credits McCarthy's unexpected primary victory there partly to that fact.)

In both political conventions in 1968, women were present —as miniskirted greeters, secretaries reading the roll call, delegates' wives and girl friends. Fashion shows were held to entertain them while the men met in the smoke-filled rooms. I met a few serious women at both conventions whose political abilities would be of great use to the women's movement.

Standing outside the Conrad Hilton Hotel in Chicago while troopers helmeted in gas masks clubbed down the long-haired young (my own son among them) chanting "Make love, not war," I began to sense a further political connection between our movement as women and those young men saying no to the masculine mystique; both represented a new kind of political power which was the converse of, or an answer to, that violence erupting in the nation and excreted by it. The night of Humphrey's nomination, I shared the bitterness and despair of the betrayed young massed on the steps whose efforts and primary victories were not even allowed to affect the system. I ducked under the barrier that protected the press and went into the dark park with the weeping young. I did not vote for President in 1968.

After the election, I began to check the Gallup polls, and by calling up Gallup headquarters, would learn that for the first time women were beginning to vote differently from men. In both parties, women, in significantly higher proportions than men, had supported candidates who were more dove than hawk in their support of peace and human priorities.

Women had never voted differently from their husbands before. That's why no one ever took the women's vote seriously. Women had to have some economic, psychological independence—our new consciousness of ourselves as people—to exert any real political power, even to use the vote in our own interests as women.

The first time we tried to use that vote in any campaign in New York was Ellie Guggenheimer's run for City Council President in 1969. She called me up early one morning and said, "I'm appealing to you as a woman." She couldn't get any help from the reform clubs—much less from the old Democratic machine—in getting her petitions filled. Would NOW members help? They might, I said, if she would campaign, at least in part, on the women's issues then being ignored in city politics. So, standing outside department stores and supermarkets on a Saturday noon, NOW members got the petitions signed easily—and just under her deadline. And for the first time, on Ellie's sound truck, we talked about the need for women's voice to be heard at City Hall.

We didn't win that one, but when Bella Abzug wanted to run for Congress—and the men were saying she was too "difficult," her personality too "strident"—she also asked my help to get the women together. And I helped persuade the women who, severally and separately, had been doing much of the work in the New York Reform Democratic movement without ever receiving much of the decision-making power, that it was to all of our interests to elect Bella, no matter how difficult her personality.

In February 1971, the supposedly progressive arm of the

Democratic party in New York State—the New Democratic Coalition—held a convention to begin discussing the issues relevant to the 1972 Presidential election and the need to build a new political coalition. The political implications of that unprecedented turnout on August 26th had begun to make some dent on the reform bosses. They asked me, at the last minute, to be on the panel on building a new coalition. And Bella Abzug was to be a member of another panel, in the afternoon, on foreign policy. But none of the major speakers at any plenary session was a woman. Only a small upstairs room was allotted for a workshop on women's issues, to consist of speeches by women party regulars. I got to that workshop, and it was so crowded it filled the whole corridor outside. Dispensing with the workshop agenda, dispensing with the speeches from party regulars, we decided that women would take over the platform at the final plenary session to repudiate such a token role for women in any political coalition for the future. A lot of liberal men who considered themselves great friends and supporters of women were horrified that we would use such tactics against them. We took over the platform, made our point, and then moved to the nearest bar to start organizing the women's political caucus.

It seemed to me that the women's political caucus needed to be organized nationally by women representing all political elements, from young and black and radical to white-haired Midwestern Republicans. I thought they all could agree on the common need for women to speak for themselves, finally, in the halls of government. The organization of such a national caucus would stimulate organization at the grass-roots level in every state, and except for the common aim of electing women, the issues and priorities to be stressed would be decided locally.

The range of women who would be reached by this caucus would be broader than the membership of NOW or of "women's lib" groups; it would reach some who had not yet identified themselves as feminist. And it would not interest female chauvinists and political extremists who wanted nothing to do with mainstream politics.

And sure enough, in the course of about two hundred long-distance calls, I found that a lot of those politically oriented women who hadn't been interested in women's rights before were ready now to organize such a caucus. They included Elly Peterson of Michigan, who had been the most powerful woman in the Republican party—its traditionally powerless lady vice-chairman—and Rockefeller's assistants Evelyn Cunningham and Virginia Cairns, who'd been such powerful allies in the abortion fight; and women "regulars" from Minnesota, and insurgents like Fannie Lou Hamer in Mississippi, Midge Miller in Wisconsin, and Sarah Kovner from the McCarthy campaign; Kay Clarenbach and Aileen Hernandez and Karen De Crow from NOW; Shana Alexander, who came to see me one evening in utter frustration at the cabal she encountered as the first woman editor of *McCall's*—she brought in Liz Carpenter. And there were new women in state legislatures who identified with the women's movement, like Mary Ann Krupsak; Beulah Sanders of the welfare mothers; women union leaders; the newly conscious women leaders of the national student associations; and the newly militant younger women lawyers. I talked at length to Martha Griffiths, who was leading the battle for the Equal Rights Amendment, and Shirley Chisholm. I even asked Priscilla Buckley, editor of the *National Review*, whom I had known in college and knew had to be a feminist now, even though her politics were more conservative than mine. And of course Bella Abzug.

Who screamed at me over the phone that I had no business interfering in her turf. When she heard about the other women who had already agreed to be convenors of the national women's political caucus, she was outraged. Well, of course I hadn't called Bella first, because protocol would dictate calling Martha Griffiths first, who at that time was the outstanding and senior fighter for women's rights on Capitol Hill. It was Bella's first term. I had helped get her elected; I resented being accused of invading her turf for organizing what I considered the logical next step of the women's movement.

Later, I learned that inadvertently I had upset a scheme of hers and Gloria Steinem's to organize a coalition of the "outs" —the poor, blacks, youth, women and gays—as the crux of the McGovern campaign. This was not the same as my concept of

women uniting in caucuses within—and across—political
lines to elect women, and focus attention on women's issues.

An enormous breadth and variety of women responded to
my simple idea that women should have their own voice in the
larger political decisions of our times. I went out in the field
that first year to help organize the Women's Political Caucus
in the various states—Arizona, Oregon, Missouri, Minnesota,
Ohio—and they responded, old and young. Inexperienced suburban housewives, and bitter, divorced grandmothers, and eager young women out of law school got themselves elected as
convention delegates, three times as many as before, and, improbably, ran for Congress against supposedly unbeatable political Goliaths like Emmanuel Celler of Brooklyn, archenemy
of the Equal Rights Amendment. He never understood how
he got beaten by a quiet young lawyer named Liz Holtzman
who went out to the subway stops every morning, with only
other women to help her, and just talked to those constituents
which his machine was supposed to deliver automatically.

The undeniable passion driving women to raise their own
voice in the American mainstream seemed to me a new political phenomenon. It implied a larger, broader political force
than the constituency of the Old or New Left. It was alienated
by the absence of concern for people's real problems displayed
by the old machines. But it could not be appealed to by leftish
jargon or by issues that were relevant to the thirties, but not to
the real concerns of most contemporary Americans.

The appeal of the women's movement, and its political significance, was its reality: women's new need to be "in" society,
to have an active voice, no longer to be "out," passively
manipulated by others. The real needs and yearnings of people for purpose in life—and their real fears evoked by the frantic pace of change in the sixties, were met, for women, by
participation in the movement itself.

It was with these thoughts in mind that I helped found the
National Women's Political Caucus.

The Next Step:
Opening Remarks to the
Organizing Conference of
the National Women's
Political Caucus

 (July 10, 1971)

The time has come for the women's liberation movement to be transcended by a massive new movement: women's participation in political power. Even more than the eighteen-year-old vote, the women's participation movement could upset all the old political rules and traditions in 1972, with a new human politics that bosses won't be able to contain nor polls predict.

It was just five years ago in Washington that some of us met late at night to organize the first and largest women's liberation organization—NOW. Today we meet to take the next decisive step for women—the formulation of a new National Women's Political Caucus.

Last August 26th, fifty years after winning the vote which we as women have never yet used for ourselves, we discovered how many millions of us there were, marching on the unfinished business of our equality. We do more than march this year. We prepare to take our share of political power: the power which is our right, as 53 percent of the voting population of this democracy, and a necessity if our new consciousness of ourselves is ever going to be more than talk for most of us.

At an analogous moment in the early sixties, the civil rights movement had to demand black power if the rights were to become real for most blacks. Women's participation in political power will change the politics of this nation in 1972 and thereafter, more deeply than the black movement or any minority movement or ethnic bloc of the past ever has. Until now, the politics of our two-party system, the politics of bossism and machines, has been based on manipulation of minorities, often against each other, by the male, white minority with power. What unites women as a majority is the refusal to be manipulated any longer. What unites women across the lines of race, class, generation and man-made party politics is the demand for participation ourselves: our own voice in the big decisions affecting our lives. This will be quite a change from the token role that women have played in American politics until now—the *few* who got beyond the menial chores.

I used to be invited to the White House during the Johnson administration to be on a "women's committee" with other "prominent" women, usually just before elections. But the women were never asked to *speak*, only to have our pictures taken with the President, or more usually, to have tea with the President's wife. Last August—frightened, I guess, by the specter of all those women marching—the House passed the Equal Rights Amendment which had been bottled up in committee for forty-seven years, but when the march was over, the Senate quickly took it back, even though a majority of senators had "promised" to sponsor it. President Nixon didn't even want to release the report of his own appointed task force on women's rights and responsibilities. He still hasn't done anything about it.

Women who have done the political housework in both parties, who have been ignored by the very men they have elected, know what we in the women's movement have learned when we've tried to get priority or money appropriated or even legislation enforced on issues like child care, abortion or sex discrimination: what we need is political power ourselves. With men composing 98 or 99 percent of the House, Senate, the State Assemblies, and City Halls, women are *outside* the body politic.

The concept of the National Women's Political Caucus has been fleshed out over five months of discussion with women from the different groups and constituencies in this nation who have, over the past few years, begun to work together on social issues. The National Women's Political Caucus will include women who are Democrats and Republicans, women disgusted with both parties and young women turned on to neither. If it succeeds in uniting women to elect women, it will have the power to confront the bosses and the machines in either party, and to change the power structure. If it uses the woman power that has been used for all the detail work (mimeographing, envelope-addressing, canvassing, doorbell ringing) and for all the coffee klatsches, lunches and teas which have helped to elect men, and uses the speeches we have written for men, and the brains we haven't been asked to use by men in the smoke-filled rooms of party decision-making—to elect women, women will finally have their rightful share of political power. Any woman against any man? Of course not. But certainly a qualified woman should be run against less qualified men. There's been too much nonsense about there being "no qualified women" available to run. Thousands of women have had educations equal or superior to men's in every way. Working women, now 43 percent of the population, have acquired technical and business experience matching or exceeding that of men. All the women who have run men's campaigns and legislative offices have political expertise, and a whole new group of women have qualified themselves for the new politics by leading, outside the party structures, the great movements on social issues.

One rainy night this winter, I went to the suburban five towns area of Hempstead, Long Island, to help launch the first women's political caucus at the grass-roots level, where the real work, the real decisions and the real organization will have to take place. Yolande Quitman, a mother of two teenagers, and a few of her neighbors who had virtually no experience in politics had contacted every women's group: Catholic, Protestant, Jewish, the P.T.A., the League of Women Voters, the A.A.U.W., students at local colleges, even the women's auxiliary of the Veterans of Foreign Wars. These women were so turned on at the prospect of getting some real political power that the meeting had to be limited to two women from every organization, and still cars were parked for blocks

around. They didn't waste time arguing about women's liberation. They made plans to run women for town councils, for
supervisory and regulatory boards to which women had never
even been nominated before, even in suburbs where women
and children formed virtually the entire population. Within
three months, they got the first women nominated for the 1971
elections by the regular Democratic party, and it now considers them one of the most powerful political groups in the district. Already beginning to search for many more political
nominees for '72—judges, convention delegates, etc.—they
have begun a voter registration campaign aimed at women and
at the eighteen-year-olds of both sexes. If, as the latest census
shows, the suburban population is becoming the decisive one
in the United States, then the women's participation movement is surely the key to the new politics of suburbia.

The women's liberation movement has crested now. If it
doesn't become political, it will peter out, turn against itself
and become nothing. Can we really make it political? Women
old-timers with a lifetime on the party fringes worry, "Women
will never get together to elect other women"; "You can't get
women to run for anything." Idealistic young radicals turn up
their noses at "Establishment politics," "women with political
ambitions of their own," or electing anybody for anything.
They call it "elitism" or an "ego trip." But the new women in
Congress today, Shirley Chisholm, Bella Abzug, know it was
women who elected them over the opposition of the professional politicians. Even the most powerful women in Congress
today, Martha Griffiths and Edith Green, were elected without much help from the regular machines and with a lot of
help from women across regular party lines.

Such women have increasingly outnumbered the few
women who might still say, "I wouldn't vote for a woman
senator." Politicians, even the Aunt Toms, will have to realize
that the old male machine bosses have become obsolete.
Women politicians in office who think that their power rests
on being the only woman there are making a serious mistake.
Such women will have no more than token power. They will
have real power to change society and to create the conditions
all women need only when there are many women there.

As we put the caucus together, now even women who have

made it with "tried and true" political methods realize that the tried may no longer be true or may never work for women. I remember when Edith Green decided not to run for the Senate because she couldn't raise the money to do it. Could the National Women's Political Caucus raise the money women need to run for the Senate or for the Statehouse, or could it provide the equivalent of money? Women and students can be mobilized to go into districts as needed, to augment local political woman power. Women celebrities can speak, write, cut records for women of little fame running for offices in small towns. Perhaps the fairness doctrine can be used to get women candidates equal time on TV and radio with male candidates.

I know that in our meetings here, trying to put all these ideas together, it may look at first like an impossible job. How can conservatives, Republicans, Democrats, radicals, women so disgusted that they want to start a women's party and run a woman for President, agree on what to do and how to do it? But in meetings already held we have come to realize that we don't have to agree with each other on everything. I suggest that the caucus and the candidates in each community will decide on the issues and methods. I submit that it only takes an hour or two, or a meeting or two, for women who may otherwise be of different political views to realize that the important thing now is to unite to get women elected—women who will be committed to the rights and interests of women and to human priorities. Women do not seek power over men or to use power as men have used it. I believe that women's voice in political decisions will help change our whole politics away from war and toward the critical human problems of our society—not because women are purer or better than men, but because our lives have not permitted us to evade human reality as men have, or to encase ourselves in the dehumanizing prison of *machismo*, the masculine mystique. Shana Alexander suggests that our slogan should be "Women's Participation—Human Liberation."

I remember once hearing John Kennedy talk about "the political passion." Beginning to understand what he meant while organizing the women's movement and doing battle with politicians in Washington, I felt what a shame it was that women are only expected to experience sexual passion, and even that passively. The great philosophers from the Greeks to our own time have said that it is when men exercise that political passion and participate in the decisions that write the ongoing human story that they are most human. It was this condition that defined the free man as opposed to the slave, whose work was needed for biological survival but never left a mark behind. That work, sweeping the floor that gets dirty again, cooking the meal that's consumed, has defined women until now as it once defined the slave. It is time to move up from the menial housework of home, office, school, factory and political party. It is time to have a voice in human destiny, to find and use our fullest human power.

It is a remnant of our own self-denigration, the put-down we finally do to ourselves, to think that a woman is "pushy" or "unfeminine" or "elitist" or on an "ego trip" to want to run for political office. It is to be hoped that there are thousands of us sufficiently liberated now to take on the responsibility and demand the rewards of running for political office. It takes courage to emerge from our private hiding place and risk ourselves, expose ourselves, as we must when we enter the political world in our own right. I suspect the great desire we have to do this now goes beyond the issues we care about—the child-care centers, abortion rights, equal opportunities in jobs and education, new approaches to marriage and divorce—goes beyond the urgent need women feel, with the young, for human priorities in our government. It is not at all explained by a simple desire for power over others. I think we are finally experiencing, millions of us, the true political passion that means we have liberated ourselves to be human.

The men who made the American Revolution and the Constitution that embodied it intended to establish and preserve beyond possible threat the right to political participation. The women's participation movement seeks that right for women, seeks that full humanness, and would keep it, even if all the issues on the current social agenda were won. Whether or not we succeed in electing a hundred women to Congress and to the Statehouses in fifty states, or tens of hundreds to city and county offices and party committees, hundreds of thousands, even millions of us will experience the political passion in trying to elect them and in discovering our own unsuspected human political power. It will not be a joke by 1976, the two hundredth anniversary of our Republic, that a woman might run for President of the United States, for the women's participation movement, the second American Revolution, will have peacefully achieved government of, by and for the people, who are women as well as men.

After the organizing conference, I made my long-distance phone calls and my barnstorming trips to Iowa or Columbus, Ohio, or Phoenix, Arizona, and saw this amazing new broad coalition of women, streaming with energy and vitality, with enormous potential for real political victory and change. And then in Washington, in the monthly meetings of the national steering committee the rest of 1971 and 1972, I continually had to fight attempts to *narrow* the appeal, to take positions and stands couched in radical jargon that was okay for the East Village in New York or counterculture San Francisco, but not for the breadth of women throughout America wanting their own political voice. It wasn't the same voice. (Women from Middle America were not that interested in lesbianism, for instance.) I seemed increasingly to be at ideological and tactical odds with Bella Abzug and Gloria Steinem and Brenda Feigen Fasteau and other self-styled radicals in the caucus leadership. I and others like Shana Alexander and Martha Mc-Kay of North Carolina who shared my idea of a broad, independent women's political caucus seemed to be in their way.

The insistence on alienating positions and the increasing manipulation of the National Women's Political Caucus for personal political power gradually drove out the central force of women I had brought in—a force that wouldn't have been easy for anyone to control.

221

After the organization of the National Women's Political Caucus, the Senate finally passed the Equal Rights Amendment, and it began to be ratified by the states. And reactionary political and economic forces became more open in their flagrant opposition to the women's movement for equality. For we were now mobilizing to political independence that great mass of women which had always been manipulated by dictator, demagogue, priest and profiteer. But what I didn't then understand was the degree to which our own political mobilization of women was threatening to forces on the left, and to the ambitions of individual women who were indeed emerging on the model of the male political bosses. Those whose main concern was to get or keep power for themselves—including women who were in there first and wanted to close the door behind them—formed a female power bloc which seemed interested in building a new political force only to the degree to which they could control it for themselves. They wanted the names of the women I had brought in—as long as they would let themselves be used merely as names. Some women with a genuine commitment to feminism and an independent political voice looked the other way, because this seemed to be the only game to play to get yourself elected. Others, like me, who couldn't be counted on to keep our mouths shut had to be pushed out.

Thus, for instance, a conference was held to organize the Women's Political Caucus in New York State. The feminists who worked for Governor Rockefeller got us the state assembly chamber, and asked me to make the keynote address. A small bunch of self-proclaimed revolutionaries whom no one knew tried to prevent me from speaking—using slogans and issuing insults bound to alienate the upstate women, the Republican and Democrat and League of Women Voters types, for whom this was the first step of feminism. I somehow managed to hold the podium, and the response of the assembled women was so strong that the disrupters left. Despite continued provocations in the workshops (including physical slapping and hair-pulling), we proceeded to set up the Women's Political Caucus in the state. Mary Ann Krupsak, Shirely Chisholm and Connie Cook evoked enthusiastic support. Bella

Abzug came late. Her cohorts were opposing the state structure.

Suddenly, Sunday afternoon, the entire registration files—the total list of registrants from all over the state, their addresses and phone numbers—simply disappeared. They were "stolen" mysteriously, right off the registration table while we were holding a post-mortem in the coffee shop. It was as if all the work that had gone into organizing this broad state caucus had been for nothing. It was another two years before it was put together again, and by that time most of the women who had given it independent strength had become disgusted with the caucus altogether or had simply decided to concentrate on their own political careers. Meanwhile, the Manhattan Political Caucus, which Bella controlled, in effect spoke for the whole state.

The uses of the caucus for some women's power, and not for others, disillusioned many. In 1972 a call went out to women in the National Caucus to go to Texas to help Sissy Farenthold run for governor, and to New York to help Bella Abzug. And I, who was still nominally one of the leaders of the caucus, would get outraged calls—why weren't we helping Liz Holtzman in Brooklyn, whose race for Congress against the leading foe of ERA was one of the most significant anywhere, or the delegates running in support of Shirley Chisholm for President? I was outraged myself and expressed it in no uncertain terms to the staff and to Bella's cohorts. They said Liz Holtzman had no chance of winning, and Shirley Chisholm's delegates were a quixotic joke: it had been decided at an executive committee meeting Martha and I must have missed to concentrate our forces only on a few key races where we had a chance of winning. It turned out that Liz Holtzman did win, and Sissy Farenthold did not, and that Shirley Chisholm won the nation's respect for her campaign for the Presidency. I made a quixotic fool of myself, maybe, going into subways at 7 A.M. to run as a delegate for Shirley Chisholm in my own district, going to Mississippi to speak for Fannie Lou Hamer, and to Pittsburgh to help raise money for Republican feminist Jo Ann Gardner, who was running for City Council. I fought bitterly and expressed disgust out loud when the National Women's Political Caucus refused to endorse Shirley Chisholm's candidacy. Shirley Chisholm didn't say anything; she just resigned.

At the insistence of Bella and others, a national convention of the Women's Political Caucus was delayed until after the 1972 elections. I fought this; I wanted the women to get together first themselves. I've never been good at the politics of manipulation, machine tactics. My point in organizing the Women's Political Caucus was that women who had been manipulated so easily by those male bosses—in the name of revolution and reform as well as of reaction—should make their own political decisions. But by this, I really meant women speaking, deciding *for themselves*. I had not meant to organize women into yet another passive bloc of votes to be used by female bosses, and delivered for the purposes of the same old male political machines. I could organize inexperienced women to fight and break through the tactics of those who had always pushed them around before, but I was helpless, strangely paralyzed, when the women began to be pushed around by other women—when in fact the Political Caucus itself began to be transformed into a machine in which the new independence of women would be manipulated and contained. When I tried to warn others of this or fight against it, I guess the female political bosses had to get rid of me.

It started to come to a head at the political conventions in Miami in 1972. The obvious strategy for the Women's Political Caucus at the two national conventions was to call a meeting of all the women present as early as possible, to formulate common demands and strategy, present them to all the candidates, and then bargain the power of the women delegates—present in enough strength at both conventions to offer such bargaining power—in return for a commitment to certain real issues, certain places for women on the ticket, and a continued decision-making voice for women in the campaign and party itself.

I went to both conventions as a reporter: a maneuver by Bella had replaced the caucus steering committee by special convention "spokeswomen"—Gloria Steinem at the Democratic, Jill Ruckelshaus at the Republican. I found, instead of a meeting to organize women at the very beginning of each convention, with subsequent daily meetings to make strategy and demands, that the caucus was planning to hold one formal, ceremonial affair only, during which the candidates would be called on to give formal speeches to the women, and the women themselves would have no chance to speak at all. Above all, no attempt was going to be made to organize the women into a real independent bloc.

When Martha McKay and I and other feminists insisted on such meetings of the women, we came into open conflict with Bella Abzug and Gloria Steinem at the Democratic convention—and with Jill Ruckelshaus and Bobbi Kilberg at the Republican convention. Again, I'm not sure whether genuine differences in ideology and thus tactics were involved—maybe political feminism versus political opportunism—or something more sinister. When some of us insisted on organizing such meetings anyhow, Gloria and Bella announced that the women assembled *had no power* to make any decisions on convention strategy. And then they acted as if whatever decisions were made had never happened. That certain women went into the political caucus to deliver it to McGovern or Nixon—for their own political payoff, or to defuse political organization of women in '72—only slowly dawned on me.

The night of McGovern's nomination, in the space behind the stadium bleachers at the Democratic convention in Miami, I finally came into open conflict with Gloria Steinem. Or rather I shouted, and she said sweetly, in effect, that I had to get out or else. I shouted, because the meeting of the women delegates which should have been called by the caucus so that all of us could swing our power behind Shirley Chisholm had been called off, evidently at Gloria's instruction. And she was already organizing, on her own, as a *fait accompli*, a move for Sissy Farenthold as Vice President.

Whatever my misguided reasons for organizing the N.W.P.C., it was already apparent in Miami in 1972 that it could provide a new machine to deliver women as a bloc—unless the women could control it themselves and make it work as an independent voice for them. For my own attempts to do that I was, as they say, "crucified" by some of my sisters and in the media. (That I fell into all the traps and probably created some unnecessarily for myself, I won't deny.) I cringed at some of the media coverage, which played up the "rifts" between me and Gloria Steinem and Bella Abzug. The worst were an especially bitchy account in *Esquire* by Nora Ephron, and a virulent antifeminist male columnist for the Florida papers, who sneered that I was "jealous" of Gloria Steinem, because she was blond and pretty and I was not (illustrated by one of those monstrous ugly pictures of me, mouth open, fist clenched). And I would writhe and wonder. Was that really what it was all about—a mere petty power struggle among the girls? Gloria is assuredly blonder, younger, prettier than I am—though I never thought of myself as quite as ugly as those pictures made me. But my battles with Gloria in the Women's Political Caucus involved my most basic sense of what the women's movement was all about. Whatever she was all about, we seemed to be operating from quite different places, in some fundamental way.

I was no match for her, not only because of that matter of looks—which somehow paralyzed me—but because I don't know how to manipulate, or deal with manipulation, myself. I could try to make that a virtue, but it's also a fault, a strange blind spot. As when, for instance, Gloria would say that none of the "superstars" should speak for the N.W.P.C. Steering Committee to the press, and so I would take her at face value and bow out in favor of Jo Ann Gardner or Martha McKay. But no, that's not what she meant—and in the end it was somehow Gloria Steinem that would speak to the press. (The two black women who held the rotating caucus chair at that time—Assemblywoman Gwen Cherry of Florida and Carol Ann Taylor of New York—were not even told about some of the caucus press conferences in Miami.)

When the Houston N.W.P.C. convention was finally held, the bloc that was to contain—and divert—the real power of women from the independence it might have achieved was in effective control of the machinery of the National Women's Political Caucus. I had in good faith continued to travel to many of the fifty states, keynoting the organizing conventions of state caucuses, and in general lending my name and reputation for women's interests to the political caucus. As always, the women I helped to organize in those different states energized and justified my own efforts by their response. But the Political Caucus could be much more easily co-opted and controlled and corrupted, both in the individual states and on a national basis, than NOW could, because it was tied to the existing political power structures and had no independent and permanent membership structure in the different cities and states to which it was responsible. (Bella Abzug and Gloria Steinem had been especially opposed to any such structure for the caucus.)

At Houston, Bella and Gloria announced that the "superstars" would now bow out of the leadership of the National Women's Political Caucus; we had merely acted as temporary custodians until the real women could take over. And again I bowed out of any attempt to run for the chair of the caucus and devoted my efforts instead to supporting a slate headed by Martha McKay, who believed as I did in the principle of a broad independent political mobilization of women. But we were again hopelessly outfoxed in Houston, as Bella and Gloria twisted Sissy Farenthold's arm to run, despite her reluctance at the threat to her own fragile health and to her Texas political career.

After Martha McKay and other independents were defeated for the top offices of the caucus, some of us realized, belatedly, that the officers elected were women who would stay in Texas most of the time, or, having no independent constituency of their own, could be easily controlled by Bella and her cohorts, or who would go along from simple opportunism. However, the officers would have to be buttressed by a large national committee elected separately. Waking up, at last, to my own power to keep the caucus the independent force it was meant to be, I ignored the "superstar, get out" bit to run myself for a continued place on the committee, where at least I could keep an eye on things. It was obvious from the applause when my name was placed in nomination that I would be elected. So, tired and disheartened, I went up the aisle to get the charter plane back to New York. It didn't occur to me, in the assumed honor and trust I thought we all took for granted in the women's movement then, that it was unsafe to leave before the ballots were counted, or that there should be "watchers" and other safeguards against fraud as is customary in male elections. Just before I got to the door, I ran into the big female honcho. "Are you leaving?" she asked incredulously. I didn't understand the expression in her eyes; it made me uncomfortable.

Through the night and into the next morning after I got back to New York, I kept getting long-distance phone calls from women—some unknown to me, some known—on their own way home from Houston. They told me something fishy was going on. When the votes for the at-large members of the Steering Committee were counted, I had by far the most votes of anyone. And then there was some confusion, someone took the ballot boxes away, someone went to Sissy and asked for a recount—and over half my votes disappeared. I now was not even among the ten women elected. Sure enough, the next morning *The New York Times* listed me as one of those elected to the Steering Committee of the Political Caucus, but Sissy Farenthold called me to apologize for the "mistake." Unfortunately, the ballots had been counted wrong, she said. I was not elected. Other independent feminists had also somehow been removed from the caucus leadership to which they had been elected on the original count.

The whole thing was so fishy that I called Liz Holtzman, who got me a fine young woman lawyer from a strait-laced Washington firm to investigate. Sissy Farenthold was quite concerned herself. It was clear enough from Sally Katzen's investigation that strange things happened to the ballots women cast at Houston. If I wanted to go to court, she and other representatives of her firm were prepared to take the case. But I did not, then, wish to make a court case against the leadership of the Women's Political Caucus—I felt that the dirty tricks involved should be exposed to the caucus itself, and they could be trusted to take whatever action was needed. That tradition of "sisterhood is powerful" kept me and the others quiet longer than it should have about actions truly menacing to the integrity and existence of the women's movement. I merely asked, and was put off, and then when I insisted, finally was granted by Sissy, time on the agenda at the next meeting of the National Board of the Caucus for my lawyer, Sally Katzen, to present her findings of improper election procedures and the evidence that votes were tampered with. Just before that meeting, Bella, Gloria and Olga Madar from

U.A.W. descended on me in a menacing, moralizing cohort, and told me to keep my mouth shut.

At the meeting, in a suburban Washington college hall, Sally made her report. Martha McKay moved that all the women who had been elected when the ballots were counted first be put back on the committee—without removing those who replaced them on the subsequent ballots. A counter-resolution was introduced, deploring the irregularities of the election procedure and suggesting watchers in the future and other remedies, but accepting the results of this election despite the admitted irregularities.

The council voting on this had already been pruned of most of the women who had been around long enough to understand what was happening or who were bold enough to resist the forces clearly now in power. Shana Alexander had long since resigned; Elly Peterson, Ellie Guggenheimer and Connie Cook now stayed away. Martha McKay and others protested till the end, but most went along. Many months later, some of the women present at that meeting drove a hundred miles to my house in East Hampton, one summer midnight, to ask my help; they complained in confused, frustrated, helpless bitterness that the Women's Political Caucus was somehow being destroyed as any real vehicle for women's political independence. In 1975, lecturing in Little Rock, Arkansas, I was accosted by a woman saying, "You and I were on opposite sides that first year of the Women's Political Caucus. Unfortunately, you were right. It's become worse than nothing for women here."

I don't think that's true in every state. At the grass roots, the women in some states are still using the Women's Political Caucus for the purposes for which I helped organize it.

But nationally it seems to many as if the fix is in. If we had known then what was revealed when the Watergate "dirty tricks" were exposed, and the subsequent revelations of CIA's "Operation CHAOS" and the FBI's acknowledged, massive infiltration of the women's movement, I might not have dropped the matter so easily. Not knowing all this, I did not choose to take the case to court. I simply dropped out of all activity in behalf of the National Women's Political Caucus. I did not trust its integrity. Or to be more blunt, I was scared.

Political infighting is one thing; outright illegality, tampering with votes, contempt for ordinary standards of honesty, and intimidation that prevents protest or recourse to court or public opinion is something else. Above all, I felt helpless because the perpetrators of those "dirty tricks" were sister leaders of the women's movement, and sometimes they even got black or Chicana women to do the actual dirty work for them.

In fact, I was scared enough by the tactics used against me to stay away, for the next three years, from any confrontation whatsoever with Gloria Steinem or Bella Abzug. That meant, in effect, bowing out of politics, personally. Earlier, I had thought of running for Senator in '74 against Javits, or in '76 against Buckley. A number of people approached me about this. But as one of my male political friends put it, "I see the shadow of a certain large-brimmed hat." I didn't even want to fight that hat. I wonder now, if I hadn't ever talked, even half-seriously, about running for that Senate seat, whether the wearer of that hat (whose principles had never seemed all that different from mine) would have been so determined to blot me out of existence in the political arm of the women's movement which I had helped start, and to whose strength she owed her own access to power.

Those questions, those realities of political power, are things I and other women have been naïvely reluctant to face —especially about one another. I think we can face them in all their ugly, sweaty, human reality, and still make a case for electing women committed to women's interests and human priorities. A *case*, a moral, political case, in terms of democratic right and justice—but not a simple-minded, misty-eyed, mushy mystique that women are so much better than men that just electing them will clean up politics, or that women, by definition, will not use political power as men have always used it.

It's a matter of simple justice and political right that women share political power, share, as half the population, in the decisions that affect their future and their lives, and contribute their own voice—which is not the same as man's voice —to the decisions of the whole society. But in achieving such power and using it, women have to face the same realities as men do. It is better for women to share power in the open democratic mainstream, with all its dirty pressures and temptations and compromises and impossibly complex problems, than to be absolutely powerless—to be manipulated passively by others, or to wield power by covert manipulation of men, which has been women's only way in the past. But there is no guarantee that women will be any purer or less corrupt in their use of power than men.

At this particular moment in history, women, having been denied power so long, share a common political passion to have a voice in society's decisions, and to put on the agenda their own interests which have been ignored. I doubt that this will constitute women as any special political bloc once they begin to be elected in real numbers. Still, the mere election of women to constitute not a token 1 percent or 2 percent or 3 percent but a substantial third or more—if not yet their actual 53 percent—of any political body, will, it seems to me, almost automatically change its agenda in a more human direction. Not only, as I keep saying, because women are closer to the concrete realities of life, but because equality, the sex-role revolution, will also liberate men to concrete human experience and to sensitivities hitherto considered "feminine."

In the transition period, why should anyone be surprised if some of those previously powerless women turn out to be just as ruthless in their drive for power, or even more ruthless, than most men have to be? How many men in politics today are strong enough to risk the kind of honor women would demand of themselves? I might dislike Bella Abzug or kick myself for having been so easily outfoxed by her, but she, at least, has so far kept her faith to fight for the principles for which women elected her. And a woman still has to be so much more "qualified" than a man to get the nomination, to win the election, to be appointed to the governmental post, that she can be expected—for the immediate future, at least—to do a more conscientious, principled job, and to be more sensitive to the human reality of political decisions, than the political hacks still acceptable among men (though that is also changing?).

As for my recent personal disinterest in politics—I now see in that my own cowardice, my faintheartedness, my unwillingness to compete in a really rough fight (that timidity I share with other women), plus the political cynicism affecting us all after Watergate.

During those next few years I retreated to try to come to new terms with the political as personal, in my own life. I had already begun the process with my column in *McCall's*, "Betty Friedan's Notebook," in which I tried to share whatever visions I might have with other women and men—bowing out, at least temporarily, from the power struggle.

Afterword 1985— see page 497

PART III

Betty Friedan's Notebook

Struggling for Personal Truth

It's ironic, maybe, that I would use a mass woman's magazine like *McCall's*, that was (and is) still servicing 8,000,000 women with the staples of fashion, beauty, home decor, child care, entertaining, cooking, and making men happy, to test the rhetoric of the women's movement against my personal truth. But it seemed a personal dead end to keep on battling within the organized "women's lib" movement against other leaders whose rhetoric seemed to be getting further and further away from the reality of women. Not that I wanted to go back, or to turn my back on the women's movement. It had been important, necessary, to do what we did. As more and more women kept saying to me, "It changed my life." But just as in the beginning I felt alone in my uneasy nameless doubts about the feminine mystique, so in the early seventies, I seemed alone, at first, in a certain uneasy discomfort with the new feminist ideology. It began to seem more and more detached from the life and problems and feelings, old and new, of real women.

So from late 1970 to 1973, I went back to my beginnings as a writer, to make new notes on my personal experience, which now included the women's movement. But if I was going to be really honest, my life also included those traditional aspects of women's experience—clothes, food, home decor, entertaining, hairdos, kids and even happiness with men—which "women's lib" ignored. I wanted to deal with the whole of our changing lives; those traditional parts couldn't stay the same, but I couldn't just leave them out, either. The movement rhetoric was fueled by and expressed our personal rage when we were saying no to sex discrimination, but it gave no answers to the new problems I was now facing in my own life—the economic burdens of supporting a single-parent family, the loneliness, the need for new roots and new patterns of living. I had no answers, but once again I moved to share the experience and the new questions as honestly as I could with other women.

I was often asked why I was writing such a column for an "Establishment" magazine like *McCall's*, instead of for *Ms.*, which was launched at about the same time by Gloria Steinem, and was being proclaimed as the organ of "women's lib." But it didn't interest me to talk to the already convinced, especially within the framework of a new kind of feminist conformity, which seemed to me in its way as denying to women's reality as the old feminine mystique.

I always saw the women's movement as a movement of the mainstream of American society—moving women into and thus changing that mainstream. I was interested in writing for those 8,000,000 woman's magazine readers, the suburban housewives, the women who had children and/or jobs, with husbands or without, who still had to deal with housekeeping, meals, and clothes as I did, even as we also now took ourselves more seriously as people. I'm very glad now I wrote those columns during those three years after I stepped down as president of NOW. It not only helped pay for my groceries, it gave me a way to continue to recruit women to the basic goals of equality—to say "you don't have to hate men and renounce motherhood to be a liberated woman"—and thus to help build the women's movement in the largest sense. It also gave me a forum to develop my own ideology—which is perhaps the ideology of the mainstream of the women's movement—without wasting my energies fighting the extremists who were co-opting the image of "women's lib."

I was, of course, struggling to find a new tone of voice as a writer, a more personal tone. I had to climb down off that soapbox to find the only authority I now could claim—that of my own experience. Rereading those columns of "Betty Friedan's Notebook" now, I am struck by how tentatively I raised questions, hinted at doubts that, if expressed more strongly then, might have averted the current crisis that seems to threaten the future of the women's movement. But the conformity the movement itself was beginning to impose intimidated me, as it did other women. I only hinted at certain doubts, for fear I would be "crucified," as my sisters kept warning me I would be, if I spoke them louder. And perhaps no one would have heard, then, even if I had. Maybe we were afraid to question any part of our monolithic "no," for fear our whole new strength found in battle would crumble. We didn't trust our own strength enough to face our real weaknesses—or to accept certain realities of women's existence without having to be chained by them, or feeling weakened thereby.

It was during the brief period in *McCall's'* history that it was headed by women—Shana Alexander and Pat Carbine—that I was asked to write a column for it, on the assumption that the women's movement was now part of every woman's experience in America, and thus that the Middle American readers of *McCall's* would identify with my words. When Shana was removed and Pat Carbine left to manage *Ms.*, my old colleague and editor-adversary, Bob Stein, took over and decided, as he had years ago about *The Feminine Mystique*, that the women out there "would not identify." He stopped my column unless I got a headline-scoop like the interview with the Pope. Still, I don't believe *all men* are incapable of sharing or of understanding women's new consciousness. I have never been edited as sensitively, and respectfully, as I was by Don McKinney, who edited my column during my three years with *McCall's*.

The problems I was beginning to face, no matter how tentatively, in those columns were more serious than I let even myself know, then. I thought we could surmount the divisions in the movement and somehow keep marching together every year on August 26th until we finished that unfinished business of equality. The momentum of our victories those years was so great—who could predict the dismay with which we now confront layoffs, backlash, and the resistance to the Equal Rights Amendment? I didn't realize how difficult it would be to surmount the polarities, the hatreds, the timidities and self-distrust—in our personal lives and in the movement. Some of those new marriages I wrote about did not in fact survive. It wasn't any easier to keep a communal "extended family of choice" together. That "new human politics" is still a distant dream. The extremists who want to take the women's movement "out of the mainstream into the revolution" have now taken over NOW.

A footnote to the feminist myopia: at one point Cynthia Epstein and sister sociologists went to see the editors of *Ms.* to try and persuade them to include "service" features on food, fashion, and home, like other women's magazines, to help liberated women find the new patterns they were needing in those areas of life. "After all, sometimes I am more interested in a new idea for my living room than a rehash of what I already know about sex discrimination," said the distinguished young author of *Women's Place.* But the editors of *Ms.* were shocked at the very notion of including "service" to the housewife in the liberated columns of *Ms.!*

What happened, I think, is that many women who, like me, saw the folly of such pseudo-radical smugness, retreated from active participation in movement organizations. Rather than fight the extremists, we concentrated on our own careers and gave personal or professional service to the movement, in the larger sense, but abandoned its organizational leadership to the extremists. We should all have faced our own fears and rage and weaknesses and doubts more honestly. Then we might not have been so blind to the fears of other women, who need the movement's strength as much as we do, but are now being manipulated by its enemies.

"Everything I know has come from my own experience."

I have to decide now: do I really want to do a magazine column? I have some qualms. I must make it clear that I have no intention of giving up my revolutionary credentials by tying in with the feminine mystique Establishment. I have warned them I'll be saying things they won't agree with. Some of the things I want to say were painful enough for me to face in my own life. For women in their thirties and forties who have patterned their entire lives on the idea that fulfillment can only come as wives and mothers, it has been painful, sometimes *too* painful, to endure the terrors and risks of finding their own personhood now. The longer we have been dependent, the more we have somehow used that dependence to evade risks and challenges that would enable us to trust our own strengths and capabilities. It's easier for the young. But it's also easier for them to fall into traps of pseudo-radical rhetoric, because they haven't experienced enough of the realities of life as a woman. This revolution will be carried by the spirit of the young, but if left to them alone, it might never be more than just rhetoric.

There are no blueprints for our revolution, not from Karl Marx or any of the other ideologues of exploited classes, for the relationship of woman to man is not the same as that of worker to boss, of oppressed to oppressor, of black to white. We can only find our blueprint from our own unique experience.

In the urgency of this moment, I feel the need to deal with the new questions women must confront today, and to deal with them in the context of my own life. It was only a few years ago that women felt freakish, guilty and absolutely alone because of feelings that we now know millions of us share. It's been comforting to know that we are no longer alone, to talk out loud to each other about problems and feelings we hadn't even dared to face in ourselves. But it's still easier to talk about it or write about it in the abstract than to face the implications of those words in one's own life. Frankly, I don't think we will be able to work out these problems in our own individual lives until we make basic changes in society. If we don't seize the opportunity to make these changes now, I'm even more afraid of a feminine backlash than a masculine backlash. Our revolution would abort.

So many words are being written now, so many blueprints and theories for women's liberation: this whole revolution could drown in a revulsion against rhetoric. What women need now is a true politics of experience, a politics so firmly rooted in the life experience of women that it can change the possibilities of life for all women.

In a nation as big as this, change happens through the mass media. Women have to use the media, not just be used by it. The bra-burning image which enables people to dismiss us as a silly joke can be replaced by the image we make of ourselves.

I used to think I could keep my personal experience and my ideas in separate compartments. Now I realize that everything I know has come from my own experience. And if my words are going to affect other women, then I should share the experience on which those words are based.

To begin with, I am a revolutionary. This revolution is not exactly what anyone else ever meant by the word, but it will transform society in ways more radical and more life-enhancing than any other. I also happen to be an American pragmatist, "Middle American," if you will, since I did grow up in Peoria, Illinois. I think we have the power to make this revolution happen now, the power of 53 percent of us who are women, along with the growing number of men who support us. Will I be co-opted, do I dare confront fresh, urgent questions in a woman's magazine whose advertising and contents mix the old recipe of fashion, decor, food and can-this-marriage-be-saved?

Well, I will risk it. It will either be a historic clash, or will help record and create our new *her* story. But I would be bored to write only about women's liberation. Women now are as involved with the life-and-death questions of war and peace, the crisis of the planet and our cities, the unknowns of theology and art and space, as they are, still, with food and children and home. I believe the women's liberation movement cannot remain isolated from everything else that's happening in the world today; the liberation of women is not irrelevant, but germane to the agony of our whole time: until we free ourselves and men from the obsolete sex roles that imprison us both, the hostility between the sexes will continue to inflame the violence of our nation.

It's time to face the problems in our own movement honestly. All these navel-gazing rap sessions about trapped housewives and the meanness of male chauvinist pigs, the comparisons of orgasms, the discussions about how worthless we feel

—in the end it's just wallowing in a soap opera. Deliver us from self-pity so that we can deliver ourselves from wasting time on nonproblems or from getting stuck in reactionary symptoms instead of changing the situation. Some worry that we'll lose our femininity and our men if we get equality. Since femininity is being a woman and feeling good about it, clearly the better you feel about yourself as a person, the better you feel about being a woman. And, it seems to me, the better you are able to love a man.

The pseudo-radicals talk about getting rid of love, sex, children, and men. I happen to like many men, love some, and think a one-sex world would be very boring. This is a *two*-sex revolution or it isn't anything. Even a male chauvinist like Norman Mailer is beginning to try to understand us.

The other night, reading D. H. Lawrence's *Women in Love,* I came across words that expressed exactly what I want to do in this column. Written in the foreword to his work fifty years ago, only the word *man* has to be changed to *woman* to convey my meaning: "We are now in a period of crisis. Every *woman* who is acutely alive is wrestling with her own soul. The people that can bring forth the new passion, the new idea, *this* people will endure. Those others, that fix themselves in the old idea, will perish with the new life strangled unborn within them. *Women* must speak out to one another."

* * *

I am asked to speak on November 11 at a monastery near West Point by the Graymoor Friars on "The Meaning of Women's Liberation for the Church." About five hundred priests and nuns are there. The only subject that made them uneasy was abortion. The Roman Catholic bishops of the state of New York had just been ordered to preach a sermon threatening excommunication to any woman who gets an abortion or to anyone who helps her get one. This was a direct order to the state legislators to take back the law women had fought for and won, giving women the right to medical help in abortion if they decide for any reason not to have a child in the first six months of pregnancy. I am tired of organizing marches, but we have to do something to make visible the power of women, to excommunicate legislators who would deny them this basic freedom.

●   ●   ●

I go into a Madison Avenue tea shop to get out of the rain after having my hair done. I look up and see a very distinguished-looking man at the next table, watching me. He reminds me that we met last winter at Bel Kaufman's party. We talk; I hope he calls me. I share a cab home from Magazine Writers with Helen, who has just started getting a divorce. She talks the way I felt, only two years ago. I hadn't the slightest idea what it would be like being divorced. I was so scared of the loneliness, it took me five years to get the courage to do it. (What a phony—Joan of Arc for American women and a miserable cowardly worm in my own life.)

●   ●   ●

My fourteen-year-old daughter Emily and I go to visit my younger son Jonathan in his room at Columbia. I have been scrupulous about not barging in on him since he got his room at the dorm. He likes his courses at Columbia, his teachers, his friends; but he doesn't like being in the same city as his family. He's asked for a few items—knives, forks and spoons, a rug and a table—which we bring him. Then Emily and I go shopping. I buy two long paisley dresses, cheap and colorful, and Emily buys minis of the same material. It's the first time we've shopped together on equal terms, and it was fun for both of us, I think.

I must say I like the freedom and adventurousness these long skirts give. You don't have to worry that your underwear will show, or suffer the indignity of feeling you're trying to look the same age as your daughter. I think that as women get more liberated, they are going to have more and more fun with fashion, instead of worrying slavishly about it. The way a woman dresses, treats her body, is a very basic reflection of the way she feels about herself. I'm in too much of a hurry and not adept enough to waste time on false eyelashes, and I'm damned if I'll torture myself with a tight girdle. But it wasn't women's liberation that started all that, not consciously, at least. Tights are so much more comfortable than girdles and stockings; eliminating bras that cut into your flesh is liberating. Still, I don't know of any woman who ever really burned a bra.

Walking home with Emily, I realize how lonesome it is at

the apartment now, with both boys gone. The divorce didn't end family life as much as the boys leaving. I won't be away so much, now that I'm doing the column, but even when I'm home there's not enough life, just the two of us here. I suppose that's really why I got the idea of the commune last spring, all of us sharing that great big house in the country, on weekends. . . .

· · ·

Señora Cuevas, the ambassador to the UN General Assembly from Colombia, comes for tea on November 17. The UN Hospitality Committee had been calling for months asking if I'd see her. She's one of only four women with the rank of ambassador among the thousands of delegates to the UN General Assembly. Since I don't know Spanish, I ask Jacqui to come and translate. Jacqui is worried about ugly problems in the movement, but she will make a fine president for New York NOW. Señora Cuevas wants my advice on how to start a women's liberation movement in her country: how to begin, the issues involved, etc. I think about all the women from different countries who've been coming to see me with these questions. It occurs to me we should have a world event, in a year or so, to help women in every country feel stronger. I read in a recent poll that far more women in America than men would simply pull the troops out of Cambodia and Vietnam, period. Maybe it would make a difference to the whole world if women had more political power.

· · ·

I meet with the Steering Committee of the Women's Strike Coalition and NOW members about a march to dramatize the abortion crisis and the need for child-care centers. I have been trying to think of some new way to translate our tremendous energy and power into action, and I had called a meeting to continue the coalition of women that had finally come together in our August 26th Strike for Equality. There had been a big attendance, but so much silly hair-splitting. Some women didn't want to use the word "liberation" because of the "bra-burning" image. Others objected to the word "equality"; they didn't want to be "equal" to men, just "liberated" as women. There was something about the largeness of the action last summer that brought us over these difficulties. This is not the same. Maybe it's my fault. I haven't had time to stay on top of this one. I have a feeling that just another march doesn't really lead anywhere. Still, we must do something about this threat to the abortion law.

* * * *

Thanksgiving at the commune is hilarious. Dick's three children come in from San Francisco and there are Martha's two, and Emily, and Arthur's Matthew, who's three years old now. We turn one of the biggest bedrooms into a dormitory for the six children, wall-to-wall sleeping bags. We are not used, any of us, to ordering the quantities of food this communal life requires. Dick and Martha made a roast that looked like half a cow, and not even enough leftovers remained for a sandwich. I have dreaded holidays lately. Without a big enough family for gaiety, holidays can be terrible. But this, all of us in our various states of nonmarriage, with our progeny of various ages, is almost magic. How can such strong individualists like each other even better after six months of sharing a house than we did in the beginning? The generation gap seems not to exist. The kids develop such different relationships with various adults besides their parents. Emily blossoms in a way I haven't noticed before, with Arthur's nice gallantry toward her. She and Sally are joining forces: at last, a friend who also has an embarrassingly unconventional mother.

Halfway through the weekend, I am given a lecture about not having carried my weight with the household chores. Feeling guilty, I offer to clean up after lunch, and, martyr, do all the pots and pans while the others go for walks. Barclay, age ten, worried that my feelings are hurt, tells me it doesn't matter if I'm not very good at cleaning up, because I "contribute morale."

Is it because the children share the chores at the commune or is it the lack of conflict and irritation from close confinement with your own small family that makes this kind of new family life so unexpectedly delightful? Of course, we are not a real commune. We don't pool our incomes or have group sex, and we shut our private bedroom doors. But the ties that are being created by this extended intimacy of our new lifestyle are real: an extended family of choice.

·   ·   ·

I have dinner with that new man. It is strange and exciting
—going to museum or a concert, even taking a walk with him,
a man over fifty shouting poetry on a deserted winter beach,
and following reindeer tracks. He knows so many things I
don't, like electronic music, and his views are beautifully ec-
centric. But I can't talk short-hand with him, as with Si, or feel
what he is feeling, as with David. I must say, my second adolescence is much more fun than my first was. It's fun relating
to men in ways I didn't while I was married, and would have
been too insecure to before I was married. Or maybe I was too
anxious to get married to really relax and enjoy the relationships with men before.

·   ·   ·

We have the abortion march on December 12, or rather
what was supposed to be the abortion march. In a freezing wet
sleet storm, only duty forced me out. Still, several hundred
people came. Kate Millett was the first speaker; I was to be the
last. But instead of talking about abortion and child-care centers, which is what the march was supposed to be about, she
talked about lesbianism. Women I didn't know were handing
out lavender armbands and leaflets saying that since Kate had
been called a lesbian, all women must show their solidarity by
becoming, in effect, "political lesbians." Nobody had told me
anything about this.

Without the purple armband, I climb up on the sound
truck and warn that to let this movement be diverted would
lead to divisiveness that would destroy it. I think this is more
than political expedience. I have experienced the good moments of really knowing a man, as well as a bad marriage, and
good moments with my own children and others; if liberation,
equality, personhood for women is worth fighting for, it can't
be at the price of these other goods. Maybe sexual politics are
even more anti-women than they are anti-men. Or are they
anti-life?

·   ·   ·

I wake up on New Year's Eve at the commune with a sense
of well-being that I can't remember feeling for years, or
maybe ever. And on New Year's Eve, which has always been
so traumatic somehow, I don't feel helpless, in a fog, tossed by

or dependent on any external agent any more. I suddenly realize that if I'm not miserable and shrinking inside—as I have felt, no matter what my outward show, the last few years—it's because I did risk making some decisions to change the possibilities of my own life. I have no idea where it will end. I'm not about to leave the movement, but for the first time in years I want to write again. Some women are still afraid of change, the ones who talk the radical rhetoric cop-out on the responsibility for making change happen now. What we need are serious politics, not sexual politics, to organize ourselves, to really use our power.

I get sick of being serious all the time. When I suddenly realize what has to be done next, it seems impossibly big, and why should I feel responsible? Still, it's fun, making a revolution happen. How many months do we have until the '72 elections . . . ?

"What's the point of making it if you can't celebrate being fifty?"

In the hectic last and only day I have given myself to get organized before leaving for Europe, I suddenly realize I don't have a will. Not that I'm afraid of flying; I used to be—terrified—from takeoff to landing. But after I finished writing *The Feminine Mystique*, for some strange reason, my fear of flying disappeared. I just wasn't afraid any more. Still, statistically speaking, I'm bound to die in an airplane crash the way I travel these days (better than a vegetative old age!).

Between airplanes, as it were, I rush into my lawyer's office and sign a will, for the kids. So many details, i's undotted, unfinished business. Sometimes I feel like a mother with a million children, all crying "Help!" Paged in the airport, landing from the last lecture in Florida: an SOS from the people in New York NOW, panicky in their agonizing struggle to remove the man-haters from leadership. A delegation from Columbia Women's Liberation wants to talk about the sexual red herring that threatens to divide the movement. SOS's from the Women's Strike Coalition about the abortion crisis. And Emily has decided she wants to go to boarding school. How can I possibly arrange for her to visit schools and get the applications in while I'm gone? To say nothing of my desk piled up with mail I haven't even had time to open.

Suddenly I remember I don't have to do it all myself. I can't afford a full-time secretary, but Sally can dot some of those i's. Lovely, efficient, much too intelligent to be a secretary for long, Sally is willing to moonlight for me after her job, take care of the most urgent questions, at least: that invitation to speak at the New Democratic Coalition conference—is it to speak at a plenary session, which means they understand the new political significance of women; or is it the usual token attention, segregation of all the women speakers in a sexual-ghetto woman's rights workshop that nobody takes seriously?

As for my kids, Danny may like being asked to take the responsibility of putting Emily up at his pad while I'm gone, and driving her to New England to look at boarding schools. (The next trip, though, I'm going to schedule for school vacation and take her along. Why not?) As for the problems in the movement, there are so many now to share the responsibility of leadership. This time I'm going to Europe with a free conscience.

From a personal point of view, these foreign invitations are the most exciting bonus that's happened to me. Until five years ago, I had never even been out of the United States. First the war, then little babies and no money, then guilt and conflict over foreign assignments because of Carl's hostility. Now, I'm free to see the world: I have made a deal with my Calvinistic conscience—for each foreign city I am sent to for the movement, I can give myself one foreign city for fun. I have given myself Paris and Rome; this time, I could go to London after I'm through in Holland.

But I'm not in the mood, really. The fact is, that week I will have my fiftieth birthday, which, I'm ashamed to admit, I dread. I can't seem to come to terms with it. Me, who's never worried about age or tried to hide it; me, who's been so scornful of women who dye their hair, have their faces lifted, let themselves be hoodwinked by advertisers into buying all those products supposed to make them look forever fifteen.

I don't want to look fifteen, but it just doesn't seem real that I'm going to be fifty. I don't feel as old now as I did in my twenties and thirties, my "feminine mystique" days, when I was always so afraid. Afraid of life; afraid to move. And then in my forties, writing my book, starting the movement, moving into the city, *moving* finally. Making decisions. The divorce. Finding new kinds of relationships with men, meeting new challenges with women, finding new strengths, delights in myself, opening new doors. I felt more like eighteen than when I really was eighteen. But it's clearly ridiculous for a woman to feel like eighteen when she's going to be fifty. Do I want to cross this traumatic divide in London, a strange city where I know no one, with not even the usual press of work to help me evade the fear of being alone?

.   .   .

The gray, dread mood lasts all through Holland. Press conference at the airport, TV, speeches, applause, publishers, publicists, cafés, banquets, all the hullabaloo and glamour. Even the beauty of Amsterdam, the canals, the faces out of Rembrandt, the trees and flat fields of Van Gogh, leave me cold. I perform okay, I guess: automatic gears can take over when you've done it so many times. The last morning, professional business done, I join the young "Angry Minas," the spirited new Dutch women's liberation movement members, on a barge through the canals—my first naval battle of the women's revolution. They are protesting the criminal laws which force women pregnant against their will to smuggle themselves out to England for medical help. Instead of our kind of march in the streets, they demonstrate by boat. I love the spirit and the style of the young Minas, and the men and children on the barge with them. Stuffing pillows under their coats to look pregnant (even the men), they sing words to a Dutch nursery rhyme that seem to mean "boss over your own belly." It's all very good-natured, but the prosperous Dutch Saturday shoppers get off their bikes, lean over the bridge rails to stare, smile—and listen. We pass a bank building on the main canal, which the Minas have "liberated" to be a child-care center. Instead of putting them in jail, the government decided to make the day-care center a pilot project for the whole country. My sullen, sulking spirit wakes up enough to wonder why this nation of pompous, stuffy Dutch burghers has spawned so many of these new human revolutions. The Provos, the first hippies; the humanistic revolution in the Catholic Church; an approach to sex as simply a human activity, an approach that prevents persecution of anyone, including homosexuals, for private behavior. And England is even farther ahead in a human approach to abortion, divorce, sex, medical care, aging, blood banks. All the power of those empires couldn't stop the advancing tide of people rising up in India, Indonesia. Was the death of empire they so feared the birth process of this new greening life: Provos, existential priests, Minas, these light-hearted humanist radicals that eschew rage and bombs? I decide to go on to London.

·   ·   ·

As it turns out, London isn't strange and lonely, at all. The names and places—Charing Cross, Picadilly, Waterloo Station, St. James Park—are ones I grew up reading about. My favorite books in childhood were *Five Children and It*, and *The Bastable Children*. The sense of oldness, the beautiful green squares of parks—like time rolling back in Berkeley Square—and again the sense of something new in the human pace of London, as if they are already on a frontier we're only just beginning to cross.

I uncover roots of my own in London, the kind of roots I think people will be sustained by in the future. Roots that grow, not in a place in earth, but out of human connection. I'm taken to my first pub and then given a glorious literary dinner party by Hilary, who bought my book for England after seeing one chapter in rough draft—the very first sign that my book was any good at all. Connection: I learn from Livia Gollancz, the woman who now heads Gollancz, Ltd., that it was also special for them. Mine was the first book they bought on their own as the young takeover generation in that publishing house. Now I haven't even a book for them to sell. Why should Liz Calder, their publicist, spend her lunch hours pulling London ropes for me? Connection: "I wouldn't be here if I hadn't read your book. It changed my life." I have tea with Alma Birk, who looks five years younger than when she came to see me five years ago in New York about British women's need to move. Now she's a lifetime peer, named by the

Queen "Baroness Birk of Regent's Park" for her pioneering
work as a lawyer in divorce reform and sex education; a member of the "meritocracy" that will soon outnumber the old
aristocracy in the House of Lords, as even that ancient British
institution evolves into something new. Tea in her house,
where H. G. Wells and Rebecca West once lived, has so many
interruptions from Alma's political phone calls that I feel we
are still on the same wavelength, exploding now. She invites
me to the House of Lords for the drug debate the next day,
February 4. I don't tell her it's my birthday.

I get up early for an interview at the BBC. Word is passed
to me through what seems to be a women's underground at
the TV station that leaders of the British women's liberation
movement (whose phones haven't answered since I arrived)
know that I have been looking for them and are waiting for
me right now in a loft they have just rented over a pawnshop.
By the time I find that loft, I feel like Sherlock Holmes. The
confusion, the determination, and the problems of the housewives with their shopping bags and the young girls in blue
jeans dropping in at that loft, the flyers, the phones you can't
get through to—even their worries are so familiar—we speak
plainly as sisters.

From that loft of women's liberation, improvising out of
makeshift, to the House of Lords—culture shock. In the Peers'
Gallery, I revert to pure American, reveling in, revolted by,
the pomp and circumstance. (Unless my eyes deceive me, the
privy-type toilet bowl in the ladies' john was actually lined
with gold.) Men in wigs, gold chains hanging from stiff black-
tailed costumes, Oxford accents addressing Cockney accents as
"noble Lords," and accusing each other of betraying the last
bastions of British power—Rolls-Royce has just gone into
bankruptcy. George Brown, former Labour Foreign Minister
(evidently retired upstairs to the House of Lords), bellows and
thunders about the disgrace to British business, with hardly a
mention of the workers who will be out of jobs. (Will women
be co-opted as easily as labor leaders?) The Queen's ministers
of war and defense, cabinet members, tycoons, retired generals and labor leaders, even bishops are wringing their hands
helplessly, incredulous, positively peeved that Rolls-Royce,

symbol of solid British power, should fail. It's as if the world of men and machines is crumbling before my eyes.

Then the drug debate resumes, and Michael Foote, mild-spoken former newspaperman, Alma, several other women peers, a famous black football hero of the new "meritocracy," and a long-haired, very young hereditary peer who has researched the medical data on marijuana propose laws to face the reality of youth and drugs in Britain. Some rather decrepit-looking relics of the "white man's burden" empire days in Burma and Ceylon rant and rave about the depravity of British youth. They give me the same feeling of being out of touch with human reality as our own politicans of the Agnew stripe, denouncing the hairs on the heads of their own sons with the same fastidious accuracy as they total the corpses from the Vietnam war. Is it a generation gap? Or is the real gap between the men across the generations who are somehow able to embrace life and its evolution and the fearful ones who try to hold back change and then, in impotent rage, finally vote for death?

The House of Lords "divides" physically to vote; human values seem to be winning here. But it isn't just the women and the young; except for those pompous, ranting empire relics, so many men, even in this bastion of the British Establishment, seem to have gone beyond *machismo*, the "masculine mystique." They don't even pretend to rattle sabers, hunt tigers any more.

The Cambridge philosophers, M.P.'s and detective-story writers at Hilary's dinner party unabashedly let their sensitivity show, and don't seem at all threatened by their brilliant wives. Hilary actually boasted, introducing me to Shirley Williams, M.P. in Wilson's shadow cabinet, that she would be England's first woman Prime Minister. If in liberating American women we also liberate our men from that blustering world-power *machismo* that keeps us courting death in Vietnam, we could make our cities green and beautiful and human, like London. We could make our blood banks and medical care, abortion and marriage laws human. We might even begin to have human sex—and really human politics. England is an older nation, but it doesn't seem about to die to me. In fact, they seem less afraid of life and change than we do.

• • •

I rush back to my hotel to change for dinner with John Wren-Lewis and Ann Faraday, connections within connections. My friend Al Toffler's fellow futurists turn out to be the leaders of the new humanistic British psychology. We compare our different roads to the same end. For me, I guess, women's liberation is only a way station to human liberation: embracing all we are, human body, spirit, mind, is finally the same, woman and man. This is the road I think the young are heading down. On this road, maybe there isn't a generation gap, or even fear and envy between young and old.

I end the night having a drink with the movie producer who introduced himself to me in the hotel lounge the first day. Connection: his son was in school with Danny. He's been asking me to have dinner with him. I'm sorry now I didn't. Drinking brandy at 1 A.M. with this nice man, I suddenly remember what day it was, and can't help laughing. I have gotten over my fiftieth birthday. I'm fifty on this magic day in this age of Aquarius. I'm my age and I feel glorious. What's the point of making it if you can't celebrate being fifty? I celebrate putting it all together finally, this half-century that's me, all of it, pains and roots in Peoria, Jewish ancestors, college triumphs, the good days and the bad of my marriage, my kids, the labor pains of writing, mistakes personal and political, the net I've cast for "herstory"—and what I am today: my body, as it is, is me. I celebrate using it all, finally—my passions of sex and spirit, my guts and vulnerability and glee for life. "What's the joke?" David asks. "It was my fiftieth birthday today," I say. "It was a magic day." I have no dread now of what opens ahead.

" 'Go home, Yankee lady! Stop stirring up our women!' "

It starts like a farce or a tragicomedy. *The Feminine Mystique* is going to be published in Brazil; the publisher wants me to come down and help start a women's liberation movement there. Thinking that he must be kidding, I write that I've been away from home too much this year; I don't want to leave my daughter again. The publisher cables, "SENDING TICKETS YOU AND DAUGHTER." Emily likes the idea of spring vacation in Brazil; she has never been out of the United States. I write Eric Seiff, my friend who's Counsel to the Agency for International Development in Brazil, asking if it is safe to come with Emily, with all the kidnapping of foreigners, etc. He says, "What ransom could they get for you? A pad of yellow legal-size paper?" and invites us to stay with them. I leave ahead of time to go to a psychological conference on the Yucatan coast of Mexico, getting shots at the last minute. Emily, who's to join me in Mexico in a week, will have to bring my health card and the tickets for Brazil, which still hadn't come yet when I left.

I love Yucatan, the mystery of the ruins at Chichen Itza; even try my hand at snorkeling with the equally nonathletic psychologists and psychoanalysts at this funny international conference on Isla Mujeres ("Island of Women"). But the telephone lines are always down here, reminding me of New York. No way to check that Emily is getting off okay. Saturday morning, about to leave for the airport to pick her up, I'm summoned to the phone, which is temporarily working. Emily is crying, in Miami. They won't let her into Mexico because she's a minor and doesn't have a letter from both her parents. Mexican bureaucratic red tape, worse than ours, dictates that nothing can be done till Monday. The phone is about to go dead again. I tell Emily to go to a relative's home in Miami, and I will phone her from Mexico City. At the airport at Isla Mujeres, they tell me I can take off right away in a little non-scheduled airplane. I get into the airplane. The pilot starts— but it doesn't. A boy is sent into the "terminal" for a bottle of Coke. They pour it into the engine. I begin to sweat. It's very hot. Then another boy comes and they start to *push* the plane. "Let me out of here," I scream, hysterical American lady. Collapsing an hour later into the regular plane, feeling strangely airsick, I see the boys pushing my former vehicle, which suddenly, raucously, takes off.

On the flight to Mexico City, I seem to get sicker and sicker. Is it airsickness or guilt at letting my little daughter fly alone, her mother on another continent? When I call her from

Mexico City, that helpless little daughter has already figured out that we can meet in Panama, has found an airline I never heard of and made us both reservations, and turned the tickets in to get the appropriate refunds. But since she has my ticket to Brazil, and I don't have enough money on me to buy another, they will only check my baggage to Panama. I have to fill out a tourist card to enter Panama in order to reclaim it. Airsickness gets worse. At Panama Airport: no Emily. Because I have the tourist card, I must go through immigration, but with no health card, I'm taken into quarantine to get typhoid, yellow fever and cholera shots. I protest, "It's a mistake! I'm not entering Panama, just rechecking my baggage on the plane to Rio!" So they ask for my ticket to Rio, which of course I don't have. Then, miraculously, I see Emily waving frantically outside the airport door, and I rush across the corridor, whistles blowing shrilly behind me. Just as the army, navy or whatever of Panama catches up to me, I stick my arm out the door—"The ticket, quick!"—and she hands it to me. But now, surely suspected of being an international spy smuggling a bomb or heroin, I'm taken into custody in earnest, under guard in a small room. I have the proof I am indeed en route to Rio de Janeiro, but I don't have the Spanish to explain it, and these suspicious Panamanian officials are much too excited now to understand my English.

The plane is almost due to leave. I have visions of ending my life in a Panamanian jail with my poor daughter stranded without money in this God-forsaken place. Suddenly, into the room marches my enterprising fifteen-year-old daughter, who has somehow convinced an English-speaking official that her poor mother is in trouble. He gets us and our luggage onto the plane for Rio just in time. I'm so happy and relieved to have Emily there that I immediately scold her for traveling in torn blue jeans or some such irritable token of my affection. By now the airsickness is unstoppable because it obviously isn't airsickness but some Mexican bug let in by my weakened state of mother-worry. I get off the plane at Rio and Sari Seiff takes my corpse and luggage and Emily to their lovely quiet house. It is near the Govia beach, with the mountains behind and the huge statue of Jesus brooding on the top of the mountain over us all.

The Seiffs, with whom I had only expected to stay for a day or so, cope with the publisher, who doesn't want me to see the reporters until next week, and the reporters who recognized me at the airport and tracked me down, and introduce Emily to the neighborhood teenagers, and get the friendly doctor from the embassy to cure the tropical disease I'm evidently not going to die of. When they're not home, their three children under ten translate the Portuguese for me. I adopt all the Seiffs into my extended family. Emily takes off for the beach with the other teenagers. I decide to live.

· · ·

Rio de Janeiro is so incredibly beautiful—South America, this whole continent about which I, like most Americans, have been illiterate, incurious, comes alive for me, becomes real. I have four days before my official schedule begins, to get the sense of women's situation here. I'm used to being my own "advance woman," as it's called in politics. I usually get filled in on the ride from the airport or at dinner with the faculty committee before I speak at a U.S. campus or city. But I cannot conceive of the women in a country like Brazil feeling as we do here. I feel guilty that the publisher is wasting his money giving Emily and me this vacation in Brazil.

· · ·

The first Brazilian women I meet are Sari's friends and neighbors. In their hushed, sun-shaded houses on this tropical suburban street with their young children in school, they are like the women in my former suburb, whose hesitant, haunting expressions of "the problem that had no name" started me on the trail that led to the movement. Only these women in Brazil—M'Lou, Rosalie, Nelia and the others—didn't quit college to marry and have their four or five children; they quit high school. And now M'Lou, after dropping her children off to school, goes back to finish high school herself so that she can go on to the Catholic University and become a psychologist. She says, "I was doing what women are supposed to do to be happy, but I was not alive. I feel as if I had been born again." She does indeed look alive, quite different from the faces I see in the fancy Brazilian beauty parlor where I go before the press hoopla begins; with their hair teased, eye make-up and false eyelashes in place at 10 A.M., they seem somehow dead from the neck up. The husband of one of the women going back to school, a successful engineer, tells me, smiling, "It's just a fad. They will get over it." But they have to work too hard for it to be dismissed as a fad.

•   •   •

I go to the *favela*, the famous slum in the middle of Rio. It is on the mountainside overlooking the sea, tucked between the neighborhoods of fashionable houses, a complex, powerful community of people who suddenly appear from the country looking for jobs in the city, who squat on this mountainside and build their shacks out of scraps of wood and tin. Without at all romanticizing poverty, I realize that with running water and electricity and plumbing, these houses in the *favela* would be much pleasanter to live in than the monolithic, isolating, antiseptic high rises that make life so unnecessarily barren for both rich and poor in our cities. I hope they improve what they have in this beautiful Brazilian city and don't follow our example of evicting the poor in the name of urban renewal, making our cities crumbling office ghettos that are somehow antilife for women and children.

My guide, Rose Marie Muraro—a scientist, a businessman's wife, the mother of children about the age of mine, and the leading feminist of Brazil—has arranged for a nun who works in this *favela* to get several of the women together for coffee with me. One is black, one is light brown, and one white in the racial mix that is taken for granted in Brazil. All had their first children at ages thirteen, fourteen, fifteen; they have five or six or seven children now, and are already grandmothers in their early thirties. The hostess does the laundry for four families in Rio, besides looking after her own seven children. She cleans and washes in the water she has to carry up in a bucket from the single pump at the foot of the mountain that serves this *favela*. Her husband, who makes about the same money she does as a janitor in an office building, is not expected to help her at all, not even in carrying the water. She's lucky that he hasn't left her. Many men do leave home, in this land of no birth control, when the third child is followed by the fourth and then the fifth, and the economic burden becomes intolerable.

Rose Marie explains who I am and asks the women if they

think a woman's movement is needed here. They begin to chatter excitedly; I gather they are saying yes. What would make your daughters' lives better than yours? I ask. Rose Marie translates their answer: "Birth control and education; otherwise, they will always be slaves." And she shrugs, disclaiming responsibility, because she has been so insistent that I must not even talk about issues such as abortion in this Catholic country. The nun then tells me that she does the work of a priest in this *favela*, teaching, doing health and social work—community organizing, really. But like all the other nun-priests, she doesn't celebrate the Mass. The priest, a man, must come in every month to celebrate the Mass. "I don't think that's fair," she says, as if she's saying it out loud for the first time. When I go out the door, the women from the *favela*, including the nun, clutch on to Rose Marie. They say, "She will go back to the United States, but you will stay here, and why can we not do what they are doing . . . ?"

• • •

The press conference is almost frightening. Many more reporters and cameras and microphones than I possibly would have expected in such a country. I've been warned that they will be hostile and brutal and treat the whole thing as a kind of dirty joke. I'm pleased that so many of the questions from the reporters here are serious; there may have been fallout in this country from our five years experience in the United States. The many young women reporters remind me of our growing underground of women in the media here. More and more women in the big cities of Brazil are working, not only because rents and the cost of living are so high, but because women with any education want to be part of the action, just as we do here.

I begin to get the sense that this dynamic, exploding nation poses the same challenge to individuality and enterprise that the United States did when our frontiers were still expanding and our cities building. It's the same incredible mix of people seeking refuge from other lands, or the promise and possibility of a new land. But the strength and individuality such a land develops is masked in the women by the Latin tradition of submission and passivity and in the men by *machismo*—a polarization of sex roles even more extreme than our own. "Our women are happy in their submission," Brazilian editors, husbands, party acquaintances keep insisting to me. Or, "Thank God they don't want what American women want or they wouldn't submit to us any longer."

I suppose it's a startling phenomenon in a country like this to hear a woman talking about equality and self-determination for women. The press follows me around as if I were a visitor from Mars or the head of some potentially threatening alien state. They run column after column of interviews on the front page, not the women's page, of the leading newspapers and news magazines in Rio.

The response is surprising: much stronger than it was in the beginning here. The editors send their inquiring reporters out to ask women if *they* want equality, expecting them to say that they are perfectly happy the way things are in Brazil. But the women they interview—housewife, office worker, student —say they *agree* with me. Finally, one newspaper ran a front-page editorial saying, in effect, "Go home, Yankee lady! Stop stirring up our women!"

•   •   •

After I have heard five or six men voice a fear that their wives will no longer "submit to them," I realize that they mean sexually. They evidently have reason to believe that their women wouldn't want or like sex if they had their own way. I thought, if that's true, is it because of the fear of pregnancy that can curdle sex when there's no birth control? Does a woman in that enforced submissiveness have so little sense of self that no matter how many hours she spends in the beauty parlor, she can't enjoy her own sexuality or her husband's? If that is so, then how much sad, cold loneliness there must be both in bed and out. What inadequacy must underlie that fragile *machismo* in the men and the dead, perfectly made-up faces of the women.

•   •   •

On the street outside my press conference at the hotel in São Paulo, a member of the reactionary junta that holds this country in tight control is shot. That night, numbers of students are arrested and held—perhaps tortured and shot?

From Candido Mendez, who was a member of the liberal-democratic government which was overthrown by the generals in 1964, I learn something of what happened to the Brazilian attempts to bring literacy and economic development to the desperate people of the Northeast; to end the autocratic control of the big landowners and generals; to develop and explore and settle the untapped interior of this huge land and give a share and a real voice in decisions to the people. I've been told ever since I came here that democracy didn't work in Brazil: there was turmoil and chaos and inflation, the soldiers and sailors and students were rebelling against all discipline. And it was the women, they tell me, who insisted on an end to this experiment in democracy and social reform, and ushered in the military coup that led to the fascist-like repression people seem resigned to now. The women who marched in 1964 demanding an end to democracy in the name of law and order and the preservation of God and the family were like a "gaggle of squawking geese, signaling the end of the glory that was Greece," says Candido Mendez.

·   ·   ·

Now a college president and a member of the Pope's peace commission, Mendez hints that the Brazilian women in 1964 were manipulated. Their leaders were the generals' wives. Women were frightened by the priests and their husbands into believing that rent control and other social reforms would mean the loss of their homes, their families, and the security of those *things* that for women have had to take the place of participation in life. I see again that if women don't liberate themselves, don't become an active part of the changing system, they become sitting ducks to be manipulated in the direction of fascism, their energy turned inward in impotent rage, resisting any change.

Now, in Brazil, this beautiful land, all political activity is forbidden. Students, unions, opposition parties, are not allowed to organize or assemble. Freedom of speech and the press has been suspended. No resistance is possible, people tell me, except for some priests who dare to say from the pulpit what ordinary citizens dare not say.

·   ·   ·

The night my book is launched in Brazil, I speak at the Museum of Modern Art. Several times more people come than there are seats for. The young men and young women sit on the floor in the front. Older ones, more formally dressed, stand around the walls at the sides and in the back. I describe our battle to establish the right of a woman to control her own body—to get medical help in birth control and abortion, and bear only wanted children. I express our feeling that no man —priest, doctor or husband—should be able to force a woman to bear a child against her will. They clap even before the interpreter finishes, and the interpreter herself gets so excited she starts making a speech of her own. And then I say, "There's no way for women to be liberated in a fascist nation. But in your country and mine, if women become active members of society instead of passive objects to be manipulated, they will surely be a force with youth in the service of peace and human life, and a force against the brutality of *machismo*, fascism and death." By the intensity of their response I realize I am saying things that they cannot say.

•   •   •

Home from Brazil, I feel more sharply than ever the value of the freedoms we have here in America, and the seriousness of the dangers threatening them now. I am sure that the newly liberated women of my own country cannot possibly be manipulated as "gaggling geese" for fascism like the women in Brazil in 1964. "There are so few democracies left," Candido Mendez mourned. "Our dream failed in Brazil."

I realize how much I don't want that dream to fail here. I think the participation of women in political power here will help to save our dream, and that movement of women starting now in Brazil may serve as dynamite to the repressive regimes of Latin America. And now I'm visited by Italian television, doing a documentary series on "*dònnas cèlebres.*" Evidently women in Italy are also beginning to move in great numbers. This Italian crew has just come from filming Valentina, the Russian astronaut. They tell me she has just read my book and learned of our movement. She's planning to use her fame and prestige to start a women's liberation movement in Russia. Well! I wonder if they'd let me into China?

"Remember when Casals told you to stop playing the French horn like a woman?"

Sometimes being a mother is surprising. The letters from Emily gave a clear message that she was having a really good time at camp, the same Quaker one she went to last summer. But her father, who had visited her first, said dourly that I had better "get her some pills." That perturbed me; she's only fifteen. I love her very much. She and her brothers always seem to me a bonus beyond my wildest dreams. So beautiful, so bright and brave and good, so wonderfully themselves.

When my oldest set up his own pad with his girl, I brought them a plant for a housewarming present (to the horror of my friends who thought I should at least *act* shocked at their nonlegal marriage). But I approve of the honesty and the commitment to real feeling my sons and their generation show in boy-girl relationships. It's surely an improvement over the rating-dating hang-ups, prudish hypocrisies and obsessions about sex that were our adolescent experience. I think it's better that they don't make a permanent legal commitment to each other while they are still finding out who they are themselves. But whether it evolves into marriage or not, they are together because they want to be; this is the only kind of commitment that seems real to me now. My friends would say, "Maybe you can be that way about the boys, but wait until Emily gets older." Do I, of all people, still have a double standard about sex?

The first thing I decide is that I am not going to "get her some pills." It seems to me that too many mothers and fathers force-feed their children into a preoccupation with sex or into a kind of unreal sexual behavior—like buying brassieres before girls even have breasts. Are these parents trying to live out their own fantasies through their children? Is it an attempt to make up for their own hangups or for the withering of sex that almost seems built into the roles we play? Our whole culture pushing sex to sell things somehow reduces sex to a commodity.

I would not want to deny the importance of sex in its mysterious reality. I would want my daughter to have that part of her life freer of conflict, more integrated with her whole self than it was with me for too many years. Human sex is not morally wrong, nor is it an enemy of women's liberation. Emily has been saying, "I'm my own me," since she was four, and has been becoming such a lovely, responsible "me" that surely her own sense of self can be trusted to guide her. So I wrote her: "As you're probably discovering, sex is wonderfully exciting and mysterious and powerful. It should be treated with responsibility and respect and loving care. Not that you'll necessarily heed my advice, but advance on it slowly and *only in accord with your own real feelings*." And I think it was honest and right, this advice. Nor is it an invasion of her privacy to tell about it, since she read the letter out loud to the others in her cabin at camp and they thought it was "hilarious."

Now the question was how to get up to the camp to visit her. Since it's in the middle of Vermont, it's impossible to reach except by car, and I stopped driving when I moved into the city.

Al offers to drive me up if we stop at Marlboro on the way, for the music festival and to visit Sonya Kroyt. I regret that I never got to Marlboro while her husband, the great musician Boris Kroyt, was still alive. Now Boris is dead and the Budapest String Quartet dissolved. But Al says Sonya is back at Marlboro this year as "social coordinator" and will get us tickets to the concert Friday night and a place to stay.

•   •   •

We get to Marlboro Friday afternoon. Sonya is standing outside the rehearsal hall under the trees. She introduces me to some of the musicians, to the conductor's wife and to Rudolf Serkin's daughter, Judith, who immediately takes me aside. "Will you meet with us?" she asks. "We have formed a woman's group, but we don't seem to be getting anywhere." All I wanted to do this weekend was revel in the music and the beauty of Vermont and visit Emily. But tomorrow morning Pablo Casals will be conducting a rehearsal for his big concert, so I persuade Al to stay for the rehearsal and to return to Marlboro after visiting Emily. Then I can meet with the women.

•   •   •

The concert Friday night is wonderful. I love it when people do whatever they do with intensity, passion, commitment. And when they do it together and something soars above what any *one* could do alone, I have the feeling that is the closest I get to religion. I get this feeling when I hear people making great music together, or great politics. I've had it unmistakably at the great moments of women marching together, like August 26th.

Listening to this inspired music, I feel uneasy that these women, whose exceptional talent awes me, should be looking to me for answers. I know there's great discrimination against women in music; until recently women weren't even allowed to audition for the Philharmonic Orchestra. Considering how many little girls take piano, violin and recorder lessons, why aren't there more women in the world of serious music? Or for that matter, in the world of jazz and hard rock? A young woman on the stage at Marlboro is playing a solo on the flute as I've never heard it played before. Her whole body moves as she plays. At the piano, a young man, Peter Serkin, is all pyrotechnics and theatrical gesture, but no soul.

After the concert, Al and I go up to the Dome, a geodesic hut that two students, a young man and a young woman, run for the rest of this unique music community. For what has to be love, not profit, they charge only $1.50 for a supper of fresh frog's legs and black-eyed peas, and $.60 for great slabs of homemade bread and cheese and hot apple cider. The young man comes over to me and says, "We hear you're going to meet with the women. We think the men should come too." I agree and praise his cooking.

•   •   •

In the morning the concert hall is even fuller for the Casals rehearsal than it had been at the formal festival concert the night before. When Casals, who they say is ninety-four, comes into the rehearsal, everyone in the orchestra and the audience stands, without a signal. When he begins to conduct the Haydn, I find to my surprise that tears are streaming down my face. I learn later from a lawyer on the board of trustees that men are even more surprised to find themselves crying in the presence of Casals. He leads the musicians, and with few words, humming, singing, with motions of his whole body, he communicates to them some larger sense of the music. It is awesome to watch.

Talking to the musicians later, I learn that something mystical happens to them when they play a concert with Casals. I think this religious sense, the awe and the tears, is evoked because this human being has truly grown to a full, unique human realization that somehow transcends age and defies death. They break after an hour, and I'm taken backstage to meet Casals and his young wife. He is resting. To conduct music like that, bringing the whole orchestra to some new peak, must use enormous energy. Only now that he's at rest and closes his eyes do I see, with startled shock, how old he really is.

•   •   •

I had told Emily we would get to camp for lunch and it's already noon. By the time we stop to buy the food and scarves and denim work shirts she's asked me to bring, it's after two. Emily is up on top of a mountain where the whole camp is having lunch. While we wait for them to come down, we're directed by the head counselor to the lake where the boys and girls swim. As the first returnees from the mountain come out from behind the fall and dive in, I do a double take, for they are swimming in the nude: boys and girls alike, quite unselfconsciously in the bright light of day. It's a Quaker camp; they replant forests, do their own cooking, go off for long wilderness canoe trips and mountain climbs. The lake was high and private in the mountains; bathing suits were an unnecessary nuisance.

I go back up the path, asking directions, hoping to meet Emily halfway. The head counselor says, "We're so pleased to see Emily showing such signs of leadership this summer." *My* Emily, who's so quiet and gentle? Two giggling girls introduce themselves to "Emily's mother," saying they are her cabin-mates and what do I think of "the revolution" Emily has just led? *My* little daughter leading a revolution? I have always felt my kids were so embarrassed to have a mother leading a revolution they were bound to do the very opposite. Emily wouldn't even march last August 26th. "If I were any other fourteen-year-old, I would. But I'm your daughter and I have to rebel against you." No feminist, she.

Their "revolution," it seemed, was to "desexregate" the camp. The girls' cabins were on one side of the road, the boys' cabins on the other. "It made us feel unnatural," Emily's cabin-mates explain. So she had organized them to take over a cabin on the lake on the boys' side, and after much arguing and confrontation, evidently the camp authorities had agreed. "Where's that silly Emily?" one of them says. "Your daughter makes us laugh all the time." And I say, "My Emily??" who seemed so sad and quiet and lonesome last year, a comedian too? And here she is, running down the road. So tall! "As tall as you are!" we stand back to back to discover. And so beautiful, and giggling, giggling. I have never seen her look so happy, so confident. I realize that Emily is discovering the power of being herself and the fun of being a woman all at the same time. She's not going to have to suppress one part of herself or the other, or vacillate back and forth. I'm moved by her "revolution," moved that she does identify with me as a woman. But I suspect somehow for Emily, for these daughters, the problems that forced us to this movement will simply not exist (unless, of course, we mess it up). Emily tells me she has almost decided to be a child psychiatrist. She has also decided not to go to boarding school after all, but to go back to Dalton and the job she loves at the day-care center. She has also become a vegetarian; she doesn't believe in killing animals. She hugs and kisses me twice before we drive off, toward Marlboro.

•   •   •

The women waiting for me under the trees in front of the Marlboro dining room had been talking and "not getting anywhere," they tell me. One of the young men says, "They just won't face the reality that they have to make certain choices as women: music or children." "But if you can choose to be serious musicians and can also have children, why can't the women?" I ask. "You could have a child-care center here. If the women musicians were taken as seriously as the men, if you agreed that you were equally responsible for the children, a child-care center would be just as necessary and practical as a dining hall or a rehearsal room."

"But could women be taken that seriously as musicians? Remember when Casals told you to stop playing the French horn like a woman?" someone asks a member of the group. And the blond young woman says, "I must admit I don't think I will ever be able to play like a man." Did she mean as well as a man? "Well, let's face it," a man says, "there aren't any female Beethovens or Casals." I suggest that the reasons for that are all right here in what they have been saying. When Casals said to stop playing the French horn like a woman, was he reflecting merely the denigration of women of his Spanish culture? Or is it also because women for generations have swallowed their self-denigration, so that they weren't able to play with the confidence and authority and the freedom that only comes when you're fully yourself?

That oneness of Casals with his music, the integrity of his voluntary exile from Spain when it became fascist, and the life force that led him to marry in his nineties—I wonder how many women have ever been able to have such oneness. Only when women are unafraid to risk themselves seriously in music or on any other human frontier, are proud of being women, and are no longer having to choose between children or a career—only then can there be a female Casals.

•   •   •

We have to break for the concert, but such argument continues during intermission and afterwards. We meet again under the apple tree on Sunday morning. "Why is there such discrimination against women in music?" I ask. "It's like any other business," the most hostile of the young men says. "It's a matter of competition, dollars and cents." Well, until recently, how many jobs were there for musicians in this country? In the material values of our culture which have defined men, dehumanized men, as breadwinners—for a man to be a musician was something he had to be defensive about. Did that mean he was somehow feminine? By all means, then, keep the women out. The hostile man, I learn, has a wife somewhere else on a big musical fellowship. I ask if it won't be freeing for men to not have to be superior and to not have to beat the rat race alone. I think of a man I know making a living for his family at a job he hates; he gets his real kicks out of making music. If his wife was earning too, they would both be freer to do their own music or whatever, even if it made less money.

Then I realize what excites me so about this weekend at

Marlboro goes beyond the music or any of the individuals. It is the sense of a whole community passionately absorbed in making something beautiful together. Neither the famous musicians who donate the proceeds of these concerts to fellowships for the students, nor the students themselves who work and play so passionately making music together every summer do this only for money. The fellowships assure them their minimal needs; the students together do the chores, cook for the cafeteria kitchens, sell the tickets. This community, needing only the addition of a child-care center, is organized to meet people's needs for living and working together. In our cities or our suburbs, the women and children are isolated from the men, who are chained to dehumanizing jobs, too often working for money alone. Here they live in relatively modest apartments or rooms within walking distance of their rehearsal studios. As I eat Sunday dinner with them in the Marlboro community dining hall, I see the music students, the Serkins, the conductor, the wives and children, all standing in line and serving themselves the excellent food the students take pride in preparing.

Sonya keeps jumping up and down—arranging the Monday night cabaret they put on for their own pleasure, solving people's problems, keeping her musicians a happy family. She is doing professionally what she once did simply because she was Boris Kroyt's wife. She had left Marlboro after his death, but the musicians found they could not get along without her.

What we all need is a community like Marlboro. A community where we can be free from our isolation, where we are encouraged in creative activities we enjoy, and where we can cooperate instead of compete as we do now in the isolation of our suburbs and cities. Even if the women are the first to complain about it, it isn't all that splendid for the husbands and the children either.

As we drive out of town, I wave good-bye to my new friends, the women and the men who are no longer hostile. Because it isn't just the woman problem we have been talking about. Deliver us to the new problems, they are so much more interesting than the old ones.

The sign on the road in front of Marlboro reads: MUSICIANS AT PLAY.

"My roots are in my moving."

It would once have seemed such a major decision to move. I would have brooded, vacillated, shopped around, not sure of my own judgment, torn with doubts. My apartment is so choked with accumulated possessions, papers, books I can never find when I need them, clothes I don't wear, cracked vases of reeds picked summer before last, that the very thought of moving it all fills me with dread. But I can only keep this sublet another year. The apartment upstairs is available. It has a living room large enough for parties again, a great space under a skylight where I can get at all my books, a big sunny kitchen, privacy for Emily.

In the heightening political pace of the movement, I have no time to vacillate. So on the afternoon of August 26th, 1971, while I am marching up Fifth Avenue again with the tens of thousands, my son Jonathan and his friends finished painting the new apartment, and with Emily packing, move all that stuff upstairs. He charges me by the hour and the cost of materials—cheaper and more reliable than professional movers, surely. He will use the money he makes moving me to move out on his own. Another few years and Emily will go, too.

• • • •

Having lived the first eighteen years of my life in one house —one town—I felt rootless when I first came to New York. During the early years of my marriage, in the rented apartments where I knew we would not stay, I had illusions of putting down permanent roots for the family, buying a house in Rockland County.

But these roots were false or else they rotted. The more I hung on to them for security, the more unrooted I felt. Now I know my roots do not stay put in place or time; my roots are in my moving. In the midst of change, moving as I have to— despite nostalgia for that which maybe never was and now no longer can be, for me or maybe anyone—I do not feel rootless. I realize that somehow my real roots are growing deeper and wider, that they are based not on blood or place, but on struggles shared, passion, pain, intimacy; my human roots in life.

How strange in this huge city to be neighbors again with

the Fleischmans and the Mehlings, with our common roots in Parkway Village twenty years ago: our identical garden apartments, our children in the cooperative nursery school, the rent strike, the neighborhood newspaper we put out together. Is it a coincidence that after our different suburban detours, looking for roots in physical earth, we should once again be separately drawn to this new experiment in urban community? Here, in "9G" on West 93rd Street, thirty families jointly bought nine brownstones, breaking through walls to give each space and air and light and individuality not otherwise found in this rotting city at five times the rent: a community around a common garden, in the city, not escaping from it.

We can't go back now to the large families and old neighborhoods and small towns of our childhood for the roots of continuity and intimacy and community we all still need. We need physical structures that fit the changing shape of our lives. But existing architecture, city planning, suburban zoning, the financing and ordinances and codes and profit interests that determine what we can build, buy and rent—all conspire to wall us in isolation. Our housing is still built as if we all stayed put in the little nuclear families we grew up in—Mama the housewife, Daddy the breadwinner, Junior and Janey. But the latest census shows most Americans no longer live in such families. What housing is there for the families where Junior and Janey have left—or for those young people themselves—for the mamas who are breadwinners as well as housewives, for the families without daddies, for the former daddies rattling around alone, and for all the men and women, black and white, rich and poor, who aren't daddies or mamas, who don't want to be or who have outlived that part of their lives? How can we restructure our cities and suburbs to nourish and not block off the new human roots we need?

• • •

Leaving the old apartment already stripped of our personal traces, it is reassuring to go into the hectic NOW office to check final arrangements for the march. I think we touch and renew our roots in history, our community with women, marching as we did on that fiftieth anniversary of the vote, as we will march now every year. We need to celebrate our past, how far we have come, how far we still must go. These rites of passage we create for ourselves in this movement of women are also roots. They seemed so puny at first, even a year ago, so vulnerable to the slightest storm or insect plague. Now, suddenly, they are lacing together, sprouting strong new shoots all over the place. The actions we have taken together, the struggles, the differences we have faced and transcended have given us roots of confidence in ourselves and each other. Even before the signals go out, women are organizing in a thousand towns what last year they only organized in ten.

At noon I go to lunch at Ellie Guggenheimer's with some nice, attractive, powerful men who have agreed to be Friends of the Women's Political Caucus. It is sweet for men to be willing to play the supportive role to women that we have played to men in American politics for so long. Then we go to City Hall to meet with Mayor John Lindsay. Last year he didn't even see women as people politically important enough to waste his own time on. He had a deputy read a proclamation that commemorated women's vote by banning sex discrimination in city agencies and public facilities. A year later, it is evident that proclamation is only worth the paper it was written on. Women have made no progress whatever in making decisions in the city agencies. John Lindsay is a handsome man: his packagers are counting on his sex appeal to women to help get him to the White House. We demand that he appoint a woman deputy mayor and an Office of Women's Advocacy to get women out of the sexual ghetto in his own city.

Just before we get to City Hall this year, he calls in the press and names a woman police captain. He says his budget won't permit a woman deputy mayor. So I say that *we* will constitute ourselves the Women's Advocacy—with his mandate, of course—to question every agency to find out what is keeping women in the menial jobs, and how programs are or are not working for the women of the city. On the steps of City Hall, where the television cameras are waiting, we announce the creation of the Women's Advocacy before he can change his mind.

In every City Hall, of course, women are hardly present except as secretaries or cleaning women. Who even sees the city's agony today in terms of women or their absence? The first step, at least, is to have some women in City Hall to ask new questions. I want to ask John Lindsay why his police are conducting a crusade, arresting women as prostitutes without touching the men who use them and make money off them. Isn't it a sexual red herring to go after these women, most of them black, who can't make money any other way, for a prostitution whose only victim is themselves?

How embarrassing, even for liberal politicians, when women who have been asking real questions about their own lives begin to ask them in politics.

Collapsing in bed in my new apartment after the march, I don't feel able to cope with rearranging my furniture, much less the new women's politics. Emily and I go off to the commune for a week on the beach before she starts school.

· · ·

But there is no escape now from politics: Eugene McCarthy is coming to our commune for two days to visit Arthur Herzog, who managed his campaign in Oregon. Our commune may haggle over cooking, washing dishes, and paying bills, but we share political passion. It is as much our root as our common need for intimacy, for family substitutes for our children. When Fred and LaDonna Harris and their kids came to visit, I arranged vases of leaves and flowers even for the bathrooms, and recruited LaDonna, a marvelous, warm, dynamic woman who leads her own fight for Indian rights, for the Women's Political Caucus. I also gave Fred some political advice, that he and LaDonna should run as a team for President, not the old President's wife stuff. (I think that women who become people in their own right are not necessarily always going to operate on their own, but often as equal members of such teams.)

Now, arranging rhododendrons for McCarthy's visit, I think of my own political root in his existential decision to run in 1968—when nothing anyone did—the kids, the peace marchers or petitions—seemed to have any effect on the war in Vietnam. With my sons approaching draft age, I campaigned for McCarthy despite the criticism of the "pure" feminists in my own organization. Party politics had always turned me off before, as they had most women, maybe because I didn't feel welcome or didn't want to address envelopes, or because their politics didn't seem to deal with life. The passion for life in the kids and the women and the men that McCarthy brought out, and the way they worked in that campaign were the first indications to me that politics in America did not have to be run by machines and bosses, run the old way.

Nineteen sixty-eight ended for me, as for many others, in bitterness and feelings of betrayal at the Democratic convention when we realized the rules were rigged. There was no way the people's will, their vote in the primaries in New Hampshire, Wisconsin, Oregon, could affect the convention—the great majority of the delegates had been picked by the bosses long before. Kennedy was dead and McCarthy gave up the fight, and the kids went home bloody to make their futile bombs or retreat into the cynical apathy of despair. I could escape back into the women's movement which no one took seriously enough to club or gas. But after that, when I lectured on campuses across the nation, I began to raise questions beyond sex discrimination, questions that were political, though the politicians weren't raising them, about the quality of life in America, about the frustrations built into our sexual roles that made us explode in violence and want to napalm all the green life in Vietnam, and club the long-haired young. And on campuses considered completely apathetic politically, more and more young men as well as women came to talk to me about these things. Maybe the party politics of these years has been irrelevant: abstract rhetoric; right or left, Establishment or antiestablishment; votes that don't change anything; candidates who are no different, really. Even the terms, the "issues," the old rubrics of "radical" and "conservative," somehow leave untouched the new have-nots, the alienated young concerned with the living of life and their middle-elders frustrated for lack of greening life.

I walk by the ocean for two hours with McCarthy. He is interested in my idea that, beyond the separation of church and state, Catholics may get out of their dead end on birth control and abortion by coming to new terms with the total personhood of women. He says, as a Catholic, he has "no problems" with the issue of abortion in terms of a woman's right to choose. What he says about the issues seems less important than his vision of the new politics beyond the Presidential maneuvers of 1972, and a new sense of calm commitment to the consequences of his political passion.

We have a funny thing about "leaders" in the women's movement. We have been passive followers, manipulated and denigrated so much in the past that many of us still feel too much self-hatred to be confident about ourselves. So we resent strength in others and say no woman should be a leader, and want to strike down any who emerge. But as we move enough ourselves to realize our own power to take responsibility for action, which is what leadership means, we know we need and can trust a leader who is able to act from the truth in herself to bring out that power in others. That's what McCarthy did in 1968, acting on the passionate human truth in himself when others only talked about the "issues" of the Vietnam war, bringing out unsuspected political power in the kids and the suburbanites, teachers and preachers, and the women like me who have continued to move according to our various truths.

The new human politics almost worked in 1968, despite the bosses and the rigging of the rules and the assassins' bullets. In 1972, the eighteen-year-olds will vote, millions of them, and even more millions of women are liberated enough now to act on their own political truth. According to the new rules, the bosses can't hand-pick the delegates to the conventions so easily. They must be elected in primaries in many states, and half are supposed to be women, the Republicans say—as many as their proportion to the population, say the Democrats. *That is what they say.* Can we do it? "See you on the campaign trail," McCarthy says, leaving our commune. I don't know whether or not his trail will lead to the Presidency ever, or how it will cross mine. But moving now to my own political truth, I understand only too well his earlier diffidence and dread of taking responsibility for the hopes and dreams he set loose on us, and we put on him in 1968, for the strength we demanded from and gave to him, and the betrayal we felt when the dreams were dashed.

·   ·   ·

Flying to Los Angeles for the fifth convention of NOW, I also feel an inexplicable dread. At the Airport Marina Hotel, it is awesome to see those seven hundred women, leaders themselves now in two hundred cities—remembering the half-dozen who started it all in my Washington hotel room five years ago. It is mind-boggling, the efficiency of room after room of mimeograph machines running smoothly and corridors of professional montages of photography and newspapers put out by NOW chapters in every city, when I remember how we stayed up all night drenching ourselves with mimeograph ink, putting out our first press release on a borrowed mimeograph machine none of us knew how to run. And the faces I recognize from so many struggles these few years, *all leaders* now, and the new ones who come up and say, "Your book changed my life." I had feared enemies in Los Angeles. A story planted in the newspapers almost scared me from coming. But the love from so many is scary, too. It was not that easy to change my own life; will they all be able to do it, to stick to it, if things outside don't change fast, if backlash comes?

I can bow out of offices, but not this responsibility. I am bothered this night by dirty jokes—with men the butt instead of women, for a change. Do we really need to ape men, I ask? Sex should not be a dirty joke, for men *or* women. Most agree; we move on. Even the media weren't able to manufacture serious divisions among us. The only time I take the floor is to protest a resolution condemning radical groups trying to take over the women's movement. We are such a big movement we are surely infiltrated by CIA and S.W.P., Radical Lesbians and square old Communists, but we are too rooted now to be taken over by anyone. We can waste a lot of energy fighting straw women, and sexual and political red herrings; we must realize our own strength and refuse to be divided—and *move on.*

•   •   •

That night my mother, who is seventy-three, drives from her retirement village in Laguna Hills to meet me at the NOW convention. Her third husband died last year. Before her marriage she was a newspaperwoman, then a housewife and leader of Community Chest drives. At seventy she started her second career, using her lifelong bridge skill to get licensed as a manager of duplicate bridge tournaments. At seventy-one she took up horseback riding for exercise. Now she has a third career, distributing ecological, biodegradable detergents, cosmetics and vitamins, which she claims gave her so much energy she has stopped using artificial hormones. She loves the NOW convention. I suddenly realize how many millions of men and women like my mother, still moving toward life in their seventies and eighties, must rebel against being walled up in nursing homes and retirement pens as if they were already dead. Will this be the next liberation movement, another powerful ally in the new human politics by 1972 or 1976?

• • •

Back home, I find the Women's Political Caucus is exploding across the states. But divisions are arising in many states between women who want to make the caucus big and broad and include women of all possible views and affiliations—and those who seem to want to make it narrow and "control" it. Some want to narrow it to radicals or liberals who are "pure on the issues" and keep the conservatives out. Other "pure" feminists are afraid "the political women" will take control. And some women with political footholds already in their parties want to keep out the "crazy feminists" who will rock the boat. I insist that they must all get together in a caucus big and broad enough to include everyone, and then elect their own leaders. And women in much greater numbers than I had expected begin taking me up on my promise to "speak for any woman running for office, committed to women's interests and human priorities, if my schedule permits."

• • •

Back home, finally, in the middle of the night, I move my furniture to fit my higher, airier new space. My old things look petty, cluttered, fussy; they won't do. I start throwing out the broken vases, dusty reeds, the little tables that serve no purpose. The things I really like look better now. And then I move my one beautiful antique, the red love seat, which had been protected in a corner, up front by the fireplace where people can actually sit on it and walk behind it. It warms the whole room, opens it up—and all the rest fits together.

"The starving Russian masses overthrowing the Czar . . . That's the way . . . some of our sisters see our revolution."

The campus—Concord College, Athens, West Virginia— looks like one of those Old Siwash college movies. Homecoming banners are all over the place: *Vote for Kissable Kate for Homecoming Queen, Sexy Susie, Make Margie.* I am told that each fraternity has its female candidate: the wild competition for Homecoming Queen is actually a battle among men; the girls are just objects. It's a college tradition on this and other campuses, but this year some of the women students feel uncomfortable about it. So do I.

In the face of this contest, I find it impossible to give my scheduled lecture, "Women's Liberation—Dangers, Dead Ends, Directions for the Future?" After a few opening words, I ask for six male and six female volunteers for an experiment. The men volunteer first. I tell them they are candidates for Homecoming King. They are to parade and strut their stuff according to the standards by which they are judging women in the Homecoming Queen contest. Traditional timidity keeps the six women from pushing themselves forward; they have to be urged to volunteer. I station these six women judges behind the speaker's table to pick the Homecoming King—Mr. Most Masculine of West Virginia State.

The first two boys, crew-cut fraternity jocks, strut their stuff, flexing their muscles with accurate, awkward consciousness of what sexism imposes on the male. Several say how good they are at an athletic or scholastic skill, which seems irrelevant to the standards of this contest. A long-haired young man puts on a homosexual parody of feminine hairprimping, the kind of grotesque joke that mocks both women and men when they repudiate their own sex stereotype by substituting the other. The last two say they feel "just foolish." All six then report their feelings: "I didn't know what I was supposed to be or do." . . . "I felt I was being judged on things that weren't really me." . . . "I felt I had nothing to offer in this contest." . . . "The contest seemed unfair, but I must admit I wanted to win."

Then the girls—soft drawling Southern accents, long blond hair—speak their thoughts as judges. A very gentle-looking girl puts her hands on her hips and looks the boys up and down in kind of a surprised relish, adopting instantly the manner of a judge of cattle. With delicious malice, these gentle Southern women ask the denigrating put-down questions that male judges ask women in beauty contests. Then they describe their feelings out loud: "I felt sorry for them." . . . "They were so vulnerable." . . . "Even for the winners, it wasn't a fair contest."

Suddenly, from the balcony, a West Virginia athlete and student leader who was very hostile when introduced to me shouts out, "It's not fair! Here the girls are suddenly saying they have the right to be President or anything else, but we have to pay for the dates when they go out with us, even when they have as much money as we do. And we have to hold the door open for them." Another boy says, "You talk about equality, but women aren't drafted, only men."

Well, it is almost a relief having the grounds for men's hostility spelled out aloud. Reporters everywhere I go ask me about the "resistance" and "the hostility from men" they assume I must be suffering as a leader of this revolution. Strangely enough, I myself have experienced less and less hostility from men, personally and publicly, in recent years. The war between the sexes—the hostility of American men for women, and the no-longer-suppressed hostility of American women for men—was already exploding even before I began to speak. I believe the women's movement is removing the causes of that hostility.

I tell them that real equality for women has to be an equality of responsibility as well as of privilege and right; that men will be liberated then from the burden of having to hold open the doors, pay all the bills, die ten years younger than women, and fight the wars. I say we can light each other's cigarettes if that means merely that we like each other. If a pregnant woman gets on the bus, of course a man should get up and give her a seat, but if a tired old man gets on the bus, I would give my seat to him. I say that nobody should be drafted to fight this war in Vietnam, or any immoral, unjust war, but any necessary service to society should be assumed by women and men alike: no reason for anyone to be exempt on the basis of sex. And maybe it might relieve men from unnecessary feelings of inadequacy not to have to be superior to the women they sit next to in class, office or even at home. It might be less lonely to share the burdens, take off the masks and really get to know one another. At least women able to pay for themselves are also able to love men for themselves, not their paychecks, and have less need for secret vengeance.

The fraternity jocks, the male beauty queens, and the female judges seem a little less hostile to each other as they variously shake my hand or hug me good-bye.

These questions keep coming up as every week brings new evidence of the reality of our revolution. Women's caucuses are challenging sex discrimination in jobs, schools, churches, restaurants, television commercials, even Little League baseball . . . women in every state are crossing man-made political lines to demand equal political power for women in 1972.

What will happen when women in great numbers begin to compete for the really good jobs which were once men's exclusive prerogative, when men can no longer count on the underpaid or unpaid menial services of women in their own homes or offices or churches or political parties? Will men actually accept women on equal terms in decision-making in politics and the office, and share equal responsibility for the housework and the bringing up of children? Can this revolution of women really change society without violent backlash from men?

For now, these are unanswerable questions. A revolution of women against men is one which I myself wouldn't want to win, even if we could, and can't really conceive of fighting. Maybe these questions come from thinking about revolution in the old way, like in a Western—the good guys versus the bad guys; Paul Revere and George Washington against the despotic British Tories; the French people guillotining the decadent king and queen; the starving Russian masses overtaking the Czar; the people of India seizing their own land back from the British viceroys. That's the way the media—and some of our sisters—see our revolution.

In reality, it can't possibly happen that way. After all, men are here to stay. Most of us really wouldn't like life without them. But men can't possibly ignore or even joke about what is happening with so many women now. Their own lives are affected. Will men willingly move over to share their central place in the sun with us? Or will they close ranks against us?

• • • •

Back home, brooding about these questions, I am suddenly inundated by long-distance calls from Florida, where I am to lecture at the University at Gainesville. The students say I am being used to whitewash a sexist situation. It is the big home-coming weekend at the university; the main event is the banquet of Blue Key. This honorary organization is the cradle of Florida politics and does not admit women. Muskie is going to be their banquet speaker. Virtually every Florida politician will be coming back to the campus for this banquet to meet the male student members who will be their political heirs. Because of recent grumbling about the barring of women from Blue Key, the women's honorary organization, Mortar Board-Savant, has been given money to get a big speaker of their own this year—i.e., me. I had not known about all this. Did they want me not to come? To boycott the sexist situation? Or could they somehow use my visit to expose and try to end this sex segregation? I ask them to meet me at the airport and tell me what they want to do.

Then calls begin from Washington, from Muskie's staff. "We understand you are speaking in Florida. The senator is a great admirer of years. In fact, Mrs. Muskie is coming to hear you speak." That's nice, I say, but if I were advising Senator Muskie, I would invite the women and me to join him at the Blue Key banquet, and publicly oppose sex segregation in politics. But the Senator is guest, not host—he can't do that, and he doesn't like confrontation, says the staff woman. Neither do I, I say. I didn't plan this, but now that I know about it, I am not going to let myself be used to whitewash sexism. Over the next week, the Florida women decide to leave the women's banquet and demand entrance to Blue Key, and ask me to join and support them. I also learn that various Democratic leaders in Florida are trying to find women to put pressure on me not to do this. But the Florida women leaders also refuse to play

Aunt Tom, or to ask me to. Muskie sends down three advance men in the face of the impending crisis. They negotiate that, for the first time, faculty women and their husbands will be invited to the Blue Key Banquet—but not, of course, the wives of male faculty or of other members, or more importantly, women students.

I am whisked away from the airport at Gainesville before the movement leaders can get to me. The sorority women who are my official hostesses are clearly nervous. Evidently a great deal of pressure has been put on them from university officials. Since Florida is one of the early Presidential primaries, press and TV are covering Muskie's appearance. And this is, after all, the South, where women are still supposed to sit ladylike on the pedestal.

At the reception, the sorority girls suddenly flutter, "Betty, Senator Muskie is here. Please come over and meet him." But the young student leader who has found me by now, though equally nervous, Southern and soft-spoken, whispers fiercely, "Are you really going to go to him?" "No," I said. "This reception is supposed to be for me." Senator Muskie comes over to meet me. He looks like a man of integrity and decency. "Senator," I say, "I hope you don't approve of sex discrimination." "No, of course not," he says. "Then I guess I will see you later," I tell him.

At the banquet, so many more students have come than were expected that I sit isolated on the dais about an hour while extra tables are set up. I get increasingly nervous. The militant young students had wanted me not to speak at all to this Establishment women's organization, but I intend to fulfill my contract to speak—and perhaps persuade them to help break down the barriers that keep young women out of the cradle of Florida politics.

I may not have been brought up in the South, but there is enough of that ladylike tradition in me to feel nervous about confrontations in politics. Maybe it's more than not being ladylike—a real fear of confronting hostility in power. Will Southern sheriffs who used bullwhips on young blacks marching for civil rights be polite to ladies now that they are also marching? I begin to feel strangely weak and dizzy. In fact, I have to ask the sorority leader if she can find some smelling salts for me. It would hardly do for me to faint before this Southern skirmish. I would disgrace the whole movement.

So, then, I speak to these Southern women about the urgency of this particular moment, and the fact that institutions have to be changed for the new generation of women to be able to have the equality they are conscious of wanting. I say that neither men nor women are born with their full human voice. They need experiences to attain this, such as the young men get in Blue Key. It is partly because women all over the country are barred from such experiences that there is only one woman in the Senate and none considered qualified for the Supreme Court. Mrs. Muskie's presence or my speech here are only tokens; they do not change the situation that bars women from Florida politics.

Then the young women propose to demand admission to the Blue Key banquet and invite the older guests to join them. I leave the dais and with several hundred others walk a few hundred yards across the campus to the larger hall where Senator Muskie is now speaking. Burly state troopers try to bar the door. The soft-spoken young Florida women politely and immovably wedge their ankles in the door so it can't close. A number of men have joined us now, students and faculty members, and we move into the banquet hall. I had not realized it would be so large, there must be several thousand men here. I learn later that virtually every politician in the Florida Establishment—from sheriffs and mayors to state and U.S. Senators and even the Governor—is here. The few token faculty women guests are not even visible in this sea of Southern masculinity.

As the soft, unmartial invasion of Florida women approaches the dais, the Southern politicians seem to be in a state of shock. But Muskie smiles. He has insisted we be given the microphone and allowed to speak. I tell the young Florida woman to take the mike. This is their show, not mine. Her voice is trembling. She says, "Separate is not equal for blacks or for women. Women insist on a true equal voice in Florida politics. You can't keep us out any longer. Blue Key is the cradle of Florida politics. It must be open to women. We will be heard."

I say that I support these Florida women; that while Senator Muskie can't be blamed for Florida sexism, let him and any other Presidential candidate be warned that sexist politics, political organizations or meetings where "men only" have a voice will no longer be tolerated.

I have spoken less than three minutes when the chairman interrupts, "If ah can get a word in edgewise . . ." (The students shout, "you don't interrupt men speakers like that!") "Ah just want to say we love you ladies, and if you all stop talking, we will let you stay and listen to Senator Muskie." "You don't have to love us," I say. "We don't have to stay and listen; we want an equal chance to do the politics and the talking."

But the rub—or the saving grace—is: they do have to love us, and we them. (Not every one, of course.) Why were those Florida men so strangely silent at the invasion of women into their sacred white male political preserve? Like most men, they go home to women at night. The men with whom we work or do politics don't have to love us personally. (Though the personal bonds between us may be almost as important as love.) But men are as dependent on love, whatever it means, from women as women have been dependent for things that often spoiled love from men. Those love-spoilers, which our movement for equality between the sexes would change, have made some men and women renounce the very possibility of love for the other sex. But our need for each other still shapes, enhances or haunts life for most men and women, despite the problems. Could the sexual reality, the human reality, of the bond between men and women give our revolution a power greater than the retaliating outrage of racial oppression, greater than the economic weapons of class warfare?

I am not saying that this war can be won in any woman's bedroom: it's society that has to be changed. In fact, until our movement to change society became too large to stop, a lot of women were afraid to voice, or even face, their private grievances. But now even Pat Nixon and Martha Mitchell give their husbands hell when they won't name a woman to the Supreme Court. And the fact that the young men in the West Virginia Homecoming Queen contest were able to put themselves in the woman's place meant that they could, and finally did, identify with women as people, not just as wives and mothers. And once this happens, the bonds men have with their own wives and mothers bring the men into our revolution. This is not theoretical; it is happening. More and more men at our meetings, rallies, marches, are joining, not heckling, us. Corporation executives are devoting night after night to help elect their wives to political office—or twisting corporate arms in Pittsburgh, Connecticut, California, or New York to get needed money for campaigns to elect women who are not their wives, women in whom they believe.

A young reporter tells me that she and her husband and most of their friends now actually chart a weekly who-does-what of housekeeping chores, to be sure it's divided and rotated fairly. At a party, an unemployed advertising executive, victim of recent corporate cutbacks, boasts about the cake he made to celebrate his wife's pay raise. A sixty-year-old psychoanalyst neighbor whose wife for forty years has picked up his pajamas and never even asked him to dry a dish boasts of his "adjustment" to being a "househusband." At fifty, his wife went back to school, learning social work, and now they lead marriage counseling groups together as a team. Instead of worrying about retiring, they are starting over again in a warmer climate.

I think we are waging the new kind of revolution Jean François Revel suggests in *Without Marx or Jesus: The New American Revolution Has Begun*, where there are no violent coups, where there are no bad guys or good guys in the old sense. Society as a whole has to be, *is being changed* in a revolutionary way that gives women equality *without men being either victims or enemies*. It is, in fact, a two-sex revolution for human liberation.

> *"I speak standing on a café table under the awning of a trattoria, with the manager pulling at my skirt to get down."*

The invitation to speak in five Italian cities came not from the women's movement, but from the Associazione Culturale

Italiana, a cultural organization which brings "men of letters" to "Literary Mondays" in Milan, "Literary Tuesdays" in Rome, etc. Few Americans had ever been invited—J.K. Galbraith, Herbert Marcuse, Gore Vidal—and virtually no women. The fee sounds astronomical in lire, but in dollars will just about pay for the trip. I've been taking Emily along on foreign expeditions since her brothers left home, because I don't like leaving her alone. Now, coolly organizing our baggage, tickets, schedules and currency exchange, she wonders, "How did you ever get anywhere without me, Mother?"

At the last moment, having managed to pack all our clothes in two small bags, I fill a straw carrying case with papers for whatever women's movement exists in Italy. The last, and only, time I was there, two years ago on vacation, I returned to my hotel in Rome one afternoon to find a strange woman waiting for me. It seemed that she was organizing Italian women. In that country it was a crime even to speak about birth control and abortion; she was secretly collecting the figures of how many women a year died of abortions. Italian women have no rights at all in the family, she explained. The wife can't even call the police if her husband beats her: he is *"capo,"* the head; she is his property. She grasped my hand excitedly. "But now women will get their revenge. We will be the black power of Italy, and you must be our leader." "How many are you?" I asked. "Six," she said. Well, no Che Guevara I . . .

We land in Turin, Italy's Detroit, gray with smog. My lecture will open the "Literary Fridays" season. They expect a hundred people or so; "Marcuse had several hundred, but for a woman . . ." the interpreter says, assuring me no one in Turin knows or cares about the women's movement.

We arrive at the theater. It looks like our old Metropolitan Opera House, tier after tier of balconies, boxes with red plush curtains and gold railings. It is packed. Women are crowded into the boxes, hanging over the balconies, standing up in back. And men, too. There must be several thousand people here. I explain what the women's movement is all about and why it is becoming the greatest revolution of our time. I tell them that in America we have asserted the right to control our own bodies, that we are demanding an approach to marriage and divorce that gives equal responsibility for home and children to husband and wife. "Women in my country are no longer willing to do the menial work for half or none of man's pay, while men make all the decisions. We are even questioning sex discrimination in the church: 'Is God He?' Perhaps you will raise the possibility of a woman Pope. But I cannot say how it will happen in your country."

The intensity with which they are listening, despite the continual interruptions for translations, is hungry, scary, as if something here is getting ready to burst. In the questions, when a man talks about "the threat to the family," a woman's "sacred duty to her husband and children," there is a muttering in the audience. When a man says, "It is God's will; women were made from Adam's rib, to serve man," the muttering becomes a growl. I begin to think I have underestimated the revolutionary readiness of the women in Italy.

But the revolution I am talking about is not revolution, Italian style. In Italy, revolution still means "communism," and the Italian Communist Party, the biggest in Europe, is taking almost the same reactionary line about divorce and abortion as the Catholic right-wing parties. The left-wing journalists who interview me tell me that women always were, and are, and will be, the most conservative force in Italy. "They only gave women the vote to stop socialism," a left-wing journalist said, incredulous at my idea that women are the next revolutionary force. He can not conceive of a revolution that crosses class lines.

The interpreter, a conventional "revolutionary," gets out of the car in horror when the "Reception of Signora Agnelli," on my schedule after the lecture, turns out to be at the *palazzo* of Gianno Agnelli, the owner of Fiat, the Henry Ford of Italy —maybe more like Ford, General Motors and U.S. Steel combined. In the fogginess of my jet lag, I drift through the marble floors, tapestried walls, butlers, footmen, handsome Italian men kissing my hand, women's faces I have seen in *Vogue*— like a scene from *La Dolce Vita*.

Why should the wife of the richest industrialist in Italy be giving a party for me? Marella Agnelli even seems to know what the movement is all about, and assures me Italian women are not as submissive as the cliché would have it. Women were a part of the resistance, she reminds me.

At dinner, I discuss the smog with my Agnelli host, and he asserts that it is ridiculous for everyone to have a car polluting the air, jamming the roads—mass transit is the only answer.

•   •   •

Sunday, with no lecture, we spend in Venice, off-season for tourists. Walking and walking, over the bridges, by the canals, we ache with the beauty of this city built for people, not cars. No one in Italy suggests replacing the canals with superhighways for "progress"; they are trying to save the centuries-old foundations from the erosion of currents stirred up by industrial pollution. They are experimenting with free buses to keep cars out of the inner streets of Rome altogether. I *see* the country of Italy, in the SuperRapido train trip to Milan, as I have not seen the United States in years, despite the thousands of miles I have flown over it in superjets.

Valeria Gentili, who interviewed and traveled with me in the United States, invites me to lunch at her house with her brother and some eminent publishers, political columnists, and scientists. They are worried about a return of fascism; violence is breaking out nearly every day between fascist gangs and ultraleft groups. They have lived through fascism: the tortures, concentration camps, loss of all freedoms. Isn't it frivolous, even dangerously diversive, they ask, to whip women up into a frenzy against men when there are real problems like poverty, housing, and if things got much worse, fascism?

Evidently neither the left nor the right of Italy takes the problems of women seriously. Divorce Italian style means the Italian man can just walk out, as many do, despite all the pious veneration for the family; he can live his life with his mistress, and his wife is left with the children and whatever crumbs she can get. Making divorce legal, as Italy finally did last year, is still not enough, considering the economic dependence of the wife. But instead of pushing for further protections for the wife, the parties of the left are now going along with the rightist move to repeal the divorce law—and are opposing birth control and abortion rights—because they don't want to antagonize the Catholic hierarchy. Women's liberation in Italy is just a crazy fad, a leftist journalist tells me.

•   •   •

The theater in Milan is even more crowded than in Turin. But now, I no longer assume that Italian women are any less outraged than we would be in their situation. By about the second sentence, I am saying that talk is not enough. Women are never going to have human freedom and equality unless we demand and get political power. When the man translates, I hear women muttering, "That's not what she said." I say what I have been evading: that women's revolution must challenge the Catholic hierarchy—and the communist hierarchy, too—because no man, priest, or commissar, politician, doctor or husband should have the power to force a woman to bear a child against her will. The interpreter gives his version. Women begin to stand up and scream at him and shake their fists. "That's not what she said." "We will not listen to a man!" He is perspiring, he looks terrified. I try to go on—but suddenly he is speechless, he has lost his wits. I say, "Not because he is a man, but because he is not familiar with these thoughts, could a woman come and help?" Angry women start converging on the stage. I can't understand what they are saying. Suddenly, a miracle. A woman calmly sits down beside me, whispering, "I am the Italian translator of *La Mìstica della Femminilità*. I have been trying to get in touch with you."

And now I speak to the urgency I feel at this moment in Italy, and increasingly at home: of *getting on* with women's liberation. For the impotent rage of women helps to feed the violence on which fascism breeds. And fascism is the oppression of women carried to its deadly extreme. In Germany and in Italy, one of the first acts of fascism was to reduce women to breeding machines: *Kinder, Küche, Kirche*. And the fascism which threatens again is inflamed not only by the impotent rage of economic despair, but the human despair our obsolete sex roles breed. How can a woman for whom sex can always mean another pregnancy freely love her husband in bed; what sexual revenge does this finally take on him? Aren't birth control and the right to abortion *necessary* if men and women are to be able to "make love, not war"?

The questions begin; a priest raises the horror of "murder" of the fetus. The women begin to growl—Catholic women. I say I don't know how to answer a question that puts the life of the unborn fetus over the life and soul of the grown woman. (I

want to ask if it is "murder" of the "right to life" when priests
don't use their sperm to fertilize eggs, but the interpreter
whispers she won't translate this because you can be put in jail
in Italy for making a joke about a priest.) A woman who says
she is the only woman sexologist in Italy reports that the sexual situation in Italy is even more deadly than my suspicion:
that 85 percent of Italian women are frigid. There is great
excitement in the audience as they begin discussing the relationship of all this to politics and to fascism. Suddenly the
manager turns off the sound and lights and says he is shutting
the theater down.

●   ●   ●

In Rome, no one meets me at the station. I see crude swasti-
kas on the wall and posters on the streets calling a giant emergency: mobilization of all Italy against fascism. *No Al Fascismo.*
I have a vision of my "Literary Thursday" cultural hosts assassinated or fleeing because of me. I go to the Hotel Forum,
overlooking the ancient Colosseum, where they are putting
me up. Emily sets off to explore the ruins; I find a little beauty
parlor next to the hotel to revive my own ruins. As I am trying to tell the Italian hairdresser that I don't want these tight
curls, the door opens and in march a band of determined
women who seem to be looking for something other than a
hairdresser. They zero in on my dryer: the vanguard of the
Italian women's movement. "Where were you?" they say
sternly. "We had people stationed at the airport all day." As an
American, I guess I wasn't expected to use a train.

Back in the hotel, there are clusters of women all over the
lobby. In Rome, the women's movement is already divided
into three parts. I am not sure what their differences are. I
recognize the leader of one branch, who asks me to speak at a
big abortion rally in the Piazza Navona the next day; she is my
hotel visitor of two years ago. "You are more than six now," I
say, and she smiles.

At the theater, I am ambushed by *paparazzi.* The manager
is trying to bar the press. The Associazione Culturale Italiana
people are standing backstage staring out at the crowd that has
overflowed the seats and balconies; women are sitting on the
floor up to the very edge of the stage. A woman translator this
time! I ask if she is familiar with the women's movement.

"No," she says scornfully. "I am political"—as if women and "political" were contradictions. A group down in front begins to heckle before the interpreter even begins. A man stands up and shakes his fist, shouting at me. The female hecklers, in boots and jeans and leather jackets, shout, "Down with men! Down with politics." I try to struggle on. The scornful interpreter walks off the stage, leaving me all alone. I begin to get the idea it isn't the translation: somebody around here doesn't want me to speak at all. They heckle two more interpreters off the stage.

Then a young woman with a baby face, tight short blond curls, and a miniskirt sits down in the empty interpreter's seat. "I'm Lucretia Love," she says in a Texas accent. "Don't worry, honey, I don't know anything about the women's movement. I'm an actress, but Lucretia Mott was my great-grandmother," and we are off.

The next day I had planned to shop and sightsee, but all day long women from the Italian movement and reporters crowd the lobby. A cold solid sheet of gray rain hides the view of the ruins. Who will *show up* at the Piazza Navona on a night like this for an abortion rally? I decide to beg off. The phone rings. Alma Sabatini, my responsible sister leader from the Italian movement, is calling. "Hundreds of women came to hear you despite the rain." she says. "We were going to move to a hall, but the fascists have come to break the meeting up, so we can't leave." "I'll be right there," I say.

By the time I get there, the fascist thugs and the police have driven the wet women back against a building wall and have formed a circle around them. My friend, Joan Cook, fending off thugs with her umbrella, saw a notorious fascist priest a block away handing money to prostitutes and sending them into the crowd. I speak standing on a café table under the awning of a *trattoria*, with the manager pulling at my skirt to get down. ("No speak Italian," I tell him, with a long-haired young American man—a student, I suppose—happily protecting me.) At that moment, I share with the Italian women leaders a sense of triumph and dread and terrible responsibility that the women's movement has already emerged as such a potent force for change that the fascists must come out in the rain to disrupt even this little abortion rally.

Back at the headquarters, the girls who heckled the interpreters last night attack me directly. "Despite what you say, women must not have anything to do with politics. If we become political, we will have to deal with men. Women should have nothing more to do with men. All of history so far has been made by men. We must get rid of men and start over again. Only women must make history from now on."

I am trembling now from flu or cold, or fear from my first encounter with real fascists. I have no more patience with this kind of talk, whether it comes from innocent sophomoric pseudo-radical infantilism or deliberate disruption. "What island are you going to flee to, to live without men?" I ask them. "If women are to have good life in Italy or in America, we have to deal with men, convince them, oppose them, defeat them if necessary, love them if we can, and work with them to change the conditions that oppress us. With fascism at your country's throat, and maybe mine too, if the energy of women is diverted away from solving our own real problems and the real political dangers of our nation—then the women's movement plays into the hands of the fascists. Just as male leaders help the fascists when they ignore the real problems of women or sell them out."

I go for dinner then with the responsible leaders to a famous Roman restaurant, but I am not hungry. The flu, maybe. I suddenly realize how many conferences that I have helped organize in America have been disrupted under the guise of "down with men" talk. I wonder if the real forces of reaction in Italy and America—and the media they control—may even be inflaming the anti-man extremists precisely to *prevent* the women's movement from gaining the political power that will liberate us from their control. The anti-man extremists are not the true radicals of the women's movement, if radical means the power for real change: they are its reactionary enemies. But the anger they play upon is a desperately real symptom of the urgent need for women's liberation.

"We ignore, at our peril, our need for love."

A while ago I went to a closed conference on "The Female Orgasm" held by a professional organization of marriage counselors, psychiatrists and the like. About 80 percent of the people there were middle-aged men. The female orgasm, it seemed, wasn't happening; maybe there was no such thing, some of the psychiatrists dared to suggest. In the flesh, Masters and Johnson described in detail their methods of inducing or enforcing or conditioning the proper sexual reflexes in impotent men and frigid women. Other sexologists reported enthusiastically on the potency, orgastic and profit-wise, of the vibrator and of another mechanical sexual device that operates somewhat like a bicycle pump. Counselors were warned, however, to restrain their enthusiasm for these efficient sex machines, for these could become a "threat" to the "human penis."

The few women therapists present didn't say much. I raised the question whether whatever was keeping women from having orgasms could be cured by vibrating machines. Maybe the life women led during the day, and the way that made them feel about themselves and their husbands, had something to do with their sexual frigidity or insatiability in bed at night. It seemed to me that Masters and Johnson et al., denigrated women in much the same way as pornographic advertisers, treating them literally as sexual objects divorced from their human condition.

More recently, I listened to "J," the "Sensuous Woman" tell women on a singles weekend how to be "sexually liberated." Her recipes, which turned women into sexual manipulators, made sex dull and mechanical and denigrated men.

At a women's conference in California, I thought at first it was a put-on when some pseudo-radical sisters claimed the "superiority" of the clitoral to the vaginal orgasm because it "enables women to dispense with men." They even suggested, in all seriousness, that women who still engage in sexual intercourse stand up for their rights and insist on "being on top, not the bottom." I wanted to laugh, or cry, on behalf of sex itself—which is to say, on behalf of women and men.

An observer from Mars, taking in the sexploitation films on every Main Street, the pornography on the newsstands, the best-selling sex books—*The Sensuous Woman, The Sensuous Man, Everything You Ever Wanted To Know About Sex, Any Woman Can* —the manuals and columns on eighty-eight ways to make your marriage and sex life more exciting; ads for orgies, "couples" encounter groups, partners who "swing" in new combinations—to say nothing of vaginal sprays and vitamins to revitalize the waning urge—would suspect that something is very wrong indeed in the American bedroom. Why is such industry needed to make the act of love endurable?

How explain the fantastic explosion of divorce, not only among the couples who married so young in the feminine mystique years, but in my own age group, after twenty years and more of conventional, adjusted marriage? In the fifties, when my friend Si Goode did his definitive study of divorce, in almost all cases the one who precipitated it, no matter who went to court, was the man. Now, in as many or more cases, he has the impression it is the women who want out.

A new book called *The Erotic Life of the American Wife* presents case history after case history documenting an appalling sexual dreariness, even open sexual war, between the American housewife and her husband. Most of the women interviewed, well-to-do suburban housewives, seemed to be erupting in one great explosive snarl at the husbands providing the luxuries they supposedly live for. Or wives were playing games of sexual revenge on the husbands, who were seeking refuge elsewhere. But by some strange quirk of logic, author Natalie Gittelson blames the sexual blight of these housewives and their husbands on the movement for equality which is probably the only hope for its cure. The straw women she attacks are the least liberated in our society; they do not enjoy equality. The bitter man-haters she quotes from the extreme fringes of the women's movement are the very ones who bought the feminine mystique so young and so completely that to liberate themselves they felt they had to repudiate marriage, motherhood, and every vestige of their own sexuality. And their exploding rage and the vicious snarl of their unliberated kept sisters are not the only threats today to a masculine potency which she equates with domination. She thinks this mess can be cured by a return to the very roles—subservience in women and domination in man—which are producing the inadequacy and torment.

I protest—on behalf of women and men and my ever-deepening respect for the power and the glory and the mystery of human sex. I protest that passionate sexual human love cannot be experienced if it is divorced from what we really are ourselves. Those obsolete masculine and feminine mystiques—the masks we've been wearing which didn't let us be or know ourselves—made it almost impossible to know each other. The Biblical word for sexual love is *knowing*.

Locked in those iron masks, we finally choke with impotent rage and become immune to each other's touch. Or when we do touch each other, it is only to hurt, in the very frustration of our longing need for love. That need is real—our human bedrock. It is not going to be met by Masters and Johnson or vibrators or impersonal orgies—or by panicky playacting of the old roles, with mutual contempt for our own duplicity and the ones we dupe.

We are in a state of transition now. The bitterness, the rage underneath the ruffles, which we used to take out on ourselves and our kids and finally on the men in bed, is out in the open now, scaring us in its scorching intensity, goading men to exasperation and despair. And now the men are letting it hang out, too: how they really feel about female parasites, the dead weights, alimony, the sexual nothingness, the lonely lovelessness of the manipulated breadwinner. "Everything I made was hers, and it was never enough," a divorced man said on that "singles" weekend. "And when she went to work—to express herself—everything she made was hers, and everything I made, too."

This is not equality, nor is it love.

• • •

I think of friends of mine who playacted for twenty years the Mama-the-housewife, Daddy-the-breadwinner, Good-Housekeeping-seal-of-approval marriage, mortgaging their souls and talents and all their dreams for a glamorous house and four children, two of each. As a commercial artist, he could make the money needed to support their expensive ménage; it was the reason, or excuse, for not risking his own art.

He was respected by his colleagues—but she made him feel like a failure. She had really married him to get, as the wife of a Great Artist, the glory she never dared to seek by any talent of her own. He loved his children, whose lives she only let him enter as a not-quite-adequate money machine. She would boast to me about the good act she put on in bed—but he never felt he gave her joy. She might go through all the tricks of *The Sensuous Woman*, but she didn't feel good enough about herself to enjoy being with him. When the rage broke through the charade, she wanted at first to sell the house and leave him, with or without the children. He resisted. She went back to school to train for work of her own. The fury between them shocked their friends, whose own façades were shaky, but it strangely helped rather than hurt their children. Maybe the honesty at last relieved the children of the burden of all that role-playing, which had made them even doubt their own reality. Honesty and respect for their own lives will eventually end their soap opera, unless some underlying root of love, or simply the will to save what they had, carries them through to the point where they can touch each other with real pleasure.

• • •

Lately, in the movement, I feel it is necessary to spell out, half-humorously—"man is not the enemy, he is the fellow victim"; some of my best friends are men, etc. Some think I say this for public relations, to sweeten the image of the movement. Others aren't sure. "The trouble with you, Betty, is that you really like men." *Don't they?* Am I lying to myself? Or have I come out the other end of women's liberation?

I am not dependent on a man now—for economic support or status or my identity. I move on my own, and worlds are open to me on my own. I no longer playact or feel stifled by enforced passivity. I am myself. I like myself and other women better now—and suddenly find I like men better, feel more comfortable with them, even delight in them.

I admit that I still need and want to love and be loved by a man. Would I finally settle, after all, for love, one man; would I get married again? Or is that a remnant of obsolete nostalgia—a dream to be abandoned with our chains? I'm not sure. The part of me that is still passionately involved with the movement is fired into higher gear than ever by the exploding pace of political '72. The other part of me is discovering new emotions about men. With apologies to Joan of Arc, *all that I am, I will not deny.*

·   ·   ·

I think in our move for equality, we ignore at our own peril the reality of our need for human love. That need can't be met by playacting or by exchanging obsolete masculine and feminine roles—any more than by orgies or vibrators—but by becoming so truly ourselves that we really can know and love each other without excessive demands or sacrifices or need for revenge. I'm not sure that need for love has to be channeled into marriage, sanctioned by the state. Can any sanction of state or morality keep marriages together that do not let us love or be ourselves?

A friend, a woman married twenty years, says, "I was going to have the perfect marriage. I saw the mess my mother made of it, always discontented, and thought I knew all the answers. I graduated from college at twenty and gave up a Fulbright in Paris to get married. I concentrated on being a good wife and mother. Two years ago, I had a fantasy of myself on a hospital bed, dying, with all the people mourning around my bed because I had been such a good wife and mother. I realized then that I had to save my own life before it was too late. I don't know how much I've messed up my kids, devoting my life to them that way. I've been giving my husband a very hard time these last few years. All my hostility is coming out. And now he is a successful lawyer, he has made enough money, he wants to have a good time. He wants me with him, sailing, skiing, entertaining, and I'm in school, making up for lost time. I'm alive again. I don't know what's going to happen to my marriage. My husband is a handsome, successful man. A lot of women are after him. If I have to choose between my own life and my marriage, I have to save my life and take the consequences."

Are these the choices women really have to make? Or is the false role-playing which brought us to such desperate choices the real evil from which women, in fact, are now liberating both themselves and men? Our kids seek commitments, one to one, more clearly and honestly than we did, and live them out with mutual sharing of housework and money, respecting each other's work and dreams, in marriages whose only sanction is their love. They don't even demand the illusion of security—that it will be for life. In my own age group, even those of us who have dropped out of the role-playing charade still seek personal commitment beyond the casual sexual encounter —all but the most bitter women, the most defeated men.

• • •

Would my bitter friend now back in law school have felt such resentment over her husband's success if she hadn't given up her own law school twenty years ago for the "good wife and mother" façade? They might have shared more closely the times of hard work then, and the freedom to play more now, and timed and raised their kids to a different tune. If the timing is different, as it can be for our kids, will it have to end the same way? Will it be different for the older ones brave enough to try again, if they do not wear the masks that keep us from ever knowing each other?

• • •

I sit in my living room listening to a friend, a man, telling me about a crazy scheme that will probably never pan out; he thinks of maybe twelve new schemes to save the world or his own fortune every month. Still, two or three of them seem to work. Maybe this one will—and I laugh and encourage him, and delight at his indomitable spirit. Strange, how apprehensive and discouraging I used to be about my husband's crazy schemes. But I wasn't earning or even risking my own talent then; our whole suburban façade, our illusion of security might collapse if his scheme didn't work. I can even comfort my friend's self-doubt over a scheme that failed, because he is not part of me, it doesn't mean my failure; he is simply a man I love and respect. Is marriage then at fault, or marriage for any other reason than just wanting to be together?

• • •

We begin to wear the sexual masks very early. My father, who loved me, saw in me the dreams that circumstance did not let him realize himself. His armor against the pain a man can't admit he suffers doomed him to early death, but he could not bear my pain as a woman. He teased me because I did not walk easily in high heels, because I would not use those feminine wiles on the telephone. He knew I would have to wear the mask.

I remember walking up Main Street hill in the sunset, and the boy with whom I started a magazine in high school put his arm around me and said, "If you were a boy, you would be my best friend." There was no way to know, then, that I wanted him to love me as a girl and *also* to see me as his best friend. In all the years that followed, dating boys, up to and during my marriage, I learned to wear the mask and never saw through theirs.

$$\bullet \quad \bullet \quad \bullet$$

I sometimes think it is more difficult, more lonely, more vulnerable to be a man today than a woman. I watched a friend of mine take a terrible defeat in the corporate rat race— and, hit in the stomach, straighten his shoulders and go back for more. His wife was completely dependent on him—and he perhaps dependent on her dependence. But as his world got bigger—and he loved that world and meeting its challenges— hers got emptier. Whatever her own resentments, wishes or abilities, she no longer had the confidence to do anything about them. He could meet his own terrors, but the helplessness at hers almost killed him. Divorce, I suppose, was her revenge for the self he could not give her.

All this time, he would tease me about the women's movement for equality. But he is still growing after fifty—the way men do, the way women are doing now. He used to be outraged at his kids' repudiation of his values. Now he listens to his kids—affirming, even sometimes changing his own values. "I'm not sure it's what I want any more—power, money. I want to feel, share more life." As proud as he is of his corporate eminence, he suddenly admits he doesn't like it when I introduce him by his corporate title, "as if that is the only reason you like me."

One chilly weekend I go to visit him on the farm where he is trying to figure things out for himself. I suddenly feel a peace there, away from all the hectic demands, the in-fighting, and the power maneuvers which, now that our movement is big business, women must also suffer without admitting pain. I admire his unpolluted mountain stream, and we begin to talk across the masks of twenty years. He is not the corporate boss to me, nor I the famous liberator to him; we are best friends.

The phone rings. I have given this number to my service only for emergencies. The phone is for me. The Prime Minister of India would like to see me at seven that evening in the city, to talk for half an hour about women's liberation. My host, with an ominous gleam in his eye, says he will drive me to the nearest airport. But much as I admire the Prime Minister of India, I do not want to go from this place—this rushing, peaceful mountain stream I have finally reached. I arrange instead to talk to her by phone during that half-hour. While the details are being worked out, he goes outside to chop wood.

We go for a walk up the mountain. He walks faster than I do, but stops every now and then to wait for me to catch up. I'm terrified of height but love to climb mountains. It is fun climbing with him. We pass a troop of Girl Scouts, a man leading them, and exchange pleasantries. As we sit on a rock at the top, really talking, finally, to each other, the Girl Scout troop appears again and the man leading them comes over to me and says, "Haven't we met?" Oh, God, I think, not here. And he calls the girls over. I wish I had worn a blond wig. Halfway down the mountain, my friend makes some arrogant comment about the impossibility of loving women who are so high-powered they get recognized on top of mountains. And I tell him he has a terrible double standard still, because he is plenty high-powered himself in his business, and neither of us is that way with each other. And, I think to myself, do I really want to run for the Senate?

•   •   •

A new man invites me out to dinner, and in between shared reactions to divorce and the doomed institution of marriage—and Walter Mitty dreams of exploring the farthest reaches of the Amazon—he gives me political advice. "I like the idea of your running for the Senate," he says, making a date for dinner the next week.

Can I, after all, be me, all that I am, and still love and be loved by a man? This has to be so, for women's liberation to be real. For this is part of what I am: this need to love a man. But

I can only love him, I know now, if I can be who I really am and let him be who he really is himself!

"To marry now is an act of hope and courage."

I was having lunch with a young man I have known very well for most of his twenty-four years. I had been lecturing at Princeton where he was doing graduate work, and I felt pleased with the evident interest and warm support the young men there had shown toward the women's movement. It was hardly the reaction one would expect from "male chauvinist pigs."

"What's so surprising about it?" said my young friend. "Even if we didn't want to in the beginning, we'd have to be for the women's movement. I mean, we have ties to them, we get attached to them [women, he meant]. It's not like a boss and the workers he can forget about at night when he goes home. You get to like them too much."

I asked with some delicacy about one particular woman to whom he had been very attached. They had lived together two years or more. Now they had parted. I wondered if he was sorry they had broken up. I spoke, in the tentative way one approaches the personal with one's own young, of the new attitude toward marriage in his generation—of living together because you want to without feeling the necessity of a sanction by the state. I mentioned Erik Erikson's view that intimacy is only really possible after identity has been achieved, in which case it's better not to make a legal marriage while still in the process of becoming yourself.

But to my surprise, he didn't agree. "That's all right if only one person is having an identity crisis," he said. "You can weather it. But if both of you are having one, it's better to have something that keeps you together through it. Otherwise you break up even when you really love each other."

He and Ellen had been very good together; he is lonely now without her. "I wasn't very good for her for a while," he said with some new, mature self-knowledge. He wishes they'd had that kind of commitment that would have made them weather the bad time together—he wishes that they had been married.

It surprises me to hear his generation defend marriage. His own parents had made his adolescence a hell as they screamed and swore and even became physically violent until they finally got divorced, leaving him the sense of no family to love or fall back on for comfort, and no sense of assurance that he would ever be able to count on love himself. Perhaps that's why he and his friends needed and made these strangely serious and monogamous nonlegal marriages—"spontaneous union," I've heard them called—so young. I was glad he could get from her the warmth and comfort and love he had been deprived of too soon by a mother locked in her own torment, and was sorry for him that it was over. But could he possibly be right, after witnessing the horror of his parents' marriage and the disastrous legal and financial and emotional bitterness of their divorce, that it still would have been better for him and Ellen to have been married?

•   •   •

The last few years, without even needing to consult the mounting divorce statistics (in some cities last year, there were as many divorces as marriages), one could toll the death knell of marriage. "Marriage as an institution is doomed" is the feeling of many women in the movement for whom the essence of women's liberation sometimes seems to be *liberation from marriage*. In suburb and city, marriages are breaking apart like branches of dead trees that offer no resistance to a sudden storm—breaking apart after ten, twenty, even thirty years. And for the first time in history, it's often the women who are saying, "I want out, I won't take it any longer. What's in it for me?" But the "dropout wife" is only news because before it was only the husband who had enough psychological and/or economic independence to walk out. Now, at least, it's both who feel strong enough to get out of a marriage gone sour.

When I went back recently to the suburb where we lived in the fifties and early sixties, my former friends and neighbors filling me in on all the gossip didn't even bother with "So-and-so have broken up." The "Joneses are still together" was the real news.

When I was getting a divorce four years ago, no one I knew

intimately had ever been divorced. Now not just the obviously stormy marriages but also the "ideal" ones are breaking up. "There is no real economic base for marriage any more," says a learned friend of mine. "When women needed a man for economic support, and men needed women economically to run a home, when they needed to have children to secure their old age, marriage was real then and sex outside of marriage was not sanctioned. There's no real basis for that now. That's why marriages now are breaking up as soon as the children get old enough or even before."

But does this divorce explosion really mean the death of marriage?

• • • •

I have dinner one Sunday night with two women friends; one, in her mid-forties, visiting from the West Coast, getting her degree as a psychotherapist after twenty years as a self-effacing wife and mother of five, is frankly envious of the two of us—women her age, divorced, successful in our careers, leading, in her opinion, divinely glamorous, free, and independent lives. She is annoyed that she has to rush to the airport to get home tonight—some problem with her youngest son, her husband at the end of his rope over an absence she has kept prolonging.

The other two are in no hurry and order cocktails, debating over lobster or duck. Sunday is the longest day; the children are not due back from the fathers until nine o'clock. One is talking, with some undefined emotion or its absence, about a man she has been dating all summer. He is divorced, the right age, eminently successful, very rich, and she wants to get married again—she panics even on a night like this at the prospect of being alone. But she does not really like him. Not that much.

The other says humorously that she has no such problem. She is currently involved with two married men in two different cities. Over the last week she has seen both, spent two intense days with one, several with the other, but does not quite know when she'll see either one again. This has been going on for several years. Neither has any interest in leaving his wife, nor would she really want to marry either one of them. Other than the fact that neither is available on weekends, Sundays or holidays, or for long vacations or dinner every night—her relationship with both is quite perfect. Marvelously intense conversation, sex, emotion, dinners, letters—more intense surely than if they were together every day. She is not at all jealous of their wives.

"What could be better?" asks her married friend. "You can enjoy all that, the closeness, the emotion, the sex, the fun and games—and you don't ever have to do the laundry, so to speak, or stop doing your thing to make his dinner. You live your own life. You only have yourself to think about. How I envy you!"

Her friends look at each other and shrug. How to explain that you might long for that very thing, to *have* to think about someone beside yourself. One of them announces she has just gone on a Weight Watchers diet, although she is already thin. "I'm just sick of being so self-indulgent," she explains. "I never have to think of anyone beside myself. I want some signposts, some texture to my life. It's like an endless hot-fudge sundae."

•   •   •

Lately, strangely, some of my most sophisticated, cynical friends are, of all things, getting married, while some of my most conventional friends are getting divorced. Lois, for instance, and Nancy R. Both beautiful, intelligent, successful—and successfully, valiantly evading marriage into their thirties, despite conventional pressures from parents and friends. No lack of men, either. Both doing better and better in their careers. Both strongly committed to women's liberation, and to a profound skepticism, if not downright repudiation, of marriage as an institution.

Lois, a tall, sparkling redhead from a large Irish Catholic family, became my friend and ally in the fight for women's right to abortion. Her mother had died young in a fourth childbirth, so Lois spent her adolescence bringing up her younger siblings. She had been devoting her own time as well as her professional time to fighting discrimination against women; she fully enjoyed the rewards of her own career in communications. And now, suddenly, she is going to get married to a Republican businessman, long divorced.

I go to their wedding on a Saturday afternoon. The groom

is in his late forties, the essence of WASP dignity in a conventional formal wedding suit, his silver sideburns not noticeably longer than those of his business and political colleagues and fox-hunting friends in the conservative Republican counties his business serves. His teenage sons, her sisters and brothers and her father, her former bosses, her motley friends and movement sisters are all there. It is a happy wedding.

Dressed in off-white and carrying flowers, the bride comes down the stairs. But the ceremony, as read by the Presbyterian minister, was personal, not conventional, and composed as carefully by this "mature bride and groom" as they put it, as the most offbeat, do-your-own-thing marriage ceremony of young hippiedom. The commitment Martin and Lois made to each other went beyond the requirements of church and state. She finally risking marriage she had so long avoided, he taking the risk again after the bitterness of a long marriage destroyed. They have the minister open:

"We have gathered here today to participate in joining this woman and man in marriage . . . We do not live upon the earth in isolation . . . You have known Martin and Lois as individuals. After today, you will know them as a family. They have stated this to you by inviting you to the wedding. You have stated your intention henceforth to consider them as a partnership . . . Rejoice with them that they have found each other."

Then Lois and Martin each make a "statement of freely chosen responsibility" that they "expect to know sufficient rewards from this relationship," that they are prepared "to limit their own freedom to the required degree" of their "own free will" because of their love for each other "and not for any lesser motive."

Taking each other "to be my wedded husband" and "wedded wife," Lois and Martin made this vow: "Insofar as I know my own mind, I intend to be faithful to you in word, thought, and deed . . . I promise to bring to you what the past has made me, and I intend to grow and develop henceforth in partnership with you . . . I promise to respect you as an individual in your own right and at the same time as the half of my life. I intend to love you and live with you in plenty and in want, in joy and in sorrow, in sickness and in health, as they befall us separately or together. I intend to live with you . . . until death do us part."

After the ceremony, as we stand chatting on the lawn, drinking champagne, the words of their vow are much discussed. Some of the men seem more shocked than the women at the unsentimentality of their clear-cut, carefully qualified commitments to each other. But I think those who have lived through the death of their own marriage or who have feared marriage as their own death are deadly serious now in every such word of commitment. To marry now is an act of hope and courage, not just an expected convention.

•   •   •

I go back to the city to help celebrate the "nuptials" of John and Nancy, members of our weekend commune. She is a sophisticated writer and TV reporter who refused to marry and become a housewife. She was writing an article, "The Case Against Motherhood," when we became friends. She and John had been making chic jokes about their relationship for three years now; they were *good* with each other, but so tense somehow; his view of marriage as a doomed, outdated, unnecessary and unnatural institution was even more vociferous than hers, since he had tried it when he was very young and again when he was not so young, and failed.

None of us had believed they would go through with it when they left for Europe to get married, inviting us to celebrate when they got back. It is a cheerful, irreverent, funny celebration. The "nuptial" guests watching the bride and groom for signs of impending doom are confounded by the strange fact that both seem less tense, more relaxed, more secure—yes, happier with each other than before they were married. How odd! "Not at all," says the liberated bride. "What made us tense before was being afraid to get married. Now we've done it, we can relax." They are so comfortable together now, sometimes they even let the tenderness show.

•   •   •

In Ira Levin's horror novel *The Stepford Wives*—more chilling than his *Rosemary's Baby*—when the suburban "Stepford Wives" stop playing housewife all the time and begin making noises like people, the men are so terrified they replace the obstreperous real women with Disneyland robots who can make hot breakfasts, wax floors, shop supermarkets, drive cars, sing lullabies to children, and even fill brassieres and put on lipstick more efficiently than women who are people. Just as robots, automation can now do more efficiently most of the big muscle work that used to be the basis of masculine *machismo*. But the marriages of my friends that weekend, with their statements of "freely chosen responsibility," are not based on the old economic roles.

Neither Lois nor Nancy needed to marry for economic support, nor will they submerge themselves in the housewife role as others I know have done. Their marriages are based on human equality and human need, alike for men and women, as Lois and Martin stated in their vows. A kind of support that can't be replaced by robots, a kind of commitment that took my other friends through their time of trouble and enabled them even to transcend the hate that had piled up. These needs are real and may be felt more strongly and voiced more clearly in the years to come by our sons and daughters. The increasing pace of change and mobility of mass society and our rebellion against the plastic makes us need more than ever that mysterious, complex warmth and strength of human intimacy —okay, call it love—which is both sexual and finally personal —human sex.

The other night in Vermillion, South Dakota, lecturing to a crowded auditorium of townspeople and students, I expressed my own feeling that the women's movement of the sixties and early seventies was merely the conscious first stage of a sex-role revolution of men and women alike. Throughout my speech, here and there I would see a woman lean over to pat her husband's hand, or a man give his wife a squeeze, or a young student put his arm around a girl's shoulder.

I think we are all frightened, men and women alike, to face the anger we have been shifting on the other, and all the more frightened because we do need each other. It took an act of courage for every woman who risked coming out from the cover of the feminine mystique. It takes an act of courage now also for women and men who are sick of playing games and scoring bitter little revenges within sham marriages to get out —and maybe even more courage to risk marriage without sham.

Remembering my friend who found her freedom like "an endless hot-fudge sundae," I cannot believe that the need for marriage is over. It is changing, as it had to, and it may emerge stronger than ever.

"Female chauvinism is dangerous."

At first the danger signs seem unconnected.

At a party in Beverly Hills, a woman, fortyish, obviously well-to-do, gushes about "women's lib" in a way that makes me uncomfortable. She has left her husband the week before along the lines of the women in a recent *Life* cover story on the "dropout wife—a striking current phenomenon. . . . Wanda Adams left home and family for a new life."

She is taken aback that I do not see *Life*'s "dropout wife"— who has moved with her daughter into a women's commune, leaving her husband to bring up her sons—as a heroine of the women's movement. I am taken aback when it turns out that her dropping out of her own marriage, which she sees as the heroic culmination of this whole movement of millions of women, is a kind of fantasy playacting, a domestic one-act drama with herself as heroine, mooning around the swimming pool and making "dates" with her suffering husband. She tells me that she sympathizes with her husband's pain and loneliness, alone in his hotel room . . . She sends the bills to him, as before . . . She is outraged that he wasn't waiting in his hotel room the previous evening when she telephoned. He has no right to take another woman to dinner! How long can she expect him—the villain in her play—just to sit still, suffer and support her?

• • •

A letter "To Julie and Abigail" appears on the Op Ed page of *The New York Times*, from their mother, Shelley List, forty-one, "divorced . . . and fairly well liberated," as she describes herself. "But what concerns me now, with your young womanhood approaching, and my 'fulfilling' myself as a writer more and more is . . . priorities. When you say to me, as one of you did recently after sharing an intimate confidence, your arm covering your eyes so I wouldn't see your pain, the tears escaping under your elbow down your cheeks, 'Do you know this is the first time you have really talked to me in a long time, and I feel so much better just for that,' I am taken aback . . . and I think about Gloria Steinem. . . . I wonder what she would do at those moments when a daughter just needs her mother and whatever wise womanly self that woman can muster, and she is not there, but out fulfilling herself. And when I pull your arm away from your eyes, and look at the moist brown, and kiss away the wetness, I wonder about liberation. . . . I wonder at those feminists who decry having husbands or fathers for their babies. . . ."

Why does she have to apologize to Gloria Steinem for moments when wiping her daughter's tears takes priority over "fulfilling" herself as a writer? Why does "liberation" or "feminism" imply to her the elimination of husbands or fathers, the exclusion of her "womanly self" as a mother?

• • •

When Bella Abzug announces she is running in the Democratic primary on New York's West Side against Congressman William Fitz Ryan, who has a long and excellent voting record on peace and women's rights and recently underwent throat surgery, liberal male journalists and other men who had previously supported both women's liberation and Bella Abzug react with "a genuine male backlash, the first in American political history," as Shana Alexander describes it. Why are they so outraged at Bella Abzug's "cold-blooded" act?

• • •

On a recent evening, over coffee in a barely furnished New York apartment, the forty-five-year-old male recipient of an act of female banishment absentmindedly plays with a sharp paper knife as he talks of Gloria Steinem's proclamation of "Sisterhood" in the new magazine *Ms.* With a tone of cold, measured outrage I find positively startling (previously he has identified completely with the women's movement) he says, "I think we have had just about enough of this." I am not sure whether the knife is meant for Gloria or the woman in his own life following Gloria's model. I ask him to please put away the knife, and I reread the article to find out why it makes him murderous. Is it a certain tone implying that women are special and pure, forever wronged by men, the dirty brutes? "I get the feeling that we are speaking Urdu and the men are speaking Pali . . . ," the article says. "Women understand. We may share experiences, make jokes, paint pictures, and describe humiliations that mean nothing to men, but *women understand.* . . . Any woman who chooses to behave like a full human being should be warned that the armies of the status quo will treat her as something of a dirty joke. . . . She will *need* sisterhood."

Can sisterhood be carried too far?

• • •

When our movement was small and weak, we thought it necessary to hide whatever arguments we had amongst ourselves: "Sisterhood Is Powerful"; alone we were weak, our solidarity is our strength. But now we must take the responsibility of strength and honestly confront our own differences. What we are doing has too many consequences in real life for women—and men and children—for any of us who have gained a voice as spokeswomen to acquiesce, by silence or for fear of losing popularity, in our going in a direction that will lead us off the track, to a dead end.

If I were a man, I would strenuously object to the assumption that women have any moral or spiritual superiority *as a class,* or that men share some brute insensitivity *as a class.* This is male chauvinism in reverse; it is female sexism. It is, in fact, female chauvinism, and those who preach or practice it seem to me to be corrupting our movement for equality and inviting a backlash that endangers the very real gains women have won these past few years.

As a woman, I object to female chauvinism, not only because it is dangerous, but because it is wrong. Just as it is wrong to denigrate women as a class by defining them as sex objects, it is also wrong to elevate women as a special class by yet another sexual definition, one that distorts a concrete fact of human life—female sexuality—into an abstract ideology. Such sexual definition, whether it seems to put us down or glorify us, denies us human identity, personal definition—the right to spell our own name as people by our own actions in society—which is what this movement is all about, and *all* it is about.

Female chauvinism denies us full humanity as women in another way, too, one that threatens backlash among women even more than men. Those who would make an *abstract ideology* out of sex, aping the old-fashioned rhetoric of class warfare or the separatist extremists of race warfare, paradoxically deny the concrete reality of woman's sexuality, mundane or glorious, burden or pleasure, exaggerated or repressed as it has been in the past. When Gloria Steinem dismisses marriage as "prostitution" in a speech to the League of Women Voters, the assumption is that no woman would ever want to go to bed with a man if she didn't have to sell her body for bread or a mink coat. Does this mean that any woman who admits tenderness or passion for her husband or for any man has sold out to the enemy? A female chauvinism that makes a woman apologize for loving her husband or children—or that defines "self-fulfillment" as a contradiction of her "womanly self" as a wife or mother, instead of *including* it—denies the real feelings of too many women.

A similar female chauvinism perverted—and aborted—the first wave of women's revolution in America. What began as a struggle for equality ended with the notion that women as a class were purer and morally superior, and thus, just by getting the vote, they would clean up America. Those earlier feminists had more reason than we to want to forget women's sexual reality: women were people who had babies, in sexual relation to men, which meant, then, complete economic dependence on men. They were denied too much because of their sex; they had to fight too long to get any rights at all. I think they finally got tired of proving they were as good as men and rationalized their isolation from society into a moral virtue, to crusade instead against the evils of drink and the depravities of men. So they won the vote and wasted it on prohibition instead of going on to restructure society to make equality possible.

That's the job we are doing now, after nearly fifty years when women stood still, or went backwards, as the pendulum has swung from feminism to female chauvinism to the feminine mystique. I predicted, starting our movement six years ago, that if society didn't restructure to permit women who have babies to move out of housewife drudgery into its mainstream, the most spirited women would begin to repudiate marriage, motherhood, children, even their own sexuality. Female chauvinism is a reaction to the very denigration of women that our movement seeks to change. But instead of changing our situation, I think female chauvinism will exacerbate the old conflicts which caused the pendulum swings in the first place.

I have always objected to rhetoric that treats the women's movement as class warfare against men—women oppressed as a class by men, the oppressors. I do not believe that the conditions we are trying to change are caused by a conspiracy for "the economic and social profit of men as a group," as Gloria Steinem sees it. The causes are more complex and burden men as well as benefit them. My definition of feminism is simply that women are people, in the fullest sense of the word, who must be free to move in society with all the privileges and opportunities and responsibilities that are their human and American right. This does not mean class warfare against men, which denies our sexual and human bonds with men, nor does it mean the elimination of children, which denies our human future.

It seems to me that *all* the women's movement ever was, or needs to be, is a stage in the whole human rights movement—bringing another group, a majority this time, into the mainstream of human society, with all the perils and promises and personal risks this involves. No more, no less. Women needed, and still need, to organize separately only in order to break through the barriers that prevent our participation as people. There is no need to shackle ourselves in a new mystique of specialness, glorifying the traits resulting from our isolation from society—some good, some bad—into virtues. No need to create an abstract religion rationalizing or dictating our continued isolation, or justifying special privilege, which exempts us from the risks and tests of merely being human. Female chauvinism is dangerous now because it could keep us from using the gains we have won, moving on through the door we have opened. It could make men slam the door in our faces.

•   •   •

My male friend on the verge of switching from supporter to enemy of the women's movement is paying $17,500 a year alimony to his first wife. He is sharing, indeed hungrily fighting to share, personal responsibility for his children with her, as well as responsibility with his second wife for the housework and her children. In this, of course, he is not like many other divorced men—only some of them. Men are *not* a class; more and more middle-aged men who played the old masculine role in their marriages and jobs are joining the long-haired young who say no to the brutal and obsolete masculine mystique of domination.

My particular friend is still being chivalrous. He shows much greater support and respect for his new wife's professional work than she for his. He had always assumed that because of her sex she was more vulnerable than he. Now he is not so sure. "I like everything about her except the way she always puts me down. It's like she is supposed to be free to really be herself now, but if I'm not always the big, strong, perfect man, I'm no good. I'm sick and tired of being treated like an enemy, a brute, no matter what I do. I want a woman who really likes me. My first wife *had* to like me, she was dependent on me. That didn't count." He asks if I have read the book about the dropout husband (*Letter to My Wife* by John Koffend, who describes becoming impotent sexually and then leaving his wife, children and executive job to escape to Pago Pago, "the story of a man who had to stop being a husband so he could get back to being a man," the book was advertised.) "Maybe Pago Pago is carrying it too far," my friend said to me, "but impotence is the masculine backlash."

•   •   •

If we *make* men the enemy, they will surely lash back at us. If we deny them their humanity, and their need for love. If we insist on our freedom, but keep them in jail as our breadwinners or scapegoats . . . If we demand, and even win, fair and equal treatment from them, and still insist on special privilege —such as exemption from the draft . . . Or if we replace the double standard which said a woman had to be twice as good as a man to get the job, by a double standard which says a woman deserves the job of *any* man, no matter how good, just because she's a woman. Or that it's all right for a woman to hit below the belt, but he can't hit back because she is a woman. The women's movement will become bankrupt if it goes that route, because our basic capital is the human rightness of our cause, and men's need for our love—and our votes. They also depend on our underpaid or unpaid menial work, but the machines or the men they have displaced could take over that. We can win men's support against the injustice to our humanity, now that they finally can see us as people. They even see an end to their own loneliness if we can really like them, instead of just *depend* on them. But if, in the name of our own moral superiority, we do not abide by even the basic customs of honor and decency, then we deserve the backlash. They are hungry for the soft qualities they've suppressed in themselves in the name of masculinity. It would be ironic if we ourselves gave up those qualities, the one part of our humanity we were freer to express than they, in liberating ourselves from the enforced passivity of femininity.

•   •   •

Is it any worse for a woman to be hungry for power, and to go after it with no holds barred, than for a man? It may be more threatening because of all that buried impotent rage which women took out on themselves, and covertly on their husbands and sons, when they had no possibility of power except through men. We even hesitate to criticize one another now, knowing how destructive women used to be when they felt such contempt for themselves that they would not even vote for other women and wanted to strike down any woman who achieved.

But only a female chauvinist would say that no matter how good a man's record is—on peace or on women—that women must support a female opponent just because she is a woman. That would invite men to vote *against* women simply because they are women.

The essence of political power for women, as well as men, has to be some principle of reward or support for those who fight for us and revenge on or defeat of our enemies. We must fight for the defeat of senators and state legislators who tried to stop the Equal Rights Amendment and to take back women's right to abortion. To get more women into Congress and to achieve real victories, not just headlines, on child care and the right of women to choose childbirth or abortion, we have to make alliances with men. The possibility of gaining actual political power ourselves—of women making policy, not just coffee—is undermined by female chauvinism. For it separates the millions of women who marched together on August 26th from the female chauvinist few.

•   •   •

Some male backlash is probably inevitable. Some men are going to have to be defeated or move over as women begin in larger numbers to compete for jobs or political offices that men now hold. But if we avoid female chauvinism—and obey at least the minimal unwritten rules whose breach men don't forgive each other—men may not find it any worse to be defeated by a woman than by a man.

In the new human politics ahead, female chauvinism will be as obsolete as the Playboy Bunny. I ran as a delegate to the Democratic National Convention—not just to champion women's rights, but to have a voice on all the urgent problems of this fascinating, fast-changing time. Politically, I'm not a woman first; like Nora, when she left the doll's house, my first responsibility is simply human, just like a man's is.

•   •   •

Female chauvinism may only be a temporary self-indulgence, an excess reaction of rage too long suppressed. In the consciousness-raising groups, female chauvinist rhetoric can be indulged in for a while without even touching the test of reality. But if the strident fringe rhetoric is confused with the reality of the movement—if it affects decisions as to personal lives or movement tactics—it could abort the entire movement. We ourselves can only be seduced by our own rhetoric for so long. If our actual situation is unchanged—or if the changes do not open the new life or self we have dreamed of, or even make life worse—we will sink into even further depths of self-pity, self-disgust and impotent rage. And we will vent that rage on men who can and must be with us, not against us, if we are to change society.

According to the Virginia Slims poll, the great majority of men and women in America now support the real goals and gains of our movement, even those who don't like "women's lib" (I no longer use the term myself: it has been too corrupted by the media and the female chauvinists they exploit). Those real goals—equal pay, equal opportunity for good jobs and the training for them, our own voice in decisions of church and state, an end to practices that discriminate against us or put us down, and the restructuring of work, home, marriage, child rearing, and our very morality that this involves—are too important and precarious to jeopardize now. Our movement has grown so big so fast because of these real needs of women, wants that most men now support. But now that they are within our reach, the forces of reaction are mobilizing against us—from the Catholic hierarchy to the bosses, political, union or business—the forces whose power rests on women's passivity.

Brooding on the danger signs of corruption and backlash, I feel that the women's liberation movement has had enough of sexual politics. The women's caucuses and NOW, the actions geared to concrete breakthrough against sex discrimination in every field—schools, churches, professional organizations, corporations, political parties—must continue until the job is done. But the consciousness-raising groups should open to men—like the group in Cambridge where each woman is now bringing in a man who is a friend, not necessarily a husband or lover. It's time now for the women's liberation movement to be succeeded in our consciousness by a two-sex movement for human liberation from the obsolete sex roles, the feminine and masculine mystiques which torment us mutually. And leave behind as dinosaurs, or isolate as lethal freaks, male chauvinist pigs and female chauvinist boors alike.

"We have become independent enough to admit our need to be dependent, some of the time."

I have been on too many airplanes lately. I have traveled too far and fast, and I feel unrooted, disembodied. Sitting on a 747 that is paralyzed in the Detroit airport because a single computer part has blown a fuse, I only wish I were home. But where and what is home for me? There is my apartment in New York and dinner with Emily, if by chance Emily is also home. My sixteen-year-old is already two feet out the door, mysteriously involved in her own "interpersonal relations,

Mummy"—as she spells it out for me with the exasperated tolerance our young feel for us as they find their own wings.

Stalled in this huge technological monster, the stewardess tells me that she was one of those forced to resign when she got married and now has been rehired although she is a mother. I smile, but I am tired of the 747s and the strangers who are all my comrades in this battle in which I seem to have traveled so far. Concepts that began as fanciful thoughts, as a yearning sense of possibility in my own mind and in the minds of others, are being accepted as commonplace, becoming law. I suddenly feel disoriented, at loose ends, tired.

Back home in my empty apartment, I pick up a pile of the hundreds of letters women have been writing me in answer to my attacks on female chauvinism and sexual politics. I don't feel like going to the NOW board meeting or the Political Caucus; I am sick of fighting the power brokers and manipulators of the women's movement; I am even sick of trying to explain to the endless reporters our real differences in ideology and direction.

Have I, unthinkably, lost my own nerve for this battle? A song nags at me, and I dust off the record player. Simon and Garfunkel sing, "I'm sittin' in the railroad station,/Got a ticket for my destination./On a tour of one-night stands/My suitcase and guitar in hand/And every stop is neatly planned/ . . . Every day's an endless stream/Of cigarettes and magazines./And each town looks the same to me,/The movies and the factories/And every stranger's face I see/Reminds me that I long to be . . . Homeward Bound . . ."

But as I start reading the letters from women across the country, my spirits begin to rise. It seems that once again we have all come to the same place at the same time. Perhaps I can find the answers to my own search for new directions in your letters—letters that look to me for answers. I realize that many of us, at the end of 1972, are somehow trying to catch our breath. After so much change in the sixties, we are breathless, tired after nearly ten years of nay-saying. Not that we want to reverse it, wipe it all out, go home again; not that at all—we had to do what we did, we couldn't stay the way we were. But now that change is suddenly more than *words,* now that it is happening—we suddenly want something familiar to hold on to. We realize we don't want to say no to everything, nor do we have to.

The relief you describe reminds me of the sudden sense of almost overwhelming relief in the letters I received after *The Feminine Mystique* was published in 1963. You said then, "It changed my whole life just to have it put into words." You said that no matter how much you wanted to be your children's mother, your husband's wife, you needed to put yourself in the equation as a person in your own right, that you were tired of confessing guilt on the analyst's couch because you no longer felt as happy in your role of mother and wife. That need to realize ourselves as human beings by our own actions in society had been so suppressed I called it the "problem that has no name." Just giving it a name made women realize they were not guilty and alone, and enabled them to take themselves more seriously—to get a job, to go back to school, to confront the discrimination against them and organize to change the things in society that must be changed if we are to enjoy real equality.

For nearly ten years, then, our consciousness has focused on all the barriers that have kept us from being full people. We acted out our rage at the put-downs we used to accept, and in acting out that anger in public we made headlines, magazine-cover stories and sophisticated cocktail-party humor. We also changed laws and have begun to change institutions: colleges, offices, unions, political parties—even the way we are portrayed on television. It took courage for a woman to act this way in public, and sometimes it seemed to require turning against her old way of life and the people in it, leaving a marriage or a home or a job. The reverberations of the movement and the results have been real and complex and not always comfortable for anyone.

We are almost afraid to face the uncomfortable part of it because we don't want to risk going back to what we were before. We had begun to feel that to be liberated we had to be more independent than any human being can really be—completely independent of our men, our children. I think it is a relief now to realize that we can admit our need for love and home, that we can be soft as well as hard with our children and our husbands, that we can admit our dependence on them without giving up our own identity. We have become independent enough to admit our need to be dependent, some of the time.

Realizing now the course we don't want to take, we can move again on our real course; realizing what we don't want to change, we regain our spirit for the changes we really need. In changing ourselves, that which we thought we wanted to get rid of may also have changed enough so we can see how much we really want to keep it.

A woman from Philadelphia writes:

"I am a woman in my forties who decided to seek 'fulfillment' outside the home. As I began accomplishing my goals, something seemed wrong. I was unconsciously pushing away the very 'male shoulder' I had come to lean on in times of need. I came to expect him to be there only when *I* chose: to help with the dishes, entertain, pay the bills, understand me, fix a leaky sink, be a lover. Slowly he was moving out of my way. While I was accomplishing my goals outside the home, my roots enmeshed in my marriage were becoming loosened. I was not happy. I was frightened. While I could not give up what I had gained as a human being outside the home, I was unable to walk away from my family. . . . I have watched many of my sisters in the liberation movement win their battles. They have alienated themselves from their husbands and children. It seems to me a hollow victory. . . ."

A woman from Sacramento, California, writes that the new dialogue "has helped clear up the many contradictions I've been battling within myself. My lack of conviction that we, by virtue of being women, are morally pure, whereas men are heartless exploiters, left me with the fear that I could not see reality. When I was told by a man that I couldn't possibly be a woman's libber because I was affectionate and wanted to please him, I wondered why it was necessary to choose between loving a man and being accepted as an equal by him."

Some of you are worried that by admitting these new questions we will give up our will to go on fighting the real and still unfinished battle. "You are mistaken if you believe women as a whole have won very real gains in the past few years," one writes. "Little has changed for the majority of us."

And from Havre, Montana: "The message is that we should

slow down or stop much of what we are doing for fear of male backlash. Not so. Women are coming alive, are growing, and I don't think this can be reversed. It seems better to live through the temporary backlash and to come out on the other side and start putting things together in a new way. We must become conscious of ourselves first."

      •   •   •

The majority of your letters, however, confirm my own feeling that many women and men who now support the goals of equality for women will be (or have already been) alienated by the rhetoric of sex-class warfare—especially the young, who are already breaking through the old mystiques of masculinity and femininity. A Mount Kisco, New York woman writes: "I am twenty-six and recently married. My husband is thirty-one. Marriage just suddenly happened for us after knowing and loving each other for two years. We were married with definite feelings of 'my being me and he being he.' He constantly encourages me to pursue my career (art) and understands and respects my ambitions. My point, as you also expressed, is that I have always felt the need for love, and in a world where role-playing so very much exists, I feel lucky to love and be loved by my husband, who puts our individuality above all else."

From Bowie, Maryland: "So glad to realize that women's lib is not just another way of saying 'Make War—Not Love With Men.' Many of my friends and I have found ourselves turning away from anything labeled women's liberation for the very reasons you mention. Most of us have a profession, we are all fairly well educated, and all of us want the *real* goals women's lib set out to attain. But to sacrifice love, home and men to do that is a little bit too much."

      •   •   •

By the end of 1972 the backlash that I predicted six months ago has surfaced. Two respected, serious writers—Joan Didion and Midge Decter—have published devastating attacks on the women's movement that they equate with the rhetoric of sex-class warfare. Joan Didion's attack on the women's movement (*New York Times Book Review*, July 30, 1972) was based on the writings of Kate Millett, Germaine Greer, Shulamith Firestone and lesser-known radical feminists, as well as on the magazine *Ms.*: "At that exact dispirited moment when there seemed no one at all willing to play the proletariat, along came the women's movement and the invention of women as a 'class.' . . . If the family was the last fortress of capitalism, then let us abolish the family. . . . Small children could only be odious mechanisms for the spilling and digesting of food, for robbing women of their 'freedom.' . . . Increasingly it seemed that the aversion was to adult sexual life itself: how much cleaner to stay forever children. . . ."

Midge Decter, in a book called *The New Chastity and Other Arguments Against Women's Liberation*, tries to dismiss the whole movement for women's equality on the grounds that it is antisexual, anti-child-breeding, anti-housework, anti-individual and anti-freedom. She seemed surprised when I pointed out the realities of the women's movement: the fight for good jobs and equal pay, maternity leaves, income-tax deductions, the right to abortion and child-care centers, the ability to get a credit card and a mortgage, economic protection in divorce, running for office and being yourself with men. But as a successful editor and wife of one of the leading editors in the literary establishment, Midge Decter, like the antisexual female chauvinists whose rhetoric she attacks, does not identify with the majority of American women whose real problems at the job or in school or in the home can't be solved by pretending they don't exist.

On August 26th, 1972, the anniversary of women's vote, in New York where in the previous two years more than 20,000 women and men and children had marched for women's equality, less than 5,000 marched. Radical lesbians and other adherents of sex-class warfare took over the march, alienating suburban housewives, working women, welfare mothers, churchwomen, Junior Leaguers and high school girls who had previously joined forces in unprecedented numbers. If those who preach the rhetoric of sex-class warfare succeed in taking over the women's movement, Midge Decter's literary attacks will be mild compared to the fury of the disillusioned and alienated women who were ready to take on the real problems. You who wrote me letters, all who read and understand these words, share responsibility with me not to let this happen.

We must continue to spell out clearly that it's not necessary to turn your back on husband, children, home or even the beauty parlor to be a liberated woman. In fact, in this era of stalled 747s, bombs in the mail, incessant and bewildering change, a very equal liberated woman can and should be able to admit a need for someone to love and "comfort me."

Your letters have deepened my own sense that the women's movement has reached a plateau from which it must find a new direction or retreat in disarray and panic. This whole movement started in the first place because love and home and child rearing had been spoiled when we tried to make them our whole life, because we had been retreating from the fears and challenges of society. But now I think we also fear that society has become too large, cold, frightening, unfamiliar, too fast-changing to endure without warmth and love to come home to.

The plateau women are stalled on is part of the larger plateau on which all of America seems to be stuck during this strange political winter. In one of the innumerable polls taken before the election, President Nixon got a slight majority over McGovern, but almost as many people voted for "neither." I think we are all suffering from future shock, all turned off by the rhetoric of hate, the old slogans of class and race polarity—as we have been benumbed by the senseless bombing in Vietnam, the violent murders, the revelations of deals, sabotage, corruption in high places and the decay of our water, air, schools and hospitals.

In the bleakest month of my own stalled spirit I was asked to lecture in Peoria, Illinois, my hometown. I have not been back in nearly ten years.

Coming in from the airport I recognize the old street names, but there is a McDonald's now on Western, around the corner from our old house. The trees in the park look smaller, the streetcar tracks are gone on Main Street, the hotel is now the Peoria Hilton.

I speak in the gym of Bradley College, and though I am used to large crowds now, I can hardly believe so many people, surely over a thousand, have come out to hear me. I recognize faces in the crowd—old people's faces, my parents' friends, neighbors. I see my kid brother on an aisle: he looks very elegant with silver streaks in his hair.

The thought of coming back to Peoria in this capacity had scared me; not for how they would receive me, but what I might revert to. I always thought I hated Peoria, couldn't wait to get out of there. Now, suddenly, a powerful emotion that I cannot even name makes my chin tremble, and I say, "This is not an ordinary lecture for me. I grew up in this place. My father came here as a boy from Russia, and my mother's father came as a young doctor. My mother went to this college. My roots are in this place. My sense of possibility, whatever it was in me that started women moving, comes from here, from Peoria. They say you can't go home again. And yet you must go home again, affirm your own roots, to know where you are going. It is profoundly moving to me that this revolution that I helped start brings me home, finally, to Peoria."

"Homeward Bound" keeps running in my head as, back home in New York, I move out of my bleak mood, teach my new class at Temple, plan strategy to defend the abortion law, discuss colleges with Emily and stop playing unnecessary power games with a man I love. I also stop feeling so helpless, hopeless about the women's movement—and about America. When my father and my mother's father and all the men like them from Poland or Ireland or Italy found their way to towns like Peoria, what blueprint of the future did they have to create a way of life for themselves and their children?

Against the shocks of the future, we must keep rooted in our own present, in whatever of our past has nourished us, in whatever warmth and strength and love we get and give from our old and our young, our friends and comrades who share our experiences and those whose differences we finally respect in our new battles as women. Finally, we must be able to join with the men we can now know and love as friends as well as lovers, and the strangers who will become our friends. We take our roots with us as we move into the unknown, and I think we may be strong enough to make it if we admit that we are unsure and afraid and still need to depend on each other.

PART IV

Transcending
Polarities

New Power in the World

In the winter of 1973, on the tenth anniversary of the publication of *The Feminine Mystique*, I addressed the NOW convention in Washington. At a gala entertainment the night before, a dramatic celebration of our herstory closed with the song "I Am Woman"; suddenly women got out of their seats and started dancing around the hotel ballroom, joining hands in a circle that got larger and larger until maybe a thousand of us were dancing and singing: "There is nothing I can't do. . . . No price too great to pay. . . . I am strong. . . . I am invincible. . . . I am woman." It was a spontaneous, beautiful expression of the exhilaration we all felt in those years, women really moving as women.

The next morning, I was given a few minutes to address the members of NOW. I spoke of the distance we had come in those ten years, and of the new strength we had found in ourselves and in each other—the strength symbolized by that great circle of women facing each other so joyously. I said that we were strong enough now to turn our circle outward; that while not losing our bonds with each other, moving from the strength of our new sisterhood, we could now face men, our brothers, in a new way.

I proposed that we begin to look at and speak to men not as our masters and oppressors, not as our breadwinners or husbands, but as themselves, the people we had to live with, work with, fight with, even love in new freedom, if we were to move on in the real world we had opened. I got a warm ovation from my sisters in NOW, but the message was premature. The organized women's movement was caught up in the rage, and the exhilaration, of uncovering, defining, confronting all the ways women had been oppressed and exploited in every profession and local community, across the country.

The popular image of "women's lib" was now preempted by *Ms.* magazine without reference or responsibility to the organized women's movement and the actions for real change in the world. "Women's lib" was becoming more and more a kind of retreat into a separate world of women, one that seemed to define itself simply in *reaction against* the values of the world-of-men and the qualities of women cherished by or cherishing men. This turning one's back on men and their values had seemed to help women define and affirm themselves in the early consciousness-raising stage. But now the celebrations of unshaven legs and underarms, of orgasms free from dependency on any man's penis, of a humble sisterhood liberated from men's need to achieve, to reap economic reward, status, power—"cultural feminism," as some called it—seemed to me a schizophrenic retreat from the necessities and actual possibilities of the modern women's movement.

There was beginning to be talk that "women's lib" didn't and shouldn't mean "equality" with men, at all. Rage against men for real grievances—that was something almost all of us experienced as we liberated ourselves. But repudiation of men altogether, and of the whole world of things and values which until now men had indeed run and created, was now not only leading women into personal and psychological traps, but also causing the movement to lose its momentum toward real equality in the world.

The energy of our "no" to sex discrimination had opened up new doors to women, had given women new aspirations and expectations, but that "no" could not in itself give us the blueprint for the new world we wanted. You didn't say no just to say no. What was the virtue of standing there forever howling at the once-closed door, even after you'd gotten them to open it a crack? You had to move in and take it from there, settle, redecorate, refurnish, take advantage, make it the house you wanted. How could we or our daughters live our new aspirations if the women's movement got stuck in the middle, in reaction and retreat from equality into separatism?

At that NOW convention in Washington the major preoccupation of the media, and of many of the delegates, seemed to be lesbianism. But NOW had already taken an unequivocal position in defense of lesbian rights—of sexual privacy and sexual preference—and no one had proposed departing from it. That position was not even controversial. What my speech warded off was a move to disavow "equality with men" and "partnership with men" as purposes of NOW—and even to eliminate men as members of NOW.

I could see the temptations of separatism. Women getting out of bad marriages in the United States still couldn't support their children or afford lawyers to collect child support. A few women had been promoted to good jobs and directorships—tokens—but the economic crisis was already being used to justify abandonment of affirmative action programs against sex discrimination in universities and industry. With unemployment growing in the United States, how could more women expect to get good jobs? How would it all end—promotion or election of those few token women and frustration for the rest of the generations now infused with new aspirations? It was seductive to retreat into delusions of Amazonian, "mother right" women's worlds. Jill Johnston came out with a book called *Lesbian Nation—The Feminist Solution*. There were some bitter movement jokes about "the final solution." At least it was a way to avoid facing the harsh realities of economics and power and competition in the world outside, of the new complexities of power in the family, of the difficulties of juggling profession, children, home, and husband when all the world was still geared to the services of a full-time housewife. Nothing had to change, no one was really threatened as long as that circle of women faced inward. And the women's movement would be destroyed, and with it, many women's lives.

Because there was still so much momentum in the actions against sex discrimination, the crisis in movement strategy that began to show itself in 1973 did not become public for nearly three years. Because I had to teach I spent those years studying psychology, sociology, and our own history again, traveling in other lands and cultures, and searching all the while for hints as to how to deal with those impossible dilemmas and no-win power struggles.

In investigating the implications of the women's movement for specific institutions—and for other cultures—I began to see glimpses of a "new yes," of forces converging to help transcend the polarities which were worrying me more and more —not only strategically and ideologically, but personally and psychologically as well. I began to distinguish between what were simply reactions to unequal sex roles of the past and what were genuine new directions. I began to see this revolution as something both less and more than an overthrow of power—as a restructuring of institutions, a transformation of power.

When you think about it, the power of the women's movement to change our lives, to break down age-old barriers in vast institutions, in those ten years can hardly be understood in the conventional terms of political and economic power. We had no guns, no bombs, no billions for bribes or blackmail . . . no money at all . . . no violence or even threat of it. It was a different kind of power.

When I was asked to teach—first as Visiting Professor of Sociology at Temple University in 1973, then at Yale, and Queens College—I chose not to teach "Women's Studies" but "The Sex-Role Revolution, Stage II."

In Sweden and Finland I had seen feminists approach many of our dilemmas not as a "woman's question," but as a "sex-role" question for both men and women. In India, I saw a culture less violent than ours, where sex roles were not polarized, where ancient gods were women as well as men, where sex was holy, not a sin, and a woman prime minister was not a dirty joke. In Czechoslovakia, Hungary and Israel I saw that equality for women doesn't happen—no matter what the abstract commitments of Communist doctrines or Socialist kibbutzim—unless there are concrete and specific steps to eliminate sex discrimination and restructure institutions involving both men and women, home and work. I saw that in the end equality for women confronts the whole system—every system—and implies changes in them all, cutting across the conventional lines of right and left.

With my students, I explored hints from many different disciplines as to how the energies of life and sexuality are blocked or turned into passive, impotent rage by the hostilities built into those polarities. We traced ways in which those blocked energies are manipulated by profiteers, priests and political demagogues to build growing reserves of family pathology, hate and violence.

I also pursued the implications of women's equality and the sex-role revolution for specific institutions, engaging in dialogue with and holding training sessions for broadcasters, architects, urban planners, doctors, lawyers and counselors. Meeting with marriage counselors or family therapists, or lecturing to medical students on "human sexuality," I would try to distinguish between the pathology created by those sex roles, the reaction against them, and real liberation. Are "sexual suicide," male impotence, female frigidity or frustration, clitoral orgasm or masturbation with vibrators and other sexual specters raised by recent doom-saying critics of "women's lib"—and a few of its own ideologists—the real sexual implications of equality of women with men? Is a head-on, losing battle with men for jobs the necessary economic result of the women's movement? Will the economic crisis send women home again, shut the doors now open? On every side, the women's movement seemed to be leading to impossible confrontations with power—insoluble economic, psychological, sexual, even theological dilemmas. And yet our new strength and hopes as women also imply value changes in the way we, and men, will love and work and live, earn and buy; maybe the very terms in which these insoluble dilemmas are defined are obsolete, unreal. Is it possible to transcend the polarities? I began to realize that equality—and the larger values revolution of human liberation—can't be lived unless we do.

Visiting the Pope in the Vatican, I had the full sense of the powers massed against us—and also of the fragility of those seemingly impregnable barriers. The mere fact of my reception by the Pope already revealed the new power which the women's movement has in the world, if it understands it.

That power must confront economic realities, but can lead to a transformation of values that will help us overcome our subservience to economic manipulation. It is more than the old sexual power of women to manipulate men, but its dynamics can't be understood by denying the reality of the force of the sexual bond between women and men: the sons, and fathers and lovers of women. The power of human sexuality—and the human misery of its denial or subversion, and the growing awareness and expectation of its human enjoyment—is part of the new power. Whether they understand it or not, the reactionary forces now massing against the women's movement are threatened not only by the emergence of women from dependence and passivity, but by the resultant liberation of human sexuality which, when suppressed and distorted, they have been able to manipulate for their own ends.

I began to speak to men in a new way myself. Even with cadets at the U.S. Air Force Academy and readers of the he-man magazine *True*, I found that hostility to "women's lib" could be transcended. There was a readiness, a yearning. Sometimes, I would worry that my sense of psychological complexity—of the personal vulnerability of women, and the strength of the bonds between us and men and children—was interfering with my revolutionary zeal. But I knew we also had to face the outside world and find new allies among men, even to protect the economic gains we had already made. I tried to create an Economic Think Tank for Women—bringing together movement, labor and black leaders with women and men economists and corporate planners. The restructuring of work and education necessary if women and men were to really share the work and the joy of society could never be done by women alone. It had to mean more than a few women getting better jobs and professional degrees. If women weren't to go home again, we had to work with new allies for different economic policies than those coming out of Washington and President Ford's Council of Economic Advisers. Was the women's movement going to be pitted against the unions over seniority? Or accept, again, women last hired, first fired? Weren't the real implications of sex-role equality shorter hours for everyone, which might mitigate layoffs?

Academic backlash was already beginning; the government was weakening in the enforcement of affirmative action programs against sex discrimination, even before the guidelines were dry on the new breakthrough law, Title 9, covering education. How could the women's movement protect the women being laid off, as educational and corporate budgets were being cut down? Why wasn't the women's movement working with the teachers' unions, and far-sighted educators, for some sort of lifetime Educaid or Educare that would give every adult a chance for new or renewed higher education sabbaticals? Instead of shutting down the huge new educational plants we had built for the young, why weren't we transforming them from youth ghettos into lifetime learning centers? More productive surely than welfare. I couldn't get funding to establish the Economic Think Tank for Women, but I kept on trying to raise these issues in the women's movement—and to forge new bonds with future-minded thinkers in different fields.

One year I devised a course called "Women and the City" which I taught at the New School for Social Research in New York. I felt that the relationship of women to the increasingly agonizing problems of the city had not been understood or even explored by academicians, theoretical or activist urban planners, policy makers, or even, in its larger implications, by women themselves. In the class, about ninety-eight women— married and divorced, single, searching, employed, job-hunting, on welfare, white, black, brown—held dialogues with various experts involved in policy making, and administration of basic city problems—problems which the experts had never looked at before from the viewpoint of women. When we discussed financial problems, we saw it was not just a question of women earning more money, but of getting some control over the money they earned, and of getting credit and keeping it, in marriage and in divorce, as people in their own right, whether their work was paid, underpaid, or unpaid. I raised the question of a women's bank, and of the legislation we needed to outlaw sex discrimination in credit and mortgages. By the end of that evening, that Greek chorus of ninety-eight women was talking about "our bank," and several of the women present that night—as students or banking experts—began moving to start one. That it took three years to break through the red tape to start the First Women's Bank—that the $3 million capitalization was raised among an unprecedented 7,000 individual stockholders mostly women, when the failure of conventional big city banks scared off Wall Street financing—that the opening of the First Women's Bank, on 57th Street in New York, in October 1975, somehow coincided with the announcement of new federal and state regulations prohibiting sex discrimination in credit, mortgage, loans, and a new flurry by commercial banks to treat women as serious customers—all this is new power in the world.

The real world women have to live in as we change our lives does involve mundane necessities like money, credit, housework, meals, a house or apartment, or room of one's own. How should we live—alone, or in families, or in new kinds of communal, extended families? In my class on "Women and the City," we discussed housing; the Greek chorus talked about loneliness, and the impossibility of finding the kind of apartments, houses and services women needed now. The experts present had truly not considered the needs for new kinds of housing and services for women and men who were not living in conventional Good Housekeeping ways. The "new yes" of sex-role equality surely implies new concepts in housing, community, appliances, services; changes in architecture, design, planning of home, office and city. Virtually all available existing architecture, urban and suburban planning, and the regulations and codes governing their financing, zoning and design are based on traditional polarized sex roles: the feminine mystique solidified into the brick and concrete wall of the suburban home and isolated city high-rise apartment; the masculine mystique of office and plant, and the polarization built into urban planning and suburban sprawl. Earlier I had begun to explore alternate possibilities, the service housing begun in Sweden, and what could be learned from kibbutz and commune living in Israel and the United States. At the International Design Conference in Aspen I got the architects and planners to play a game with me—figuring out the new kinds of housing needed for sex-role equality, and the problems involved. Lately I have been exploring these questions further with young women moving into architecture and planning.

•   •   •

At the International Women's Year Conference in Mexico, not only the old reactionary powers and Communist commissars but the despotic rulers of the Third World seemed threatened by the women's movement. They outfoxed us, manipulated us, co-opted International Women's Year—in effect, they used the United Nations to try to stop the women's movement from spreading world-wide. But the very reaction against and to us, in Mexico as in this country, confirms the fantastic real power of the movement. I believe, through all the confusions, that it's an unprecedented new kind of power in the world, one that threatens the old control of political and economic power by church and state in ways we ourselves are only dimly aware of.

I sensed in Mexico—and have become more sharply aware as the crisis in the women's movement surfaced late in 1975—that those powerful external enemies cannot succeed in stopping the women's movement and the new kind of power unless we are divided and weakened from within. It is not only agents of the FBI and CIA, which the Church Senate hearings and the Rockefeller Commission revealed were infiltrating the movement, that we have to worry about. It is our own unadmitted personal betrayal—of our own truth and the truth of our movement. It is the weakness that is afraid to trust our own strength. It is the remnant of our own self-hate that makes it so hard to trust each other. It is the naked inexperienced desperation for power that we have not faced in ourselves, as women who have been too powerless too long, which is turning the movement away from its real strength. For the millions of women in the mainstream of America who are ready to move now in real life, in the unfinished movement for equality—and who need the movement to change their own lives and find the "new yes"—are alienated by the hate rhetoric, the extremism and manipulation coming now from other women who would keep the movement small and powerless so that they can manipulate it for their own power: the old kind of power.

They would keep that circle turned inward, the easier to manipulate it with pseudo-power—a female *macho* mask of rhetoric and rage that is at best a reaction against the old helplessness but is not the new power. It is weakness masquerading as strength, evading the real tasks of restructuring institutions, of creating the "new yes." Somehow we have to transcend the polarities in ourselves and in our own movement, to find that new power, and move on.

By the end of 1975, I, and all of us, had to face that polarization of our own movement—that unadmitted weakness, desperation, self-hate, cowardice, and betrayal that will surely divide and destroy the women's movement if we don't understand it for what it is. We have to uncover the enemy within—our movement, ourselves—in order to confront the enemy without.

Are we going to throw away that new power in the world? After ten years, I admit a period of wanting to turn my own back on the women's movement—of wanting to move on in the world, leaving it behind. But that is surely my own weakness, my failure of heart and responsibility, in the face of questions so complex I don't have any easy answers—in the face of risk to reputation, popularity, perhaps my own power if I raise these questions now. As I write these words, I feel the anxiety and awful responsibility of women looking to me for leadership again, and of not knowing what to do, wishing someone would tell me. I only know that, whatever the discomfort and risk, we have to face the reality of these new problems and transcend the polarities or we will lose that new power in the world, the movement that encircled and empowered the liberation of each one of us, and whose strength is still essential to our own.

One of the problems we face as women is our sheer lack of experience with the realities of power. Until recently we have had no direct voice in the decisions of the world, and partly as a consequence, have had to wield too much covert power in the family. I don't have much patience with the idea that feminism must abjure all power as men have used it in the world, or that women will somehow, mystically, use power better or differently from men. Women can't evade its realities in any system. I joke about this: "Power may corrupt, and absolute power corrupts absolutely, but absolute powerlessness is worse."

When Indira Gandhi was elected prime minister of India in 1966, I went to India to see for myself how she would use that power. As usual, the experience in India raised more questions than it answered. In Indira Gandhi, I did indeed see a woman wielding real authority in a style indubitably different from men. And Indian men were not threatened, did not react to that power as we have always assumed men must react to it in women. But then even during those few short weeks traveling with Gandhi through India, I also saw that for the whole people, there was a definition of masculinity and femininity that was not as polarized, not as unequal as in the West.

The Indian men were not *macho*. The relationship between their value of the female—their gods are women as well as men, or half-woman, half-man—their reverence and celebration of sex, and the nonviolent power with which they overthrew British colonial rule—all this fascinated me. Equality between the sexes was not the main problem in India then and is not today. Other problems are more terrible. I felt and feel an almost inescapable arrogance in trying to deal with any of India's complex economic and social problems by American standards. These problems even as I saw them are insoluble in American terms, in terms of all polarization of the past. But in India, I saw a woman prime minister deal with such complexities, sensed a style of thought and action that is different from win-or-lose, yes-or-no solutions.

I also felt hostility from many Indians toward American arrogance and power. Like most Americans, though I protested the war in Vietnam, it remained remote to me, except for my draft-age sons. When Indians said, "It is your presence we object to," I realized that for them, for many Third World people, there may not be any "good Americans" after Vietnam, as for many of us there were no "good Germans" who acquiesced in the Holocaust.

From the beginning, it seemed to me Mrs. Gandhi got a bad and prejudiced treatment from the American media. It is a cliché to come back from India horrified at the poverty, the dirt, the cheapness of human life: it makes us uncomfortable and rather mad at them for making us uncomfortable, the anger being a substitute for facing our guilt at our own affluence. I think American newsmen and embassy types are also uneasy with the nonpolarized, "feminine" thinking of Indians. They were certainly uneasy dealing with a woman prime minister.

I delighted in and respected Mrs. Gandhi's style. And, I suppose, we became friends—in trivial woman ways, as well as serious ones. My last day in India, after covering Mrs. Gandhi at the Congress party convention, I went shopping for presents for my children, and then came back to my hotel to pack. The phone rang; the prime minister's secretary said accusingly, "Where were you? The prime minister has sent out a search for you." I envisioned some horrible, inadvertent breach of protocol. What was the problem? "Tell me," said the prime minister's aide conspiratorially, "do you have more than one coat with you?" "No," I said. "That is too bad," said the aide. "Tell me, that cape you were wearing on the plane, do you think we might borrow it for a few days?" Designed by Rudi Gernreich, it was a marvelous irregular sort of cape, reversible black on one side, camel on the other; it would be perfect over saris. But it was the first original I'd ever bought —reduced to half price at a sale just before I went to India— and I loved it. Should I offer to give it to the prime minister? "No, no," demurred her aide. "that's not necessary, we just need it a few hours."

When I got back to the United States, I called Rudi Gernreich, whom I'd always admired, and told him about this. "What do you think I should do?" he asked, fascinated. "Send her an original cape," I said. "Surely you must like the idea of the first woman prime minister wearing your cape." "Oh, dear," he moaned, "That was last year's model. We've only got one left. Can she wear a size six?"

A few months later, the prime minister of India came to the U.S., in need of aid in the country's famine. I went down to Washington to give her moral support, and was waiting with other reporters on the White House lawn when Mrs. Gandhi landed by helicopter. Wearing our cape, she stepped out to greet the President—and as she passed the press on her way into the White House, she saw me wearing mine and gave me a big broad wink.

When the United States supplied arms to Pakistan in the Bangladesh war—and the use of rape as a weapon by soldiers in that war left many Bangladesh women in the plight of Untouchables—Indian women asked my help, and I led a delegation of women to Washington to protest, and to demand aid for the victims of Bangladesh and an end to U.S. intervention. People were now saying, "How can you propose more political power for women when the two states headed by women already are at war?" I felt no need to be defensive about Golda Meir or Indira Gandhi just because they were women—but I felt a particular delight at the shortness of that war, the speed with which she led her troops in beating back the Pakistan invaders, and the rejoicing with which the victorious Indian soldiers in the freed villages blunted their guns and bayonets with marigolds.

In Mexico City last summer, my Indian friends were effec-

tive and essential in whatever little we accomplished toward
uniting women and advancing world-wide equality, at the International Women's Year Conference. They were as dismayed
as I when crisis flared in India, and the prime minister suspended those democratic freedoms and instituted martial law.
They rushed home to confront their own problems. I don't
know what is really happening in India now. But I'm not sure
that an American has any right to judge. The Indians have
long suspected—and recent revelations of CIA intrigue have
confirmed those suspicions—that the U.S. and British governments were somehow involved in stirring up or exacerbating
the corruption, and religious and tribal dissensions and moves
against Mrs. Gandhi's regime, in undermining the unification
of India and its emergence to independent power in its own
subcontinent. I liked the passionate democracy I saw in India,
and the vitality of its response to those complex, impossible
problems. I can't help mourning her retreat from democracy.
Being a woman is the least of Mrs. Gandhi's worries at this
moment—but I would hope that the new kind of power I
sensed in her will somehow take her through, and help her to
withstand the giant superpowers raging over her subcontinent
—dividing and manipulating—and to find the food and resources her people need, without giving up forever the freedoms she herself has cherished.

Madame
Prime Minister

It was her first week in office. I heard no Indian say out loud that a *woman* should not be prime minister. They merely commented on how "frail" she looked, at the great Republic Day parade, with her white sari half covering her head in the manner symbolic of the submission of Indian women. As helicopters strewed rose petals and proudly strutting Indian soldiers showed off the artillery with which they had defended their border against Pakistan and China, the politicians and dignitaries in the V.I.P. section paid court to Kamaraj, the walrus-mustached king-maker who had engineered her election.

Madame Prime Minister Indira Gandhi—young, at forty-eight, in a land where the old rule—sat alone. "The king-makers wanted a weak king," I heard a quip. "She is too weak, surely, for the problems of the world's largest democracy at this time."

Those correspondents and photographers who had flown in from London, Paris, Bonn, Toronto and New York to cover her ascent to power were even more skeptical. They watched, incredulous, that first morning at 8:00 A.M., as she introduced her policy of *"dharjan"* (communication) with any Indian who wanted to see her about anything. With a personal prayerlike *namaste*, she greeted Untouchable street sweepers, angry squatters whose huts and temple were being demolished by a building project, schoolboys declaiming warlike poems, and

339

men and women from villages. Disposing, then, of five different television interviews from as many countries in a half-hour, in the bare sunlight, she went to her office in the grandiose Red Fort to cope with the crises she had inherited: famine and rioting in the South, frozen American aid, the withdrawal of troops from the Pakistan border, India's grim population explosion, the final details of the third Five-Year Plan, and the face-saving insistence of the two men she had defeated, each to rank *first* in the Cabinet.

Suddenly, at noon, she left her ministers and advisers to visit the camping ground of the folk dancers who had come to New Delhi from all over India. When I caught up with her, in a haze of dust and flies among the bullocks, donkeys, goats, men, women and children crowded between the tents, she was having her picture taken with the dancers from riot-torn Kerala. Suddenly there was a blare of sound, and the men from Kerala were shouting and jumping, waving spears inches from the prime minister's head, doing a dance around her. I had visions of Dallas, of our FBI having a mass heart attack. Over the heads of the photographers, who were swearing in heat and hysteria, I saw her giving holy hell to her security for trying to close in with big ropes and get those spears away from her head. Then, smiling, looking cool in the heat, the prime minister of the world's largest democracy kicked off her shoes and joined barefoot in the dance—looking natural and not a bit afraid, as if, despite her Oxford education, she enjoyed this. Maybe she is going to surprise them all, I thought. She saw me staring at her, and winked . . .

I had come to India with the questions we all have in America, where the thought of a woman president is still so inconceivable that its very mention is a joke. How is it possible for a woman to be elected prime minister of India, where enforced seclusion of women in purdah, child marriage, and burning of widows alive on their husbands' pyres outraged Christian missionaries less than a century ago? In the United States, women, supposedly so long emancipated to equality with man, can at most aspire to adorn the White House, more or less decoratively, as the President's wife, making headlines according to her flair for fashion; she may move into humanitarian spheres, above the political battle, second a political nomination as the "woman vice-chairman," or hold some nominal token appointment, but can she occupy the seat of power in her own right?

Indira Gandhi is, of course, Nehru's daughter. But could a female Kennedy, Roosevelt, Eisenhower, Truman, Churchill, De Gaulle or Adenauer even be imagined in a similar situation? Could the Congress Party, the enormous, loosely united vehicle of India's struggle for independence from Britain, be in such trouble today that it had no alternative to Nehru's daughter?

Knowing that in India, as everywhere, power is hotly fought for, I also wondered what price she had to pay as a woman in competing with and surpassing men in this political struggle. Did she face enormous resistance from the hostility of men? How did she acquire the strengths and abilities necessary to lead 480,000,000 people, to take political command of the giant apparatus of modern nationhood which has always been considered man's world? Is she, to put it bluntly, a battle-axe who has forsworn her own femininity and become, in everything but name, one of the boys? Is she torn by enormous conflicts between the exercise of her political power and her basic nature as a woman? Has she had to pay a price as a wife and mother, to renounce happiness as a woman (as many here claim a woman must when she takes a position of any power)? Or does she, on the other hand, draw on unique strengths and abilities as a woman in her political life?

And finally, what chance does she have of staying in this position and of having other women follow in her footsteps? It's not so strange that a BBC commentator joked, that week in London, "What is wrong with you girls that you are not heading for No. 10 Downing Street?" And more than one U.S. television commentator, for the first time, suggested: "Perhaps it is not a joke, that a woman might one day be President of the United States."

In those hectic first three weeks of the transfer of power in New Delhi, I received almost incredibly open-hearted, soul-baring, painstaking help from Indians, from Indira Gandhi's closest personal friends to her political enemies. I felt almost guilty of "Ugly American" arrogance in even bothering them with such questions at this time, but their honest fascination, the way they invited me into their homes and told me bad things as well as good, seemed to indicate that they, at least, didn't think a woman prime minister was a joke—and that they were delighted at the notion that there was something on which they might be less "backward" than Americans.

Finally, I had the unique opportunity to get to know Indira Gandhi personally, traveling with her by plane, helicopter, and jeep 2,330 miles across India on her first trip among the people as prime minister. I was the only American, and one of the two women in her small party of fourteen. She talked to me, alone and at length, about her life, the conflicts in her marriage caused by her rise to political power, her feelings about womanhood and her country.

What concerned me first was whether Indira Gandhi had become prime minister only because she was Nehru's daughter, or whether her story does in fact have implications for women generally. Political insiders in India seemed to feel that if Nehru had died in 1954 rather than 1964, his daughter never would have been considered a possibility for prime minister. Until that time, though politics and the struggle for Indian independence had dominated her life from childhood, her own importance had been merely as Nehru's official hostess, housekeeper—and the doorkeeper to his office. "I underestimated her," a shrewd Western diplomat told me. "She was sensitive to her father's every whim, saw that he didn't see the wrong people and saw the right ones. The doorkeeper to a great man's office has a great deal of power. I thought she was courted by the political officials because that was the way they could get in to see Nehru, and that after his death her power would rapidly disappear. Instead, it increased."

When Nehru was still alive, a veteran American correspondent predicted that Indira Gandhi would probably "join the ranks of anonymous offspring of famous fathers. I do not believe that her father could impose her on the country, even if he were willing to try. India would not accept another Nehru as prime minister. Nehru must know how quickly the children of giants are dwarfed, even by ordinary mortals, once the giants depart."

"Where are Gandhi's sons today, without Gandhi?" Gopal Menon, a leading Indian businessman, said. "We didn't pick her after Nehru's death when feelings were highest. She has become our strongest political personality in her own right, the best one on whom we could reach a consensus, the only one who could unify the whole country around her, if we faced a war."

An elder Indian statesman who was close to the family told me Nehru himself would not have thought his daughter could be prime minister. "In the early years, Nehru used to bully Indira in an absolutely shocking way. He would shatter her self-confidence; she was a mass of nerves. Only in the last five or six years did he begin to treat her as an equal. She accepted the role he gave her, whatever it was; she used to take the tongue-lashings. It was the jobs she began to do on her own that seemed to bring her alive. Her father will be peeping over her shoulder all her life. She'll always be trying to prove to herself: 'My father didn't think I was capable of doing it, but I have done it.'"

Indira Gandhi told me herself: "I believe what my father did for India was the right thing then, but you don't do anything because somebody else did it. It has to be the right thing now. I have my own ideas, and I am very stubborn about them. I'm sorry to say that's one of my worst sins. I'm a very determined person—I've had to be, from sheer sense of survival."

"No man or woman is born a prime minister, not even Nehru's daughter," said Krishna Menon, the left-wing leader who was supposed to have a Rasputin-like influence on Nehru. He did not support Indira Gandhi's election "until it became certain," her campaign lieutenant told me bitterly. "He knew she was too independent-minded, he couldn't influence her as he did her father." Not even her bitterest opponent, Moraiji Desai, who fought her candidacy to the end, raised the argument that a woman should not be prime minister. His supporters wanted him to, he said, but he would rather "lose than go against my principles. We are committed to the equality of women." His own wife, however, and the wives of other Indian political leaders have never been seen with them at a social or political affair.

I talked to village women ten miles outside Delhi who still live in purdah, forbidden to move outside the women's quarter of the house; to girls who are not even allowed out to go to school; to a widow, married at thirteen, who did not burn herself alive at seventeen on her husband's funeral pyre but is still forbidden by custom to remarry or move in society. Child marriage is now illegal, but everyone knows that in parts of India eight-to-ten-year-old girls are still literally being "sold" into marriage for the dowry, and are even murdered, without much fear of prosecution, so that the husband or his parents can collect dowry from another wife. The influence of purdah on India is still so strong that in elementary school, in Jaipur in northern India, I saw class after class of thirty to forty boys and only three to six girls. Nearly 90 percent of Indian women are still illiterate, compared to 65 percent of the men.

The week Mrs. Gandhi took office, the Indian newspapers carried a not unusual picture of an air force officer's wife humbly kissing her husband's feet. Frank Moraes, editor of the *Indian Express,* told me: "We can accept a woman as prime minister—there's nothing extraordinary about it. Women have been part of our political life ever since Gandhi. Yet most men in India still won't accept a woman as an equal in personal life."

But the thrust of Indian society seems to be in the direction of the kind of equality educated women like Indira Gandhi now take for granted. Every Indian I met apologized for purdah as an "alien" deformity imposed on Indian women by foreign conquerors.

In the ancient Hindu tradition, they told me, "*shakti,* the female principle, is another name for energy, power. There are goddesses for all our gods—not just mothers of Jesus, but goddesses of wisdom, wealth, light in their own right. Our history is full of brave women like Jansi, our Joan of Arc, who led an Indian army into the battlefield in uprising against the British, a century ago, when Victorian women were stifling at home. In the villages, where four out of five Indians still live, women work alongside the men in the fields. They will come up from poverty with the men, and simply skip the nineteenth century."

One thing is sure, the syndicate of big state and city political bosses who united behind Mrs. Gandhi weren't concerned with women's role, but with their own shrewd estimate of her mass support among the 480,000,000 people of India. Which means that not as an ideal, but as a political actuality, the Indian people can accept and respect a woman—this woman—in a way only the most "advanced" men and women have suggested in the West. As Indira Gandhi herself snapped at the persistent question from Western correspondents on how it feels to be India's "first woman prime minister": "As prime minister, I'm not a woman—I'm a human being."

As a tall, bearded Sikh put it: "Some of your American men make me sick, holding open the car door as if women were so special, and then keeping them out of all their important affairs. Having a woman boss does not take away my manhood."

The kind of fuss we would get into about a woman President, I found in only one newspaper in India, the organ of Jan Sangh, which hearkens back to the past like the John Birch Society here, reviving the old religious and caste hatreds and prejudices by which the British kept India divided. It showed cartoons of men's heads in women's clothes, warning that now women will wear the pants and men will be emasculated. This group is behind the whispering campaign that Mrs. Gandhi is too "frail" and "emotional." The fact is women's freedom and equality never has involved a battle of women versus men in India. It was won as women came out of purdah to fight along-side of men in the battle for national freedom. Talking to Mrs. Gandhi and other Indians, I begin to see we are bogged down here in questions about women that neither women nor men even ask there; they simply take the answers for granted as part of their whole nation's emergence from the stranglehold of superstition and "backwardness," the unfinished struggle which Indira Gandhi has had the nerve to take on.

• • •

"Doesn't it frighten you, being prime minister," I asked her the first afternoon, thinking of an American President's words about the frightening loneliness of realizing "the buck stops here."

"It doesn't frighten me yet," she said. "I've already had the experience of having the buck passed to me, though nobody ever made a fuss about it. All the things I've done were big challenges at the time, and it hardly seemed possible I could do them because I'd never done them before. But I grew up with the idea that courage was the most important thing; my mother and father both drummed it into me.

"Until I was sixteen," she told me, "I thought it would be more fun being a boy. Of course, everyone wished I were a boy. My father had no son—I was always with him. I climbed trees. Then when I was sixteen, I discovered it wasn't a handicap being a girl at all. There were so many things more important to do than climbing trees. My mother fought for all sorts of rights for women, while she was fighting for independence. I'm not a feminist, I suppose, because I grew up taking equality for granted. Both my parents were in jail so much, I had to learn to make my own decisions and stand on my own two feet."

Her ideal as a child was Joan of Arc—and her own mother. ("I learned nonviolent resistance from my wife," Nehru used to say.) But it was Gandhi who made her father a feminist. She explains: "Gandhi felt the struggle for independence had to involve the women as much as men, not only because they were half the population, but if you were asking a man to go to prison, to face the firing squad, it would be much harder if his wife said no. So he appealed directly to the women and gave them the hardest work—on the principle that, if you just put your big toe in the water, it will take you forever to swim, but if you jump right in, you're not afraid. Women rose to it and did things they had never believed they could do."

Indira Gandhi never thought of political ability as *male*—the very methods of India's nonviolent revolution were as right for women as for men: the spinning of their own cotton and the making of salt from the sea, the boycott of the British goods which enslaved India economically. With the men often in jail, the women had to take the responsibility of leadership. As a ten-year-old, with both her parents in jail, she herself organized a Monkey Brigade of children who would play in coffeehouses and outside of officials' windows to pick up information—and would help carry on the picketing. The letters her father wrote her from jail, stressed above all the message *Don't let history scare the pants off you.*

She defied her father and went against the Indian custom of arranged marriages in insisting on marrying Feroze Gandhi (no relation to the Mahatma), a fellow student in London who was a member of the despised Parsi caste. Her wedding dress was homespun *khodi* that her father had woven in jail, and her honeymoon ended three months later when she was arrested, leading a "Quit India" demonstration, in 1943. She was confined for thirteen months in jail, with twenty-two other women in a barracks that had only the most primitive sanitary facilities and virtually no shelter from the unbearable sun; she was not even allowed the letters, parcels or visitors that were permitted the other prisoners.

"The worst thing about jail was that everything was mud-colored," she told me. "After I got out, I couldn't get enough of colors, I had to touch everything I saw. After so much roughness, I had to feel soft textures."

Then came Independence. Her mother was dead and her father was India's first prime minister, it's George Washington and Abraham Lincoln combined. He kept summoning her from her home with her husband and two little boys in Lucknow to "come immediately, there must be a dinner party"—for Khrushchev, Nasser, Mao Tse-tung, or Mrs. Kennedy.

She absolutely refused to run for assembly or Parliament herself, which as her father's daughter she was asked to do at every election. Once, the home minister cabled Mahatma Gandhi to order her to run. She told the Mahatma that her children were still small and needed her around, and she would not be bullied by him or anyone else.

"I didn't really do anything much myself when the boys were very small," Indira Gandhi says. "My husband was living in Lucknow; I spent half the time looking after my father's house, and half the time with him. The boys went back and forth with me, except when I was out electioneering for my husband or my father. I didn't believe in leaving children to others. I only started doing things myself after the children went to school. Even then, I'd organize my day to be home when they got home from school."

She also insisted that she was not "qualified." Usha Bhagat, her children's kindergarten teacher and then her secretary, came to work for her in 1953, several days a week, when Mrs. Gandhi was just beginning to get involved in child-welfare projects, the sort of thing in which women in India—or America—try their wings without really planning it, when their minds are still mainly on their own children.

Usha told me: "There has been over these years a tremendous change in her. When she spoke, she used to be very hesitant, always groping for words, not confident and firm like now. When I first came to her, she was diffident, not at all outgoing; she traveled only with her father or on holiday with her husband—not on her own. The quality of leadership may have been there, but it was hidden. I don't think she thought of herself as an active political person or a leader at all. When her father sent for her to run the prime minister's house—it was her sense of duty which made her go, not just duty to her father, but her sense of what her father meant to the country. He had sacrificed his whole life to the country, and there was so much to be done, and he couldn't do it alone. She would have preferred to live in a small house of her own with Feroze. When Feroze got elected to Parliament, he took his meals and slept in the prime minister's house, but he worked and entertained his own guests in the house given him as a member of Parliament. He refused to be just the prime minister's son-in-law. He had a very sensitive man's ego, and he didn't like reflected glory. You could feel the tension developing between them.

"She is a complex person, so many sides to her, I don't know of any one person with whom she communicates on all levels. The people she talks to about her political life will not know her other side. The old friends who come in for tea, they are friends in a feminine way—they went to school together, or their children were the same age—and she just wants to gossip and discuss the children. Then there are one or two—not many—with whom she has a spiritual sort of communication; there is a mystical streak in her. Her life is in compartments. She's spent so much time listening to people's problems that sometimes she has to retreat inside herself and be alone. I have seen her do that even in the midst of a crowd. She is a very reflective person, but she has so little time that she reflects more intensely than most people.

"Anything she does, she does intensively, in a very short period of time. Time moves differently for her. I have seen her literally put her mind to four things at once—dictating a memorandum to me on a welfare project, discussing a political campaign on the telephone, while on the desk in front of her is a table plan drawn up for a big dinner. The protocol may be correct, but it's all wrong from a human point of view—she always takes great pains to put people next to someone they would really like to talk to. And suddenly, out of the corner of her eye, she sees that the arrangement of roses in the vase is not right.

"She had that same kind of concentration with her children. Even when they were little and I taught them in kindergarten, I would notice that she seemed very fond of them, but she was not fussing at them all the time like an ordinary mother. I noticed that the other mothers—who were at home with their children all the time and were always coming down to interfere at school—never seemed to feel it necessary to pay any real attention to their children. Whenever she was with the children, she paid intense attention to them. She would be resting in the afternoon, and the boys would come home from school and lie down with her. She talked to them, explained things, listened to them, discussed things in such an interested way—that when it was time for her to go, I don't think they ever felt rejected."

In her own mind, it all began the year when, still refusing to run for office herself, she promised her father would speak for another woman candidate if the district put one up. When her father wouldn't speak for the woman—he had other commitments—she got on a train, furious, and spoke herself—and discovered the people *listened* to her. The woman won with a huge majority, and Indira Gandhi was asked to join the all-important Working Committee of the Congress Party. She was thirty-five. They had to have one woman on the executive board, and as is the way with such boards and their token "woman" or Negro, they put her in charge of a previously nonexistent Women's Division. She took it seriously. Something had to be done to give women the nerve to press themselves forward as candidates, and to fight it out in the smoke-filled rooms.

"I got the committee to agree that 15 percent of every slate, in every state and town, should be women," she recalls. "They thought it was a big joke. They said men won't vote for

women, and women won't vote for women. Well, I said, we
have so many seats to fill, why not take a chance? I didn't insist
they stick to the absolute letter of the law—they averaged 12
percent, not 15 percent, but it was a beginning. They thought,
of course, that the women would all lose. Actually, the women
didn't lose—wherever a woman has lost, it's not because she's
a woman, but because the Congress Party is in local trouble.
But you had to fight them. They would say, 'No competent
women are available, so we'll just have to fill the seat with a
man.' Or they would try to put up the least competent women
in a district where there were educated, able women who
wouldn't be afraid to speak up. Or since there were also supposed to be a certain number of candidates from the minority
communities—the Untouchables—they would try to get
around the whole thing by putting up an Untouchable
woman."

She organized training seminars and camps to teach
women how to speak and act as legislators—even illiterate
women. By now, women sit on all the village councils or
panchayats—and in some cases head them. I talked to one
woman newly elected to a *panchayat* in Jaipur; the end of her
sari covering her whole head, she seemed so submissive that I
wondered what influence she could have—but evidently she
had lifted her sari in indignation to insist that a new teacher
be hired for the village so that the girls could go to school as
well as the boys. There are now women members of state
legislatures and in both houses of Parliament—fifty-nine, as
against only twelve in the Congress of the United States—
women chief ministers and governors of the largest states,
women ministers of state, planning commissioners, magis-
trates and deputies. Indian women have been ambassadors to
Moscow, London and Washington—not just Luxembourg.

This battle for women was merely her apprenticeship.

"Each member of the Working Committee was supposed to
supervise the selection of candidates in one or two states. I
came to Assam, and it was clear they weren't dealing with the
minorities and tribes as they should. I called the President of
the Congress Party and told him what needed to be done. That
seems so drastic, he said. The trouble with too many politicians is they hate to make a decision. They get out of unpopu-

lar moves by letting things slide. I really had to *yell* at him, but we were in real danger of alienating the tribes, the way we were ignoring their own wishes and forcing things on them. I insisted, and we made the changes and Assam is much more stable today."

"She has real personal courage, she has physical courage," I was told over and over again, by young correspondents, soldiers, cynical newspaper editors, tired political hacks, shaking their heads in that emphatic Indian way. She went to Bombay during the language riots and defied the local political bosses by insisting that the city be districted according to the language the people spoke—which was not the language of the wealthiest contributors to the party treasury. The political bosses were afraid the wealthy businessmen would move away. Indira Gandhi was sure they would not—and she was right.

When she was elected the Congress Party's president in 1959—taking over command of a huge political organization no longer united by ideals of freedom but rotting with corruption, opportunism, and warring state and city bosses—her first act was to drop her father from the executive committee. She also replaced ineffectual hacks with capable young workers and cracked heads together to get unity. She went to Kerala, where the Communists had won an election, and discovered that they had changed the children's schoolbooks to rewrite Indian history in terms of Lenin rather Gandhi—and though she herself had been considered "left," she didn't stop until a new election was called and the Communists were put out of office.

During the Chinese invasion and again in the war with Pakistan, to the horror of the officials she flew in a helicopter to the front lines. The troops recognized her, and their cheers reverberated through the mountain passes into the Assam Valley. "The second time I came, the Chinese were almost there," she said. "I left at 4:00 A.M., I wouldn't have been so silly as to rush into Chinese arms. But I had said I would come back if there was any danger, and I'm glad I did. I got the young people to organize a home guard. The thing is to get people to *do* something about their situation—that is what gives the courage."

When her father died, in 1964, Indira Gandhi refused the post of foreign minister. She was not "qualified," she said. Instead, as minister of information and broadcasting, she not only changed the radio and TV network from a government propaganda mouthpiece by opening it to independent commentators—including opposition-party members—but kept up morale in the war against Pakistan without permitting any note of "hate Pakistan" on the air.

Could a woman do all this without being a battle-axe and antagonizing men? Evidently, because the powerful political bosses, in whom Moraiji Desai's rigid "inflexibility" had aroused enormous resentment, were able to unite behind her. Usha rushed to the house, the night the news came out that she would be prime minister. "I thought she would be shattered—such a tremendous burden! But she looked excited, happy, as if she accepted the challenge, not at all as if it had been forced on her, but as if it had opened something in her. Suddenly, I saw her as quite a different person. And she was not at all afraid."

·   ·   ·

I went with her 2,330 miles to Assam in her Indian Air Force Viscount, smaller plane, helicopter, and jeep. It was her first trip into the remote interior of India as prime minister. She spoke five times, first to the crowds gathered around the Behar airport where we changed to a smaller plane (the crowds were still there waiting when we came back three hours later), then to an incredible crowd, half a million people filling miles of mud flats on a riverbed like the Mississippi, sitting motionless on the ground, people as far as the eye can see, a haze of dust swirling over their heads in the hot Indian noon, all staring with intensity at the slim figure in the blue sari on the garlanded dais. Her voice—so different from the loud oratory of some of her fellow politicians—carried unmistakable authority. It was high but not shrill, sometimes halting with thought, lilting in appeal, almost passionately sincere. She spoke three times in Assam as we moved further and further into the hills—flying past the Himalayas in the corridor through Pakistan, past Mt. Everest. The narrow road from the airport was rimmed by jungle, palms, mango groves and endless tea fields lined twenty, thirty, fifty people deep.

The first time I heard her whistle-stop speech, the sunset was full on her face and doves, eagles and crows whirled around her head. Her very look became vibrant, warm, alive, as if that thin frailness had been fed by the intent listening faces of the men in the diaperlike dhotis and the women, covering children with the ends of their saris, sitting on the ground. The strength of that current between her and the people is the source of her power.

What she says is simple enough: that Indians fought with nothing but the will to be free and earn their freedom, that they rose as one man to defend their borders against invasion and were victorious. But if they do not fight now with the same will and unity against the real enemy—their own backwardness, poverty, ignorance—they cannot remain free. They must produce their own food, not rely forever on foreign aid; they must conquer inefficiency, bureaucracy and sloth, and build industrial production and many more schools. This can't be done by statements from the government or by troops in battle, but only by the people—by *them*. And that means hardship and work, and continuing the spirit of self-sacrifice of Gandhi, Nehru, Shastri. They *must criticize themselves*— but the most important thing, *have confidence in themselves . . . and India*.

When they let out the cheer *"Jai Hind!"*— "Long live India!"—she teases them gently: "That is not loud enough." They laugh and say again: *"Jai Hind!"* "No, no," she says, "loud enough to sound all the way to the Red Fort." In a great burst of the good-humored national pride she has evoked, they shout, *"Jai Hind!"* and as she turns away, "Indira Gandhi, *ki jai!"* ("Long live Indira").

That night twelve people were killed in a stampede in that village in remote Assam as the great crowd tried to get a closer look at Indira Gandhi. At 6:00 A.M. the next morning, she took off in a helicopter for a meeting with the border tribes.

In the straw *pandal*—the tribal open meeting hut on stilts— she invited me back to the enclosure curtained with red and yellow shawls, where the local women senators and Congress leaders were helping her change to tribal dress. (With a clear sense that she embodies in her person the symbol of India as a nation, the prime minister religiously wears, in every part of

India, the particular local form of woman's dress—as she avidly tastes and relishes the local and regional dishes. When someone congratulated her on her "fortitude," she said "but I love it—the variety").

The Assam ladies took down some shawls from their curtain wall to drape on me. The prime minister was staring at my feet. "Are you comfortable?" I was wearing thong beach sandals, slightly incongruous with a black silk knit dress, but I had had such trouble the day before getting in and out of jeeps and helicopter in high heels. I started to apologize when she lifted the hem of her sari and showed me that she was wearing moccasin bedroom slippers. (In Delhi, she usually wore high-heeled open-toed sandals.) "On a trip like this, one has to be able to *move*."

Prime minister or not, she relishes the feminine minutiae of life as vividly as any woman—and without taking her mind off the great concerns of India and the world. "We were discussing the details of the Tashkent agreement," one Cabinet member told me, "and suddenly she said 'I think you are getting a cold.' She opened the drawer, pulled out a box of lozenges and made me swallow one. Then she went on to the next point of the agreement."

In the midst of the political exchanges with the tribal leaders, Mrs. Gandhi noted with excitement that some of the women were not wearing nose rings. "Every time I come, I have been sliding in the hint that the nose ring is not really very pretty," she told me. "The last time, the women admitted for the first time that it was really very painful. The nose thickens, and the ugly red swelling around it distorts the whole shape of the face!"

·   ·   ·

The rest of us went ahead in a regular army helicopter in order not to keep her waiting—or to get caught in the stampede of the crowds that closed around and behind her. We would hear the great murmur and swell of excitement of the crowds staring up from the dusty mud banks as her glass-nosed jet helicopter came down from the sky. Still in the air, her sari-draped head would be recognized, and she would make the prayerlike Indian gesture of greeting. I lost count of the number of times she made speeches, accepted salutes, and rode standing up in the back of the jeep the length and breadth of the crowd at each village and airfield so that no one who had come from miles away on foot, would miss the personal greeting, the *dharjan*—"communication"—which strengthens her and them. At some villages and airfields where no speech was on her schedule, the expectation of the crowd was so intense that she spoke anyhow. She spoke extemporaneously, always without notes, with the same aura of personal conviction, sincerity, strength—even the fifth time in a day, when we who were following her were tired, hot, dirty and bad-tempered.

As we were flying past Mt. Everest on our way back to Delhi, I asked her secretary, Kapoor, if he thought the prime minister might not be too tired to talk a bit with me. On the trip out, between speeches, whenever the door of her compartment had been open, she had seemed to be working on state papers. "Open the door a crack," Kapoor told me, "and if she does not look too busy, you can go in." I peeked through the door, and she was sitting in her big comfortable reclining seat reading my "Woman, the Fourth Dimension" issue of the *Ladies' Home Journal*, which I had given her in Delhi.

I said hesitantly, "If you're not too tired, if you've recovered—"

"From what?" She laughed. "This is not the sort of thing that tires me." (Those who have known her a long time say that her obviously mythical "frailty" is the way she looks when she has nothing demanding to do—her "nonfunction" look, her old friend Tara Baig calls it. In the morning, when she first gets up, I noticed that her features seem "thin and pointed"; after the *dharjan* with the crowd or a tussle with the politicians, the thinness somehow plumps up. It's as if her energy builds up the more she uses it, rather than drains away.)

"You come alive when all your powers are used, is that it?" I asked her.

"Well, yes," she said. "But if you think this trip used that much of me . . ." And of course, for her, this trip was almost a joy ride, a holiday.

And suddenly I realized that the naturalness in Indira Gandhi's authority bespeaks not only experience, but the fact that she is using to the fullest not alien abilities copied from men, but abilities which are very much her own as a woman. For instance, her ability to compartmentalize her time and thinking, to do four or five jobs at once, has always been the secret of a woman's creative energy. Not long ago Indira Gandhi's youngest son bought her a pedometer—he wanted to know how many miles a day she traveled, walking at home, while she thought, talked, decided.

"Ten miles, he clocked me once," she told me.

I asked her if her political career had involved conflicts for her as a woman. Various Indians had told me dramatically that she had had to "choose between her country and her marriage," "sacrifice her personal happiness to her political duty," and so forth. But it was very hard to reconcile her air of joyous affirmation of life with such martyrdom, despite that "sadness" people saw in her eyes, those moments in which she seemed to withdraw into herself.

"You see, I have a political personality that is one part of me, and an unpolitical personality also, and both have to come out. Actually, I've gone from stage to stage so imperceptibly, I've never really made that kind of choice. I hear these stories that my marriage collapsed and I left my husband, or that we were separated, and it's not true. In 1947, when I was spending about fifteen days a month in Delhi taking care of my father's house, it got so difficult going back and forth with the children that I moved the children there. My husband campaigned for Parliament from Lucknow, and I went back to help with his electioneering, and after he was elected he moved into my father's house with us. It wasn't a conventional kind of life, and it wasn't an ideally happy marriage. We were very happy at times. We quarreled tremendously at times. It was partly both of us being so headstrong, and partly circumstances, and also he was split in two. I wouldn't have gone into public life if he had said no. But I am so intense in whatever I do, he must have been frightened to have it all concentrated on him. He wanted me occupied. He was very occupied with his own career. (He was a rising opposition leader in Parliament when he died in 1960.) But when I went into public life and became successful, he liked it and he didn't like it. Other people—friends, relatives—were the worst. They would say, how does it feel, being so-and-so's husband, and he would get upset and it would take me weeks to win him over. To hurt the male ego is, of course, the biggest sin in marriage. Also, I don't think he could ever make me out. He was not a person who discusses these things. He was a very good political speaker on any issue, but this kind of thing, about feelings and so on, he could not speak. In the end we were somehow getting beyond all this, and becoming very close together. The summer before he died, we had a nearly perfect holiday."

An old friend of the family said, "If he had taken advantage of being Nehru's son-in-law instead of resenting it so, it might have been different. But then he wouldn't have been Feroze. He was so touchy about where he was seated at public functions. She was very much in love with him, and so crushed when he would take it all out on her. He would often be quite mean to her in front of us. And after a while she hid the sadness and the hurt, and a kind of freezing set in."

"I suppose you couldn't have turned yourself back into a little housewife," I said.

She looked quite startled. "You know, that's always been my ambition," she said. (At least, that must have been a persistent illusion; during all the time she was in actuality accepting that increasingly more difficult series of political challenges and responsibilities which prepared her for the prime ministry. Her intimate women friends had all told me, sentimentally, sincerely, "If circumstances had permitted, Indira would have been quite happy just to be a housewife, puttering around her own house and taking care of Feroze and the children.")

There never was one single choice, but a series of little choices. "Things happen so fast you don't have time to think; events, situations, you simply react to them. But it's something in you, too. The time I decided I should go speak in Himalchi when my father wouldn't—six hours later, I was there. That's when it all began really, discovering I could make the people listen. Why did I go? The good Indian would say it was just not in my stars to be that little housewife."

She gave up the Congress presidency when her husband had his first heart attack. Ironically, she was in a train coming home from a brief trouble-shooting mission for another woman candidate when her husband suddenly had his last attack. Usha, who went to the hospital to sit with him while others waited at the airport to bring Indira Gandhi, told me, "He kept saying, 'When is Indira getting back?' They were very close at the end. It was terrible for her, that she was not there."

Indira Gandhi does not think that "happiness" is the most important thing in women's life. She says quite simply that she has had "unhappy times and happy times," but she is not an "unhappy woman." Nor does she think it impossible for women like herself, who insist that they are "human beings first," to have a good marriage. She said:

"I didn't have less love because of this. I think my husband gave very deeply to me in the end, and I to him. I think giving is what makes for happiness, really. After all, one becomes what one is through all the real experiences of one's life, all the things that shape you. If you are complete as a person, nobody can be a threat to you. But if everything is a question of status, if you are insecure as a person yourself, it's always a question of who's higher or lower. I don't think he'd have been the person he was if he were married to the sweet little woman in an Indian movie; he would have been just an ordinary husband. I think this conflict helped him to grow also.

"Conflict and unhappiness are not the worst things that can happen. It depends on the person. It can either crush you or build your strength. It's all the experience one has that makes one what one is—the wider the experience, the stronger one's personality."

Perhaps when the sense of your own personal responsibility for shaping the future of your country and history becomes a very part of your personality, "happiness" as previously defined is not relevant. That sense of larger purpose is just as natural and basic to her as a woman, as being a mother or a wife. And Indians do not view this whole question of women in the either/or terms of the feminine mystique (career versus marriage, self-fulfillment versus love, individual identity versus femininity, etc.), because they do not view men in these terms. A brilliant young Indian planner told me: "Women are not regarded as something all that different here because we don't have the feeling about sex as sin—a form of lower activity, as in your Judeo-Christian tradition. In our temples, Konarak and others, the sexual act is portrayed in vivid detail as part of the religious celebration, the vibrant joy of life. You don't get the feeling of pornography, something wrong, dirty. The woman participates actively in the sexual celebration, she is not merely the passive victim. Women are also considered to have souls, and participated in celebrating our holy mysteries in our very ancient tradition. The Hindu idea of stages of man's life recognizes the first stage of celibacy, when man's life is devoted to learning; then the stage when family life is the main concern; then the stage of devotion to the wider causes of community or nation; and finally the stage of contemplation. When life is a question of stages, one does not think in terms of either/or."

Thus it is not assumed that a woman who commits herself to a larger cause is going to neglect her family or her home. They are not seen as in conflict with each other: a woman will not always be a young mother with young children; she will go on to other stages of maturity. One Indian joked: "The reason you Americans cannot have a woman President is no American woman ever reaches the age of thirty-five."

Despite her personal times of unhappiness, there is no basic conflict between Indira Gandhi's private personality and her political personality. They are *both* her basic personality as a woman. This is why she seems so truly strong that she is able to be gentle—as strong men are gentle who are not torn in two or full of fears about their masculinity; strong enough to draw out the strength of others, instead of keeping them weak. And this is why she is able to command respect from men as many American women cannot. Here, a woman who breaks into public life feels so unequal that she is afraid to listen to her own voice and tries to become one of the boys. She isn't free to use her own strength as a woman, as Indira Gandhi seems to.

"She is a superb listener, not like some women who talk all the time," one of her Cabinet members told me. "She takes in all the alternatives, and instead of either/or, black and white, somehow brings them to a synthesis—as if two things that seemed to be opposite can somehow coexist. It is amazing what a backlog of decisions she has been able to dispose of in a few weeks in that way."

Her old friend, Pupul Jayocar, had said; "She has that flexibility of mind not to judge immediately, but to take in. If there are enormous contrasts and contradictions in a country, as there are in India, the only way to resolve them is to contain both in a single act of perception. They cannot even label her modern or traditional, the contemporary mind in India has to be able to contain and resolve both as she does. That extraordinary capacity for detail—which she got from her mother, not her father—is also crucial for this country at this moment, which is too likely to get involved in abstract ideological debate. The abstract ideological statement is finally arrived at, but somehow nothing gets done."

She is also an "impatient" woman. ("She does not suffer fools gladly," someone puts it.) And vain and petulant and quick-tempered. She has stamped her feet and *yelled* at the frustrating aspects of Indian bureaucracy. She "plays favorites," a woman minister told me. "She's so determined not to be a feminist that I consider her a leader of men, not of women." As a woman, she obviously enjoys flattery "from all male creatures," but suddenly one sees her wink.

I asked her what she considered the greatest danger to India. She said: "The danger really is the politicians. I never thought I would be prime minister, not because I'm a woman, but because I have too rational a mind for a politician. Indian men are very emotional, much more than women. For some of them—well, it's very comfortable to keep sitting where you are. The difficult thing is to keep moving on, and to persuade the people they have to keep moving on. It's so much easier to sink back into a yearning for the old traditional ways—or whip up emotions in a religious revival."

Her image, as prime minister, is not Mother India, with its connotation of helpless children; it is a younger generation's eagerness to break out of tired dilemmas and doctrines, and make one's own new frontiers. Indira Gandhi said: "In the old days, the maharajah would dictate like a father dictating to a family, and all accepted his decisions. The only way we can really move ahead now is for people to think out things for themselves, to take responsibility. Otherwise, one person has to do it all. The danger is our own need for dependence. I suppose it comes from being insecure, from having been poor and deprived and dependent, ruled by others for so long."

On the trip to Assam, two men, high officials in the Indian government, had explained to me with great passion what it had done to the Indian people—the years of being treated by the British like "children," as if we "were not capable of anything except to be hewers of wood and bearers of water—until we felt we were not good for anything ourselves."

Everybody in those lands was treated as women are still treated here—as dependent, really not capable or supposedly desirous of being anything but "bearers of water"; housewives. Indians are enormously critical of themselves. But as a woman, I can understand very well why Indians resent the idea of the United States or Britian or anyone else telling them what they should do, should want or not want, now. When we say to them—raising your own food is all you should worry about; we will produce the industry, or nuclear energy—it infuriates them even more than it infuriates a woman to be told by her husband: "You just keep the house clean, and don't worry about the world."

•   •   •

During the first three days of the national convention of the Congress Party at Jaipur, the prime minister sat cross-legged on the floor at the back of the dais in her white home-spun sari, hardly visible among the powerful bosses of the "syndicate," the planning theoreticians, Cabinet members and chief ministers of the big states who were sitting around and in front of her on the straw mat, leaning against the white bolsters, chewing cigars or betel nuts, and conducting their steady undertone of political chitchat and maneuver. As Kamaraj and other speakers thundered in the traditional ham style of political oratory, the ranks of delegates, also sitting cross-legged in front of little floor-height writing desks under the huge canopy of brightly colored Indian tent material, paid no attention. Resolutions were passed unanimously, it seemed; one was hardly conscious of their being brought to a vote.

Suddenly, on Friday, rebellion broke out. A resolution on food policy had been proposed, and the suggester of an amendment refused to take it back. Kamaraj tried to railroad it through. A beautiful dark-eyed woman seized the microphone and made an impassioned appeal which brought angry shouts of defiance from the delegates. "All right, then—vote," Kamaraj shouted. "Yes, go over here." "No, there." No one moved. Looking reflective, taking it all in, the prime minister continued to sit there, cross-legged.

On Saturday morning, casually changing her seat to one of the bolsters at the front of the dais, Indira Gandhi, wearing a blue sari that stood out visibly against the men's white dhotis, *looked* like a prime minister. The politicians, the syndicate bosses, and the chief ministers who had been bowing and scraping around Kamaraj all suddenly seemed to have some reason for coming over to squat beside her. She would listen gravely, nod her head, smile, close her eyes in thought, shake her finger, lean back against the bolster and stare out at the delegates, her eyes sparkling with enjoyment at the whole scene as she had at the *dharjan* in the garden when the little schoolboys declaimed their warlike poetry, waving their arms and clenching their fists.

At six o'clock Saturday night, after the last resolution was passed, the prime minister spoke. The enormous tent was filled. For the first time, the delegates listened to the speaker. In the most gentle, ladylike way, Madame Prime Minister gave the boys hell.

"It is not good for us to keep asking for things from outside countries. We must ask ourselves, at the lowest level, what have we done to change the situation—to change, for instance, our own food habits. We are short of rice, but we are not really short of food if we distribute it equitably. Poverty is as much a peril as war to us. When America or Russia want to do something in their own national self-interest, they don't argue whether it's capitalism or communism. We have grown so defensive, we admit mistakes when we don't make them. Our great weakness is that we do not know our own strengths. People ask what is new to come out of this Congress. I say, nothing new. If only we *finish* the work we have to do, that will be something new."

There is a great laugh, and a shout of "Long live Indira Gandhi."

·   ·   ·

"She is a people person," Mukul Banerje, the loyal, hard-working secretary of the Women's Division of the Congress Party had told me, "but she makes even me adventurous."

One afternoon Indira Gandhi left the politicians on the dais at Jaipur and went to meet what seemed like a boundless sea of women in the garden of the Maharani College. Students lined the walks and driveway in pretty silk and cotton tunics, over pants tight on the leg, softly wrinkled at the ankles, their dark hair in long braids down their backs. Women kept streaming through the gate—in saris of vivid purple and pink and elegant gold-embroidered silk; beautiful young women not much older than the students, with the red marriage mark on their foreheads; a fat woman with the Kashmir wool shawl that is the mink coat of India; women carrying babies; and old widows with toothless grins. Pretty young women traffic "cadets," with red berets atop their khaki uniforms, would hold out their arms and softly push the swelling, chattering wall of women back, urging "discipline, discipline." Groups of women also stood silently, covered from head to foot in the black tentlike burka that women whose lives are still spent in purdah must wear on the rare occasions when they are allowed outside.

She did not talk to them about the problems of women at all. But the problems she did talk about—food, poverty, backwardness, peace—were, I suddenly realized, problems that will not be solved unless women take their part equally in the world with men. The passive dependence, the silent submission to fate which had been idealized for Indian women was clearly now the main enemy of all the Indian people. And of us all. There are surely American women who could lend some "people person" concrete vision to our abstract dilemmas in Washington, even if we lack the sari grace of Indira Gandhi.

•   •   •

They say India's problems are so great, no man could solve them. I don't expect Indira Gandhi can perform miracles, but her belief in the strength of the Indian people could evoke the needed thrust of new purpose. India's most dangerous problem is that her population is multiplying too fast for the people to rise above incomes of less than $100 a year. Indira Gandhi will push family planning. Just before I left India, billboards sprang up in the public squares and bazaars, proclaiming, with all the hard sell of a big American advertising campaign, "A small family is a happy family." There were two identical houses, one a mass of squalling, dirty children and miserable parents; in the other were two happy, clean youngsters with a well-dressed father and mother seeing them off to school.

A pretty woman doctor whom I accompanied on her rounds in a mobile family-planning clinic in the villages, handed out vitamins to help the living children survive and showed me proudly the graph of their first thousand "loops," which had been dispensed two months ahead of quota. Her husband, a business executive, had not wanted her to work. "So for a few years I did not enter my service. All I did was wear pretty clothes, and when he came home tired, I always wanted to go out. He finally decided he did not need all that femininity, after all."

As for the new prime minister—"It depends on whether she delivers the goods for the people, or not," said the doctor.

The woman getting the loop said, "She must do the job. If she fails, they will all say it is because she is a woman. They will watch like a hawk for her to fail, not only in the opposition but in her own party. And the problems may be too great."

"A person cannot fail in a job like that," said the doctor. "She can only grow. When the people are depending on you, you can do the job you have to do."

Afterword 1985— see page 499

One of the most powerful forces arrayed against the women's movement—and sexual liberation in general—is the hierarchy of the Catholic Church. They have used millions of tax-free Church treasury funds, edicts from the pulpit, even threats of excommunication to prevent ratification of the Equal Rights Amendment in the United States and to prevent women from exercising their right to medical help in abortion if they choose not to bear a child. New decrees from the Vatican implacably insist that sex for nonprocreative purposes is a sin, condemning and banning sexuality as it is now being enjoyed by great numbers of Catholics as well as non-Catholics, just as an early papal decree forbade Catholics to use any form of birth control.

And yet I feel more strongly than ever that the intransigence of the seemingly monolithic Catholic Church will somehow be transcended or transformed by that new power in the world—the power of women, of the young, of sexual liberation itself.

Why did the Pope receive me, and even give me a medal for works on behalf of women? The papers I had to supply in requesting the audience made no bones about my record in advancing "the right of women to choose" in the matter of abortion, and the Equal Rights Amendment. Xavier Rynne, authority on the Roman Catholic Church, wrote *(New York*

Times, October 12, 1975) that it was not "accidental," when, soon after issuing a "traditional statement on women's limited role in Catholic religious services, [the Pope] received the feminist leader Betty Friedan and told her, 'We wish to thank you, and congratulate you on your work.' " While seeming "to hold the line on strictly doctrinal matters," Rynne continued, the Pope's reception of me was part of his own campaign for "the happy synthesis of new and old, of traditions and reform, of conserving and updating."

The fact is, young priests and nuns, old and young, are intent on transforming that monolith from within. The National Assembly of Women Religious, the organized nuns in the United States, have proclaimed their support of the Equal Rights Amendment—as well as of the priesthood for women. And in my discussions with such nuns, it becomes clearer and clearer that when women do participate in the decisions of the church—and have a voice in its theology—the doctrines enforcing nonprocreative sex as sin, and women as breeders, will be transcended.

As soon as I got back from Rome, I met with Sister Margaret Traxler and other leading American nuns in Chicago. They felt reinforced in their own militancy by my reception by the Pope. Last year, the same week the Catholic bishop of San Diego threatened excommunication to any member of NOW, I spoke at Mundelein College in Chicago. The sisters running that college refused to be intimidated by threats by the local Right to Life group against my speaking. That Sunday I had brunch and Bloody Marys with several of the nuns in a communal apartment they share off Michigan Drive, out of the cloister. They told me they were working on themselves to get rid of their own "excessive humility." They had become aware of a certain amount of economic exploitation of themselves as women in the church, and they were no longer going to tolerate it. Under government contract, they had to be paid the minimum professional wage for school work or teaching, but according to the rules of their order, they were supposed to turn their paychecks back to the order—and then received a small allowance for their own subsistence. Even if they still wanted to dedicate their lives to the service of the church, why shouldn't they be the ones to decide how, and on what kinds of service, that money they earned should be spent? They had suddenly realized that their own services—and the money they were worth—should give them their own voice in the decisions of the church. That new power in the world already belongs to these nuns, if they choose to assume it.

And the 83 percent of American Catholics who now use birth control are not as opposed as the priests of the hierarchy to sexual freedom or equality. The majority support the Equal Rights Amendment. Somehow, despite all the sound and fury about new constitutional amendments giving fetuses the rights of full citizenship—and thus making abortion a crime— these amendments have not gotten reported out of committee so that senators would have to vote on them before the 1976 elections. With all the die-hard power of the Catholic hierarchy in the United States, senators facing reelection also have some sense of that new power implicit in women's right to choose.

A Visit with
Pope Paul

The audience with the Pope was granted so suddenly, so improbably, that I didn't dare wait. I caught a late plane to Rome after a Sunday night lecture at the State University at Stony Brook. The discussion ended with a student asking, "What is the most radical change you foresee from the women's movement?" "I can't tell you now," I said. "You wouldn't believe it anyhow. It's theological."

Was that why I was going to see the Pope? Lately I've been thinking that the ultimate implications of the women's movement are more profound than we dare realize. And the latest indication of this comes from recent reverberations within the Roman Catholic Church, the bastion of the Judeo-Christian tradition that has shaped the mind of Western man—and denied women—through the millennia.

Now, I am not myself religious, or so I would have said. I am a daughter of the secular city, of the generation that lived through holocaust to ask, "Is God Dead?" Lately, however, like the young, I have begun to feel uncomfortable with the conventional wisdom and sophistication that denies the experience of transcendent life, creation, and mystery, the great questions of beginning, end, and purpose—the experience that is religion, whatever name it calls God.

In these years, when the purpose transcending my own life and those of my sisters has been to write our own names as

women, religion that calls God Him seems irrelevant, or, to
the more stubbornly religious, inimical. During the months I
was finishing *The Feminine Mystique,* over ten years ago, Vatican
Council II was meeting in Rome. Even if no woman participated at that historical assemblage, the ecumenical movement
that swept the church in the sixties seemed to converge somehow with the movement of women in society generally. So
many of the problems rending the church and the Catholic
priesthood after Vatican II had to do with women: birth control, the Pill, abortion, celibacy of priests, divorce, the growing rebellion of the nuns and of Catholic women themselves,
who have composed the bulk of the faithful, against decisions
governing their own bodies and daily lives—decisions made
solely by men whose vows of priestly celibacy define women
as temptations to sexual evil.

But if women were not present at Vatican II, Catholic
women were visibly present, in great numbers and militancy,
from the very beginning of the women's movement. More and
more in recent years I've been asked to speak at Catholic colleges and seminaries, including famous Catholic men's schools
deciding to admit women. On the Sunday before the women's
strike for equality on August 26, 1970, women demanded that
the pulpits of Boston churches be turned over to women, and I
preached the sermon at Arlington Street Church in Boston
with Mary Daly, the Catholic theologian who wrote *The
Church and the Second Sex.* It began to seem as if the theological
debate topic of the seventies might change from "Is God
Dead?" to "Is God He?" For now, in all the Protestant
churches, women who before had just cooked the church sup-
pers were demanding and winning the right to be ordained as
ministers and to sit as deacons on decision-making bodies; in
Conservative Judaism, women were fighting for the right to be
ordained as rabbis and counted as persons in the necessary
minyan or quorum of ten.

•   •   •

And yet a head-on collision seemed unavoidable between
women and the Catholic hierarchy on the issue of abortion.
My most agonizing decision, in my leadership of NOW, was to
confront abortion in terms of a woman's right to choose—
whether or when to have a child—and to control her body

according to her conscience. I felt this would cause terrible conflicts for Catholic women, and yet it had to be done. The Catholic hierarchy in my own state has spent millions of dollars trying to block, and then repeal, the life-saving law giving women the right to medical help in abortion. When the Supreme Court interpreted the Constitution as guaranteeing the right of women to choose in the matter of childbirth and sexual privacy generally, thus ending the medieval criminal abortion laws in all the states, the Catholic hierarchy mounted a campaign to amend the Constitution to give the fetus the full rights of a U.S. citizen from the moment of conception. And it underlined what seemed to be a declaration of war against women by campaigning against ratification of the Equal Rights Amendment.

It began to look like war to the death, with new encyclicals coming from Pope Paul in the Vatican forbidding women to offer the mass or even serve as altar girls, much less aspire to the priesthood; countenancing no relaxation of celibacy for priests; forbidding the Pill or other birth control; even forbidding nuns to change their habits and cloistered life and become part of the community, as they were moving to do in America. And yet, and yet . . .

Despite the implacable die-hard statements issuing from the Pope, there were signs of something else happening. I had silently whistled when in 1973 I had read in the paper that the Synod of Bishops, meeting in the Vatican on "Justice in the World," had proposed that "women should have their own sphere of responsibility and participation in the community life of society and likewise of the Church." When on May 3, 1973, the Pope named the Special Study Commission on the Role of Women in Society and in the Church, it was composed of twenty-five people, thirteen of them women. *L'Osservatore Romano*, the official Vatican newspaper, announced it would study "the specific role of women in society and men-women relationships, on the basis of the radical equality of men and women" and women's "aspirations and frustrations," with the goal of ascertaining what attitudes and structures needed to be altered in order to guarantee the "authentic promotion of women." In U.S. reports, an unnamed Vatican spokesman was quoted as saying "this means the Vatican is coming to terms with Women's Lib." The commission was due to start meeting in November.

In September I spent several days in Rome, ascertaining that despite the impression of impregnable battle lines between the church and women, in the Vatican itself powerful forces were convinced that the very survival of the Catholic Church as an institution rests on a breakthrough on these issues involving women and sex.

Providing me with the necessary introductions to key people in the Vatican, Father Francis X. Murphy of the Holy Redemption Order in Washington said, "At this moment in history, it might be a good idea for you to talk to the Pope. If we don't give women control over their own future, we're not going to have any control, or future."

·   ·   ·

In the discreet offices of Borgo Santo Spirito, headquarters of the worldwide, black-robed Jesuit order, I got the strange sense that I was walking into a part in an intricate scenario already laid out. Elena Bartoli, director of the Jesuits' Visiting Bureau and one of the first women to come even close to a center of power in the Curia, picks up the telephone: "Father, I have here in my office," she says in a conspiratorial tone, and then into rapid Italian. I am sent to see Rosemary Goldie, a discreet, self-effacing woman who was one of the first brought in as an "auditor" at Vatican Council II and has since been elected head of the Congregation of the Laity. "Obviously, it had to come in the church, when it started happening to women in the world," she shrugged. "If women can never be priests, however, a woman will never be able to celebrate the Eucharist within the Catholic Church. Does this mean they will have no power in the government of the church? It's a question that has to be met theologically."

Father Vincent O'Keefe, second in command of the Jesuit order and former president of Fordham, tells me: "The Holy Father has made it clear that celibacy for the priesthood will not be changed. But is this a dogmatic question ruled out by the church doctrine, or a matter of practice that could be changed? We are a strictly male order. The voting group is male, bishops and cardinals. These things were taken for granted. All of a sudden, the roof fell in. The nuns running the schools, the hospitals, the colleges, doing the work—they were tired of taking orders from these creepy old men who know nothing about women except to keep them at a distance . . . as a danger, the temptation to sin, it goes back to the Garden of Eden. You can't make a go of it without the nuns. You have to meet them on a profound level; you do it with them or it won't get done, the work of the church. In our order, this whole question of women has been given number one priority among the Big Issues of the Day, to bring about a situation where everybody has a shot at developing into a a full honest-to-God human being. The position we push with the younger priests is to deal with women as people, as equals —it's not doing women a favor, it's a practical matter for the survival of the church."

At Borgo Santo Spirito, I got the clear sense of these shrewd Jesuits looking into the future, determined to save the church for the modern world, shuddering when "the hope raised by Pope John" was dashed by the edict forbidding Catholics to use the Pill and birth control. "A lot of men as well as women said here we go again. It was a mistake we won't be able to live with. But the church will have to come to terms with it some other way."

As I pass from office to office down huge, dark, empty marble corridors, across the vast space of St. Peters, through the stone walls of this centuries-old, vastly wealthy, state-within-a state that has been so exclusively male, I sense an apprehensiveness. The only skirts here are the skirts of the priests. The suave Cardinal Pignedoli, the Secretary for Non-Christians who they say may be the next Pope, sweeps in with a swish of his long skirts and says, "I do not know why you have come to see me. I have nothing to do with women. I am only concerned with nonbelievers, Hindus, Moslems, Jews. Women are none of my business." Bishop Gagnon, who is head of the Commission on the Family, seems nervous, uneasy, almost grim at my questions about women. "Would it really make a woman freer, give her more dignity, responsibility, to give her liberties in these matters?" he asks. Women, it seems, wouldn't accept his jurisdiction over them. "We can no longer think of women only as mothers."

Why are they so apprehensive at my slightest question? It is explained by a defrocked Dutch priest, Marc Reuver, who used to be Vatican spokesman for the English-speaking world: "Psychologically and theologically, there is an attitude of fear, a panic that the Vatican no longer controls. Before, if the Pope spoke, everyone followed him."

Now, according to the polls, the majority of Catholics practice birth control, and more Catholics get abortions than non-Catholics. But the real crisis of the church, I learned in Rome, is "the crisis of the priests" themselves: between 1964 and 1969, more than 13,000 priests gave up the priesthood. "This fear is almost polarized around the issue of women and sex," Reuver said. "They see the woman primarily as a threat to celibacy. Since the fifth century, the priests, the religious, the nuns were supposed to dedicate the whole life to the Lord. It's easier to keep them under control, married only to the Lord. And there's the practical question. If priests get married and have to support families, it will change completely the whole financial situation of the church. If nuns are no longer the brides of the Lord, they will have to be paid more. That is in back of the fear of sex and women, too. And if, as you say, women take control of their own bodies and their own lives, according to their own consciences, can they so easily be told what to do by the priest any longer? So now the Vatican says in the abstract that men and women are equal, but when you come down to what this involves in concrete reality, it's another story."

He goes on to explain: "The new Commission on Women has had ruled out from the beginning the possibility of dealing with the idea of women being priests, the questions of birth control, the Pill, divorce. There is a growing gap between the institution of the church—the Vatican, the hierarchy—and the church of the faithful, including priests and nuns. This increasing gap is precisely because of these issues. Theologically, there's nothing against women being priests, but the Roman Catholic Church is a men's society; women play the role of listening, giving money and praying. As the result of your movement, there will be a rebellion, because the church only deals with women in the abstract; it cannot come to terms with the realities of life.

"Many priests have mistresses, but to them woman is only

an object, for only a few hours, in the same way that to the celibate, woman is still seen only as sex and a little repressed love. That doesn't help women, it manipulates women. And yet our theology is built on respect for personhood. The reason for the unalterable stand of the church on these issues, besides the financial fear, is the practical fear that the church will lose control over Catholics as such."

Reuver himself married his assistant in 1971 ("for sixteen years we shook hands passionately") and they left their religious orders, but he did not leave the priesthood. From an office over the beautiful Piazza Navone, he is now secretary general of IDOC, a worldwide ecumenical communications network for those trying to revitalize the church.

In the Machiavellian atmosphere of Borgo Santo Spirito, Elena Bartoli says: "It was the women who used to go to church—how many men did you see at communion, at mass? —it was not masculine. The change is that men dare to be religious. Women used to go to church for the blah-blah-blah. Now you know what you go for. Women are not so dumb to go to church for the blah-blah-blah any more."

Reuver had told me that "many people in the Vatican take a much more liberal stand on the issues than the official church line." And so I asked Elena Bartoli if I could have an audience with the Pope. "What needs to be said," she says, "would take the kind of audience only given to heads of state. There is no point just to kiss the ring." I gave her, in four pages, the details of my life and work, so much of which concerns those issues on which the Vatican's crises and mental apprehensiveness are based that I did not really expect to get the audience.

Ten days after I got back home, the phone call came from Rome. "You said you would come back if the Holy Father would see you," said Elena Bartoli. "He will see you. What Wednesday will you come?" "Next Wednesday," I said.

•   •   •

I was briefed by the best. My priestly adviser in Washington was appealed to for protocol: "The point isn't what you say, the meeting is the message. Go buy an elegant dress. Consider it a diplomatic mission. Wear a veil on your head and kiss the ring." Well, I agreed it was a diplomatic mission, but my advisers from the women's movement pointed out that any kind of veil covering my head would be taken as an ideological statement: the veiled head has been the very symbol of women's submission to an inferior status, in the Jewish and Moslem as well as the Christian world. On the other hand, my friend Dean Joe Mulholland of Fordham warned that Golda Meir had to send a plane back for her hat to see the Pope. "It would be diplomatic but okay ideologically if you could wear a hat, as long as it didn't cover your head," said Mary Jean Tully. Mr. John, a famous hatter and social acquaintance, was appealed to. Many hats and concoctions that when you got down to it were still *veils* were tried on before Mr. John and his assistants got the point: that it had to be a hat that was a nonhat and did not cover *any* of the head. A sort of band or halo was found, which literally did not touch the head at all; they sewed on a comb to anchor it.

In Cambridge, Harvey Cox, the eminent theologian at Harvard Divinity School, suggests, "Why don't you take him a present? Doesn't the women's movement have a symbol that looks like a cross with an equal sign?" From Ohio, Elizabeth Farians, of the new breed of Catholic women theologians, sent me a compilation of all the biblical and church pronouncements, from the Apostle Paul down, denying the personhood of women.

• • •

The night before my audience with the Pope, I had a dialogue at the Loyola campus on the outskirts of Rome with American Catholic college students spending a year in Rome, and Italian and other seminarians studying English as part of their preparation for the priesthood. I needed to touch base with someone on the theological implications of women's liberation; I was very nervous about this meeting with the Pope. I talked of the personhood of women. They seemed very hungry to hear about it; moreover, in the discussion afterward, they insisted on raising the embarrassing, concrete questions.

On Wednesday morning, crossing the great square of St. Peter's on my way to the Vatican, I was stopped by a young man with a student's book bag. "I am a seminarian who heard you last night," he said. "We want you to know we are glad you are going to see the Pope, and we hope he hears you."

I walked across St. Peter's Square and to the iron gate at the

side of the Pope's great audience hall, and was passed by the
Swiss guards in their striped medieval uniforms and raised
spears. I felt quite alone and rather scared as I walked through
the Vatican courtyards past the gardens and statues of saints,
the stained-glass windows; chilled, awed by the golden ba-
roque wealth of the church and the stone images by which
man has worshiped nearly two thousand years. With all its
troubles this vast institution still encompasses one-sixth of the
people in the world. What was I doing here?

An image from Xavier Rynne's "Letters from Vatican
City" came into my mind: the bronze doors opened for Vatican II, and he saw "row upon row of bishops, clad in flowing
white damask capes and mitres, descending from the papal
apartments . . . in rows of sixes, an apparently inexhaustible
phalanx of prelates . . . and the scarlet ranks of the Sacred
Cardinals." All men. And somewhere also in the back of my
mind were all the words down through the ages saying that
the voices of women cannot be heard in the church.

Ecclesiastes: "I find woman more bitter than death, she is a
snare, her heart a net, her arms are chains; he who is pleasing
to God eludes her . . . but the sinner is her captive."

Ecclesiasticus: "No wickedness comes anywhere near the
wickedness of a woman, may a sinner's lot be hers. . . . Sin
began with a woman, and thanks to her all must die."

Paul: "In all the Churches of the saints women are to remain quiet at meetings since they have no permission to speak;
they must keep in the background as the Law itself lays it
down. If they have questions to ask, they should ask their husbands at home."

St. Clement: "Every woman ought to be overcome with shame
at the thought that she is a woman."

In the hall of the palace for private audiences, I pass a beautiful statue of mother and child. But if I had walked over these
ancient stones into these gates, less than two hundred years
ago, having said what I have said in the world, saying what I
intend to say to the Pope, I would have been condemned as a
witch, and "condemned witches were strangled, hanged, be-
headed and their bodies cast into the fire; often they were
burned alive."

In the salon, where those granted private audiences this day wait to be called by the Holy Father, I sit down between what seems to be an official delegation of Indonesians and a fat American businessman muttering about Watergate. I suddenly stop feeling nervous. Women are half the world, after all, and the other half is the whole rising army of the young climbing over these sexual barriers that have been used to keep us apart for so long. There is no way the church can survive if it locks itself behind such battle lines. I know what I have to say.

In the group ahead, the veiled women genuflect, and bow their heads and kiss his ring. The Indonesians go past me on their way out. I am finally waved into his presence and walk over the rich carpet to the throne-chair where the Pope in his white robes sits, flanked by aides in black priestly garments, intimidating with the trappings of grandeur and power. I walk close to this awesome figure, to the symbol of power that has embodied the highest visions and worst fears of the mind of man, and I see a man who is *human* and quite old, holding out his hand in a sort of half welcome, half blessing, with eyes full of the craft and authority one would expect in one who has risen to the pinnacle of such a powerful political world, staring at me, studying me. I was told that he would speak first. He motioned to an aide, who brought him a jewel box. And Pope Paul VI handed me this box and said in English, "We want to express our gratitude and appreciation for all you have done for the women of the world."

"I have brought you a present, too," I said, and handed him the chain with the gold-plated symbol of women's equality. "This is the symbol of the women's movement—the sign of the female, in biology, crossed by the sign of absolute equality. As Your Holiness can see, when women are completely equal to men, it becomes a different kind of cross."

I handed my cross to the Pope, saying I brought it "in the hope and expectation that the Catholic Church is going to come to profound new terms with the personhood of women, and that when this happens, the church and the Judeo-Christian tradition which have been a force holding women back for many centuries will become a force for the liberation of women."

There was a quick interchange with the interpreter, and

then the Pope spoke in Italian. "We want you to know that it will not be a radical approach," said the interpreter, "because the church has always upheld the dignity of women."

"It is not a question of radical, Your Holiness," I said to the Pope. "When the church comes to terms with the full personhood of women as it has with the full personhood of man, it will be new—and many problems which have long oppressed women and are now tormenting the church will be seen in a different light and can be solved."

The Pope, who quite clearly understood what I was saying, referred the word "personhood" back to the interpreter, and he and another aide seemed to be having a brief semantic debate, in Italian, on the right word by which to translate "the full personhood of woman."

The Pope put on his glasses to examine the chain and equality cross I had given him. "Is this for me?" And I said that I knew that during his papacy more has been done to give women a voice than in the 1,900 previous years, but it was not enough. And so I hoped the Commission on the Role of Women in Society and in the Church that he had named would confront all the concrete barriers to the full equality and participation of women in all the fields of society, and in the church itself. And that this would have enormous importance for millions of women who are not Catholics, as well as for Catholic women, all over the world.

The Pope said again that the church had always upheld the dignity of women, but now it was going to really study the situation of women, and not only in the family, but at work, in all the fields of society, so that women could really develop according to their aspirations and play their proper role.

He said he wanted me to understand that he personally was very disturbed and opposed to anything that oppressed women, and had been grieved to read in the newspaper a new incident of oppression of women. Leaders of the Italian women's movement with whom I consulted, before and after the audience with the Pope, said the Italian papers that night had carried a story about the jailing of the "three Marias" in Portugal, for their poems and activities in organizing women.

The Pope took my hand in both of his, as if he really meant his concern for women. He seemed much more human, somehow, than I expected, with a warm and caring expression; he evidently wasn't just going through perfunctory motions in meeting with me; he seemed strangely intent, curious, interested in this meeting, which was going on much longer than anyone had given me reason to expect it would.

He told me to open the jewel box. In it was a bronze medal with an embossed likeness of him in robes and papal scepter, with that same intent expression, and the words "Paulus VI P.M. Anno XI." I thanked him, and remembering the caution not to talk too much, repeated once again what I had really come to say: that the church by coming to new theological terms with the full personhood of women—and by bringing about the full participation of women in the church—would be able to see in a new light problems that have been oppressive lately to both women and the church. And he held out his arms—as if to bless me, I guess—and I was ushered out. When I got out to St. Peter's Square, the doves that were flying earlier were gone, and it had begun to rain.

• • •

The next day I met with various mothers superior and others in the Vatican who are concerned that the church make a real breakthrough in the participation and personhood of women, not just a token statement of pious intent.

Teresa McLeod, who holds a doctorate from Louvain University in Belgium, was the first woman to get a degree in theology from the Pontifical Institute in Rome. She is mother superior of Regina Mundi, a school now training three hundred women theologians from forty countries throughout the world, in conjunction with the vigorous old Gregorian Institute. She "regrets" that even before the Commission on Women began its work, a "veto" was issued by the Vatican Secretary of State that it was not to deal with such crucial problems as the priesthood for women or birth control. "I don't know if it's going to be just another series of pious pronouncements. I'm a little skeptical if discussion has been ruled out in advance on some of the most important questions." She feels that the question of the priesthood for women is important no matter how many women want to be priests. "It's the possibility that's important. The priesthood has been linked to power as well as service, and people who have the power don't always want to give it up. It doesn't help that the people who have the power and could lose it happen to be the only ones who have the power to make the change, and some are scared stiff at the thought of women priests, as if that would mean loss of privilege for them."

Mother McLeod, and most of the others I talked to, did not feel that the theological arguments were what was really keeping women out of the priesthood. "The arguments from Scripture, mostly the things Paul said, were based on the sociology of his time. The fact that Jesus had no women among his apostles—women couldn't have gone around in a bunch with the men then. It was inconceivable that Jesus could have chosen to incarnate himself as a woman of that period, because a woman couldn't have done what he did. The other argument—from tradition—is trickier. If it's tradition with a small 't'—custom, habit—those traditions can change. But Tradition with a capital 'T' that has been handed down from Christ through the teaching church—that is more difficult. Any religious belief has an element that is not completely rational and depends upon your acceptance of tradition. If you shake one belief basic to that tradition, you shake them all.

"Pope Paul has a great sense of responsibility for not demolishing any important tradition. I'm not sure these breakthroughs will come in his lifetime. Some of the men think we will be satisfied with some special form of consecration of women—some kind of 'setting aside' of women as teachers, nurses—as a panacea instead of priesthood. My answer to this is: how would you like special rites setting men aside as bus drivers instead of letting them be ordained as priests? Some of these men don't realize how restless the nuns are, that we can no longer be treated as children."

Perhaps, as Mother McLeod suggests, "none of the men around the Pope have told him any of the things you did." But even if the commission steers away, at first, from the crucial issues, she and the twelve other women, and in fact quite a few of the twelve men who will sit on the commission will insist that women at least be proportionally represented on all of the commissions that set church policy—those on canon law, theology, liturgy, the family. "Just getting the women there to begin making decisions, about women and everything else that concerns us, instead of just celibate men" will inevitably bring the church to new theological terms with the personhood of women.

Handsome, young Father Ivern, who is also with the commission, drops statistics to express his outrage that with 1,500,000 nuns in the Catholic world compared to only 300,000 male religious, the entire top decision-making structure is all male with, so far, women only brought in as "consultants" or "*servottore,*" secretaries, at the third level down. He himself, as adviser to the Jesuit Superior-General on social questions, is insisting on bringing in more women as advisers. "Now that we start working with women, we start changing ourselves, there's a different approach to problems; many problems can be solved with less effort by a more intuitive approach than by too super-rational an approach. It's a whole dimension that was lacking before."

●   ●   ●

How these questions will indeed be seen in new terms, when women participate as active persons in the discussions, is hinted at by the new women theologians.

I am sent by Sister Mary Linscott, president of the International Union of Superiors General, to eat lunch with a group of nuns in the world headquarters of one of their orders, outside Rome. Over wine at lunch, they dismiss the theological arguments against the priesthood for women as hardly worth discussing. "The argument isn't theological, it's prudential— that existentially it would be unwise to do it right now. The underdeveloped countries where there is the greatest shortage of priests are the areas where women would be the least accepted sociologically. The closer an era or culture is to the level where brute strength is essential, the stronger is masculine superiority. The further you get from this point, the stronger the position of women. But I think in the church everybody is learning that the human psyche can only take so much change at a time."

Then they describe to me the outrage of nuns, especially in America, Belgium and England, when their attempts to become more effective in the modern world, under the stimulus of Vatican II, were met by directives from the Vatican as to the length of the hems of their dresses, and as to what time they should say their prayers. The Vatican shook as mothers superior wrote letters to the press and came to Rome to protest "in a perfectly respectable way that we would appreciate being consulted before, not after, you issue edicts affecting our lives."

Two American orders were so incensed they moved out of the control of the Vatican altogether and reestablished themselves in the larger community. Now it is a society of married as well as unmarried nuns, and men and children, dedicated to the same service to the community as they had been before under Vatican orders.

These educated nuns are well aware that their insistence now on their own identity and self-worth rests on the fact that they have, for the first time, education equal to these men, and economic independence or bargaining power. "American nuns, at least, had to become more and more educated very rapidly in order to compete with lay peers in social work and get Catholic boys to college. Their professional standing improved their sense of self-worth at a time of a seller's market. With the educative needs, and the fact that so far it takes much less money to support a religious woman than a married professional woman, or a man, a bishop meets a mother superior, and if the bishop starts trying to tell the nuns how to teach math when he doesn't know anything about it, they can just leave . . ."

As women theologians graduate in greater numbers from Regina Mundi and other universities, and as more and more men defect from a celibate priesthood, the handwriting is clearly on the wall.

And women who are now studying and teaching theology —Mary Daly in Boston, Rosemary Reuther in Washington, Elizabeth Farians in the Midwest, Teresa McLeod in Rome— are already building a theology for women linked to concrete historical facts of life that puts currently unsolvable problems in new light.

The reverence for life may well have formed the church's original attitude on birth control and abortion, but the new theologians speak of the "quality of life" and the willingness of parents to take responsibility for the offspring they add to the polluted, overpopulated world.

"You must act according to your conscience; it must tell you what to do," young priests are saying to young parents. As for divorce, bishops now tell parish priests to send Catholic teenagers who insist on getting married (usually because she's pregnant) to the justice of the peace—so great is the likelihood that the marriage will end in divorce before they are twenty-five—so that they can remarry without embarrassing the church. On the question of divorce, the new theologians, men and women, agree "intimacy" and "genuine love" are becoming essential matters, not "indissolubility." (The Catholic attitude on divorce was usually protective of women, Vatican experts explain, "at a time when men could divorce and abandon their wives and families at whim, and women were helpless.")

The women theologians noted that "it suddenly dawned on us that certain things we were expected to do or not to do because we were religious women were not religious questions at all but sociological, based on customs of the time when the institution began. For instance, the very custom of the cloister, the nun not going beyond the walls alone—this was not a religious matter at all, but the condition of a respectable woman, at that time in those countries, who could not safely or properly walk out in the streets alone. But our tradition didn't change when conventions of society changed, and this made us quaint and picturesque. Our life stopped while the life beside us evolved—we have to join the women of our time."

On the question of birth control, Teresa McLeod points out that "the Catholic approach to contraception was worked out in a period when they did not really understand the reproductive cycle. Now it seems inconsistent to require the couple to make the decision when and how often to bring a child into the world by using the rhythm method only, and not the Pill. It's less and less satisfying to argue that one method is natural and the others science now makes available are not. Is it natural to put twelve gold fillings in your teeth? Despite the official position, many priests are saying to women or couples tortured over such problems: 'I cannot make the decision for you.'"

Elizabeth Farians figures that "respect for life during the first period of humanity meant to people the earth. Many children were needed to do the work of the land and to man the military at a time when war was the way to settle disputes. More children died than survived into adulthood. It was the quantity of life that was important. The postindustrial age is different. Most children survive; women have many years to live after their fertile period; not as many children must be born. So the production of children need no longer be the major function of women, and women can be seen as persons in their own right . . . and children valued as unique individuals. Now we are faced with the problem of survival in an overpopulated world because we have not been able to change our respect for life to concern ourselves with the quality of life instead of its quantity."

The new women theologians have also begun to trace the origins of church attitudes denying to women "creation in the image of God." Sister Albertus Magnus McGrath points out that in the original version of Creation, man as "humanity" is presented as the image ("God created man in the image of himself, in the image of God he created him, male and female he created them [Genesis 1:27]"). But the church's demand for the subjection of the wife to husband was based on Paul's statement that "woman was not made in God's image."

Also, Sister McGrath points out, "Goodness does not belong to women because of the archetypal concept of Eve as weak, deceived, sinful, the eternal seductress, less a person than a sex object. Creativeness is not hers because of the misunderstanding of human genetics which persisted until the nineteenth century—the idea that all of a child's characteristics were in the male seed, and that the mother was merely a passive instrument, nourishing the seed in her womb, 'the good earth' in which the all-powerful seed could grow. Any woman would do for this anonymous function, so that the mother does not matter except as being sufficiently segregated to insure legitimacy." She also speculates that this "view of woman as part of vegetable nature conditioned the denial of education to girls through the centuries, and the still persistent psychological conditioning of the female to a sense of herself as inferior and subservient, a mere utility."

These new women theologians share my own hunch that this denial of "full human personhood in the image of God" is linked to "the contempt for human sexuality and more specifically for female sexuality, which is both symptom and cause of a psychic sickness which has beset the church through the ages."

Their theological hypothesis parallels my own psychological one that the pent-up sexual and human energies thus diverted have been manipulated into violence for men, and passive submissiveness for women, which is violence-against-the-self. And this is the service of death, the denial of the reverence for life on which all religion is based.

The nuns and priests I met in Rome, Chicago and St. Louis who are trying to brook this great divide insist "our revolt is religious in the true sense of the word." They insist that the church cannot survive as an institution and does not deserve to survive if it does not permit women to affirm their full personhood, and men to affirm their human sexuality. Nor will they tolerate what Elena Bartoli calls the "blah-blah-blah" of an abstract religion that denies the concrete reality of life.

Women theologians like Elizabeth Farians who were not allowed to "speak" in the church itself are beginning to talk of "The Second Coming—The Coming of Woman, Christa."

"Through the Coming of Woman we will become finally human because we will accept the so-called feminine principle in our own nature—i.e., the masculine and feminine in each of us will be harmonized and balanced. Each of us will be free to be ourselves. We will no longer be restricted and truncated by sexual stereotyping. We will reflect the image of God in individualized infinite variation. The Coming of Woman will be the final humanization of the species. Man and woman will relate to each other truly for the first time."

"The future ministers of the Word will shout the Good News—there is a movement, and there is a Coming of Woman."

With all the huff and puff of threatened male priests in the Vatican hierarchy and American chanceries, I hope the Pope's receiving me is a sign that the church may embrace the coming of woman, to survive. As one of the first women brought in as "auditor" by Pope Paul at the end of Vatican II, Rosemary Goldie recalls how "bishops and cardinals came to stare at us—women in St. Peters. By the next Vatican Council, women will be included normally in the work. We will just be taken for granted as ordinary members of the people of God."

Afterword 1985— see page 500

I suppose that what really made me go to see Simone de Beauvoir was a feeling that *someone* must know the right answer, someone must know for sure that all the women who had thrown away those old misleading maps were heading in the right direction, someone must see more clearly than I where the new road ends.

The women's movement had been turning inward on itself, borrowing its ideological argument from those of other revolutions. And the result was a paralysis of action—or abortive actions growing out of rhetoric that did not open up new possibilities in life. I wanted to help keep the women's movement on its own existential course—finding the truth from the reality of our own existence. But it is very difficult for people to trust themselves like that, especially on a new road.

I had never met Simone de Beauvoir, but I had learned my own existentialism from her. It was *The Second Sex* that introduced me to that approach to reality and political responsibility—that, in effect, freed me from the rubrics of authoritative ideology and led me to whatever original analysis of women's existence I have been able to contribute.

When I first read *The Second Sex*, in the early fifties, I was writing "housewife" on the census blanks, still in the embrace of the feminine mystique. And the book's effect on me was so depressing that I felt like going back to bed—after I had made

387

the children's breakfast—and pulling the covers up over my head. Only after a dozen years of living that kind of life did I personally, concretely, analyze what had brought me and other American women to that depressing state. And then I saw it as something that could be changed.

It is only recently that Simone de Beauvoir has embraced the women's movement, professing publicly to find in radical feminism an ideological blueprint superior to Marxist-Lenin-ist-Stalinist communism. Maybe, I thought, Simone de Beauvoir could give us the authority we need.

It didn't quite work out that way.

I made the trip to Paris, meeting her with two interpreters —one French, one English—in her salon.

It was furnished in well-worn, self-conscious Bohemian ele-gance—Oriental tapestries, porcelain cats, shawls, statues, pil-lows, pictures—memorabilia of her travels with Sartre all over the world. She looked more proper, correct, Establishment, than I had imagined, somehow more prim. My mind's image of her must still have been that of the young girl, leaping over the Parisian rooftops with Sartre—as she portrays herself in the early autobiographical chapters of *Prime of Life*, which I had relished. And still I felt the thrill of meeting a cultural hero in person—an intellectual heroine of our history. And after the gracious beginning, she offered, almost cursorily, the authority I thought I had come to find. But the authority with which she spoke about women seemed sterile, cold, an abstrac-tion that had too little relationship to their real lives. I felt almost like a fool, struggling with those mundane questions that women have to confront in their personal lives and in movement strategy. Those questions did not seem to interest her at all. Somehow she did not seem to identify with ordinary women trying to make something new of themselves, or to feel at all involved with their everyday problems. And yet she ut-tered the fashionable radical phrases, repudiating "elitism," elevating the anonymous "working-class" woman in the ab-stract.

She proclaimed it quite irrelevant for women to break through sex discrimination to get better jobs or advance in professions or achieve posts of leadership. One must simply destroy the system. But how then, I asked, are women to eat—

how are they to get the technological skills, the expertise even to have a voice in changing the system? They do not have to have *good* jobs in order to eat, she said of other women. But she herself had lived a life of exceptionally good jobs and had risen to eminence in a respected profession. Other women should not seek fame or even by-lines on their own articles, she said, though she herself will continue to write, of course, under her own famous name and enjoy the royalties and the influence it has earned. The comforts of the family, the decoration of one's own home, fashion, marriage, motherhood—all these are women's enemy, she said. It is not even a question of giving women a choice—anything that encourages them to want to be mothers or gives them that choice is wrong. The family must be abolished, she said with absolute authority. How then will we perpetuate the human race? There are too many people already, she said. Am I supposed to take this seriously?

It didn't seem to have much to do with the lives of real women, somehow. Or even the reality of herself, Simone de Beauvoir, in this salon that was decorated with personal style, full of cherished objects. She was absent-minded, perfunctory, as if her mind were somewhere else, far from these problems of women. I had been told that Sartre was ill and that she would give me only an hour because she had to go to the hospital to be with him. I can respect such a bond. But when one has lived a whole life in such dependence upon a man as she has—and by flaunting the absence of legal sanction, made a stronger bond than others do in ordinary marriage—how could she then advocate that other women renounce the very need to love and be loved by a man, the security and beauty of a home, or the possibility of wanting to give birth to a child? Or did she still fight her own unexpressed dependence by urging other women to be more independent than men?

And then I recognized the authoritarian overtones of that supposedly Maoist party line I'd heard before from sophomoric, self-styled radical feminists in America. I have been told that Sartre has been embracing the Maoist approach in French politics, with de Beauvoir following him, as she did once with existentialism . . . Possibly the existential authority I was seeking from Simone de Beauvoir is something she no longer seeks in the reality of her own experience, much less in that of other women.

No matter. I wish her well. She started me out on a road on which I'll keep moving, even though it's rough going. All of us must simply keep moving on it, now, I suppose, trusting ourselves, our own experience, our own questions. There are no gods, no goddesses, no outside authorities, however radical their credentials. We need and can trust no other authority than our own personal truth. The only test of our movement is whether it opens real life to real women—to ourselves.

A Dialogue with
Simone de Beauvoir

 Friedan: I thought that it might be important for us to have a dialogue now for this reason: the women's movement, which I think we have both helped to influence by our books and through our thinking, has emerged as the largest and fastest-growing—perhaps the only vital—movement for basic social change in the seventies. But it has reached in America, and to some extent in the world, a kind of crest, and now it is floundering a little on a plateau.

de Beauvoir: Yes, I think that's true here in France.

Friedan: In the last two years in America, there has been a diffusion of energy in an internal ideological dispute. Women began to realize their political power with the passage of the Equal Rights Amendment right before the '72 elections and the Supreme Court's decision on abortion. At that point, forces on the far right began a well-financed campaign to prevent ratification of ERA in the States and to overturn the abortion decision. From testimony at the Watergate hearings, we suspect that *agents provocateurs* were also at work within the women's movement, fomenting disruption and extremism, fanning the divisive note of sexual politics—"down with men, childbearing, and motherhood!" The attempt to make a political ideology out of sexual preference, out of lesbianism, has diverted energies from the political mainstream and hindered the political momentum of the women's movement.

de Beauvoir: Well, of that I'm not so sure. Do you mean that promoting "Down with childbirth, up with lesbianism" may be a maneuver to ruin the movement?

Friedan: It immobilizes the movement politically. To some extent there are genuine ideological differences. Some women in the movement genuinely feel—and I might disagree with them—that this is a class warfare against men, that childbearing, motherhood, and sex are the enemies. But it is my feeling that an overfocus on sexual issues, on sexual politics, as opposed to the condition of women in society in general, may have been accentuated by those who wished to immobilize the movement politically. According to the Gallup and Harris polls, the majority of American women, and even a majority of men, support the basic goals of equality for women in society. But when it is made to seem that women must renounce the love of men or children, you alienate the majority of women . . .

de Beauvoir: I understand.

Friedan: . . . as well as unnecessarily alienate the men. By the way, I am very glad to see that you now call yourself a feminist. I know you now think that a change in the economic system, such as communism, does not automatically bring about the liberation of women. How do you relate the women's struggle to the larger economic and political struggle?

de Beauvoir: I don't at all think that the Communist or Socialist systems as they are practiced answer this need. But I think there is a very strong relationship between the economic struggle and the feminist movement, at least as far as France is concerned. There was a strike at a Lip watch factory, in which 80 percent of the strikers were women. The strike was led by the women and lasted for six months, giving the women a sense of their own economic, and therefore political, power. However, though they were very active in the strike, when it was a question of taking the night watch, if their husbands didn't want them to, the women said, "All right, we're doing enough for the strike without upsetting our marriages." So even in their activism they remained subordinate to their husbands and unconscious of their relationship to the condition of women in general. The great problem of the MLF (Mouvement de Libération des Femmes) here is to tie up these economic struggles to the feminist struggle.

Friedan: Is the MLF moving in a more economic direction?

de Beauvoir: It is very much divided. There are feminists who are concerned only with what you were talking about—the revolt against men, lesbianism, and so on—but there are many others involved with the Socialist movements, who try to connect the sex struggle with the economic class struggle and try to work with the women workers.

Friedan: Well, in my country the breakthrough in consciousness has been big, but we are facing a situation of economic turmoil in which women are being fired. With the retrenchment of budgets in universities and corporations comes a backsliding of the gains women have made. It is being asked, "How can we enforce the rules to hire more women when there is unemployment and there are more serious worries?"

de Beauvoir: It is not quite the same here, for the time being. On the contrary, the government tries to give the impression that the women are being integrated. Women are received at the Polytechnique, women are named presidents of universities, but the best of them understand that these are just tokens given by the reactionary forces. One woman resigned from a high post because she didn't want to be a token.

Friedan: We feel that women should take all the jobs they can get as long as they keep fighting to open the door wider for women and have no illusion that the tokenism takes the place of a real breakthrough.

de Beauvoir: This attitude is very much questioned in France. Certain women think this, but very often they are accused of being "career women," "elitist," "privileged." Those who refuse are better liked because they don't believe that they widen the gap, but rather that they become alibis.

Friedan: Would you agree that it is not just a question of breaking through the overt sex discrimination, but that it will be necessary to change the rules of the game, the very structure of work—the class separation of secretary-boss, nurse-doctor?

de Beauvoir: Yes, that's why many women think they should not play the game, not the game in its present structure.

Friedan: How are they to eat?

de Beauvoir: They don't have to have the leading jobs. They don't have to be presidents of universities; they can be simple schoolteachers.

Friedan: Do you agree with that?

de Beauvoir: I ask myself the question. I think there is some truth in it, because if you want to really change society, it's not by accepting "honorable" jobs or important posts that you'll do it.

Friedan: On the other hand, if women are to be in a position to change society, they have to have the confidence and the skills to move in an advanced technological society. How are they to get those if they do not break through the barriers against them and actually move in the society? Your argument can easily be used to rationalize a position of continued inferiority —to reject education as well because it is tainted by the system.

de Beauvoir: Education is a different matter. One can have an education in order to have the instrument, but refuse to use it in order to be amongst the "elite" of a society we reject. Many of us think, and I do, too, that if society is to be changed, it must be done not from the top, but from the bottom.

Friedan: We are writers, so we can achieve some higher post in society by writing critically about the society. Your position gives you the voice and the ability to influence millions. Would we be serving the cause of women if we did not use this power in ourselves?

de Beauvoir: Because of the way I was brought up, and because of the situation in my time—there was no feminism—the idea was for women to be the equal of men! But there are so many women now who are so profoundly feminist they refuse to be the equal of men. They don't think that the aim is to acquire a name or a place in this society, but to fight and destroy it. For example, there is a general refusal of what is called the "star system." These feminists don't sign their articles in the feminist newspapers; it's a collective system and no one signs. They refuse the idea of competition, masculine glory, ambition, and fame.

Friedan: Are you no longer going to write books under your own by-line?

de Beauvoir: No, of course not, because I was formed differently. I began under a different system, and what I have achieved I am going to use. But I understand and sympathize with those who don't sign their names.

Friedan: I think that it would eliminate the "star system" if there were a thousand Simone de Beauvoirs and a thousand Betty Friedans. If *we*, who are known, tell the others to stay nameless, that doesn't eliminate the star system.

de Beauvoir: I'd be sorry if there were a thousand Simone de Beauvoirs. What I mean is that the basic work women should be doing is not each one trying on her own to make a name for herself.

Friedan: In the women's movement, in the student movement, and, I think, even in the black movement, the argument of elitism has been used to get rid of democratic structure and effective leadership, to manipulate and prevent effective action. This doesn't remove power; it just makes manipulating power easier when there is no structure of clear, responsible leadership. That was the way that the student movement was ruined.

de Beauvoir: I think that in France the women's movement is much more spontaneous and very real, very fundamental, on the part of all the young women who try to live their state of being women differently. Naturally there are inconveniences in having no structure or hierarchy; it can lead to dispersion and hinder unity of action. But to refuse bureaucracy and hierarchy has the advantage of trying to make each human being a *whole* human and breaks down the masculine idea of the little bosses.

Friedan: I don't want women manipulated by male power machines or co-opted by female imitators, either. A guerrilla army is harder to take over. You need the maximum amount of autonomy for local groups with just enough national structure to be able to take massive actions that have an effect on the whole country.

de Beauvoir: That is what we did with abortion. We managed to mobilize Paris, the provinces—all over. But that is an issue which interests all classes of society. All women—peasants, workers, as well as the *bourgeoises*—are concerned about the abortion issue. But there are issues around which it is much harder to unite everyone. For example, the question of housework, which I consider very important for feminists. Housework takes up so much time, is nonsalaried, and is exploitation by men of women. Well, on that subject, you will get an echo from the *petites bourgeoises*, certainly from the intellectuals, and perhaps from working women. But from the nonemployed wives of workers, there will be no support; it is their reason for being. That is going to create a great division among women.

Friedan: I have been putting together an Economic Think Tank for Women, and one of the questions is how to put a minimum wage value on housework. This could be recognized for Social Security, for pensions, and in the division of property if there is a divorce. Surely the poor and middle-class housewife would identify with that.

de Beauvoir: There I don't agree at all. It makes for segregation; it puts the woman in the house even more. I and my friends in the MLF don't agree with that at all. It's keeping to the idea of women at home, and I'm very much against it.

Friedan: But don't you think that as long as women are going to do work in the home, especially when there are little children, the work should be valued at something?

de Beauvoir: Why women? That's the question! Should one consider that the women are doomed to stay at home?

Friedan: I don't think they should have to. The children should be the equal responsibility of both parents—and of society—but today a great many women have worked only in the home when their children were growing up, and this work has *not been valued* at even the minimum wage for purposes of Social Security, pensions, and division of property. There could be a voucher system which a woman who chooses to continue her profession or her education and have little children could use to pay for child care. But if she chooses to take care of her own children full time, she would earn the money herself.

de Beauvoir: No, we don't believe that any woman should have this choice. No woman should be authorized to stay at home to raise her children. Society should be totally different. Women should not have that choice, precisely because if there is such a choice, too many women will make that one. It is a way of forcing women in a certain direction.

Friedan: I follow the argument, but politically at the moment I don't agree with it. The fact is, we have hardly any child-care centers in the United States. We're fighting for them, but there is such a tradition of individual freedom in America that I would never say that every woman must put her child in a child-care center.

de Beauvoir: But that's not how we see it. We see it as part of a global reform of society which would not accept that old segregation between man and woman, the home and the outside world. We think that every individual, woman as well as man, should work outside and have the possibility, either by communal living, collectives, or another way of organizing the family, of solving the problems of child care. Not keep the same system of crèches, but change the system so that the choices that are available are different. Something along these lines is being tried in China. For example, on a certain day everyone in the community—men, women, and children, as far as they are capable—come together to do all the washing or darning of socks; it would be all the socks, and the husbands would darn them, too. Encouraging women to stay at home will not change society.

Friedan: I would tend to think more in terms of a pluralistic situation of real options. I think that the sense of individual family and the values of motherhood are so strong in people that I don't see any viable or even valuable political attempt to wipe them out. If people should choose a communal life style such as you spoke of, that possibility should be open to them. But I would like to see the creation of new institutions in society so that men and women who choose a nuclear-family life style can be liberated from the rigid sex roles we have been locked into in the matters of housework, child care, and so on. And those who wish to continue in the conventional roles should have that option. The problem has been no other options.

de Beauvoir: In my opinion, as long as the family and the myth of the family and the myth of maternity and the maternal instinct are not destroyed, women will still be oppressed.

Friedan: Now, here I think we do disagree. I think that maternity is more than a myth, although there has been a kind of false sanctity attached to it.

de Beauvoir: As soon as a girl is born, she is given the vocation of motherhood because society really wants her washing dishes, which is not really a vocation. In order to get her to wash the dishes, she is given the vocation of maternity. The maternal instinct is built up in a little girl by the way she is made to play and so on. As long as this is not destroyed, she will have won nothing. In my opinion, the abortion campaigns as such are nothing except that they are useful in destroying the idea of woman as a reproduction machine.

Friedan: You do believe, then, that women should not be mothers?

de Beauvoir: No, I'm not saying that, but since you're talking about choice, a girl should not be conditioned from her childhood to want to be a mother. I don't say either that men should not be fathers, but I do think it should be a choice and not a result of conditioning.

Friedan: I believe with you that it should be a choice and that women should have the choice when to have children if they decide to do so. We are trying to change society so that women, who do happen to be the people who give birth, can be full people in society. A whole new approach to child rearing needs to be created—not just mother, but mother, father, society as a whole, the communal situation, if you wish, and the child-care center and so on. Then I think many women may more joyously and responsibly wish to have children. I think that motherhood is a good value in life. I found it so; I think many women have . . .

de Beauvoir: Why tie up maternity with housework? In this way, housework is encouraged by a sort of token—motherhood. No, we do not agree, because you express the idea of remunerating housework, while I think that women should be freed from housework. At what age do you give a girl the choice? If she is conditioned from birth to think that she *should* have children, when she is twenty she no longer has a choice.

Friedan: She should have other choices, but don't eliminate that as a possible choice. When you got your Ph.D., you were a very exceptional woman; you were the only woman in an intellectual circle. Now society is a little different. Is it possible that in your generation, motherhood was seen so strongly as something that would prevent a woman from really using her abilities in society that it seemed necessary to make a choice between one thing or the other?

de Beauvoir: I thought I couldn't have children because I wanted to write. But we are getting away from the subject. I think that if housework is paid, it is a way of accepting segregation and the structure which, through maternity, condemns women to housework. I am totally against this.

Friedan: You would not put any value on the work women have been doing?

de Beauvoir: I think that the value is such that it should be shared by the men—by everyone—and that women should not be forced to do it.

Friedan: There I agree . . .

de Beauvoir: Then it must not be specially paid. Society should be organized in such a way that this work is done as a community thing—as a public service, perhaps. A Chinese man said, "I clean my own teeth; I don't ask my wife to do it." Mending socks should be the same thing; there should not be a special sector for housework—that is what I consider scandalous. There could be laundry centers that would do the washing for a whole building. We are moving more and more toward that sort of specialized division of labor.

Friedan: Are we talking about society today or about some remote future? In some of the Communist countries, instead of restructuring jobs to take maternity into account, it has been decided to pay the women to stay at home and pay the men more to keep the women at home. I think this is a reactionary move. But that's not the same as women in America, now, who have been at home for ten and twenty years, having the right to Social Security and retirement pensions, for example. Some value should be put on the work they have been doing.

de Beauvoir: If you put it in the past tense, yes, but society must change. Just as you don't pay someone for cleaning his teeth or his hands, so in the same way each one will have his own work: wash his own dishes, clean his own corner, make his own bed, and so on. Thus the very notion of housework will disappear.

Friedan: A point on motherhood. I think that it is neither good nor necessarily desirable to renounce all of the values of motherhood as long as one has a choice and as long as girls are not conditioned to think they must, or should, spend their whole lives in that role. Then one can affirm whatever values really exist in motherhood.

de Beauvoir: There are values in fatherhood, too, but no one ever mentions that. Yes, there are values, but doubtful, dubious values, because at the same time one must see how the child is treated. The liberation of children is a very interesting idea. Now, the child becomes the object of the parents. The relationship between parents and children is very difficult.

Friedan: How then would you suggest that we perpetuate the human race?

de Beauvoir: There are enough people on earth!

Friedan: I want to talk a minute about love and marriage and sex in their relation to the women's movement. I think that a sexual relationship with a man is not something that is necessarily bad or negative or the enemy of women's liberation. One should be able to really enjoy it. What subverts sex is woman's inferior role in society all day long, her lack of self-worth. The dehumanization of sex, the exploitation of sex, and the *machismo* of the male are bred by women's inequality. When this is changed, there can be real sexual liberation.

de Beauvoir: One must achieve a sexual or love relationship that is not an oppressive relationship, one that would no longer be a "caste" relationship. As it is now, the relationship is one of a higher caste in relation to a lower caste.

Friedan: When women have real economic independence, when we have our own identity, when we feel as good about ourselves as people as men are able to—which may also make it easier for men to feel good about themselves—we can then relate on a basis of equality and mutual respect for each other's person. Would you not then believe that the need and the possibility of love and sexual intimacy could be fulfilled?

de Beauvoir: Of course, but we're so far from sexual equality.

Friedan: I think you tackle the question of sex by tackling equality, not by renouncing or urging women to renounce love or sexual relationships.

de Beauvoir: Of course not, but a woman can love a man or a woman as she wants in a world of equality. While it is not equal, she takes a big risk.

Friedan: I have often quoted something I first read in your work. You said that a woman feels debased in sex because she has the underneath position. You felt, and I agree with you, that she was merely expressing her resentment at being underneath in society generally.

de Beauvoir: Certainly, it's a cultural fact.

Friedan: So it is not sex that reduces women; it is society.

de Beauvoir: Absolutely. But sex becomes the symbol of what society does.

Friedan: When we change society, we can choose our sexuality.

de Beauvoir: I quite agree.

Friedan: To get back to the political: it is my opinion that women, in liberating themselves from passivity, will no longer be so easily manipulated and will no longer be a conservative and reactionary force. That is what I think the threat to the established power groups is. But can women liberate themselves if they do not also relate themselves to the larger political questions of the time?

de Beauvoir: I think that politics as it exists does not interest me. Personally, I do not vote. What interests me is the work that certain feminist movements and certain young revolutionary movements can do—to sap this regime but not play their game. Their politics is not to take part in politics. They feel that feminist politics is not to take part in this man's fight. Up to a certain point I agree, depending on the fight in question.

Friedan: But if feminism means not to take part in politics, what becomes of women when men become fascists or make nuclear war?

de Beauvoir: Up to a certain point, I said. Of course, if I were an American, I would have fought against the war in Vietnam. But there are means of not entering into the fight of men, into their political deals, which is very feminist.

Friedan: How?

de Beauvoir: That becomes a much too complicated question; to know how to fight against a nuclear war—that would really take us too far. Before all these questions that you raise can fall into place, society has to change.

Friedan: But how is it going to change?

de Beauvoir: We are already moving it. There are black movements, the young people, the women. These are not minorities. Women are not a minority—marginal forces if you prefer.

Friedan: Now, that is exactly what I am leading up to: that we should somehow join forces with other movements forwarding human life, to make society move. Otherwise, we remain outside and there will be, I think, fascism.

de Beauvoir: Not join forces, but each one should do its work in its own place, in its own way, in its own group. . . . Each group will explode its own part. There is need for a liaison between this or that to do the work; for example, doing women's work.

Friedan: We are shaking society in one way or the other.

In January 1974, despite a blizzard that shut down airports and made highways hazardous, some thousand women came from all over the East Coast to a weekend conference on the divorce crisis called by the NOW Task Force on Marriage and the Family. I was supposed to keynote it, but my own plane was delayed, so I closed the conference instead, and those thousand women stayed until I finally got there Sunday afternoon. Brilliantly conceived by Betty Berry—who was "just a housewife" until her own divorce crisis catapulted her into the women's movement to become a nationally respected innovator on marriage and divorce—this conference confronted lawyers, social workers, judges, marriage counselors, therapists, and other comfortable experts—or profiteers—on divorce with the uncomfortable reality of women's experience.

Ordinary women—wearing masks so they wouldn't lose custody of their children, or be faulted for speaking out in divorce cases still in the courts—spoke their full bitterness at the *reality* of the divorce crisis. This bitterness was directed not so much against men as against the blindness, the lack of help anywhere for their problems, and the increase in those problems caused by so-called reforms in divorce law.

There had been a 1,000 percent increase in the divorce rate in the state—and the divorce rate nationally has more than doubled—in the last ten years. In 1974, there were over a million divorces in the United States. For a lot of reasons. Some experts blamed "women's liberation," but in fact, the geometric increase in divorce was caused by many of the same factors which brought about the women's movement. A similar increase in divorce has been marked in all advanced technological societies, and in communist as well as capitalist nations in this decade.

The old economic bases for lifelong marriage, the length of life itself, the religious proscriptions, the psychological and sexual expectations—all these had changed, so drastically, so fast. The new independence of women—or the movement of women toward it—was certainly one factor in the increase in divorce. Studies had shown that marriage in the United States worked out much better for the health and well-being of the husband than of the wife. And in almost all cases in the past, divorce happened because the men sought it. Now, for the first time, some women had enough independence to want out of bad marriages.

However, the equality women now sought was still not a fact, and the "no fault" divorce laws recently passed in almost every state were not helping. In all but a few states, they permitted people to end marriages with no mandate—or even provision—for judges to divide the property equally, or to give equal consideration to the contribution of the wife if she had been working in the home during all the years her husband had been building his profession or business.

A recent poll by Market Opinion Research showed that only 14.9 percent of divorced women were awarded alimony, and even of these few, less than half collected it. Of 44 percent who were awarded child support, less than half collected it regularly. In fact, in New York State, it had just been found that no matter what child support had been ordered, most husbands didn't pay it after one year, and almost no husbands paid it after five years.

And I knew this was true, personally. For the first time, I relaxed my own pride and admitted to my sisters in the movement that after five years of divorce, and despite a much-publicized court decision, I still had not been able to collect a penny of child support from the father of my children. And besides the full cost and responsibility and now college bills, I also had several thousand dollars in legal fees. The condition of other women, less able than I to earn their own living, much less carry the full economic, as well as psychological, support for their children, was worse (at least, I didn't need and never sought alimony).

Much was being made of the new trend that, when divorce happened, the husband should have equal consideration when it came to custody of the children. I believed that was good; that's what equality should mean, that in divorce neither spouse should automatically be given the responsibility for the children. The mother is not necessarily better than the father; it should depend on the wishes, situation, and needs of the whole family. But the bitter fact is, too many divorced women had no choice but to leave their children as well as their husbands, because there was no way they could support themselves and their children, and take care of them as well. And other women, who couldn't or wouldn't give up responsibility for their own children, were going on welfare.

For older women, who were more likely to have spent their married lives as housewives, the situation was even more drastic. If a woman was divorced after nineteen years of marriage and her husband remarried—and she had spent those nineteen years as a housewife, working in the home without pay—she was not entitled to one penny of old-age insurance from the Social Security system in her own right. She had been insured only as her husband's wife; now his second wife collected on his old-age pension, or upon his death.

And now, with the passage of "no fault" divorce laws, husbands were in fact walking out more frequently, because it was now so much easier to evade the economic burdens of supporting two families.

Equality was our aim, but women didn't have equality yet, and in the transition to it, divorced women were suffering more than society, or women themselves, wanted to admit. They were suffering not only loneliness and guilt and hostility —the psychological scars of that inequality that had been responsible for destroying so many of the marriages in the first place—but real economic deprivation.

The fury some women expressed, in the rhetoric of "women's lib" extremism, against marriage and the family itself as the oppressor of women provided no answer to the real problems women were facing. Neither, in fact, did my own insistence, in theory, that new kinds of marriages based on real equality were down the road, promising more real happiness and fulfillment for women and men. Women who did not yet have economic equality were being faced with insoluble economic problems in divorce, whether or not they had sought such divorces. They voiced their bitterness, on that weekend of blizzard, not in vindication against men or husbands—what point was there in that?—but at the lawyers who charged more money than they collected and exacerbated the conflicts; at the landlords who evicted or wouldn't rent to divorced women; at the social workers and welfare officials who violated their privacy and dignity; and at the therapists who had no answers for their problems.

The experts present were shocked into new awareness by that conference, and by the similar work the NOW Task Forces on Marriage and Divorce were doing in other states. Some NOW chapters did set up such divorce or family crisis centers, as I suggested, in New York's Westchester and Nassau-Suffolk counties, for instance. But more to the point, the new ideas and innovations needed were taken from the woman's movement into the social agencies and even the churches, and embodied in legislation. Senator Mondale held hearings on the crisis in the family, and his aides consulted Betty Berry, me and others on those issues we had raised. Representative Yvonne Burke and Senator Tunney introduced Displaced Housewife legislation in Congress. And investigations were begun in other states on how the "no fault" divorce law was really working.

Betty Berry and I got one of the major insurance companies to do a feasibility study which showed that marriage and divorce insurance and survivors' benefits would indeed be feasible—and even profitable for the insurance companies—if they were compulsory for everybody, by law, in the manner of no-fault automobile insurance.

Economists have seriously begun to study concrete economic means of measuring the value of the work done by the housewife—or house spouse—both in terms of insuring housewives in their own right for old age, and of valuing their years of unpaid labor for pensions or severance in divorce. They are even thinking of measuring it in the Gross National Product. In my opinion, this is an issue of utmost priority for the women's movement now, and should be linked to the campaign for the Equal Rights Amendment. Legislation has been passed which is supposed to enable women to collect child support from husbands who have skipped the state or otherwise evaded paying, by means of automatic enforcement by the IRS. But it turns out that women can only use that means as a last resort, by personal order of the Secretary of HEW himself! Which women have enough money—and time and chutzpah—to get the kind of expensive legal help needed to get such a case to the personal attention of the President's Cabinet!

A lot of women—I among them—are becoming convinced that the whole matter of marriage, divorce, child support, and property settlement should be taken out of the hands of the legal profession, even if it does put a lot of lawyers out of business. At a recent conference in Florida sponsored by state legislators and the Women's Commission, it was found that judges were extremely inconsistent in such matters and inadvertently biased in the direction of men's financial needs, contributions, and estimates of the situation. This needn't be. Formulas could be worked out and fed into a computer—formulas which would take into account the actual contribution of the woman, the minimum wage value of her unpaid years of service and all the other factors involved in estimating needs, responsibilities, and the practical realities of divorce.

As a matter of fact, in the last few years insurance companies—for their own profit—have begun to put a value on the "replacement cost" of the housewife's services. The insurable value of the housewife was recently increased to a maximum of $50,000 by the Manhattan Life Insurance Co. Until now, the amount of insurance on the nonemployed spouse had been limited to $1,000 to $5,000—to cover funeral expenses. Now the idea is that the working widower should have enough insurance to pay for child care, washing, cooking and other services that the wife had provided—and also to offset tax advantages he loses from marital deduction and joint filing. (The company states, "as with any truly 'liberated' plan, it works equally if the spouse to be covered is the male.")

"What's the real answer?" I asked Betty Berry, in futility over these economic problems. "A woman should never give up her job," said that formerly happy housewife. "She shouldn't stop working. Love is not enough." The answer, of course, is simply the equality that our whole movement seeks: that women should be educated to do the work society rewards, and should be paid for that work. And since women are the people who do have children, there should be maternity leaves—and paternity leaves—and child-care centers, and full income tax deductions for child care and home maintenance. And each woman and man should be insured in her and his own right for old age, illness and the like.

Lately, I have been trying to warn the sociological experts on the family—and some of my seemingly more radical feminist sisters—not to mistake the pathologies resulting from unequal sex roles, the extreme reaction of the moment to them, or the current explosion of divorce—for the wave of the future, and foredoom the end of marriage and the family. Or, on the other hand, to use the specters of such doom as an argument to stop the women's movement, or the Equal Rights Amendment, prematurely in midstream.

At an international conclave of sociologists on the family, in Paris in the fall of 1974, and at the prestigious Groves Conference on the Family in Hot Springs, Arkansas, that spring, I sensed what could be a dangerous tendency of experts on the family to blame the divorce explosion and the dissolution of the family on the women's movement—and to project the present divorce rate into a straight line of continued increase into the future, with a consequent decline in the birth rate, until the human race ceases to reproduce altogether and the human family, the race, is doomed—unless, by implication, the women are brought to heel again.

At the Groves Conference, sociologists and marriage counselors bewailed the fact that in a time of frantic change and economic turmoil, when men and children need more nurturing than ever—the symbol given was a calm, soothing, full-time wife-mother waiting with Bloody Mary or chocolate milk shake for the husband and child to come home—the women's movement was somehow inveigling those otherwise nurturing drink dispensers out into the frantic rat race themselves. They forget how the very ability to nurture soured in women who felt like "service stations" to their husbands and children in the years that led to the women's movement in the United States, the hostility that caused some finally to walk out on husbands and children.

Are marriage and motherhood "endangered species," as Columbia sociologist Amitai Etzioni warned in *Human Behavior*, August 1974? He predicted that the end of the family might be the next American crisis—that America might be running out of families as fast as we are running out of oil. The number of single-parent families has risen 31 percent since 1956, he said, about triple the growth of two-parent families. Some twelve million Americans now live alone. Nearly a third of all schoolchildren are now children of divorce. The birth rate has fallen to an all-time low of 1.9 children per family as more women seek careers other than motherhood. Professor Etzioni warned that if these trends continued there would be few families left by the mid-1990's, and he blamed the murder of the human family—no less—on the women's liberation movement—and on the increasing emphasis on personal self-fulfillment and growth over duty to spouse and children. With the end of the double standard and of the husbands' control over property and credit, women are becoming less economically and sexually dependent on their husbands, he complained; even marriage counselors and clergymen no longer advise couples to stay in a "bad" marriage for the children's sake. And he was appalled by a recent life insurance survey in which three out of four agreed that it was perfectly all right for couples to choose not to have children. And one out of four approved of people living together out of wedlock, in communes or in open marriage.

But I see no evidence that Americans, including liberated women, have lost their need for intimacy, commitment, love, emotional and economic support. The structure is merely changing, has to change, in the direction of equality—and probably for the better, not only for women, but for the whole family. The fact is, more Americans are married now than ever before, not counting all the young and old who now live together in nonlegal marriages. Most divorces now end in marriage—which, contrary to doom-and-gloom predictions, do not always repeat old patterns; these new marriages often last till death. In a seventy-five-year life span, child rearing can't be the basis of a lifelong marriage. But studies show that in childless marriages, both husband and wife are happier than in conventional child-rearing marriages (which may say something about those old sex roles women and men were locked into).

Women are beginning to pick and choose their futures more carefully. By 1974, the census showed women in the United States marrying later (21) than their teenage-bride sisters of the 1950's. (In 1974, only 60 percent of the women in the age bracket 20–24 were married—partly because three times as many women were enrolled in college than were a decade earlier) And this year, there has been a slight upturn in the birth rate, because women in the 25–35 age bracket were having more children.

My daughter and her generation in college want to have children—and professions. They will probably have fewer children, later, than full-time housewife-mothers. They and their husbands will share the satisfactions and burdens of the work world, and their homes and families with more equality, less resentment, and more mutual dependence-independence than their parents.

Not that this will solve all the problems of women, men, families, marriage and human sexuality. Lifelong marriage will probably be an enviable achievement in the future—as the values of long-term intimacy and commitment are savored. But it will be less traumatic for people to leave bad marriages, as it is already less traumatic for children of divorce. More and more people will have experiences of conventional marriage, and unconventional communal living arrangements, and periods of living alone. And perhaps, as women get over the hostility and superindependence caused by their reaction to their passivity, they will become confident enough in their own strength to be able to relax and be tender, loving, nurturing when the situation calls for it, as they are able to be militant and determined and assertive when the situation calls for it.

I doubt the family is an endangered species. I think it is just evolving to new forms. Otherwise, like the dinosaur, it would become extinct. The women's movement has been a necessary part of its evolution. But the danger now is getting stuck in the middle, in reaction, in the sexual hostilities that were bred by our dependence, in the economic and psychological scars. One of those scars was a lack of trust in ourselves as women, a lack so great that it is hard to trust any man. The rage that dependency bred in our mothers, exploding in us, was sometimes too awful to admit; it made too many of us project that rage as a weapon against men, because its enormity was too great to face in ourselves, and thus we became even more guilty and self-destroying in our marriages. This tangled mess of scars, of reactions and defenses and rage, of economic consequences and human needs—the polarities here may be hardest of all to transcend.

The Crises of Divorce

(NOW Marriage and Divorce Conference, January 1974)

I think that here today we can see the reality of the women's movement—not the rhetoric, not what the media makes it, but why we really need it. And we can see also our responsibility to use the power we can see here—the power we clearly have to change the conditions that have tortured our lives and brought us to this hour.

I got divorced five years ago. I should have gotten divorced ten years ago. It would have been better for my children, probably better for my former husband, certainly better for me. To show how far we've come in this short time, let me tell you that ten and nine and eight and seven and six years ago, I was warned by my publisher, editor, agent, and my dear husband that I would be ruined, I would be destroyed, if I got divorced—that my whole credibility, my ability to write in the future about women, and the credibility of the movement would be destroyed—and I didn't dare say boo. At that time, I didn't know personally a single woman who had gone through the experience—who I could dare to ask the things that you can't ask a lawyer or trust the lawyer to tell you the truth about. And then somehow the women's movement began to

413

give me the strength that it has given all of you. And I said, I don't care, I have to do something about my own life.

I was made to feel so guilty, as were many of you, about losing my femininity, about undermining somebody else's masculinity by earning money, that I didn't have the nerve or the knowledge to protect the money I earned. I didn't know the things that you are making common knowledge—the rights we have, the rights we all should know about when we go into marriage—much less the rights we want to secure further by the reforms that are needed now.

If there is any one thing that makes a feminist it is to grow up believing somehow that love and marriage will take care of the rest of your life—and then to wake up at forty or fifty or even at thirty and find it isn't so. And then to face the world— the reality of it. Divorce has increased 1,000 percent in this state in the last few years. Don't blame the women's movement for that—blame the obsolete sex roles on which our marriages were based. Perpetuating those obsolete sex roles will only lead to the end of marriage. Our movement to liberate women and men from those polarized, unequal sex roles might save marriage. And marriage is probably worth saving. The intimacy, the commitment—the long-term commitment of marriage—is something we still need. Even here at this divorce conference, the workshop I attended this afternoon on the Status of Marriage was so crowded that you could see that even those of us who had been through the bitterness of divorce still believed somehow that there had to be a way to make marriage work—but on a different basis. Meanwhile, we must face the reality of the hundreds and thousands and millions of women and children, and men too, in this state and in this nation, who are suffering terribly from the dissolution of those marriages that were based on obsolete sex roles.

Now, I want to suggest some concrete ways by which we may use the reality of the power we have here to make the changes that are needed. Reality both in the long-term sense and in the immediate sense of the suffering of real women who can't be sacrificed to the future, and of real children who are dependent on them, and of real men. The paradox, of course, is that it is the best of men that are suffering. There *are* good men—and I must admit that some of us haven't had too much to do with them—there are men who feel an obligation to support their children, an obligation toward the family that they helped bring into the world. And those men are suffering, as are the wives in the new families that they may make.

It isn't women against men. That's not going to solve it, despite the hostility that some feel here—and with reason. I'm proud of this conference, that it didn't wallow in that hostility, but got on instead to the hope, the reality of making a future where hostility isn't necessary.

Now, I propose, first of all, that we insist immediately on statewide hearings dealing with basic reform of marriage and divorce laws, and that we demand live television coverage, rebroadcast on prime time on every network. The women's movement had just begun when the so-called divorce reform law was passed. At that time, we were so concerned with principle—that equality of right and opportunity had to mean equality of responsibility, and therefore alimony was out— that we did not realize the trap we were falling into. It is a trap for thousands, hundreds of thousands, if not millions of women, when they face a no-fault divorce law—in which a separation begun before the law was even envisaged becomes de facto divorce—with no provision for economic support or division of property. My phone sometimes rings early in the morning or late at night, calls from women all over the state who just find my name in the telephone book and who are desperate in the plight in which such a law leaves them. I wonder how many divorced wives of prosperous men are now on welfare. Statistics indicate that a child in a family now in poverty, headed by a man, has a fifty-fifty chance of getting out of poverty by his or her maturity—but that a child in a poverty family headed by a woman has no chance.

Now, for the future of our children and ourselves, we must insist on immediate legislation—not that brings back the fault divorce, because that only benefited the lawyers, but that enforces economic provisions for a dependent spouse and children. These must be realistic provisions and realistic machinery to enforce them, including payroll deductions that could be collected automatically, like Social Security, and enforced bonds for the self-employed, who otherwise so easily might default.

We must also write into such legislation provisions for putting an economic value on the service of the woman or man who has been primarily in the home. She should be insured in her own right for Social Security in old age and severance pay in divorce, for realistic educational programs or other aid to enable her to become self-supporting. There should at least be a law that when a wife has put her husband through graduate school to get his Ph.D. or M.D., then he owes the same to her upon divorce.

At the same time, being realistic and understanding the economic dislocation that our whole country is facing, we have to thoroughly explore marriage and divorce insurance. It is a possibility, insurance experts tell us, but it has to be mandatory. It is now public knowledge that the great majority of men, a few years after divorce, do not pay any child support, whatever amount the lawyers agreed on or the court ordered. It's not that these men are evil, it is just that there's an economic pinch and the cost of living is getting higher and higher, and if they don't have to do it, out of sight is out of mind. They suppress the whole thing and finally simply desert their children emotionally as well as economically, because it makes them feel too guilty if they really face their abrogation of responsibility. But there are economics involved here and we have to find a system. Alimony? Forget it—it's a sexist concept, and doesn't belong in a women's movement for equality. But that economic equality we seek is not a reality yet. Half of all women are unpaid housewives still, and the ones who work still earn barely half what men earn, and are still expected to take the entire responsibility of the kids, as well. Maintenance, rehabilitation, severance pay—whatever you want to call it—is a necessity for many divorced women, as is child support. Maybe marriage and divorce insurance should actually be built into Social Security, like survivor's benefits at death.

At the same time, we need new forms of the marriage contract, and knowledge of your rights when you marry, and maybe something making it more difficult to marry. Maybe there should be a large first premium for marriage and divorce insurance—a price of marriage, like you have to pay under no-fault automobile insurance to buy an automobile. To get this legislation passed, the political will of women, who are 53 per-cent of the population, can be joined by men who have suf-fered from the divorce law the way it is now.

But while this is happening, there is something that we can do right now, beginning tomorrow in all our NOW chapters. I propose that we set up divorce or family crisis centers. Women who have been through the experience could tell a woman now getting a divorce how to handle her lawyer or how to find a good one, or what's a waste of money and what isn't—all sorts of practical things that we didn't know until we'd gone through the experience. They would need some training. We would have to get a training program funded to train such women, or men, as divorce counselors—para-professionals, if you will—working under the supervision of professionals—lawyers, therapists—who are also feminists. It would be better than the do-it-yourself kits that can lead you into legal traps. Also there could be some real counseling, if needed, not the phony stuff that goes on now under the New York law in the name of conciliation. That just wastes more money on law-yers. Women now beginning to feel their own sense of identity and to see through the role that they've been playing can be temporarily misled, or swamped by the hostility that women have a right to feel, the rage that they used to turn against themselves, to take out on their own bodies. Now the hostili-ty's out there in the open, and they might temporarily feel—when it wasn't necessarily so—that their marriage was the enemy, or the husband was the enemy, whereas he was just trapped in the same situation they were.

I'm not saying that all marriages can or should be saved, but maybe some are unnecessarily broken in the heat of break-ing out of the role trap. Or perhaps a woman who has found her own identity and who isn't going to take certain things any more becomes temporarily very threatening to a man who has been similarly brainwashed by the masculine mystique. And yet he also might prefer to save the marriage if there were a chance of finding out how to do it. If there is a residue of love and mutuality that makes it possible for a marriage to be saved, then let us have consciousness-raising groups or what-ever you might want to call them for such people, of men and women together, or for men and women separately and then together, to see whether the marriage can be saved. Because some women have made mistakes—walking out too quickly; thinking that the marriage was the enemy, the husband was the enemy, when the situation was the enemy, the roles were the enemy. And some men, temporarily threatened, have walked out too quickly, and know now what they've lost. So maybe we could save some marriages or make it possible for them to resume on a better, more human basis: NOW's idea of equal partnership in marriage. And that would be real and not phony.

If there is no possibility of resuming it on a different basis, then there could be the counseling that all of us sometimes need, no matter how strong we think we are. No matter what battles we take on in the outside world, we have to admit that sometimes we feel terribly helpless, and I speak from personal truth, and we could use some help and some support. Having originally been trained as a psychologist, despite my knowledge of the way Freudian psychology was used to mess women up with the feminine mystique, I would never say to any woman, "Don't go near a psychotherapist because they are all trying to get you back in the trap." You can't deny your own need for help when you need it. And there are more and more women and men therapists, even analysts, whose own consciousness has been changed by the women's movement, who can—without denying or defying or denigrating your own identity as an individual and the importance to you of coming into your full personhood—help you to, if not save the marriage, at least have the minimum of the inevitable bitterness and conflicts and emotional turmoil that happens to all of us when we break up those marriages. And this we could have in the family crisis center. And while we are getting the law with mandatory enforcement machinery, we could contribute some help there meanwhile; we could make a list of accountants or set up our own corps to collect that child support so that women wouldn't be at the mercy of the lawyers who charge them more than they ever really help—until most women finally just give up. And I've personally been just as helpless, in this matter, as a lot of you.

Okay. We could set up a network of divorce centers, use the NOW machinery for it, get some foundation help for it. If the foundations are so senseless that they don't understand the need for that, we could do it ourselves, as we did with abortion clinics. Even fees based according to ability to pay that such centers might charge would be much cheaper than legal fees. It would take business away from the extortionist lawyers. Furthermore, it would have an impact on the legal profession as a whole—bringing down the legal fees, cutting out the extortionist practices and the denigrating-to-women processes— similar to the women's self-help health movement's impact on the medical profession.

Finally, and this is long-term, I think that the situation that we are in now, this fantastic divorce explosion that brought over a thousand women to this conference despite the blizzard, to speak from such personal pain, is a temporary crisis. I think that this is an explosion of the void—that everything we are doing in the women's movement, not only the specific reforms on marriage and divorce, but everything we are doing in the women's movement for equality should make it possible for our daughters and our sons to have different and better marriages and families.

That call to my NOW sisters in 1973—to turn that inward-staring circle outward—seemed premature at the time. It was dismissed contemptuously by the new radical feminist spokeswomen of "women's lib" in their stance of permanent professional rage against the male oppressor. But more and more women were in fact speaking in a new way to men. And more and more men, even some who had seemed hostile to "women's lib" and threatened by it at first, were listening to women in a new way, taking them seriously.

I saw increasingly more men in the audience at my own lectures around the country. Sometimes, I'd speak to previously all-male groups—an executives' meeting in Minneapolis, a press club in Detroit, the foreman's association of the U.S. army arsenal in the Adirondacks, an exclusive businessmen's luncheon club in Philadelphia, where the only women present would be wives and girl friends, or a token few female colleagues invited because of me, just for the occasion. Or it would be a men's college in Virginia or a Jesuit seminary in Texas inviting me in their own anguish to break down the barriers that kept them isolated from women.

From the beginning, I'd been more surprised by the intensity of support some men felt for the women's movement than by the hostility it evoked from other men. The hostile catcalls and crude jokes had almost disappeared by 1973. The polls showed a *majority* of men in the United States—a slightly greater majority of men, then, even than women, supporting equality of the sexes, the Equal Rights Amendment, and the goals of the women's movement generally. The support came first and most obviously from the gentle, long-haired young or from older men who had suffered in their deviation from the masculine mystique: the robed priests at the Greymoor Seminary; artists and writers who didn't want to play like Hemingway or Norman Mailer, fighting those bulls. And male homosexuals coming out of the closet. A doctor in Syracuse or a disk jockey in L.A. who had felt the pain of his mother's or his wife's withdrawal from life, her dependence on him, even the revenge she took on him. A long-haired young reporter on the East Coast, who told me what a relief he felt in his relationship to a woman, now that he didn't have to pretend to be something he wasn't. A disk jockey on the West Coast who talked about his wife's nervous breakdown, and how different it was with his second wife, who worked as he did, and with whom he shared the housework.

And then this note of understanding, support, relief began to be apparent in unlikely places, the haunts of workingmen, executives, Middle American and Rotary Club types, the heart of *machismo* itself.

I was asked to talk to the Foreman's Association at the U.S. Army Arsenal in Watervliet, New York. I heard they got calls all afternoon: Was that "woman's libber" going to use pornography? Attack the family? The men were not so young, they were both blue and white collar, of various ethnic origins—and they did not wear their hair long. Their wives looked tired and sensible, nodding their heads after almost every sentence. In the beginning the men just sat there apprehensively. And then something happened. A current flowed. And the wife would lean over and touch her husband's hand at one point; or he would pat her shoulder.

One night, lecturing at Augsburg, a small church college in Minnesota, I learned that a man I had loved had died, at not much over forty. He had destroyed himself—drinking, daring dangers like parachute jumping, reacting in defense against that *machismo* which had made him always feel so inadequate, vulnerable, a failure before he began. That night for the first time I felt the personal pain of men, as well as of women, in the war between the sexes, the war which neither of us can really win.

The young women, newly admitted to this college, complained that the men shunned them, calling them "Augie Doggies." And I understood all too well the pain and the writhing the girls felt at this name-calling. But what made those young Midwestern boys—the first in their families to go to college—so angry, so threatened by the women in the class, that they were so cruel? "Augie Doggie"—and I thought of Catholic mothers and grandmothers for whom sex could mean the burden of unwanted pregnancy and another child to care for, and who thus turned against sex, and nuns for whom sex was sin, making little boys feel dirty—and lonesome and unworthy of love. You were a sissy to cry when someone blacked your eye, and you had to win. Who cared what women thought anyhow —among the boys. And then having those girls next to you in class, and just as smart as you, maybe smarter. And you couldn't black their eyes. Maybe you even had feelings about these girls, soft feelings you were ashamed of having—"Augie Doggie."

As I talked that night above the tears I wasn't free to cry for my own friend's loss, I kept repeating that bitter phrase, "Augie Doggie," and like a catechism, counterpointed the insults, indignities, and discriminations against women in the towns and homes they grew up in, with the pain and loneliness and helplessness, and the need to strike out in cruelty that many of them felt. I talked of boys who can't ever get the love they need from incomplete, bitter or resigned mothers, and then can't love themselves as the men those mothers and our society say they have to be. Their grievance against women damns such men to loneliness in that need for love that is inescapable in both of our humanity. I had not meant to give a talk like that in Augsburg, but by the time I was through—and could go back to my hotel room and my own grief—those crew-cut tormenters of the "Augie Doggies" were openly crying, and the girls were looking at them in wonder.

I was asked that spring to speak at the U.S. Air Force Academy in Colorado; the young cadet officers who met me at the airport told me that those future colonels and commanders were near open rebellion at the ban forbidding them to wear their hair long. They felt a hunger for the new values the rest of their college generation was experiencing—the "greening of America," as Reich embarrassed many by naming it out loud. Those cadets in Colorado—the brightest of those training for future military service in America—were rebelling against the *machismo* that symbolizes, and that expresses itself in, U.S. foreign policy, military invasion, and subjugation of weaker, alien people in foreign lands. Some of those cadets felt that "life was passing them by" in their modern fortress school. And some of their officer-professors agreed and welcomed the coming day when women were going to have to be admitted to the service academies as an opening also for new values—those values hitherto despised as feminine.

There were some catcalls when I was brought into the dining room, where several thousand young military men were eating dinner: men among men. At the close of my lecture, the Air Force cadets stood up and cheered! But that week in Colorado, I tried and did not succeed in getting the local "women's lib" group to continue a dialogue with the young cadets who, in good faith, were eager to go on discussing the questions I had raised.

My father, and all too many salesmen-businessmen fathers, died too young of heart attacks that were indeed related to the rat race he couldn't win, the debt impossible to stay on top of, the exploitation he couldn't let himself fight back against—and the unease of a wife whom nothing ever satisfied. My mother seemed to have all the power in our family; only later did I understand why she had to have that power and used it so against him—the bitterness she always felt at her own economic dependence and lack of identity, the sheer waste of those abilities and energies which the house and the driving, the shopping and entertaining, couldn't get rid of. The power those Jewish mothers, Catholic mothers, Irish, Italian, Latin, WASP mothers held—exerted overtly and covertly in those little houses and apartments they so easily dominated for lack of constructive use of their energies—became a destructive power, to them and to their husbands, daughters and sons. It was a defense against dependence, a female kind of *machismo*, masking vulnerability, weakness—and, in its revenge, creating and perpetuating more vulnerability and weakness and lonely alienation in their sons, which the sons in turn would defend with *machismo*. D. H. Lawrence, in *Women in Love*, got the whole dynamic right—the cruelty of the young mine owner mirroring the cruelty of the alienated mother recoiling from the husband on whom she was dependent, and from her own son; the son then unable to love even the spirited woman whose freedom and independence might enable them both to give and receive the fullness of human sexual love.

The masculine mystique, as many men are now telling us, is that cowering little boy shrinking from the punishment of those dependent mothers in their secret bitterness—and getting his revenge beating down the softness of his need for them, eternally proving his hardness among the boys. To say that *machismo* is the cause of all war is silly and evades the complicated reality, the dynamics, the economics, but we can now see it—as opposed to real strength—in LBJ sending those boys to Vietnam to "bring the coonskin back for the wall," and in Kennedy bringing the world to the brink of nuclear holocaust proving himself a "man," not a "boy," to Khrushchev in the Russian roulette of the Cuban missile crisis, and in Nixon nearly turning the United States into a police state in his terror of the "effete" pansy liberal intellectuals and the long-haired young.

Is it more than a hope that the women's movement could be a way out of this warfare between the sexes, transcending the extremes of *machismo* and dependent femininity, and their exploitation in the violence raging in the world?

In December 1975, Pete Hamill, a tough Brooklyn ex-sportswriter, wrote "A Farewell to Machismo" in the *Village Voice*. The song he saw as nearly ended went

> *Yeah, the Kid is his name*
> *And he's too tough tuh tame*
> *He's the fastest the meanest, the best!*
> *Just blam! blam! blam!*
> *And he don't give a damn*
> *He's the Savior of the West!*

[Robert Coover, *The Kid*]

For me, the Kid was machismo. And he's almost gone now, and God-damnit, in a lot of ways, I'm going to miss him.

The style was full of exaggerated masculinity, peacock pride; brutal vanity and the language of stunted boys . . . The Kid always wore the mask of chivalry, appearing tough, resourceful, brave and solitary, and his image seduced generation after generation of Americans, including mine. Statesmen and steamfitters, prizefighters and presidents, foot soldiers and Harvard men: few were immune.

And now, at last, it's over, the chivalric mask has been removed. In the end, we saw Richard Nixon's features crawling underneath; we saw the dead of too many wars speaking from the eyes of The Kid; we saw marriages dissolved into bitter personal history, bodies lying on the streets of a dozen cities, macho princes filling up the prisons, all of them moving around behind the mask. The Kid could not stand exposure. Bothered by long attacks from the female citizenry, deprived of crucial support from some of the men, and worst of all, subjected to laughter, the Kid is riding off into what might prove to be a permanent sunset. . . .

The last James Bond film did not do well at the box office.

• • •

So sometime in 1973 a young woman called me and asked, in a tone of urgent importance, if I would consider writing an open letter to "*True* Men," the readers of the he-man magazine *True*, catering to hunters, fishermen—tight-lipped, monosyllabic straight square men. She was top assistant to the editor of that magazine; I think they'd just given her an editorial title. Committed to the women's movement herself, she convinced me that the Middle American male readers of *True* had a distorted image of "women's lib" and should be told what it really was all about. If, that is, I was interested in convincing straightforward Middle American men. More importantly, if I wanted to know how such men were responding to the movement and its message, they would run the questions I thought up and compute the answers, and I could write a second article responding to what they said.

Before the deal was set, I had to come in and talk in person with the editor of *True*. He was a straight no-nonsense man, a conservative, as opposed to a rabid, male chauvinist, who seemed remarkably perceptive once he discovered I was not a witch with two horns and was not particularly interested in

either attacking or shocking him—but in writing that letter to
"*True* Men" and getting their answers.

The "Open Letter to *True* Men" duly appeared in January
1974, and the response to the questions—from those red-
blooded, even red-necked he-men—was amazing. But Ellie's
boss—that decent, open-minded, changing male chauvinist—
was fired shortly thereafter. I have no idea whether he was
fired because of his departure from *machismo* in opening his
columns to a leader of the women's movement—or because the
appeal of that old *machismo* to American males was waning so
fast that the troubles of his magazine required more drastic
treatment.

In any event, Ellie somehow held on to her job. (As long as
women are handmaidens, assistants, they weather the power
shifts, because their sheer enterprise keeps the enterprise going.) And Ellie got me the results of the first thousand ques-
tionnaires returned by the "*True* Men."

"How do you really feel about the women's movement?" I
had asked. Only about 9 percent felt "it's a joke," and only 6
percent that "it's a bunch of man-hating bra burners." And 4
percent felt "uneasy" and a bare 2 percent considered it a
"menace to all men that should be stopped." Of these stalwart
males, the great majority said "I agree with a lot of it, but not
the extremists" (45 percent) or that "it's going to change men's
lives for the better as well as women's" (20 percent) or that it's
"very important and necessary for women even though it's
making life uncomfortable for men" (10 percent).

More felt it had changed their wives, their daughters or
their mothers "for better" than "for worse"—they were having a little more trouble about the change in their "women
friends."

"How do you feel about your wife or woman friend having
or getting a job?" I'd asked. The great majority, 75 percent,
felt either "proud of her" or "it makes life better for her and
me and the kids," or "relieved that the whole burden is not on
me." About 10 percent said, "it's good for her but hard on me
and the kids."

If a woman could get a job "as good or better than yours,"
again, most (75 percent) would feel either "proud" or "I'm not
sure, but it's an interesting thought" or "it could give me the

chance to do something I couldn't risk before." Only about 4 percent would feel "less of a man in the world's eyes."

How "willing" were these he-men to share the housework? The answer checked by most (nearly half) was: "We are both equally responsible for our kids and our home, and I respect her responsibility to her job as she does mine, but it's not always easy to work it out." Most of the rest felt "willing to help with the dishes, the shopping, take out the garbage, and take the kids off her hands some of the time, but basically the home is her responsibility." Only 4 percent felt, "It's a woman's business to keep the house clean and take care of the kids —no real men would have any part of it"—fewer than the 7 percent who would "gladly stay home all day, keep the house clean, cook and take care of the kids, if she would get a job that could support us all."

Nearly half of these men said they sometimes "feel lonely," even when they are with their wife and kids. *Most* of these "true men" felt their "main function, in regard to the wife and kids, is to be the breadwinner, the man who pays the bills." Only one out of four said they ever "resented" this, and one out of three that they ever felt "anxiety about carrying the whole responsibility for all of them." But six out of seven "would like to feel needed and loved for yourself alone."

More of them liked their wives "as a person" than felt their wife "liked herself" or that she "really liked" him. More liked "going to bed with your wife" than felt she "enjoys going to bed with you." The overwhelming majority of these men— over 75 percent—felt "a true man's masculinity" was measured by "his ability to be fully and freely himself." Only 7 percent said it was "his physical strength," 6 percent "how he dominates other men;" 6 percent "his sexual prowess," 4 percent "how much money he makes," and 3 percent "how he keeps women in their place." But only 50 percent felt "a true woman's femininity" was measured by "her ability to be fully and freely herself"—about a third felt femininity was her "physical attractiveness," 10 percent her "ability as a mother." And eight out of ten said if they "lost out on a job to a woman who was damned good," they would feel "no worse than losing out to a man that good." Only 3 percent would feel it "an attack on your manhood."

The last question was: "American men are dying much younger than women. If women's liberation relieved you of some of the killing economic pressures and enabled you to enjoy more of life, would you buy it—even if it meant women holding business and political jobs that usually have gone to men?" Four out of five said yes.

Invited to give their "own personal thoughts about women's liberation," a fifty-year-old policeman said "more power to them." A twenty-four-year-old electrician said: "One must demand a lot to obtain their due." A twenty-four-year-old auditor said: "I feel *equal* to a proud, independent woman. I feel superior to the loud-mouth idiots that the press spends so much time covering."

A thirty-one-year-old trucking manager said: "I'm happy to see the way it has helped to develop women to a self-awareness of their total potential."

A forty-eight-year-old rancher said: "Women are not equal!"—and if he "lost out on a job to a woman who was damned good," he would feel "angrier than if another man that good had gotten the job."

A railroad worker: "To each her own." A laborer: "Right on!" A superintendent: "Women, like men, are human beings."

A forty-six-year-old meter inspector: "If you are sure of yourself as a man, it doesn't bother you that women are treated equal."

An electronics technician: "It is a refreshing attitude change on the part of women which can benefit all of humanity."

And a thirty-eight-year-old athletic coach: "In general it is good, but some women's groups are as exclusive as men's. There must/should be a dialogue between the sexes."

An Open Letter
to *True* Men

The word is that you feel threatened by the women's liberation movement. You thought it was a joke, at first, but it's begun to get to you—through your wife, girl friend, daughter, even your mother, to say nothing of the women in the office who say you shouldn't call them girls any more.

Well, it's not a joke, and I don't think you can turn it off, or even that you would really want to, if you understood how the women's movement is going to affect your own life—how it can liberate you to be more truly yourself as a man than ever before.

Before I go further, I want you to know that I am taking a risk, myself, in writing this letter to you. Because some of my sisters think you are the enemy, in which case it is a waste of time, or dangerous, or treason, to venture into enemy territory like this. And some of you are the enemy, or think you are. But I think you don't have to be the enemy of the women's movement. For if this were a class war of women against men, women could never win it, not just because men have too much power—which they do—but because most women wouldn't have the will to fight such a war. Most women wouldn't want to live without men, most want to be able to love men.

But what the women's movement actually implies, in change or risk or promise, for all our lives, both women's and

429

men's, is serious enough, and maybe even slightly frightening, to us both. Before we lock ourselves into fixed positions we might never find our way out of, I'd like to know what honestly frightens you, or makes you mad, about women's liberation. And I'd like to tell you honestly what has been making women madder and madder. Because it seems to me we'll come to a dead end soon if we keep on talking just to ourselves —men to men, women to women. But if we can talk honestly to each other about what we fear, resent and want, those bitter battle lines of sex might look a little different to us both.

First, what you have heard about "women's lib" may bear only a slight relationship to what the women's movement really means, to me and to most women in America. A freaky bunch of bra-burners? Bitter losers who couldn't get a man and have it in now for all men—uncombed hippies who won't take the responsibility of home and kids? That's the image the media has been giving of "women's lib," though no woman in the movement, to my knowledge, ever burned a bra. (A number of researchers and reporters have been assigned the job of tracking down the original "bra-burning" by major news agencies and encyclopedias, and have never been able to find evidence it ever happened. The braless fashion was actually begun by a *male* fashion designer in the mid-sixties, about the same time as the women's movement began making headlines.) The people who started the women's movement were hardly hippies: they were women in their forties and fifties and thirties, housewives with children who'd gone back to school or work, or women who had worked for years. Most were or had been married; some were single, divorced, widows, even nuns. Most were white, middle class, and middle-aged, in the beginning—Middle American, really—though black women were among the founders. (Most black women at that time were putting their energies into the black civil rights movement.) Then more and more younger women began to rebel at women's role in the student movement, even among the hippies— those "chicks" at the mimeograph machine.

The women's movement exploded in America in the mid-sixties not because I or any other witch of Salem seduced otherwise happy housewives who would still be putting on false eyelashes to wax the kitchen floor if we hadn't put other ideas in their heads. It happened because women couldn't live their whole lives through husband and children any more. With women's life span now stretching seventy-five years, most of those years will not be filled with kids at home to care for, and too many marriages end in divorce for a woman to count on a man to take care of her all her life. And with so much work that used to be done at home now being done in offices and specialized professions—the teaching of kids, baking of bread, butchering, canning, doctoring, the making of clothing, all of it costing more and more money—a woman had to be able to move, work, earn, out in society where the action was, where the men and the children were most of the day now, whether or not she was married or had kids herself.

Women began to take themselves seriously as people, and to realize they weren't freaks when they resented being put down or exploited, or taken advantage of in the office or at home. We began to organize, using the law and the tactics of demonstration and confrontation that had worked for blacks and workers—and invented tactics of our own.

But "equality" for women—equal opportunity, human dignity, individual identity, freedom of choice, which is what all the American revolutions have been about—really can't be seen in quite the same class-war terms as workers striking a boss for a pay raise, or blacks sitting down at a "whites only" lunch counter. Some of the man-hating image of the movement comes from this extremist ideology of sex-class warfare —and the temporary explosion of hostility which fuels it. But the media, in its hunger for sensationalism, plays up the extremists and their exhibitionist tactics far beyond their importance for the movement as a whole.

The movement has grown much too large in ten years to be contained in a single organization or single ideology. By now some 3,000,000 women have bought my book *The Feminine Mystique*, which many regard as having started it all in 1963; they consider themselves "liberated," have changed their lives and the way they think about themselves whether or not they belong to an organized group. Recent Gallup and Harris polls indicate that the *majority* of all American women now agree with the basic goals of the women's movement for equality— even those who say they don't like "women's lib."

The actions women have taken together to change their lives in recent years are the real women's movement, not the rhetoric or media image of "women's lib." The movement is women at the telephone company, who were never allowed to apply for jobs beyond operator, winning over $100,000,000 in back raises for the better jobs they now can get. It's airline stewardesses, no longer forced to resign at age thirty or thirty-five or because of marriage. There are over 1,000 lawsuits against universities and other institutions who will lose their government contracts if they continue to keep women out of the better jobs. Little girls in Midwest towns are getting the right to be in the Little League—or on high school track or tennis teams. It is now illegal in many states to discriminate against women in mortgages, credit, loans, to set different quotas and standards for men and women for admission to college or law school, to ban women from restaurants where male-only business lunches take place. The movement is winning maternity leave, and even paternity leave, clauses in union contracts, and a demand for child-care centers in both national party platforms. It's demanding income tax deduction for expenses of working women, such as child care and housework, in the same way that men can deduct martini business lunches; attacking pension plans and Social Security laws that don't give men and women the right to retire at the same age with the same benefits, and that deny the husband of a deceased woman worker who has paid Social Security all her life the same benefits as the widow of the male worker.

And it's women from Texas and Georgia arguing and winning a historic case in the U.S. Supreme Court attesting as a constitutional right a woman's right to choose whether or not or when to have a baby, and therefore have medical access to abortion, according to the privacy of her own conscience. It's women calling themselves Ms., whether or not they are married, single or divorced, as all men are called Mr. It's objecting to Janey and Junior's readers and television programs which show women only with aprons on, cooking supper or bandaging children's knees; never as doctor, lawyer, or space explorer. It's women beginning to go to law school, and medical school, and business school, not yet in equal proportion to men but *many* times the one or two women in the classes before. It's many daughters of policemen, not just their sons, entering the police force in New York this year, women breaking through the barriers that have kept them out of major sports and varsity programs and physical training, from grade school on, and women getting ordained as ministers, priests, deacons, rabbis; twice as many delegates to both political conventions as ever before. Women are getting elected to state offices which women never ran for before, and are seriously running for President and Vice President—and are demanding, in all parties, the chance to "make policy, not coffee."

It's also the young couples beginning to really share the work and the fun of the home and children they make together. And girls in high school, or college, or working, not expecting the boys always to pay, when they go out . . .

All of this cannot be summed up as equal pay for equal work, or as women wanting to be just like men.

Where does this leave men? Does it really threaten your masculinity, your power, your sense of your own importance, all that's made life worth living for a man? It seems to me the real result will be to relieve you, as men, from some burdens that have become almost too difficult to bear, the way things are. I think you will live longer. And certain pressures that can make a man's life seem not worth living will no longer be, at home or in the office or at school. Maybe you won't have to be so touchy about your masculinity, because you will be able to feel more important for who you really are yourself.

Men have been dying ten years younger than their wives because of the heart attacks and ulcers brought on by the burdens a man is supposed to carry by himself, the rat race he has to keep running to win, the tears and fears he's not supposed to feel. You grew up knowing you were going to have to take complete care of yourself, your wife, whatever children you had, until death or until the kids went off on their own. It was unfair that a woman could grow up expecting to be taken care of all her life—and unfair to her if death, divorce or circumstance ended that dream, and she had never gotten the confidence or skills to take care of herself in the world. It's only when the subject of alimony comes up that you bewail the unfairness to you. But aren't there times, even in a good marriage, when you panic at the burden? Wouldn't it be a relief if your wife could get a job that paid well enough to ease that burden on you? Or that you could be free to take more time to do things you have always wanted to do?

As for your relationship with your wife—or any woman— has it ever seemed to you that whatever you do, it's wrong . . . that nothing ever satisfies her . . . that whatever you give her it's not enough? As if underneath she has some secret complaint or grievance against you? Or do you feel lonesome sometimes, left out when at home with her and the kids, uncomfortable, as if you're an outsider, that they're ganging up against you, so it's a relief to get out with the boys? It might be a greater relief for you if your woman could just feel better about herself. When you feel as if you're nobody yourself, you can't feel good about other people. A recent study of Long Island housewives showed that they saw their husbands first of all as breadwinners, then as fathers, then as husbands, and last of all, as themselves. When women no longer have to depend on husbands first of all as breadwinners, and no longer feel so bad about themselves that they can't see any good in their husbands, they will be able to love you for yourselves. There would be less nagging, less guilt, fewer problems, more love from the woman with whom a man feels at home.

As for that masculinity supposedly being threatened, wouldn't it be a relief if it didn't get measured any more by the big-muscle bluster some aren't born with—and all can lose —or by winning the rat race that is always stacked against you? It's the sexual and economic *testing* that can make a man feel inadequate even before he begins. I think it might be just as much a relief for true men to break out of that iron mask which makes you so unnecessarily vulnerable—and other men your enemies—as it has been for women to break out of our false, simpering, ruffled masks which made us feel such contempt for ourselves and other women, and feel such rage and fear of men. Beneath the phony togetherness, wearing those masks, we are both alone.

You've heard, of course, that "women's lib" wants to destroy marriage, the family, motherhood, and take the pants off men . . . that it's turning women against their own husbands, children, homes, even sex. There is a lot of bitterness and rage exploding in women today, with good reason. It may turn, temporarily, against the very husband, children, marriage and home women were supposed to live for. Because she wants nothing to do with men, it may even temporarily turn a woman off of sex. The women's movement is not the cause of this exploding rage, but it may be the only hope for its cure. Because all this hostility is a symptom that something is terribly wrong with the way marriages, family and home are structured right now, built around those separate, obsolete and unequal roles women and men have been trying to play.

Medical and psychiatric experts have noted that marriage, the way it is structured now, works out much better for men than women, even though the men die younger. On scales of happiness and general well-being, married men and single women are much better off than married women. Police and missing persons bureaus report an enormous increase in runaway wives. In one instance, the husband was asked by the police to describe his wife. "Sort of average." "What color are her eyes?" "Blue, I guess, or is it brown?" He couldn't remember, it was so long since he had looked at her as a person, really seen her. But if a woman feels like nobody—"a service station," as one woman I interviewed put it—it's bound to rub off on her husband and children, even if she doesn't get desperate enough to run away. And it's bound to affect the way she feels, or doesn't feel, in bed with her husband at night. And not all the sex manuals, sexploitation films, pornographic titillators, vibrators, Playboy Bunnies, or Masters and Johnson techniques may cure what seems to be happening, or not happening, in the American bedroom at night. Can they change the conditions of women's lives, the routine all day, every day, at home, in the office, that have driven them to this desperation?

Only the extremists think women's liberation has to mean the end of marriage and the family, but it certainly will change marriage, the family, the way we raise the children, even the architecture of the home, when we liberate ourselves and each other from the old sex roles. I hope, and believe, women will *enjoy* being mothers when they stop living through and for their children, and feel better about themselves. (And it may be better for the kids to take the bus themselves and butter their own sandwiches and do their own homework instead of mother's chauffeuring them, doing it all for them.) I think marriages may last longer, and we may find in them the love, comfort, intimacy, peace, and support we still need and seek from each other, and so rarely find today.

Can you finally look at your woman in a way you've never looked at her before—not as the old lady who gets you breakfast, or as your kids' mother, or as a sex object—but as the person she really is herself? Are you afraid to do that, true man? Well, let me tell you she is even more afraid than you are. When all we were supposed to be were wives and mothers, we never had to face the world, to be tested as individuals. It's easier to blame things on you than to face that lonely test of who we are ourselves in this fast-changing human world. This test you can no longer take for us, true men, we have to do it ourselves. When we know who we truly are, as women, you'll be able to be truly yourselves, as men. When we break out of the roles that have kept us from being ourselves, and know each other for who we really are—woman and man— then, and only then, will come real sexual liberation, and the end of loneliness—and men and women will truly be able to make love, not war.

When reality itself becomes more lurid than one's most paranoid fantasies, judgment suspends. This account of the International Women's Year Conference in Mexico was written immediately upon my return in July 1975, and it gives the terrible, mystifying frustrating flavor of that conference as I experienced it. But it was only later that I realized how outrageously women had been misused by those who control the United Nations. For the maneuver that tied the World Plan of Action for Women to the elimination of Zionism led to the full-scale use of the United Nations to sanction a new world persecution of Jews, in the General Assembly, December 1975. The disruption of the Tribune in Mexico, where I and other feminists would have protested this wrong political use of women's just cause, was not accidental, and my sense of something very wrong wasn't paranoid. It was very hard to convince Golda Meir, this winter, that *women* were not responsible for the equation of their cause with the new wave against Israel. Most of the women at the official conference voted the way they were told—as at any government conference—and those of us who spoke in the name of that new power of women had been, in effect, run out of town.

The realization that governments are now trying to manipulate, co-opt, blunt or even infiltrate the women's movement is not comfortable. How does one deal with it, and not be paralyzed from action, or diverted by suspicion from the energy and will to keep on moving? Just before I left for Mexico, someone came to see me to ask me to hold a press conference in Mexico, to expose the links between Gloria Steinem and the CIA, which had recently been documented and released by the Redstockings group. I refused. I had had nothing to do with that research or its release, was worried about its implications but personally was afraid to touch it. I had discussed it with Liz Holtzman, who thought it should be taken seriously. I put it to her: "If those Select Committees on Intelligence are finding out how the FBI and CIA infiltrated every other movement of social change in these years, let them find out who the agents were, or are, in the women's movement. We can't all start suspecting each other." Anyone who respects the women's movement and values its integrity has to take such charges seriously. But whose interest would it serve to publicize a seeming link between the American women's movement and the CIA on the eve of Mexico?

I continued to be harassed about the Gloria Steinem business. I began to get cables and long-distance calls from the States, advising me to make an announcement from Mexico that even to discuss the Gloria Steinem matter was betrayal of sisterhood. On a weekend respite between the two weeks of the Mexico Conference, in a hacienda on a mountain-ringed valley, in a thunderstorm at midnight, a strange woman knocked on my hostess's door. She said she knew I was there and had to see me with urgent information. What was that urgent information? That I had to stop the talk about Gloria Steinem—how did that woman even know I was there? (She turned out to be *Ms.* correspondent in Mexico.)

After I got home, the pressure increased—my friends were harassed by telephone calls warning that I would be "destroyed," in real danger, if I didn't silence the questions about Gloria Steinem. Why me? I kept saying. I didn't start these questions, I'm not pushing them. But if you are talking about my responsibilities to the women's movement—they are serious questions. During this period, I also received obscene telephone calls threatening to publish sexual rumors about me and some man in Mexico that I doubt ever existed. I was genuinely scared when UPI in Washington received a call that I had a massive heart attack.

I have no idea whether Gloria Steinem had anything to do with these calls or whether the CIA or FBI was really involved, and I do know that the women who passed the threats on to me were genuinely concerned over divisiveness in the women's movement, as well as my own safety. But if the charges were true, no appeal to "sisterhood" could gloss over the implications and dangers to the movement, and I would not be intimidated into silencing the questions. I sometimes wondered if I was becoming paranoid—except that it all happened, and just about that time, new witnesses before the Church Committee told about similar kinds of things happening to Martin Luther King before his assassination.

The women's movement is important, but I surely don't intend to die for it. I want to live that "new yes" myself, already.

Scary Doings
in Mexico City

 It still feels unreal to me, far-fetched, like a poor imitation of a James Bond novel or the movie *Z*. It would be called *The Feminists Who Went Out in the Heat*, a new mystery spy thriller of international intrigue and Gothic horror, with women, as usual, the helpless victims walking innocently into the sinister villains' clutches . . .

I went to Mexico City this summer of 1975 to help advance the world-wide movement of women to equality. While the official United Nations-sponsored World Conference of International Women's Year filibustered, I helped organize "global speakouts" among the 5,000 women at the unofficial Tribune across town, most of whom had paid their own way. Despite every effort to keep the women divided—including violent disruptions played up by the media—we women united in Mexico City—women from the Third World, Latin-Americans, Africans in turbans, Indians in saris, antifascists from Greece, feminists from Japan, Australia, Mexico and women who didn't want to be called feminists from Nigeria and Ecuador, as well as Americans, black, brown and white—to insist that women's equality couldn't wait on a "New Economic Order."

I still don't understand why, or which, world political powers were so afraid of women uniting at Mexico City that they sent men with guns to disrupt our "global speakouts." I still can't believe that I was followed in Mexico City, interrogated by the Attorney General of Mexico, bolted in a hotel room after midnight with an unidentified agent in the lobby supposedly protecting me from kidnapping, warned that my life was in danger, and finally rescued physically by three women from Detroit when the men came in with guns . . .

• • • •

Some background may be relevant. When the UN declared 1975 as International Women's Year, I got an SOS from the women's underground at the UN that no full-scale conference was even planned, such as Stockholm had had for the environment. In my naïveté, I went personally to see UN Secretary General Kurt Waldheim, to convince him of the value to the UN of such a World Conference on Women.

Just before the crucial UN vote on the conference, I had a curious luncheon invitation from a woman involved with the old-time Communist women's group, the International Federation of Democratic Women. The other luncheon guests were Soviet women delegates. They said a UN Conference on Women would be dull, wouldn't I rather help them organize a vital international women's congress in East Berlin for the fall of 1975? And did I know, by the way, it was they who introduced the resolution to make 1975 International Women's Year? I hadn't known that, but said I thought a world Congress of Women ought not be dominated by the United States or by the Communists either. The only way to do that was through the UN. Still, Arab and Soviet delegates had voted against such a conference, which originally was to be held in Colombia. The Arabs twice tried to call it off. Then Mexico moved to host the conference; Princess Ashraf of Iran started the funding. It was rumored that Mexico's President, Luis Echeverría, wanted to become the next UN Secretary General . . .

Last summer I went to the World Population Conference in Bucharest to prepare myself. I saw a curious alliance of the Vatican, the Communists and the Third World nations (Latin-America and Arabs especially) oppose woman's right to control her own body and equality for women as "irrelevant." Our feminist buttons, "My Body Belongs to Me," were eagerly snapped up by Roumanian women, for whom abortion, their main form of birth control, was illegal if they were un-

der forty and had not had four children. I heard firsthand
from Communist women in Bucharest of their fatigue from
carrying the double burden of jobs in which women got the
worst shifts and dirtiest work-loads and then the full burden
of the housework at home—and of the lack of campaigns
against sex discrimination or for men to share the housework,
because Communism itself was supposed to be all that was
needed to liberate women. I realized that maybe you couldn't
have women's liberation in a country where women weren't
free to organize on their own behalf.

Both at Bucharest and in the months before Mexico City, I
received several strange letters warning me not to speak
"where I was not wanted" or I would be denounced "first as
an American and then as a Jew." Our NOW representatives at
the UN were also told that American feminists were not
wanted in Mexico City.

• • •

Cosmetically, Mexico City went all out to welcome the
World Conference on Women. Huge signs in electric lights
blazed the length and breadth of skyscrapers, office buildings,
and banks all along the Reforma—"*Año Internacional de la
Mujer 1975*"; the fat dove with the female sign on its breast and
the equal sign for a tail, in neon like a beer commercial;
"*Igualdad, Paz y Desarrollo.*" But from the beginning, attempts
to use real women in Mexico without risking their infection
by those ideas of "*igualdad*" backfired. On my way in from the
airport, I learned from Mexican feminists that market women
who peddle cigarettes and trinkets on the streets of Mexico
City had been hired to throw flowers at the feet of the arriving
delegates at the opening ceremonies at the Olympic Stadium.
That demonstration was supposed to set the note for the Conference—Echeverría, the hero for poor Third World women—
but there were delays: in the Mexican rainy season, the
women got cold and wet waiting, and wanted to get into the
conference they were supposed to welcome to get warm—and
to hear what it was all about. And blue-uniformed women
police, whom we later learned had been specially trained to
handle the likes of us, had used the necessary degree of muscle
to keep their country sisters out. Those market women, whose
banners said "Welcome Women of the World to Mexico, Land

of Liberty" and "Plan Your Family" and "Equality" and "No to *Machismo*," had been organized by the Mexican government and they had upset the scenario by being real women.

In fact, said Esperanza and Anilu, our own Mexican feminist friends, they too had been hired, by the Attorney General of Mexico, to organize Mexican women for the conference—but had gotten into trouble because they took him seriously. They had wanted to have a march of Mexican women during the conference, as we had had in the U.S.A. The Attorney General had said there would be violence, if they tried such a thing. But if world-famous feminists marched with them, *macho* Mexican policemen might disgrace the country by shooting us—with the whole world watching! So the Attorney General had trained women to break up any demonstrations that might arise, they warned us. Well, my own son had studied in Mexico, and his friends and teachers had told me all about the students shot and jailed in the students' demonstrations in 1968 and during the Olympic Games. Echeverría had then been Minister of Internal Security.

Only two weeks before this conference, two students had been shot in the back of the head; the police involved were under the direction of the Attorney General of Mexico. And now this Attorney General, Pedro Ojeda Paullada, had just been named president of the conference, without a dissenting vote (though one Mexican newspaper did print a cartoon showing a man with handcuffs looming over the women at the conference). My first day in Mexico City, I was stopped by at least a dozen women from different countries to proclaim their outrage at a man being made head of the first World Conference on Women—and a policeman at that! But not one delegation had protested. Rita Hauser, brilliant New York lawyer/feminist/Republican, was already so disgusted, she didn't intend to stay.

The trouble was, though the majority of the delegates were women, for the first time at a UN conference—the men took the chair in the Third World and Communist delegations when anything significant came up. (Many of the women had never been to an international conference; some didn't even know what a resolution was. Many of the delegations were headed by presidents' wives.) And official delegates, women or men, voted as they were ordered.

Thus Echeverría, to enormous applause, decried efforts of women to win rights within the system, hinging the liberation of women on "transformation of the world economic order" and "global revolution." Imelda Marcos, wife of the Philippine President, sounding like "Fascinating Womanhood," said all Philippine women wanted was to enjoy their own femininity and God-given difference from men (which was embarrassing for the brilliant Philippine women who helped draft the World Plan of Action). The Soviet cosmonaut Valentina Tereshkova proclaimed the equality of women fully achieved in the Soviet Union, but failed to mention how many women, besides her, sat on its supreme governing bodies. And Mrs. Sadat, first lady of Egypt, extolling the high status of women in Egypt from the goddesses of prehistory, except for times of foreign invasion, got the conference's ovation when she hinged the issue of women to Arab "liberation" of Palestine. When Elizabeth Reid of Australia warned that if the nations never got around to confronting the real problems of women, then Mexico City would be a mockery of women, no one seemed to be listening.

•   •   •

It took me nearly an hour to get from the official UN conference, at Tlatelolco, to the medical center, where I spoke at the unofficial Tribune on the first Friday. Was it deliberate, situating the Tribune five kilometers across town from Tlatelolco so that the thousands of women who had come to Mexico really concerned about women's conditions couldn't get near where the real decisions were being made? It had been announced from the beginning that the Tribune of nongovernmental organizations (NGO's they are called) would not be permitted to take any action. The format, controlled by UN and Mexican officials, kept the women from getting together. Only one room held over 1,000 people—though nearly 5,000 were registered, 7,000 after they finally let the Mexican women in. Every time frame was filled with speeches by "experts," too often on "nutrition" or "crafts"—like "one big home economics class," as one disgusted delegate put it. Panels were scheduled simultaneously, dividing the women into

rooms of 100 or less, with facilities for simultaneous translation only at large, official sessions. From the very first day, the
women's frustration was extreme. I was given twenty minutes
on a panel on "Feminism" that first Friday—to get it out of the
way before most of the delegates got there, I suspect.

I said that I did not speak as a delegate of my government
but for the women's movement which had started in the
United States in the sixties, that no one gave equality to us, we
had to fight for it ourselves, as in all other revolutions, and we
did so in a unique movement, uniting women across lines of
race, class, education, generation and man-made politics. I said
that women's liberation obviously couldn't be accomplished in
isolation from the economic and political situation of the society generally; that women in abject poverty, or fleeing from
bombs, or under fascist or other repressive dictatorships
couldn't liberate themselves; that, in fact, without freedom to
dissent and organize we could never have had the women's
movement in the U.S.A. And I said that while man was not
the enemy as such, our movement as it has grown has confronted real enemies: reactionary forces, of state and church
and corporate power, massing to block our Equal Rights
Amendment and to reverse the Supreme Court decision giving us the right to choose in the matter of childbearing and
abortion. I said that women—the largest group in society—
had been easily manipulated by dictators, demagogues, priests
and profiteers in the past, and now our movement from passivity to active self-determination was threatening to those who
have been controlling and exploiting us, in all governments
and economic systems.

I also warned that the forces that control the governments
of the UN might try to use International Women's Year to co-
opt or control the women's movement. If we women of the
whole world could get together in our own interest in Mexico
City, it would represent a new kind of political power.

I received an amazing ovation, considering the rift among
women that was supposed to take place in Mexico. The Russian woman I had met earlier came up to me and joked: "You
are too eloquent. I do not agree with you. I think you may be
dangerous."

At a press conference afterwards, I was asked how the ex-

perience of American women could possibly help liberate
women in underdeveloped countries. I said I wouldn't be so
presumptuous as to tell women in any other country how they
could liberate themselves, but they could learn from our experience, at least, that "development" alone is not enough. For in
this technologically most developed nation, we women still
have to fight concretely against sex discrimination in every
field. At this press conference, I was also asked a question
about Gloria Steinem and CIA attempts to infiltrate and control the feminist movement. The Redstockings document link-
ing Gloria Steinem and *Ms.* to the CIA had been released in
Mexico before I arrived, and she had left the conference. I said
I didn't know whether the charges were true, but that anyone
responsible to the women's movement had to be concerned
over increasing evidence of governmental attempts to infiltrate and manipulate it. The CIA taint is even more anathema
in Latin America than in the United States, and it was being
used to discredit American feminism generally.

It was bad enough just being an American. One had to keep
repeating: *I and feminists generally are certainly not agents of
American imperialism . . . We are exploited by the same multina-
tional corporations that exploit you . . . have opposed U.S. foreign
policy . . . marched against the war in Vietnam . . . believe in
your right to control your own economic resources.* I could even
boast that I'd been on both Johnson's and Nixon's "enemy
list."

But the fact is, I am an American, and in Mexico City I
realized that acutely. I've understood before that shame at our
country's evils comes from commitment to its values. But in
Mexico I suddenly had the insight that the women's movement itself was based on the values of American democracy—
the belief in individual dignity and freedom, equality and self-
fulfillment, and self-determination, as well as the freedom to
dissent and organize.

• • •

On Saturday morning, the Mexican newspapers carried
front-page headlines and even editorials claiming that "la
Feminista Friedan" had insulted the president of Mexico by
accusing him of *"machismo"* in the appointment of
"Procurador General Pedro Ojeda Paullada to preside over the

World Conference of Women." I had merely repeated what every other woman was saying about the appointment of a man to head the women's conference—that it was "symbolic" of less than complete sincerity about equality for women, but perhaps it was enough that such a conference on women be held at all, in the land of *machismo*. (Consciousness was already raised at Mexico City, for powerful Mexican men to respond to "*machismo*" as an insult.)

It began to seem as if the real enemy at the Mexican Conference was the American feminists. Some of this seemed simply anti-Americanism, even if deserved, and some of it was something else. On Saturday morning the U.S. delegation invited all American NGO's to the embassy for an "informal dialogue." By the time I got there, a succession of women, brown, black and white, were venting their frustration at not being allowed any voice in the Mexico City Conference, to say nothing of the sins committed against them at home. Some were simply frustrated leaders of black and chicana civil rights groups, and some were very frustrated feminists—Carole De Saram, president of New York NOW, Ronnie Feit of the National Women's Political Caucus, Jan Peterson and Thelma Daley of the Coalition of Labor Union Women, Dorothy Height of the National Council of Negro Women, Dorothy Haener of U.A.W. But others, whose faces were not familiar, seemed only intent on trashing the United States—not only the official U.S. delegation, but me and other American feminists.

Nobody could figure out why these women had come to the conference, because they broke up every meeting or caucus or briefing every time it really began discussing the problems of women. They never wanted to say where they came from. "I am a citizen of the world" would be their identification. Or, "I am an African, but I happen to be living in San Diego, California." One group said they were from CORE, but black feminists wondered. They had an expensive hotel suite at the Fiesta Palace and an inexhaustible supply of liquor to hand out, and the men in the group were writing the women's speeches. An NBC correspondent asked where they got their money, and was told they were "assisted" by Colonel Amin, the dictator of Uganda. Watching a white American feminist being

driven to tears by a member of this group, who claimed talk of
equality for women was "imperialist" and "racist," a brown
feminist from Ecuador said to her black sister: "Are you a
woman or aren't you?" The other one said, "I am a victim of
American racism and imperialism." The Ecuadorian said,
"Well, honey, you are at the wrong conference. How come
you spent all that money to come here and for this hotel suite
if you don't want to even talk about the problems of women?"

It was the question one often felt like asking the official
delegates up at Tlatelolco using that supposedly historic Conference on Women as a mere excuse for their own political
agenda. There began to be talk that the Group of 77 (the Third
World and Communist countries) weren't going to let any
World Plan of Action come out of the Conference on Women.

I was sitting in the back of the plenary chamber in
Tlatelolco when Leah Rabin of Israel got up to speak, and
there was a mass exodus of Arabs and Communists, many African and some Asian delegates. I admired her calm and her
courage in reacting to that exodus. (Among those walking out
on Mrs. Rabin, with a spiteful sort of smile, was that same
woman who had threatened, at Bucharest and before Mexico,
that I would be denounced "first as an American and then as a
Jew" if I dared to speak for women where I was "not wanted."
She was supposedly compiling a "clearinghouse" of all Third
World women's groups for A.I.D. Or was someone else financing her "Women's International Network"?)

Personally outraged by that walkout on Mrs. Rabin, I
walked the length of the hall to shake her hand. I was outraged
as a woman for such use of that Conference on Women, and I
wasn't the only one to feel that way. Back at the Tribune,
turbaned Victoria Mojekwu from Nigeria was sounding off:
"Is the conference supposed to be for the women of the world
when they tell me, an African, to walk out on a woman because she is from Israel—when will they walk out on me because I am African?"

•   •   •

For nearly a week, while the official delegates filibustered,
the 5,000 women at the Tribune stayed meekly divided in their
separate panels, hotels, and supposedly unbridgeable cultural

differences. Attempts to organize a "feminist caucus" at first found mainly Americans talking to other Americans.

Other meetings held in small hotel rooms at night, under the title of "Coalition of Unrepresented Women," tended to be dominated by other Americans, or rather those mainly interested in attacking the U.S. delegation as "elitist." I thought this was a futile diversion of women's energy at this international conference, as if the U.S.A.—for good or ill—were the only issue. True, the Republican administration had not appointed the most militant feminists to represent it here. But most of the delegates, alternates and advisers had been organizers or leaders of women's caucuses in the State, Justice, and Labor Departments, the Republican party, and trade unions and bar associations. The U.S. delegation would vote in the interests of women because the women's movement is so strong in the United States it wouldn't dare otherwise—and the U.S. government's championship of women was a lot like the kiss of death at a UN conference!

All week Tribune officials refused to let us have the only room large enough for even half the 5,000 women to meet together. Crowded into small Room 3 on Monday morning, several hundred hot, frustrated women at the first "global speakout" proved that women could bridge that supposed chasm between our worlds when they spoke from their own experience as women, instead of mouthing political rhetoric. That was the one rule I proposed—and that women from no one nation (i.e., my American sisters) would speak twice till others had had a turn. Then I handed the chair over to Sudha from the All-India Congress of Women, and sat down on the floor.

At first it didn't work. Those mysterious "citizens of the world" got the whole room mad, hogging the floor mikes with that political rhetoric, lumping "feminism," "racism," and "elitism" into one anti-U.S.-imperialism bag. Shaking with rage, Sudha stood: "We all know there is racial discrimination in the United States, but black or white, you are better off than we are. In my country, women and their families must live on a per capita income of six dollars a month. Can't we see ourselves as women fighting the discrimination against us in the whole world?"

And then Latin-American women began to speak "simply for ourselves as women." "I, a woman from Peru, want the right to control my own body, but my government says it is an imperialist plot to limit births, that women must wait until Peru is more developed to decide for ourselves how many children to bear." A woman from San Diego matched her with the account of her bishop's threat of excommunication for housewives who claimed the right to control their own bodies.

A Canadian woman said her delegation had been briefed to oppose discussion of a New Economic Order, but she herself understood that most women couldn't hope for equality without such development. Another spoke of "the great humility any white American woman must feel knowing the government and corporations of our country have been responsible for exploitation and oppression in the world. It is a fact that because the United States has in the past exploited the resources of Chile and Bolivia, women of the United States enjoy a higher standard of living. It is also a fact that this same imperialism oppresses people of color in the United States, and exploits the great majority of women, whatever their color, and that neither imperialism nor exploitation of women is confined to the United States."

That night, at a meeting of several hundred NOW members in the Del Prado Hotel, the idea of a march was again broached, not by me. The idea was beautiful—a march of the "women who are more than half the world" carrying banners of their nations to Tlatelolco like our march in New York on August 26, 1970. But in Mexico City, I said, it would be irresponsible for U.S. women to organize such a demonstration—especially considering the students so recently shot, and the warnings of the Mexican feminists. The important thing was to get space in which the women of all countries at the Tribune could unite—not to risk bullets. I have no taste for martyrdom.

The next morning, still crowded into small Room 3 at the medical center, real work was begun. Jacqui Ceballos and a chicana leader named Graciella—operating in Spanish and English simultaneously, since there were no official interpreters—got the Tribune women organized into six groups to tackle the specifics of the World Plan of Action, which the official delegates at Tlatelolco had not yet even begun. Suddenly Marcia Bravo, the unflappable director of the Tribune, rushed frantically into the room as if she expected to see God knows what instead of women studying papers, and called me out. The Attorney General wanted to see me, at once. There were rumors that I was going to lead a march of 5,000 women to the palace to demand his ouster as president of the conference. When I went back to tell this to the meeting, the blue uniformed policewomen wouldn't let me in. I panicked, a bit . . .

The Attorney General of Mexico, a suave man, did not have me beaten or tortured. He merely questioned me intently on whether anyone had approached me in New York, any Mexicans, to organize a march. I told him that no one had, that I personally had no intention of leading a march to demand his ouster, and would be glad to deny that rumor if he would give me the large room at the Tribune the next morning. That got the global speakout moved up from Room 3 to Room 2. And, as if orchestrated (only it wasn't), no sooner had I reported on the Attorney General's accusation when Jan Peterson from Brooklyn said, "Why shouldn't we have a march? Otherwise nothing may come out of Mexico for women at all." For up at Tlatelolco, China and the Soviet bloc were now insisting there could be no World Plan of Action for women's equality until colonialism, neocolonialism, racism and foreign domination were eliminated.

I said the Tribune officials had better give us that large Room 1 at once, to approve some Plan of Action on behalf of all the women whose interests were being ignored by the UN delegates—or we might have to march.

• • •

At one o'clock Wednesday afternoon, we finally convened in the Great Hall, and with calm intensity and no disruptions approved paragraph by paragraph the specifics of a Ten-Year World Plan of Action, adding the machinery to enforce, on a world scale, bans against sex discrimination in education, employment and political decision-making and against other violations of women's rights. Eight of us, from six continents— including black and white Americans—rotated the chair. Pat Keppler of Harvard Divinity School and Ronnie Feit coordi-

nated the working committees which lined up at the floor
mikes, and in two hours several thousand women at the Tribune—right to left, all four worlds, under- and overdeveloped
—came to a concrete consensus on the Plan of Action for
Women which our official counterparts at Tlatelolco had been
filibustering for seven days. No one left the meeting for lunch,
no woman fought any other for the mike, and there was no
nit-picking or political rhetoric. When it came down to the
specific actions women needed, we were surprisingly unanimous.

When it was discovered that a separate caucus of Latin-
American women was also working on the plan, we sent a
delegation to merge our work with theirs. And before we had
to vacate the hall, the body unanimously demanded that their
"united voice as women of the Tribune" be heard by the UN
Conference. There was talk of "all the women" going up there
in buses, to stand outside Tlatelolco in massed support while a
delegation presented our plan to the Attorney General or to
Helvi Siipila, whose patronizing treatment of other women as
Secretary-General of IWY had angered many women.

The unity of that climactic meeting of the Tribune was a
politically transcendent experience for the thousands who wit-
nessed it, but it was not reported by the press. It went against
the image they were giving of Mexico City, of women in a
ludicrous global catfight. Peggy Simpson of Associated Press
told me she had filed the story, but had received instructions
to give them, instead, details to go with a picture the next day
of two Latin-American women fighting for the mike. That
unexpected unity of women must have been very threatening
to someone; it wasn't allowed to last . . .

•   •   •

Assembling at the Tribune at 9 A.M. on Thursday to take
our demands to the UN, we discovered that the dozens of
specially chartered buses which went back and forth every day
from the Tribune to the hotels and Tlatelolco had completely
vanished from the streets. So the delegation and a token escort
went up to Tlatelolco in three cabs, while the others secured
the big room again for us to report back to at noon.

In the cab going up, Dr. Marjorie Bean of Bermuda read
her speech to Victoria from Nigeria, Sudha from India, and

me. She said our delegation represented the "united women at the Tribune, feminists and other groups." "Not feminists!" screamed the previously militant Victoria. "I said, feminists and other groups," replied tall, black Dr. Bean in her haughtiest Oxford accent. It was lovely to hear a black woman insist on saying the word "feminist" without apology.

Helvi Siipila received our document, but seemed shocked at our "unprecedented" demand to speak to the UN ourselves. (True, the women's liberation movement is not an official government body, but not so long ago the UN had received Arafat, wearing a gun, on behalf of the Palestine Liberation Organization.)

Going back to the Tribune on the bus, which had suddenly reappeared, I sat next to my new feminist friend from Egypt. I had drunk borscht with Leah Rabin at the Israeli reception the night before. I have never bought the mystique of women as any special force for peace. But when it came to action on our special concerns as women, suddenly everyone back at the Tribune was now suggesting that we couldn't really trust any of our governments or the UN itself to do anything unless we were organized ourselves, in our own nations and across the political barriers dividing our man-made worlds. At noon on Thursday it was proposed simultaneously from all sides of that chamber to set up a permanent World Tribune of Women to continue the magnificent unity we had finally achieved here.

That night I got myself a car and driver, pinned my press badge on my slinkiest black evening pajamas, and headed into the whirl of receptions and dinners being given for the official delegates. At India's reception, I ran into American Ambassador Jova, who sat me down on a couch and told me gleefully he'd had a call from the Mexican Minister of Internal Security to *shut me up!* Said the ambassador humorously, "I explained that in our system we can't do that to a private citizen who hasn't committed any crime. And besides, if I told you to shut up here, it might be counterproductive." Did I understand that the reason the buses had disappeared that morning was that the Attorney General wasn't taking any chances. "He didn't believe you weren't going to march. He told me they were fully prepared to do whatever was needed to protect you."

"You mean we really could have marched?" I asked the ambassador, kicking myself for being so faint-hearted. He laughed and shrugged. But protect us from *what?* "From the terrorists they would have blamed if you were shot," a Mexican journalist explained.

At a seated dinner for 3,000 my friend the Attorney General was throwing at the anthropological museum (to which I wasn't exactly invited), I joined Jill Ruckelshaus of the U.S. delegation in a frustrating try at a dialogue with the women delegates from the People's Republic of China. They wore blue uniforms and no make-up; the head of the delegation had short square-cut black hair; a younger one had light-haired pigtails; and they were flanked by men in identical uniforms. We ascertained, through the interpreter, that the head of the delegation was a mayor and vice-chairperson of a provincial senate—and we toasted to that! We found out that she had a daughter, and since I did, too, I proposed a toast to our daughters. Then I asked her if she knew of our women's liberation movement in the United States. She said, "There is no point for women to liberate themselves under capitalism." I said it was necessary, and good, for women to liberate themselves, no matter what the system, and our movement was one of the things now changing the capitalist system. And wasn't it possible that in advanced industrial societies like the U.S. today, the women's movement might be the same kind of revolutionary force as the working class, or proletariat, in the days of Marx and Lenin? She looked puzzled and turned to the man, the Chinese ambassador. He barked out something that sounded authoritative. And the three women, who had seemed as intent as Jill and I in having a conversation, visibly withdrew. The leader didn't answer, she just smiled sarcastically, as if she were saying to herself, "capitalist pig."

And yet she was a woman. I didn't accept the impossibility of talking to her. Maybe if I could sit next to her, some woman-to-woman things would get across. I asked a UN interpreter if he would change seats with me, and stood up to move closer to the Chinese women. At which point, the Chinese ambassador suddenly stood up and, like blocking a tackle in a football game, put his whole body between the Chinese lady and me. And then, improbably, there was the Attorney General standing by our table, effusively embracing the Chinese sister and making it impossible for me to talk to her. I smiled at him and said, "You see, I haven't organized a march against you, after all—not yet." The party was over.

• • •

And now strange things began to happen to disrupt that unity at the Tribune. Now the Attorney General and the Mexican press were accusing me of "manipulating" the Tribune. Several times, when I was being interviewed by foreign television, that same woman who had warned me not to speak for women or I'd be denounced as a Jew would break in. "She does not speak for American feminists," she told a Danish cameraman. "I speak for myself," I said. "Who do you speak for?"

The Mexican feminists kept dragging me and other NOW leaders over to their own conference, held in a huge posh bank, with all the earphones, translators, and engraved programs we lacked at the Tribune (we had to write our meeting notices and distribute them by hand). Only there never seemed to be more than a few dozen Mexican women, extremely well-dressed and polite. The night after our speakout, they insisted that Jacqui and I meet them far out in the Lomas section for an emergency discussion. When we got there, an old caretaker finally opened the locked gate of a very dark mansion. Only one Mexican feminist was there. What was the emergency? That it wasn't safe for us to stay at our hotels, which were bugged; we must move out here where we could be "secluded" and "rest," said Celia Negretti. And how would we get back and forth to the Tribune and the conference? The Mexican feminists all had cars, she soothed. I was so annoyed by the ineptness of the idea, and by being dragged away from the Tribune and now too late for a bath and dinner, that I didn't wonder until later whether these Mexican feminists were real, or agents assigned to watch us and keep us away from the action.

On Friday noon I was on my way back to the Tribune with the gloomy news that now even the Australians had no hope of getting a Plan of Action out of the conference unless it was adopted without even considering any of the amendments. I was waylaid by a group of women—some I recognized from the disruption at the U.S. embassy—who had a television crew with them and wanted it on television that I was a "racist" because I had not shown up for a meeting with black women that morning and had insulted Latins and chicanas by my "language." I said let's go over and sit on the wall and get to the bottom of this right now, and forget about television. I knew of no appointment to meet with black women that morning and did not know the Spanish language, but if I had inadvertently insulted anyone, I honestly apologized. (It seems maybe I *had* affronted chicanas, because I kept saying, "black and white" Americans, and they had been trying to tell me I must say "black, white and *brown*.") The TV camera was now taking pictures of a large sign saying "Lesbians Go Home" that had suddenly appeared.

By the time I got into the meeting, the "United Women of the Tribune" in the big hall were in chaos, with what looked to be two Latin-American women fighting each other for the mike—that picture which the world's media carried as typifying the disunity of the women at Mexico City. Only that picture did not just *happen*, it was arranged.

The "united women" were quietly going over the Plan of Action and waiting for Ms. Siipila when, as if at a prearranged signal, a Latin-American said over the loudspeaker: "The Latin-American demands are not in this document." And the crows outside poured into the hall, occupying whole sections of seats, filling the aisles, and taking over the stage. Someone must have tipped Mexican television this was going to happen because they were already there, in strategic spots. One of the women trying to take over the microphone was said to be the daughter-in-law of President Echeverría, Rosa Luz, who is a Communist. I recognized the other as one of the well-dressed Mexican feminists from the bank. Were they trying to get the meeting back to order—or egg on the disrupters? The translation system seemed to have broken down. On either side of the hall, two men in work jackets seemed to be directing the disrupters, and giving signals for slogans. One woman was recognized as a prominent rightist Argentinian refugee, and others as rightist Cuban refugees. As before, that mixture of left-radical slogans and the far right was puzzling. A UN official later found a literal monkey wrench behind the chair, which had evidently been used to shut off Marjorie Bean's mike.

"If you had been up there and kept the meeting going, I'm sure you would have been shot," said Carole De Saram cheerfully.

At this point, Helvi Siipila arrived, and the disrupters as if by signal again stopped and let Dr. Bean and the rest of our rotating chairpanel back on the stage. (All except me and Emily Moore, my black American sister. By unspoken agreement, we stayed down on the floor.) Ms. Siipila said that the decision had been made that the women of the Tribune could not be heard because "You are not united." And as soon as she left, the disrupters started again, more violently than ever. The planned discussion on setting up a permanent World Tribune of women couldn't take place.

I sat on a stone bench against the wall outside, and women from other countries kept coming up to me and saying it isn't all over, is it, why can't we go on and set up a World Tribune of Women, expecting I would know what to do. And I sat there trying to pretend that tears weren't streaming down my face—not, as rumor had it, because I had been clubbed by a disrupter, but from rage, helpless, frustrated fury at whoever was going to such lengths to destroy that beautiful unity women had achieved at the Tribune. And I didn't know who or why, or how to stop it. Later I asked Dorothy Height of the National Council of Negro Women about the rumors trying to make me a "racist." "It's part of the same setup," she said.

• • • •

Around midnight, walking back from a party of Mexican feminists (another group, there seemed to be at least five—this one wanted to be a NOW chapter), I stopped to have a drink at the Angel Bar on the mezzanine of the Maria Isabella with Catherine East, a stalwart Washington feminist serving as the technical adviser to the U.S. delegation. Sitting on little stools around a mushroom table, Catherine kept looking over her shoulder. "We are being watched," she told me. "I think we're being followed." Two men were standing by the deserted hotel desk at the foot of the stairs in the empty lobby, not doing anything, just watching us.

When we stood up, the two men disappeared. Then when we got to the foot of the stairs, we saw one man in the corner by the elevators, the other outside the hotel entrance. Catherine put me in a cab, and I saw her looking for the license number: it must have been a special hotel cab, it didn't have a taxi sign. And then, out of the hotel driveway it turned right— the opposite direction from my hotel. *Now I've had it*, I thought. Maybe it was a one-way street. That cab took fifteen minutes to get me to the Montejo; I walked it in less than five. But no matter—Catherine was already on the phone when I got to the hotel desk. She said the men watching us had gotten into a yellow car parked in the middle of the street and had followed my cab! And she said she was sure now it wasn't safe for me to stay in Mexico any longer. I asked the hotel clerk if he could get me the airline ticket office, and he said "not until the morning." He noticed that I was upset. He said, "Do not worry, there is an agent here to protect you!" And he pointed to a man sitting in an armchair in the corner of the lobby, watching television. And I realized he'd been there every time I came in or out.

I locked and bolted the door and the shutters on the window, and sat shivering on the edge of the bed. I tried to get through to one of the NOW women, but the phone was dead. The few hours I slept that night, I had terrible dreams. I was really scared. It was like the joke "wolf, wolf." It had seemed a joke—CIA agents, the KGB, spies that came in from the cold —but this was happening. The newspapers lately had been carrying more and more strange tales of kidnappings, hostages, shootings for political reasons, terrorism. I didn't want to be a coward, but I didn't want to be kidnapped in Mexico, either. Who would ransom me?

I couldn't get a plane to New York the next day, but if the two eminent Mexican journalists with whom I was to have breakfast thought it was really dangerous for me to stay, I'd fly to Texas. The Mexican journalists thought that was exactly what "they" wanted me to do—and "they" was probably the Mexican government, whose fascist core is masked by a left façade. They recognized a familiar pattern, the way movements are broken up in Mexico—the government organization of feminists to supplant real ones, the seeming radicals who

have also been hired by the government to disrupt, and provide the government with an excuse to suppress, jail or shoot
the real leaders. But if I do not move anywhere alone, I probably will not be shot, they said.

They told me I must realize how I had been set up, personally, as a target even before I got to Mexico, and that all those
rumors were surely more than coincidence. But even with the
exaggerations and the false rumors, we were having a tremendous, maybe unexpected effect on Mexican women. One journalist, Helena Fabian, told me that at her hairdresser's that
morning, an elderly woman in her seventies had been reading
the newspaper report about the conference. Helena had said
she was going to breakfast with me. "That revolutionary!"
said the elderly señora, raising her eyebrows. And the hairdresser had interjected, "But, you know, she is right." And so
I decided to stay.

●   ●   ●   ●

In the sunny courtyard of the Cortes, I ordered garlic soup
to give me strength, and tequila with hot peppery sangrita
juice, and brought my American sisters up to date. And said
that somehow we had to get rid of our own jealousies and
close ranks against whatever force was operating against us
here, because this was probably as crucial a moment for the
world-wide movement of women as 1966 was in America. And
I told them how I had panicked and my feelings had been
hurt, and how I had lost my temper over the "racism" rumors,
the charges of "manipulating" and all the other personal sins
I'd been accused of the past week. And there hadn't been time
to consult enough when I took advantage of the Attorney
General's charge so we could take over the Tribune. And I had
had far more media attention than I wanted, and I knew it
made them mad. "But don't you see, it's the women's movement that's the real threat, and they want to divide us and
they're setting me up as the symbol. And there's no way I can
fight it, alone." And damn it all, I was crying again! But I
guess that made the others feel better.

And then we all went to a lunch being given by the
Domecq brandy refractory in honor of the Mexican feminists
and International Women's Year. We persuaded the Mexican
feminists that they should have a press conference on Monday

to make it clear that the women at the Tribune are united. And we, or at least I, would stay out of it. By now I didn't care if these Mexican feminists were the government-organized ones; they were feminists. (They wanted to take pictures of their little daughters with me—even the blue-uniformed women security agents wanted to take each other's pictures with me!) One of the Domecq executives said to me: "Do you have any idea how much money is being spent in this country this week to offset the effect you people are having on Mexican women?"

*   *   *

On Monday, at Tlatelolco, at the official conference, Arab, Communist and some African and Asian nations moved to link the Ten-Year Plan of Action for Women to the abolition of "imperialism, neocolonialism, racism, apartheid and Zionism." A European woman delegate told me: "That is clear anti-Semitism, and we will have no part of it." It was also clearly anti-woman. The women in the U.S. delegation were very bitter, because if this declaration remained, how could the U.S. support the World Plan of Action for Women? As a bitter footnote, when the spunky woman delegate from New Zealand tried to get "sexism" added to those evils the world must eliminate before women could be free, she met opposition from the Communists, Latins and others. The men said they "didn't know what sexism means." "Then you have no business at a Conference on Women," said that sister from New Zealand.

I was hurrying to the sidewalk to get a ride to the Tribune, and a reporter, a woman whose press badge I didn't really see, kept running beside me, asking me, of all things, if I planned to go to the Conference of Women in East Berlin this fall. "I don't know that I'll be asked," I said. "Judging by what's going on here, the Communists don't like feminism."

"But if you are asked, will you go?"

"It would depend on whether I could talk freely," I said, "or whether I would be merely being used as a decoy for other women."

*   *   *

Esperanza Marti, Mexican feminist, opened the last of the global speakouts. "There have been rumors that women at this

Tribune are divided," she said. "We are not divided. Mexican women know we cannot wait until development is finished to demand equality. They have told us in every kind of voice that we should not unite with our sisters in the developed countries, that they are our enemies. This is a lie. They say that women under capitalism and women under communism and women struggling free of colonialism have nothing in common. But you cannot prove to me that liberation of women is automatic in any ism. I am a feminist."

At this point a group led by men came in organized formation from the corridor into the meeting hall, carrying a huge bedsheet banner reading *"Mujeres y Imperialismo."* Shouting, they marched down one aisle, marched up the other, marched outside, and marched back in again, shouting and pushing closer and closer against the back row of seats where we were sitting.

A woman from Japan said: "This conference is being manipulated to make it seem impossible for women to unite. Japanese women are taught to be modest. We are bitter because they have tried to make us fight other women." And the disrupters shouted her down.

And then a woman from Greece spoke up passionately: "I fought in the resistance. Greek women fought equally with men against fascism, but when the dictatorship took over, women were not equal. The feminist movement will make women of the whole world a force against fascism and dictatorship. They are trying to make us think that American women, feminist women who are fighting against fascism, are our enemy. In my country we have seen agents of provocation disrupt meetings of people in this very fashion."

And the men led the disrupters up the aisle, and one passing me raised a fist. Dorothy Height spoke out: "We black women know what oppression is, what it is to be discriminated against, exploited—and that we need equality, sisters of every color, all races—we can work in unity." And she was shouted down, even more viciously.

Then someone grabbed my arm and said the Tribune officials wanted me to get out of the room, it wasn't safe for the American feminists to stay. They had discovered the men leading this disruption had guns.

But now I was pinned against the wall, and a television light was turned on me, and a Mexican TV man was insisting on a statement acknowledging defeat. Wasn't it clear now that Latin-American women didn't want our message of equality? He was rather ugly about it. I said it was clear that someone didn't want women, in Latin America and the world, to unite for equality. It was no defeat; the power of women's unity at the Tribune prompted this violent disruption—but they wouldn't be able to stop the women's movement from spreading over the world, after Mexico City.

Then Dorothy Haener of U.A.W. and her friend Sarah Powers appeared at the edge of the spotlight, and a black woman with them, a city councilwoman of Detroit, told me to take her arm, and they got me into one of the work offices with half-partition, half-glass walls, and told me to keep my head below the edge of the partition so that no one could see I was there. And I could tell they were serious, so I did it, though I didn't know yet about the guns.

•   •   •

I'm still not sure what we did wrong or right. A quiet woman from the World YWCA said: "The real explanation is so far-out you won't believe it. It was because you really got the women united, including the Third World women. And then you began talking about a World Tribune of Women. That did it. You see, the Communists are planning this huge world conference of women in Berlin. They want to get the women's movement under control, so that's why they set up International Women's Year."

I left the next morning. The World Plan of Action was passed without the amendments for its implementation even discussed, and was linked by the Declaration of Mexico to the overthrow of imperialism, Zionism, etc., so in the end the U.S. delegation voted against it, and others that had been for a real Plan of Action for women abstained.

In the corridor, after the last Tribune speakout was broken up, Jacqui and Carole and others tried to talk individually to some of the women who had been used to disrupt. And just like those market women paid to give the phony welcome that first day, some of these women began to get really interested. They were, after all, women: brown, black, white. And the men with guns didn't like that and told my friends the Spanish equivalent of "Stop messing up our women."

⁎   ⁎   ⁎

Well, it is not a James Bond story. It happened, though I still can't believe that the women's movement, which we started ten years ago out of the desperations of our everyday life as women, could be such a powerful threat to forces of the left or right on a world scale. (It could be significant that Echeverría had a session with the Pope before the conference on women, and that Philip Agee's book *Inside the Company* includes, in the alphabetical list of CIA agents and contacts, "Luis Echeverría, Minister of Government [Internal Security].") Can the women's movement really threaten the dangerous, ruthless men playing those games of ideology and oil and nuclear bombs and territory—the real power games? If women did unite across the world, as they began to do in Mexico City, the unprecedented new kind of power unleashed would be harder to control or contain than the spread of communism among the workers of the world, one hundred years ago.

All I know is that the women who went to Mexico City will never be the same again. And if we began to realize that our own power was greater and more threatening to all the old powers than we ever dreamed, we now know that we will need all our wits and guts to keep their agents from co-opting it.

In the fall of 1975, another supposed world conference of women was held in East Berlin, controlled by Communist groups who had instituted International Women's Year for that purpose. American feminists were not welcome. The few who managed to get there could not even get feminist resolutions on the floor for discussion. As was already clear in Mexico, the Communists do not like the women's movement for equality.

On a trip to Czechoslovakia in 1967, I got some insights into the failure of women to achieve true equality under the Communist system as well as in the capitalist system.

It was in 1967, shortly before the Russians came in. The women's organizations had been disbanded when the Communists took over many years ago. Communism was supposed to be sufficient. But a woman journalist I'd known years before had sent word to me that women there were now facing something similar to the feminine mystique. At first, as I learned from her and others, women had been needed in the labor force and had been admitted to universities and medical schools on an equal basis with men. Of course, in the early days of the Communist regime, the big emphasis was on heavy industry and the idolization of the proletariat; the university degree and a profession like medicine was not valued as highly. It did not make you a member of an elite or give you a voice in decision-making.

But now, suddenly, Czechoslovakia had evolved, and professional skills, university-trained managers, even doctors were becoming more important to the economy than Ivan, whose muscles could be replaced by machines. And suddenly it was discovered that the pregnancies and other mysterious female diseases of the women doctors were disrupting the hospital schedule. Institutions with too high a percentage of female doctors or professionals had to take steps to counter this new evil *"feminizasce."* It was suddenly also discovered that children were suffering from maternal deprivation—*"deprivace"*—they needed their own mothers home all day. Child-care centers were too expensive, anyhow. Better to pay the men more, and have the women stay at home!

My old friend Hilda Scott has since left Czechoslovakia and described the plight of women there in a cogent, brilliant book, *Does Socialism Liberate Women?* (Beacon Press). She asked me to come there in 1967, because the women were getting so tired from the burdens of their half-equality that they were in danger of acquiescing to that feminine mystique, Communist-style.

The men practiced male prejudice unchallenged; the women somehow got the worst shifts, and then they had to go home and do all the housework without the appliances and labor-saving devices we have here, much less any new communal arrangement to liberate them from the housework. No attention, no priority was given to such matters by overwhelmingly male commissariats. There was never any consideration that men should share the housework and child care if women shared the work in the factory and office.

Too few women were sitting in decision-making spots even to make the commissars aware of the problems. The women were so tired they didn't have the energy to advance professionally or politically. By the time I got there, quotas against women had been openly resumed in apprenticeship training programs and professional schools. When I asked the political commissar I was interviewing how many women sat on his central committee, he said, "Many, many, you may be sure." I said I would like to know how many. His secretary brought in the list and he read the names—Ivan, Karl, Otto—not a single woman. He shook his head, muttering that I must understand the difficulty of finding qualified women, that it is not right to ask women to take so much time away from husband and children.

Some of the women I talked to that winter in Czechoslovakia were so tired, they liked the idea of staying home and letting the men run the factories and the hospitals. Others tried it for a while and became restive out of the action, and suffered economically as well without the extra income. So they had decided women needed to organize again in Czechoslovakia.

The commissar thought it was a joke when one of the women said of me: "You had better be careful. She is a Karl Marx for women." The next year, in fact, the women in Czechoslovakia did try to organize a woman's movement. They wrote asking me to write for their newspaper; they wanted to publish my book. Then the Russians came in.

It is not possible to have full equality for women without a sex-role revolution for men. I wonder if that ever will or could be done in any system where women are not free to organize and liberate themselves. Castro's historic speech last year denouncing *machismo* in Cuba and some programs being started in East Germany show the beginnings of awareness of a woman problem in the Communist regimes. I don't suppose that women in any part of the world can be isolated from the germs of women's movements spreading from the West.

From discussions with political scientists, I see that the women's movement and feminism are threatening to Communists because (1) they cut across class lines and go against a strict class analysis of history and revolution; (2) they put too much emphasis on the individual and self-fulfillment, on a woman's right to control her own body and her own destiny, on the fact that she is not just a sexual or economic instrument; (3) if women began to understand the concept of "personal as political" in Communist lands, and arose from their tired passivity, it would shake more than women's lives; (4) sexual liberation itself is threatening; the permutations of women's passivity and rage into everybody's sexual alienation are as basic to acceptance of Communist oppression as of capitalist exploitation; (5) the women's movement is a real mass movement for revolutionary social change, and it is spreading world-wide. And it didn't come from and can't be controlled by the Communists.

I don't think any existing Communist model can give us a blueprint for the "new yes," because all the Communist regimes are stuck far short of real equality for women, further from sex-role revolution than we are.

China may be another story, but they don't seem very eager for me to come and see.

Afterword 1985— see page 501

PART V

An Open Letter to the Women's Movement—1976

An Open Letter to the
Women's Movement—1976

From all sides, now, they are tolling the bell to mourn the death of the women's movement in America. I could say to the doomsayers "You are premature—the women's movement is not dead, not by a long shot. We've had a few setbacks maybe, but why this curious, indecent haste to bury our movement?" I could warn our enemies: "Don't celebrate too soon. We have a few minor differences, but don't try to move in on our weakness. The women's movement is stronger, healthier than you suspect. ERA will be ratified in 1976." I could say to all of you in the movement, "This divisiveness is dangerous. It is a betrayal of the movement to question any leader now. Remember, sisterhood is powerful." But the bell would continue to ring. If I kept on saying such reassuring words, I would be lying to you and to myself.

We must ask, we must listen, we must no longer blind ourselves to the danger signs. The women's movement is in danger, from within and from without, and those who wish it dead will indeed move in on our weakness. And if the women's movement dies—or becomes weakened, is no longer the vital, strong, moving force that enabled all of us to change our lives—what will become of each of us, and our sisterhood, our new hopes? Would we have to go back to the way we were before?

Consider the crisis as it has been brought into the public

consciousness over the past months. It became public in mid-November 1975, after two weeks during which:

(1) There were three days of all-night voting, stolen registration books, and accusations of fraud at NOW's National Conference in Philadelphia, October 25–27. Then, for the first time in the women's movement, the American Arbitration Association was called in to police an election, which culminated in the chaotic victory of a so-called "Majority Caucus" vowing to take NOW "out of the mainstream, into the revolution"—this, in the crucial, and only, national membership organization of the American women's movement.

(2) On October 29, on the tenth anniversary of the founding of NOW, a "general strike against the system" was called by the self-styled new "revolutionary" leadership of NOW and was a disastrous failure. Called "Alice Doesn't" (from the movie "Alice Doesn't Live Here Anymore"), the strike was supposed to protest the entire system as it oppresses women: Alices everywhere were not to go to work, not to shop for groceries or cook, not to sleep with their oppressors. Newspapers reported gleefully that women were, in fact, working, "because they had to, or lose their jobs," and were also shopping and cooking. Nothing stopped. Several thousand women marched in Los Angeles; teach-ins involved other hundreds; there was street theater and consciousness-raising in Philadelphia and Detroit. Other than that, even NOW chapters ignored or were embarrassed by the day. And the newspapers chortled over its failure.

(3) On November 4, state ERA's failed by large margins in New York and New Jersey—progressive ground where the women's movement is supposedly strongest and where the federal Equal Rights Amendment was ratified earlier with virtually no opposition. Headlines and commentators claimed that women—fearful women—were responsible for the defeat of the ERA. Editorialists proclaimed the certain doom of the ERA nationally—and moves to rescind began in some of the thirty-four states which had already ratified it. In the key state of Illinois whose ratification of ERA in 1976 could take it over the top, legislators virtually refused to enter into serious discussion with leaders of the several thousand women who came to Springfield that week. In the State of New York, failure of

the state ERA was used as an excuse by the legislature to remove further funds from child-care centers. A massive march on Washington to rescind the Supreme Court decision giving women the right to choose in the matter of abortion was called by the Right to Life groups.

The newspapers—and even the women's movement's own press—began to headline "Does the Women's Movement Still Have Clout?" "Is NOW on the Brink of Then?" (*Village Voice*, November 17, 1975) "Can Feminism Survive the ERA Defeat?" (*Majority Report*, November 15, 1975). And to the fury of radical feminists, the *New York Times* even ran an editorial pleading: "Save the Movement."

I read that editorial on the plane to New Orleans, where Sunday, November 9, I had agreed to meet with the "independents" on the NOW board and with former NOW leaders to finally come to grips with the crisis in the women's movement.

Earlier, those of us who saw the danger signs didn't want to do anything. We whimpered timidly, bound by the pact of silence of "sisterhood," of that inward-staring circle. The erosion of that circle had to weaken us so seriously that the enemy actually began to move in before we finally forced ourselves to face facts. There is a panic now in our belated admission that the women's movement has been in serious danger from internal enemies for some time. Some still don't want to admit it. It had to erupt to public notice before we could take it seriously ourselves.

The meeting of thirteen of us in a motel room in New Orleans on November 9 was neither formal nor secret nor meant to start an organization rival to NOW or otherwise to split the women's movement further. We all agreed that the women's movement was in crisis, that real differences in ideology as well as the destructive power struggles had to be dealt with, and that it was essential to have a national feminist organization committed to the goals of equality. The idea was to save NOW as the mainstream of the American women's movement, and make it more responsive to the needs and problems of women in that mainstream.

It was stunning to me and to others, and a reminder of the true strength of the women's movement, that "Thirteen NOW

Leaders Form Dissident 'Network' " would merit front-page
headlines in the *New York Times*. *Time* magazine (November 24)
called it "Womanswar," coming "at a time when much of feminism's early momentum is gone." The *Washington Post* (November 30) headlined "NOW Faces Major Crisis," stating:
"They campaigned under the banner: 'Out of the mainstream,
into the revolution.' While they won control of the National
Organization for Women . . . the victory of the group called
the Majority Caucus has not yet eased a year-long war within
the nation's largest and most powerful feminist organization.

"The crisis may be unparalleled in NOW's twelve-year history. And ratification of the Equal Rights Amendment which
has stalled four states short of the number needed to become
part of the Constitution, may be in jeopardy if NOW's support
for it is weakened by internal dissension."

The headlines proclaiming the New Orleans meeting—and
the events that led up to it—as a serious "split" signaling the
death of the women's movement were both exaggerated and
premature. But the division within NOW had been building
for several years. There have always been differences, divisions, disagreements of ideology—and seeming ideological differences masking simple power struggles—in the short life of
the women's movement. Why wouldn't there be? The remarkable thing about the women's movement, up to now, has been
our ability to come together from all our different starting
points, with all our differences of belief and style. The remarkable thing was that in those early years women were able to
get together and work together with a singularity of purpose
and focused effort men have seldom equaled.

When did divisions and power struggles, even radical "crazies" become dangerous to the women's movement? The much
respected newsletter *Spokeswoman* (December 15, 1975) provides one clue:

> In the middle of the worst economy since the Great Depres-
> sion, women are literally *watching* their hard-won gains being
> stripped away from them. . . . We are facing an uphill battle
> against well-organized, well-funded opposition on the right—
> from the corporations that have never wanted to pay for past
> and present discrimination, and from their "cultural" right-

wing allies who promote the idea that we are responsible for our own problems, that our institutions may not be taken to task. . . . The women's movement has, in fact, had a few too many successes for the opposition's comfort, and might have a few more. . . .

Rumor has it that the Ford Administration will try to rescind the executive mechanism requiring affirmative action by federal contractors. . . . HEW is moving right along with its now-aggressive agenda for dismantling equal opportunity machinery in the academies. . . . The government is being less cautious about its always covert alliance with corporate interests: equal opportunity is a luxury "we" just can't afford right now. . . .

In part, our diversion into in-fighting and dead ends has been a by-product of the opposition economic equality—with all its implications for power—faces from big business, church and state.

If we are honest, we will face the fact that while many women have new aspirations, have gone back to school or moved into work more adventurously, many other women have been fired in their fight against sex discrimination. If we allow the laws against sex discrimination in education and employment to be loosely enforced or even taken off the books, if we let the ERA slip by with its constitutional guarantee of equality—we can expect to see other women laid off, not promoted, blocked again by sex-discriminating training programs and professional school quotas.

To move on to the next stage in our development, we must forge new alliances with male labor leaders and far-sighted public and corporate planners, take new approaches to hours, public service employment, negative income tax, education, seniority, welfare, Social Security, and old age. There is immense resistance to these changes from some quarters. Aside from the direct economic threat to institutions like insurance companies—who profit by paying lower benefits to women and who are beginning to be seriously annoyed by all the new laws and regulations undoing sex discrimination against women in credit and mortgages, and all the rest—there is a pervasive threat to all corporate profiteers in eliminating that substratum of helpless, anonymous, unorganized female labor:

the women who used to be brought into work when needed and laid off or persuaded to go home again in tighter times, the virtually invisible women who quit when they got married or had kids and never stayed around long enough to fight for their rights or accumulate benefits. The new generations, not expecting to quit, demanding promotion and benefits equal to men, and knowing sex discrimination is against the law are a danger.

Similarly, in the religious sphere, the women emerging from the passive, helpless fear of unwanted pregnancy shadowing their lives—once they find that power to control their own bodies, how blindly will they follow other dictates from the priests? When women get so independent they define their own sexual terms, will they ever again acquiesce in John Birch campaigns against pornography or in any questioning of freedom?

It is not an accident that the forces of reaction financed by big money have converged to stop the women's movement—money which the government bloodhounds tracking down other pernicious corporate influences on American life have somehow not bothered to investigate. But this is only one enemy. There is another enemy within—ourselves.

A cannibalization of leadership has set in at the core of the women's movement, both in NOW and in the radical women's groups and the women's centers. It is a power struggle so acute and finally so vicious that, finally, only those who can devote twenty-four hours a day to the movement can play— women who have made the women's movement their sole profession, their career, their sole road to glory, even their personal life.

Even as the new aspirations of women clashed with economic reality—and with the powers massed against us that made the sort of victories we had won so easily before harder to gain—*the struggle for power in the movement itself* focused energies further inward, away from the tough economic problems, onto sexual issues that threatened no one. And not only that, the struggle within NOW corrupted everyone to the point where they evaded dealing even with their real differences on those sexual issues.

For instance, for several years no one in NOW has dared

speak out against a preoccupation with the issue of lesbianism. Neither I nor probably anyone else left in NOW disagrees with the rights of sexual privacy and sexual preference, and the need to end statutes or practices oppressing or discriminating against homosexuals. However, lesbian rights as one issue among many on the agenda of the women's movement is one thing—lesbian rights as the main issue, the hallmark, is something else. It got so that no one running for office in NOW dared say out loud that lesbian rights was one issue being twisted way out of proportion to the danger of the movement as a whole, though many thought so. In New Orleans, we finally began to discuss the misuse of the issue of lesbian rights in the women's movement—and women who happened to be lesbian were as definitive about that misuse as the no-longer-intimidated straight women. (When the account of that meeting appeared in the newspapers, Mary Jean Tully and I got letters demanding that we repudiate our implicit "heterosexism"!)

Does it help a woman liberate herself, does she become more equal, when she makes love to a woman instead of a man? I doubt it. I think it just evades the issue. It's something any woman can do without breaking through barriers in the office or school, or threatening those in power. It doesn't require any ability, cost or earn money, risk any test or change any institution. As an expression of sexual preference, to each her own. But as a political statement, it's a copout.

I think the main reason so many women came up to me in the noisy chaos of that convention in Philadelphia, or have written to me in despair and outrage, is simply that *the real differences were never articulated* there, for the women themselves to discuss and decide. If my crisis meeting in New Orleans with past and present leaders of NOW finally made us face these differences, so be it. The danger to the movement of women in America, to the gains we have made in ten years, to the ability of our daughters to live out their aspirations, can no longer be denied.

Can we, or they, continue to live out our aspirations for equality in the mainstream of American society if, in fact, the women's movement is destroyed as an effective force? Will individual women in the next ten and twenty years continue to be able to change their own lives if there is not an effective women's movement to support them?

These are the questions that I have been asking myself lately. And these questions have begun to make me uneasy. They are not rhetorical questions. I am not at all sure of the answers. I tell myself, what does it really matter if a makeshift organization like NOW should in effect go down the drain as new leaders fight each other for power because they have lost heart to fight the external enemy; lost heart to find new allies among former "male chauvinist pigs" in unions, black organizations, even corporations; lost heart to reach out to those formerly timid, frightened, even antagonistic women who now want to join and feel part of the women's movement, but don't identify with the rhetoric of "revolution against oppression"?

I came down from my own ivory tower to the messy real world of NOW to plead "unity, unity." I now believe that "unity" is a specious plea unless the real differences of ideology and strategy that have split the movement apart—and have kept it from reaching out and bringing in the new power embodied in all those women out there—are faced.

They should not be swept under the table any longer in a mushy, anxiety-ridden need to hang on unquestioningly to "sisterhood": no matter who says what—no matter if it all slips away. Our responsibility is to the truth that will make our movement grow. Consciousness is connected to energy, action, the burning wish to change one's life. Consciousness doesn't happen in a vacuum. Self-pity and the prejudices of hate do not change anyone's life. There is a terrible temptation to stay put, shouting the old "NO" in a louder and louder voice, shaking one's fists in anger and maybe even talking of guerrilla warfare in the streets, taking karate lessons, playing at toy bombs—or else to transfer one's energies altogether into the creating of "alternate" perfect feminist-Amazonian institutions, because it is so much less dangerous to fight other powerless women than to take on the institutions and complexities of real power in this world. But the power of the movement comes from the desire of women, tens of millions by now, to change their own lives, and if the energy is not directed at the real world they live in, there will be no power worth fighting for.

I am not the only one to see this as the crux of the crisis. As the *Spokeswoman* put it (December 15, 1975):

> We are people of high energy, energy that must be expended *somewhere*. The first places we turn are our own institutions and organizations. We have correctly and consciously tried to identify and reject those structures of male society which are unjust and oppressive. We have experimented in our institutions with non-hierarchical, non-authoritarian systems; we have rejected 'media star' leaders, elites. We have had some success in making these concepts work for us, as we have had some success in making traditionally organized institutions in the larger society more responsible to women. The problem comes when we are not so successful and, needing to place blame for our own failures, begin to place it on each other. We begin to believe that the significant fight must be waged *first* internally. Frustrated by our slow progress in building the new society outside, we work, at least, to make our own smaller "societies" embody our principles—*with absolute purity*. Because of this demand for purity, our rejection of elites can become a rejection of all leadership; our discomfort with hierarchy, a distrust of all structures; our belief in democracy an intolerance for representation. We feel that no one speaks for us. Each of us is too important.
>
> The sphere of action gets smaller, and can get smaller still. Where consciousness causes great personal upheaval, there is great need for resolution. *The idea that one's own life can embody the future society is a very attractive one.* It resolves all of the tension between public and private actions: divorcing one's husband, having an abortion, sleeping with women thus become revolutionary acts.
>
> But apart from our lives, they are not. Changing consciousness is a lifetime process, the basis for political struggle, not the struggle itself. . . . Political consciousness turned inward is dying consciousness. Sisterhood means little if it cannot alter the conditions of our lives. . . . Our lives are shaped by outside forces. We must act together against those forces or we cannot win.

•   •   •

I have been reading the previous history of the women's movement in this country and in Britain. There was consciousness as acute as ours, maybe more acute, among those who first fought for the women "before God and the law" in the seventeenth through the early twentieth centuries. And time and again over these centuries, when the victories were incomplete the pendulum swung back again—and the new consciousness was blotted out as if it had never existed. And the heroines of herstory were buried out of history, or their very lives were revised into images of witches and monstrous freaks. And fifty years later, women like me would emerge, and in frustration and agony would start to invent the movement all over again, and would in wonder rediscover those heroines, the minutest traces of whom had been so obliterated that the premises on which they had moved were no longer even dreamed of by their granddaughters.

The same danger is seen by thoughtful radical feminists. "Sister," an article privately published in New Haven because *Ms.*, which commissioned it, refused to print it, points out:

> Even if the ERA is passed, with no organizations to insure that it is implemented, it will be a hollow (although necessary) victory. The first women's movement won suffrage at a time when its vital organizations had disappeared. Despite the vote, the position of women began to decline steadily.
>
> Our national organizations are moving towards deepening factional convulsions; our mass-based local organizations, present just a couple of years ago in so many cities, have disappeared, or have become so small and splintered as to be almost invisible. . . . Women's liberation is not for a few hundred or even a few thousand women. It must be for millions of women.
>
> The present inward focus and demand for total twenty-four-hour dedication are among the reasons . . . feminist collectives, coffeehouses and print shops in existence six months ago are gone now. What appears at first to be a flowering of institutions is also a needle scratching back and forth across a broken track, a revolving door of misspent energy, a failure to accumulate and build . . . a dodge, a feminine mystique, a refusal to hear the cries of a movement treading water, an abdication of responsibility. . . . Our organizations and our alternate institutions die from internal bleeding long before they succumb to external pressure. . . . They die because we deny the reality of our conflicts and fail to provide formal, open, democratic channels for their resolution. . . .
>
> The idea of a women's consciousness which is unstoppable is a collapse into mysticism. There is absolutely no historical, sociological, or psychological basis to assume that without our

bringing about real changes in the social order our consciousness will continue to grow, or even that it will continue to be
maintained. . . . The consciousness articulated at Seneca Falls
in 1848 vanished. What will happen to ours? Without a movement to support it, consciousness veers off, turns inward toward self-hatred or destructive mysticism, and finally, dies.

I hear you, Sister! The vote for women was won in the
United States the year before I was born, after a century of
passionate struggle. In the year 2000, will some harassed,
guilty daughter of my daughter's generation have to start all
over again?

• • • •

I don't necessarily think such pendulum swings are automatic in history. Too many women have changed their lives—
and would have had to change their lives, whether or not we
ever said those words. This time it's not a question of a few
rights on paper, a few laws or philosophical arguments. The
great majority of women are now working in jobs outside the
isolation of their homes because they have to. How can they
go home again when half work to support families for which
they are the sole provider, and the other half because their
second paychecks are essential if the whole family is not to
subside into poverty? In a front-page warning the *Wall Street
Journal* advised (February 2, 1976):

> Does your wife work? No? Then maybe you'd better try to
> get her a job. The age of the two-paycheck family has arrived in
> a very big way. And, whatever impact it may have on such
> things as child care and household maintenance, its economic
> impact on family income is tremendous. The "man of the
> house" whose solitary toil still has to bring in all the family
> cash is at an increasingly severe disadvantage. It is no longer a
> matter of the Smiths keeping up with the Joneses. The big one
> is the question of Mr. Smith keeping up with Mr. and Mrs.
> Jones.

The close of 1975 saw more adult women at work than ever
before—more than before the recession, while a million fewer
men worked than before the recession. Working wives now
number 19,835,000 in the United States, up 205 percent since

1947, when only 6,502,000 wives held jobs. Tracing this "massive shift in the family breadwinning department" since World War II, the *Wall Street Journal* says:

> In 1947, the working husbands outnumbered the working wives nearly five to one. In 1975 it was less than two to one. And presumably, the trend will continue. The muscle civilization is gone. Women can shuffle office papers as well as men. . . .
>
> One thing is certain. If the income brought into family coffers by the womenfolk of the country were suddenly cut off, the nation's high-flying "standard of living" would collapse overnight.

Add to this picture the enormous increase in single-parent families and the great number of women now living alone—and the great weight of economic necessity supports our movement for equality. The nation depends on it. The economic crisis may be making it tougher and tougher to make new gains for women—but this time the women can't go home again.

However, in that year 2000, a lot of women may be bitterly working outside the home and in it as well, and cursing our name in history if our movement gets stuck in the middle. This revolution always meant more, has to mean more, than a few women getting jobs only men held before, and a lot of women wearing themselves out with long hours of office work on top of the same long hours they have always worked at home. Saying no to the feminine mystique, and organizing to confront sex discrimination, was only Stage I. We have somehow to transcend the polarities, even the rage of our own "no," to get on to Stage II: the restructuring of all our institutions on a basis of real equality for women and men, the "new yes." The dynamics involved here are both economic and sexual; the energies whereby we live and love and work and eat, which have been so subverted by power in the past, can be truly liberated here, in the service of life for all of us—or diverted in fruitless impotent reaction.

The paradox could almost be charted mathematically: to the degree that we turn inward in unreal sexual fantasy and shadow warplay of hate against each other or men—to that degree we alienate the real sources of new energy waiting out there. But if we turned our own intense energy outward again, we could at last mobilize in numbers sufficient to overcome the last-ditch forces now massed against us.

Consider! A month after the defeats of the state ERA's in New York and New Jersey, the Harris poll reported that 65 percent of all women endorse "most efforts to strengthen and change women's status in society," but only 17 percent feel "most organizations trying to change women's status in society are helping the cause of women." Reported Louis Harris:

"One significant clue to the gap between the popularity of the cause and the relative coolness toward women's rights organizations is that a 62%–29% majority of women does not feel that women are an 'oppressed group' in America. . . . It is clear that if women's organizations campaign for women's rights in the name of 'liberating women from oppression' they are going to ride into a storm of disbelief."

In earlier Harris surveys, more men than women advocated greater opportunities for women. "However," says Harris, "this has now changed drastically, and women feel much more strongly than men about achieving equal rights and opportunities for women. But as women have become more conscious and articulate about their status, they have also become more selective about the leaders and groups they want to speak for them. And the early rhetoric describing women as a downtrodden, oppressed and largely disenfranchised sex increasingly strikes most women as neither accurate nor a rallying cry they will respond to."

Women, like most other Americans, have become cynical about mere rhetoric from right or left, adherents of the feminine mystique or a mystical "Mother Right," *McCall's* or *Ms.* Waiting on line at 3:00 A.M. to vote at the NOW convention in Philadelphia, a woman in front of me from Michigan was saying, "But I want to be in the mainstream. That's what I've been out of, as a woman. That's why I'm in the women's movement." And a student in New York, working as a paralegal in order to raise money to go to law school, said, "They may say the women's movement is dead, but I think the movement of women has gone beyond the ones who thought they

were the women's movement. Your organization, using slogans that sound like the sixties, seems backward to me. But the
women's movement can't stop. I want to get into law school
and I want to get married and have children. I'm not sure I
can pull it all together as easily as all that unless more real
changes are made."

•   •   •

The division within the movement—or the seeming division between the leadership of the movement and the majority
of American women who now support equality, but not
"women's lib"—may simply reflect different stages of the liberation of that enormous energy of women, so long suppressed. Some have so little confidence in their ability to really
change their own lives, much less the world, that for them the
hate, the rhetoric, the little power they can achieve in the
movement itself is all. They are the ones who seemed wedded
to the most vengeful, purist, zealot dictates of feminist
"revolution"—and who are most scornful of "male ego trips,"
"power trips," and "elitism" when it comes to mundane matters such as fighting for job or professional decision-making
opportunities. They make women feel guilty who are advancing in their own profession, or who even dress well; they de-
nounce with scorn the "white, middle-class" existence of most
women in the movement, which is the existence of the majority of women in America. They are the ones who say the
movement should turn its back on the backlash against affirmative action progress in universities, and the threats to sex-
discrimination programs that have enabled women to advance
into professions. They say the movement's main concerns
need to be racism, poverty, rape and lesbian rights, everything
and anything but the problems of white middle-class American women. But in fact they themselves are usually white middle-class American women, and sometimes it seems as if they
are using the women's movement as a game to escape the reality of their own problems as women—instead of accepting the
responsibility and power to do something about those problems.

People wondered why "Alice Doesn't" failed to mobilize
women almost anywhere to "strike against the system,"
whereas five years earlier the women's strike for equality

brought out women in joyous, effective displays of energy and action across the nation. The very success of our movement is the reason for the difference. By the very nature of our progress, women now have more to lose.

It was a profound misunderstanding of the reality of the women's movement to believe that most women in America would strike "against the system." To want equality, a voice in the mainstream, to be a part of the action of the system: that is what the women's movement is about, and these things in turn liberate new values from female experience, which changes the system.

The strike on August 26, 1970, was for equality. In those years when our movement was young, women were in such a mood to act and so few had been anywhere near an organized group that all it took was a small enthusiastic core group and a call all women could respond to. There were only thirty NOW chapters then, but, with the larger coalition I put together in New York, that was enough to spark a national action in the style of the sixties. As the media covered the action, we in effect discovered our own movement. If it had failed, there would have been little to lose. The women's movement was still so small then that nothing serious was expected of it.

By October 1975, the situation was quite different. Women were organized in their fields and professions, and were moving ahead seriously on equality. As the newspapers reported, those who had mobilized in Chicago or in Colorado coffeehouses in 1970, or who had marched down Fifth Avenue, were in the library working on Ph.D. theses or trying cases in court in 1975. Further, NOW chapters were now in seven hundred cities, and were beginning to have some power, working on specific issues. The 1970 action had been endorsed by the convention membership of NOW, to whom I presented it. There is a reason why strikes are voted by the memberships of unions before they are called by the leadership. There is too much to lose—in bargaining power—if the members in fact don't follow. Strikes are called only on demands of some urgency to the workers, when normal bargaining fails.

If I had been consulted by the leaders of NOW I'd have advised against "Alice Doesn't" despite the fact it reproduced the outer form of my own idea five years earlier. But we were in a different place now.

Women moving into those good jobs we'd demanded were now threatened by layoffs; they were organized into groups at work with real demands which would have been jeopardized by a strike "against the system." "Alice Doesn't" seemed frivolous to them; it embarrassed them.

In New York, with ERA on the ballot, NOW leaders would have nothing to do with "Alice Doesn't." They called to warn me that, if asked, I shouldn't *knock* it—but I should just say that in this state we are not taking part, our concern is ERA. Unfortunately, a national strike which fails weakens the power of women everywhere. I now believe that we who knew it was a disastrous idea should have said so in time, because those who went along, rather than cause further dissonance of sisterhood, in fact colluded in a failure of responsibility of leadership.

The women's movement loses its power when it no longer energizes, and is energized by, great numbers of real women. But those who have used the women's movement for their own power or profit or personal glory make a serious mistake if they think they can now proceed ahead alone on that glory road, take the gains, and let the movement go. Certain female politicians who were in fact elected as champions of women somehow conceived the notion that the ERA would only succeed if its skirts were cleansed of any taint of feminism; the women's movement wasn't needed any more. A very broad coalition of the sort that *Ms.* had put together on paper for a so-called National Women's Agenda—stretching from Hadassah and the Junior League to the Girl Scouts—was supposedly going to put ERA across.

So the energy of the women's movement was not solicited —was in fact discouraged from the campaign.

True, the women's movement was also involved in internal battles. But the point was, we who were responsible for the emergence of the Equal Rights Amendment and for the general rebirth of equality between the sexes were told by those whom our own new power had elected that our energies were no longer needed. The reason ERA was defeated in the fall of '75 in two of the most progressive states of the union, where in fact the women's movement is strongest, is that political bosses wanted to use the power they got from the women's movement—without the substance or the energy of the movement itself! It was not just the overpoweringly financed campaign of lies spread by reactionary enemies of ERA that did the amendment in, it was the misappropriation of the movement by its own political friends, including women elected in its name. But their own political fortunes faltered with that ERA defeat.

I hope they now understand—those who have been elected to office or who reaped profit or glory from the momentum of the women's movement—that that new power in the world is only yours as long as you truly serve it and respect it. And if you think you can take that power and let the movement go—what really is your power then? And, now that we are being honest, you who owe your new progress in law school, medical school, businesses, professions, and art to the women's movement—if you don't acknowledge that debt by action and commitment to the movement, where will you lose your momentum?

A woman recently divorced, struggling, working, starts to tell me about her new life and all its problems. I say, "Would you go back?" "Of course not," she says, "I'm alive now. But I must admit, the problems do increase geometrically. It's not like I thought it would be." My own daughter, at nineteen definitely not a radical feminist because, being my daughter, she has to be "my own me," still takes it absolutely all for granted—that she will go to medical school or be a research scientist, and have *her* two or three children which she will bring up equally with her husband without all her mother's stupid conflicts and problems. Then suddenly she learns from the newspapers that the women's movement is in trouble. She subjects me to worried, accusing interrogation. "What went wrong? Is it serious?" She might joke about all those childhood hours collating NOW stencils in her infancy—but her very confidence takes for granted the women's movement. "For instance," she says to me, reproving my neglect, "how can they continue doing all these things, the women in places like Spokane and Peoria, if the whole thing falls apart in the middle?" But if your future is involved, daughter mine, as indeed it is—

though I'd never say I did it for you, we all did it for ourselves
—don't you think it's time you got in there and took responsibility for the next stage, too?

                          •   •   •

The alternative, again, is to get stopped short of real equality. When that happens, disillusionment sets in, and with it
comes backlash. The women who are already moving in backlash against us are the most afraid, the weakest, the ones who
have most reason to feel insecure as women in this complex,
changing society.

Have you ever spoken head-on to one of the followers of
Total Womanhood or the Pussycat League or the League of
Housewives? They are truly vicious, the fearful sisters; they
make the most rabid feminist seem loving and serene. They
are afraid their husbands won't support them any longer if the
ERA is passed, afraid their husbands will leave them without
the threat of alimony. If they learn how to play totally passive,
to greet him at the door bare-ass or draped in ostrich feathers,
to pretend to swoon with ecstasy while icy cool, will that
great, big, wonderful man they were brought up to expect
would take care of them for the rest of their lives still be there?

Maybe not. Those ladies are right to be afraid. Because
without ERA, marriages *are* ending in divorce, men *are* leaving and not paying child support or alimony. In the present
economic situation men are losing jobs and are failing to keep
up the payments on the house or the car. Phyllis Schlafly need
not be afraid, though. She has taken advantage of the new
possibilities opened to women by our movement to go to law
school. She gets well paid for telling other, more frightened
women that all they have to do is stop the likes of us who dare
to ask for equality. Lately their hate squads seem to turn up
wherever I speak; those well-dressed women with teased, set
hair seem consumed in some way by an icy, burning rage, like
dry ice. Once one spat at me.

There is a phenomenon of a certain kind of hate called
"ressentiment" described by a famous European sociologist,
Max Scheler. It is a phenomenon experienced by a people or a
group who over a period of time are so continually and hopelessly frustrated in human dignity that they no longer experience the unfulfilled need as a specific frustration. They are in a

permanent state of hopeless, free-floating rage or anger, which can be manipulated by the powerful with whom they identify into lynch-mob fury against persons or groups who try to be free. What distinguishes these hate-filled sufferers of *"ressentiment"*—besides the scorching intensity of their own permanent, free-floating hate—is their craven, obsequious subservience to the ruling classes: they identify with their own oppressors. Thus it was in Germany that the clerks and civil servants and the lumpen proletariat provided the reservoir of *"ressentiment"* that was ignited by Hitler and the Nazis into the holocaust which sent six million Jews to the gas chambers, along with trade unionists, intellectuals and others who dared to speak out and organize against their real oppressors.

The women whose fearful dependence makes them buy Total Womanhood and wear those slavish ostrich-feather masks, what do they really feel in bed at night? When women's assertive, life-affirming energies are turned against themselves, the sexual source of love is perverted into hate, and this is transmuted to men in a reservoir of violence that finally serves death. I would like another lifetime to trace down the clues to this process in psychology, anthropology, and history, whereby energies turned from the service of life become diverted to the service of death.

The real revolutionary importance of the women's movement is that we are breaking that vicious circle. We are liberating women from that *"ressentiment"* which finally subverts her very power to love. By freeing women to move in the mainstream, we are also liberating the sexual energies which have been manipulated by dictators and demogogues. As I wrote in the epilogue of the tenth anniversary edition of *The Feminine Mystique:*

> I think the energy locked up in those obsolete masculine and feminine roles is the social equivalent of the physical energy locked up in the realm of $E=MC^2$—the force that unleashed the holocaust of Hiroshima. I believe the locked-up sexual energies have helped to fuel more than anyone realizes the terrible violence erupting in the nation and the world during these past ten years. If I am right, the sex-role revolution will liberate

those energies from the service of death and will make it really possible for men and women to make love, not war.

How do we find the new path? How do we break that vicious circle? We cannot do it by turning away from the world of men and power, by playing revolution, by creating Amazonian communes, by telling ourselves that women are really the first sex ("Who wants to be president of General Motors?"). We can't break the vicious circle by treading water or losing our movement's momentum and vision while we concentrate on fighting for power within our own organizations.

What we have to do as a movement is set up simple democratic channels for open, even impassioned discussion of basic issues and strategies, instead of trying to manipulate each other covertly. Let the members decide—and may the best woman win! And if the differences are really irreconcilable, let those who want to talk of guerrilla action in the streets and feminist violence have one kind of organization, and those who believe that equality for women and participation in the mainstream is the real revolution have another—like the British suffragettes did, when one group could not go along with the methods of violence the others finally resorted to.

At this writing, I believe the open differences in NOW will be resolved and ways will be created for representation and for decision-making by the membership on the future organization which the woman's movement still needs. Maybe room will be found for both approaches to serve goals like the ERA, and younger women will take over leadership from older ones. And some will begin to find new ways to work with men on Stage II: the restructuring of institutions.

The powers against us need not prevail if we can get ourselves together. The men who need that second paycheck from a working wife, wives themselves, the daughters with new aspirations, all the women who have to support themselves and/or families—they are the overwhelming majority of this country. And if the *Wall Street Journal* sees it, the rest of the capitalist Establishment or at least its intelligence must realize that if the women went home again, this whole inflated economy would collapse overnight. Sure, sex discrimination was profitable—still is for some companies. But for the economy as a whole—yes, even under rotten old capitalism, which may or may not have the power to regenerate itself—equality between the sexes, participation of women, with all the rewards thereof, is becoming one of the main sources of new energy.

I can see the horror mounting in my fellow revolutionaries: "Are you arguing that the movement of women to equality won't die because capitalism needs us to make money, now, to buy their goods?" Partly. But we might not be so easily manipulated now to buy what we don't need if that audience of pent-up, helpless, greedy women no longer sits there living vicariously in front of the television set.

More to the point, the movement of women from passive objects to active participation is converging on other movements that together hold the clues, the dynamism and the power to restructure the institutions. On a plane back from Tennessee where I was debating ERA last week, I picked up the *Mainliner* magazine United Airlines provides for its business-executive travelers. It was a special issue on "The Changing American Work Ethic," and the cover story was "Why Should Sammy Run Anymore?" It was certainly not a feminist tract. In it, Studs Terkel reported the rebellion of men in occupations ranging from "sanitary engineers" (garbagemen) to "account executives" (salesmen) against meaningless work in euphemistic disguise. After interviewing 133 working people, Terkel concluded: "The widely held idea that only youth is questioning the work ethic is a myth. Today, most people want more leisure time for their families, for studying, for hobbies. Above all, people are searching for daily meaning in their jobs. They want recognition and the satisfaction of a good job well done. . . . The new work ethic, it if works well at all, may mean changing the four-letter word—work—into a six-letter word—growth. And that may just be the carrot that will keep the system functioning smoothly for both generations." And a section in that same magazine on "the shrinking work week" sketched as trends here to stay the four-day, forty-hour work week—and even three-day work weeks—as well as Flextime, where workers decide what time they will come in to work and leave, instead of that rigid nine-to-five day.

In the beginning some critics used to say that women were fighting to get into the mainstream, the rat race, the job world, just as smart young men—and old ones too—wanted to get out of it. But women as well as men need the security of enough food to to eat, and the skills and opportunity for meaningful work, and the recognition and reward for it, to be able to choose to live life for human values. When a man no longer shares the whole breadwinning burden, he can think in terms of work satisfaction, not just of the paycheck. And one of the meaningful parts of life men want to share more of now is the family—those very chores which became burdensome to many women, when they were chained and isolated by them.

It is not easy to transcend polarities. There is a dialectic to it, as Marx said: thesis, antithesis, synthesis. *Reaction*—the mere overthrow of power, the exchange of roles—is not real revolution and finally turns against itself. But the creation of the "new yes" can only come from strength. When women turn away from that inward-staring circle and use their new energies to confront and restructure the institutions in which they live and work, they discover a new power in themselves that comes from the participation, the equality. No woman is born with that power, nor men either. It comes from testing oneself and realizing one's human potential in the tasks and challenges of society from which women had been barred. (I doubt that strength can ever come from consciousness-raising alone—or from "assertiveness training.")

In *The Uses of Literacy*, Richard Hoggart quotes Chekhov:

> "Do, please, write a story of how a young man, the son of a serf, who has been a shop boy, a chorister, pupil of a secondary school, and a university graduate, who has been brought up to respect work and to kiss the priest's hand, to bow to other people's ideas, to be thankful for each morsel of bread, who has been thrashed many a time, who has had to walk about tutoring without galoshes, who has fought, tormented animals, has been fond of dining at the house of well-to-do relations, and played the hypocrite both to God and man without any need but merely out of consciousness of his own insignificance—describe how that young man squeezes the slave out of himself, drop by drop, and how, awakening one fine morning, he feels running in his veins no longer the blood of a slave but genuine human blood."

When that finally happens to women—and I sense it is happening in many of us, I sense it in myself—I doubt we'll wake up one morning, any of us, as a "Female Man" (the brilliant science-fiction novel by Joanna Russ which describes the polarized manworld/womanworld we create in reaction, trying to climb out of that world. That's merely female *machismo*.)

Science fiction has fascinated me lately in my search for the "new yes." In a wonderful book called *The Left Hand of Darkness* by Ursula LeGuin I found this passage:

> How to break the circle? They say here: "All roads lead to Mishnory." To be sure, if you turn your back on Mishnory and walk away from it, you are still on the Mishnory road. To oppose vulgarity is inevitably to be vulgar. You must go somewhere else; you must have another goal; then you walk a different road.

In *The Left Hand of Darkness*, there is no sex-role polarization. There are human beings who in "kemmer"—the period every few weeks when all are infused with sexual passion—variously become man or woman to each other's man or woman, and father or mother to a child.

We don't reach the "new yes" of sexual liberation—human liberation—just by saying "no" to male power. The road away from Mishnory—the reaction against an excessively powerless femininity and an excessively dominant masculinity—is still the road of sex-role polarization.

I keep remembering how some years ago at a conference on the female orgasm held by marriage counselors, sexologists and other therapists in Chicago, I heard a bunch of balding, authoritative male experts decry the absence of female orgasm, and Masters and Johnson reported for the first time on the amazing results that could be achieved with mechanical devices. I shocked that conference by saying they might do more for sex—and the female orgasm—by considering the conditions of women's lives, as they affected her feelings about herself and men, than by promoting these mechanical contraptions to bring a twitch out of her.

In the years that followed, as women began to share their real feelings with each other, they expressed a mix of revulsion against and obsession with sex epitomized by a famous essay called "The Myth of the Vaginal Orgasm." There were conferences and workshops on sexuality where women taught other women how to masturbate with vibrators so they wouldn't be dependent on men, or the human penis, at all. In *Fear of Flying* Erica Jong had her heroine move from masochistic, rape-and-humiliation fantasies and sexual obsessions to the "zipless fuck"—where she reduced the male to a dehumanized sex instrument, the Playboy Bunny in reverse. Was this the sexual dream of liberated women?

I didn't think a thousand vibrators would make much difference—or that it mattered who was in the missionary position—if the unequal power positions in real life weren't changed. The "zipless fuck" was simply sexual revenge. The question is: How can we enjoy the true human differences of sex—male and female, yang and yin, passive and active—all the facets of male and female we each possess in varying degrees and can express in love or life, in passion or poetry? How can we evade the final fact that our humanity is *ours* as male and female if we are to truly realize ourselves? It was the *economic* imbalance, the power imbalance in the world that subverted sex, or made sex itself into a power game where no one could win.

Work and love, Freud said, are the two essentials of the human condition. The trouble is, the polarization of the two sexes in human society has also polarized work and love—economics as the male world, and love the female. Concepts of power ignore sex or treat women as a commodity. The sex therapists treat them like things too—as if sex, mechanized, could be divorced from love, or both from the world of work. In the real world of home and kitchen, bedroom and office, where we all live, economic power and sex are inescapable, and converge.

In unlikely places—doing a piece of film criticism on the movie *Husbands* for the *Sunday New York Times Magazine*, or participating in a panel discussion on masochism for *Viva*—I have tried to put into words my sense of how sex and our human needs for love were being distorted by these sex roles and their economic imbalance. I feel like a grim spoilsport sometimes, always insisting to my sisters in the movement on that dull economic basis that had to be changed for any woman to be able to enjoy her own sexuality, or to truly love anyone. It was so much easier and more fun just to talk about sex, vibrators, women, men, underneath or on top. But to extrapolate sexual joylessness and lonely need, masochism or cruelty as the permanent condition of women is in my opinion to give up the battle. This is the sexual pathology bred by our inequality and the reactions to it. The only way off the Mishnory road is equality.

*   *   *

I know now that I have fought for women because I did not find it good being a woman, and I wanted to. I knew my mother didn't like being a woman, and had good reason not to. And reacting in my determination not to be like her, I embraced the feminine mystique and for a while denied the very abilities and opportunities she had fought to inspire me to. I knew that she had such good reason to dislike being a woman —because of those abilities and energies like mine that she had no way to use—that she could not really enjoy her husband, her children, her home. Reacting against her, I would have forgone the use of my own abilities in society and sunk deeper into that vicious circle of *"ressentiment."*

Neither I nor any woman could break that vicious circle alone. We found our strength by confronting the conditions that made us what we were as women, and by acting together to change them.

"It changed my life," the women keep writing me. And they're right. Without the women's movement, how many of us could have had the strength to change our own lives, could have freed that energy we were turning against ourselves and used it to break through those barriers and move out to life?

I will wake up tomorrow morning having finally finished this book, and I will feel good about being a woman. And I will share the good news with a man whom I feel strong enough sometimes now to love quite helplessly, without defenses and even transcending the poles of myself, loving him.

And I will call my daughter, who already takes it all for granted. And then I will rearrange the furniture, buy a bathing suit, treat myself to an island vacation, get to work on the presidential campaign, decide not to do anything much about this crisis in the women's movement because I see you are beginning to solve it yourselves. I want to get to work on Stage II of the Sex-Role Revolution, the restructuring of our institutions. I want to move on now and change my own life.

And yet I think some day we may look back and realize that these years of our passionate historic world-opening journey have been the most intense life we, or anyone, could ever experience. And men who never had such problems, and women who were too ladylike to get involved, will envy us. For we have lived the second American revolution, and our very anger said a "new YES" to life.

Afterword 1985—see page 502

Afterwords

Afterword to "The National Women's Political Caucus" (pp. 221–32)

In 1984, the National Women's Political Caucus—which had grown strong, developed many good leaders and helped elect many women to office in the different states and to defeat their enemies, in the twelve years that followed those birth pains—was joined by NOW in demanding a woman on the national ticket. NOW had never endorsed a presidential candidate before, but Reagan's war on ERA and abortion, his gutting of sex discrimination laws and social programs, and above all, the threat of nuclear war in his macho foreign policy, seemed to demand this political move. The machinery the Caucus had in place for a floor fight, if necessary, at the Democratic Convention, helped make NOW's "outside" pressure for a woman on the ticket invincible, although NOW, as usual, was criticized for its unladylike "toughness."

Even after 1984, however, when women's political power got a woman nominated for vice president by a major national party for the first time in history, the questions implied here remain. The "gender gap"—the difference that emerged in 1980 and 1982 between women's vote and men's for various candidates and on various issues—was not so clear in 1984.

But the fact that a woman on the ticket was not a major

consideration one way or the other meant that in one important way the work begun with the founding of the National Women's Political Caucus had already achieved its aim: as a matter of course, from now on women will be a part of the pool from which candidates will be selected, by any party, for city, state, or national office. Women, by rule, constitute half the delegates at Democratic conventions—as a result of Caucus efforts in the past—and the Republicans had to make real efforts to bring women in, to compete for that "women's vote" in 1984. We must remind ourselves that the gender gap did not even exist before the women's movement.

So women now have to face new concrete realities of political power in the United States. After 1984 we must face up to questions that go beyond the simple matter of getting more women elected, getting that first wedge in the door, that first voice, which we needed the Caucus for. For not only women but men who have concerns for peace, democratic rights, and human values recognize the need for "new ideas," new political thinking—in the Democratic Party, the Republican Party, the labor unions, even the leftwing groups—relating the values of equality, concern for life, peace, and freedom to the economic, technological, and demographic realities of the last quarter of the 20th century. We must acknowledge politically what we ourselves have helped to create—the desire to share the good life that now drives all the millions who make up the American mainstream, the "middle," including countless women who are using those rights and opportunities we won. A central question is whether women will be better served by maintaining separate caucuses or by insisting that we be an integral part of the search for a new political center that is taking place now, in city, state and nation, in both parties.

Women constitute more than 50 percent of Democratic voters now; they should be the vital heart of Democratic policy-making. But since the '84 election, I sense that women are being dealt into Democratic policy-making even less than before; some male politicos would even make feminists the scapegoats for Mondale's disaster, as if, again, the "white male vote" is all that counts. As of this writing, few women are taking part in these discussions—and "women's issues" are not being discussed. But child care and abortion are now more than "women's issues." Should women themselves still be addressed in "special interest," "single issue" terms?

Can any *woman*, facing the dilemmas of survival in this nation and world, at this end of the century, be persuaded that women's rights, women's equality, is the most important issue requiring her energy and passion—especially if she is already enjoying a measure of that equality, the exercise of those rights we won? And yet, with those rights in danger now, if she does not join with others to save them—and raise her voice to demand commitment to those rights from any candidate or party who wants her vote—where will she be in 1994, who will fight for her?

Afterword to "Madame Prime Minister" (pp. 339–64)

I was planning to return to India in the spring of 1985 to see for myself how Indira Gandhi was using her power, in the face of her nation's complex problems twenty years later. I had been disturbed by the various reports of her incursions on civil liberties; she had seemed such a great believer in democracy. I admired the Indians' zest for democracy, despite the severe problems that could make them easy prey to authoritarian solutions. It has always seemed to me that Indira Gandhi got a bad press in America because of her insistence that India remain independent, unaligned in the polarization between the two great superpowers—and possibly because she was a woman.

I wanted to see what enabled her to hold her country together, keep her people's confidence, despite all the predators from without and warring religious and political factions within, which she had managed to keep in uneasy unity for her nation to survive. Those religious differences, I had learned when I was with her in India, have often been fanned into zealotry and violence by political enemies of India's independence, who have their own agendas for the subcontinent. How tragic, then, for Indira Gandhi to be assassinated this winter of 1984, in her prime, by a guard in her own household, in a new wave of religious zealotry. I last saw her, at the UN

General Assembly a year ago, as a leader of the nonaligned nations, pleading to the superpowers for an end to the nuclear missile buildup.

Even that brief firsthand glimpse of India's complex terrible problems of poverty, and of a population whose growth dooms it to even deeper poverty unless it learns to control its own reproduction, left me in incredulous awe at the complex, flexible leadership demanded of—and given by—Indira Gandhi to help her people keep control of their own destiny. She made me realize that women could have a different political style from men's—though, in a world still ruled by men, they have to survive against, and learn to use, the tactics and weapons of men's sometimes brutal political games.

Afterword to "A Visit with Pope Paul" (pp. 368–86)

Ten years later, in 1985, the Vatican and the Catholic hierarchy, under another Pope, have still not come to terms with the personhood of women. This Pope and his new archbishops in America are adamant that women cannot be priests, that women must not use any form of birth control, including abortion, that will enable them to choose when or whether to have a child, and that there is no debate or dissent on this monolithic doctrine. But more and more openly, nuns and priests, prominent Catholic laymen and women, and the National Council of Catholic Bishops in America are posing broader questions about "the right to life" and are, in fact, raising their voices in debate and dissent. That a believing Catholic woman was nominated for Vice President of the United States in 1984 and took a position, despite the opposition of a few archbishops, that women had a right to choose childbirth according to their own religious conscience, was a historic breakthrough.

But the bombing of abortion clinics, while law enforcers from the president down look the other way, is an evocation of brutal force against women's right to choose—so basic to her new personhood and her political and economic independence —that hints of Hitler's *Kristallnacht*. If neo-fascist forces con-

tinue to grow stronger in America, will women be the new
Jews?

Afterword to "Scary Doings in Mexico City"
(pp. 440–67)

Awaiting the end of the UN Decade on Women with a conference planned for Nairobi in July, 1985, women in various
parts of the world are less naïve. Women in the U.S., in pre-
liminary meetings; Yvette Roudy, Mitterand's Minister for
Women's Affairs in France; Jihan Sadat in Egypt; and women
I met with this past summer in Israel are determined to see to
it that the UN Conference on Women sets up some real machinery for advancement of women's rights the world over—
and makes some real statement about peace—instead of being
used as pawns for others' political agenda, as were the UN
women's conferences in Mexico City in 1975 and Copenhagen
in 1980.

In Copenhagen in 1980, it became clear to me that certain
powers in the world—Third World despots, Communist commissars, neofascist dictatorships, and even Western democracies that pay lip service to women's equality—manipulated or
allowed the so-called UN Conference on Women to become a
vehicle for another, much publicized attack on "Zionism as
racism" (the only news that came out of Copenhagen) as much
to prevent any real world organization on women's rights as
to voice another attack on Israel.

In Copenhagen in 1980, whoever was controlling arrangements for the UN Conference made sure that the women from
various parts of the world wouldn't really be able to get together to discuss their own interests, even as much as we were
able to in Mexico City. Every meeting of the Forum or Tribune held in a large enough hall for more than fifty people to
attend was disrupted as soon as any serious motion on wom-
en's rights or equality was entertained. Well-trained young
women shouting slogans against America, against capitalism,
and against "Zionism" broke up every serious discussion of
women's needs for more rights, education, literacy, or their

own organization. The only sessions that were not so disrupted were the clearly "non-political" seminars on the family, or the elderly; on those questions women from Africa, Asia, Eastern Europe, the Soviet Union, East Germany, France, England and the U.S.A. were allowed to talk freely to each other and easily found common ground.

In the formal governmental meetings, the only important vote was on the Zionism-as-racism resolution, for which men were flown in from many capitals to replace the women delegates who had been allowed to sit there during the meaningless pious resolutions on women's rights. An American proposal for UN affirmative action machinery against sex discrimination in employment and education, to be set up in ways suitable to the development of different nations, was not even allowed to surface.

Afterword to "An Open Letter to the Women's Movement—1976" (pp. 471-96)

The disruption of the women's movement in the mid-seventies —the diversion of women's energy into seemingly ideological battles over sexual politics and internal battles for organizational power—paralleled, if it was not actually maneuvered by, the organization of a powerful, well-financed backlash against women's rights that doomed the ERA. It seems more than coincidental to realize in retrospect that ERA, which had passed Congress overwhelmingly in 1972 (354 to 23 in the House, 84 to 8 in the Senate) and had been ratified by thirty states by the end of 1973, came to stalemate in 1974 and 1975 and began to be rescinded, in Georgia, Nevada, Oklahoma, Nebraska, as NOW and the women's movement generally was torn apart by the battles and issues I warned about in these letters.

The hearings that followed the Watergate break-in had just begun to reveal the "dirty tricks" of government agents infiltrating and acting as agents provocateurs in the peace and student and black civil rights movements as the bitterly divided NOW convention in Philadelphia in October 1975 was electing officers committed to taking the flagship of the women's movement "out of the mainstream into the revolution." That same year only one state, Indiana, ratified ERA; the list of states rescinding grew, and state ERAs were defeated in the states of New York and New Jersey.

After Nixon resigned, and Ford pardoned him, and then the nation turned in revulsion against the corruption of Watergate and the desecration of Constitutional rights, and voted that government out, the "craziness" in the women's movement came to a halt. I tried about that time to get my own file from the CIA and FBI under the Freedom of Information act. All they sent me was newsclips; the rest was still classified; the explanation was that its release might endanger agents still on active duty. Were we paranoid to suspect that government agents—or agents of industries with much to lose if ERA ever got into the Constitution—might have been stirring up much of that dissension and disruption that used up NOW's energies in internal battle when crucial time was passing for ERA? That does not excuse those of us who allowed ourselves to be thus diverted.

We learned a lot, too late. We learned not to let sexual politics divide us. I myself seconded the resolution on lesbian rights at the International Women's Year Conference in Houston in 1977, to get it passed quickly, without the hours of bitter discussion that otherwise would have preempted the airwaves. The headlines and newscasts focusing on lesbianism were especially alienating to Middle American and Southern states which were the only hope for ratification of ERA before the time ran out. Sexual politics is always good for a headline —but the movement as a whole, including responsible lesbian leaders, came to see that it does not empower women or enable them to change their lives. And, still, it is not that easy for women to wield real political power, as we learned in 1984, even with a woman on the presidential ticket.

The women who fought the battles recorded in these pages were empowered thereby, whichever side we were on. We all changed our lives—became professional, political, displaced housewives, divorced, remarried, and spelled our own name, finally, as person. But will the young women who start now from that different place take that torch from us? Will the women's movement as we made and knew it, in the peak moments recorded here, move on into a second stage, as I have elsewhere suggested, restructuring institutions so equality can be lived, in office and home, by women, men and children? Or will the movement retrench and bring in the young to defend, once again, the basic rights we thought already won, now under such attack? Or will the young who've grown up enjoying those rights and opportunities we fought for remain preoccupied with their private pleasures and ambitions and let those rights die, for another generation to start over again? The women who still say "it changed my life" would not want to go back. I hope these memories will help daughters who don't even realize what life was like before avoid that forced retreat. I would not wish them such pains.